History of
The Royal Navy

History of
The Royal Navy

Edited by

LIEUT.-CMDR. P.K. KEMP, O.B.E.

G.P. PUTNAM'S SONS
New York

CONTENTS

FOREWORD

To write a detailed history of the Royal Navy in 120,000 words is clearly an impossibility. Four centuries of continuous life, added to two or three hundred years of a previous spasmodic existence, presents a canvas on which the very limited paint available must inevitably be thinly spread. This would be true of most navies of most nations, but is particularly so in the case of Britain, for throughout her existence as a nation her national economy, more so than that of any other country, has depended upon the sea and her ability to use it to her best advantage.

In the 17th, 18th, and 19th centuries Britain amassed an empire that covered much of the globe. Partly by conquest, partly by exploration and discovery, her influence in the world expanded, based upon the supremacy of her Navy and its ability to protect and encourage her maritime trade. Throughout its history the Royal Navy has always, therefore, been at full stretch. Ten long sea campaigns within the compass of only a little over two centuries is some measure of its total involvement in the political realities of Britain's place in the world. It is indeed total, for without the sea, and without the freedom of movement which the sea permits, Britain dies as a nation.

In this book therefore the aim has been to paint a picture on the broadest lines, concentrating only here and there to describe an action of particular interest, a battle of particular importance. Seven authors have combined to write the text, and where space has not allowed them to write at the length and detail they would have wished, an attempt has been made to fill part at least of the gaps with pictures and photographs.

The authors I have asked to assist in the writing all have a considerable claim to be recognised as naval historians of distinction. Professor Christopher Lloyd has spent much of his working life in teaching naval history at the Royal Naval Colleges at Dartmouth and Greenwich, and was Professor of History at the latter college until he retired two or three years ago. He has written many books on naval subjects and for several years was Secretary of the Navy Records Society, at the same time editing many

of its fine volumes. Professor Bryan McL. Ranft succeeded Professor Lloyd as Professor of History at the R.N. College Greenwich, and is, like him, well known in the Navy Records Society in which he is a member of the Council and an editor of one of its volumes. At present, in addition to his duties at Greenwich, he is engaged in a study of the anti-submarine operations of World War I with a view to the production of a volume of relevant papers for the Navy Records Society.

Oliver Warner is equally well known as a naval historian, particularly of the period of the Revolutionary and Napoleonic wars, and he has written all the chapters in this book which cover those vast campaigns in which Britain reached the maritime heights. He, too, is a member of the Council of the Navy Records Society.

Captain Donald Macintyre is the author of a number of books of naval history and biography, particularly of the First and Second World Wars, though his naval interests lie wider than that. He is a member of the staff of the Naval Historical Branch of the Ministry of Defence. Captain Geoffrey Bennett, too, has written many books of naval history, and a recent biography of Admiral Lord Charles Beresford aroused considerable interest and acclaim. His interests in naval history have, perhaps, been focussed more on the First World War than on other periods, and the three chapters which cover this campaign all come from his pen. Vice-Admiral Brian Schofield is a historian of the Second World War and a well known commentator on post-war naval events. He has been a frequent contributor both to the Proceedings of the United States Naval Institute and to its annual publication, the Naval Review.

Finally, a word about the editor himself. He was Naval Librarian and Head of the Naval Historical Branch of the Ministry of Defence, until he retired in August 1968, and at the same time editor of the Journal of the Royal United Services Institution. He has written a number of books of naval history and is currently a vice-president of the Navy Records Society, having edited two of their volumes. He has written five of the chapters of this book.

P. K. KEMP

Opposite: A First-rate building in the dock at Deptford. The three-decker in the foreground is believed to be the *Royal George*. From the painting by T. Cleveley the Elder

CHAPTER 1

*First steps towards a Navy – The Cinque Ports Navy –
The Lord High Admiral – Early Wars against the French –
The Understanding of Sea Power – Growth of Fishery and
Trade – The Merchant Adventurers – English Voyages of
Discovery – Reprisals against Spain – The Drift to War*

PETER KEMP

It has been claimed that the Navy of Britain first came into being in the reign of Alfred the Great. It is true enough that in the year 896 King Alfred built warships and used them both to blockade the Danes in their Northumbrian fastnesses and to discourage Danish seaborne raids into the English kingdom of Wessex. Perhaps the most that can be said is that Alfred was the first Englishman with any appreciation of the value of sea power in war, but it is straining at the truth to believe that, in Alfred's few ships, we see the birth of the British Navy. We need to step forward 600 years for that.

Not unexpectedly, it was the growth of maritime trade which dictated the need for a regular navy. Until about the year 1300, English shipping played a very minor part in world trade, even though, by that date, a fairly important export had been built up in English wool and English tin, both at that time the best in the world. The carrying trade at sea was largely in the hands of the Hanseatic League, which controlled the shipping of the Baltic and north European coast, and of the Italian states, first Genoa and later Venice, which dominated the Mediterranean trade. The rest of the world was still a closed book.

The profits of the carrying trade began to attract the notice of English merchants during the 15th century, and it was in these years that they began to form themselves into companies of Merchant Adventurers, building bigger ships and competing against their foreign rivals. By the middle of the 15th century they had captured almost the whole of the wine trade, based on Bordeaux, and much of the wool trade to France and the Netherlands.

The fishery, too, became a considerable source of maritime growth. This could perhaps be called fortuitous, for at the beginning of the 15th century the huge herring shoals moved out of the Baltic and into the North Sea, where they were no longer under the territorial control of the Hanseatic League. But at the same time as this drift of herrings to the North Sea coasts of Britain took place, the great cod fishery off the south-west coast of Iceland was almost entirely exploited by English fishermen from the east coast ports.

During the centuries between about 1200 and 1500 there were continuous wars with France, and for these the king needed ships. Almost all the Plantagenet kings owned a few ships and galleys, but the main burden of providing a navy in war lay with the private ships belonging to the Cinque Ports of Hastings, Romney, Hythe, Dover and Sandwich. Under a charter which granted them certain privileges and relieved them of certain statutory dues, they were required to provide 57 ships, fully manned, for 15 days every year whenever the king required them.

These ships, both those owned by the king and those provided by the Cinque Ports, comprised the navy of Britain, such as it was. But it was never a navy in the sense in which we recognise a navy today. The ships themselves did no fighting; on not one of them was a gun mounted. They carried fighting men, almost always in the role of transport to and from France, but very occasionally for the purpose of what one can best describe as a land battle at sea. Such a one was the battle of Sluys, fought off the Netherlands coast on 24th June 1340, between an

Opposite: A typical Tudor merchant ship of the Armada period, the ship *Griffin*. She was of 200 tons and carried a complement of 100 men. Owned by William Hawkyns, she was one of the merchant ships appointed to serve under Sir Francis Drake during the campaign against the Spanish in 1588. From a line drawing by Visscher

GENESIS OF A NAVY

English fleet of some 250 ships commanded by Edward III and a French fleet of about 200 ships commanded by three 'admirals', two Norman and one Genoese. The 'battle', if it can be called such, was fought by ships grappling one another and the armed men on board, swordsmen, axemen and pikemen, boarding the enemy under the covering fire of archers. The slaughter was prodigious, the French losing between 26,000 and 30,000 men, the English about 4,000. One of the Norman 'admirals' who was captured was stabbed to death and hanged at the masthead of one of his own ships taken in the fight.

These were still very small ships. Edward III himself was embarked in the cog *Thomas*, a bluff-bowed, broad-beamed, single-masted ship of about 200 tons. It was the typical 'round' ship of northern Europe, built for trade and taken up for service in war as a transport for soldiers. The cog was the largest ship in either fleet, the remainder ranging down to small vessels of only 20 tons. The French fleet was said to include galleys, mainly Genoese, but the probability is that most of the so-called galleys were in fact barges.

The King's ships were always under the administrative control of a Keeper (or Clerk) of the King's Ships. The appointment, in the beginning, usually went to the Church, and the first holder of the post was William of Wrotham, later Archdeacon of Taunton. There was nothing unusual in this, for the Plantagenet kings appointed their bishops mainly as political advisers, their bishoprics only acting as useful sources of income. Indeed, most Archbishops of Canterbury doubled their holy office with the appointment of Lord Chancellor, standing next to the king as chief administrator of the realm. Many people have seen in this appointment of William of Wrotham, which was made in 1205, the seed from which grew the office of Admiralty, but this is an over-simplification. The Admiralty grew much more from the later appointment of a Lord High Admiral than ever it did from the appointment of a Keeper of the King's Ships.

Executive control at sea was vested in two Admirals, one of the North and one of the West, the dividing line being the banks of the River Thames. These were royal appointments, only made in times of war or threatened trouble. On occasions Edward III appointed one man only to command all the fleets, and in the course of time the man appointed

became known as the Lord Admiral, or High Admiral, and later as the Lord High Admiral. The first appointment was in 1360, and spasmodically thereafter until 1391, when the appointment became permanent. He became one of the Great Officers of the Crown, with a permanent seat at the Council, responsible to the king for exercising the military command of all naval forces of the country and for administering justice in all actions and suits arising out of sea affairs.

It is in this appointment that the birth of Admiralty, as we know it, exists. One could therefore say that the British Navy was officially born in 1391, when the appointment of Lord High Admiral embarked upon its permanent status. Yet here again one would be guilty of over-simplification, for there were many long periods subsequent to that date when there were no royal ships for the Lord High Admiral to command. He kept his appointment during those years because of the legal duties attaching to his position.

With the growth of English maritime trade there came an inevitable technological advance in the science of shipbuilding. The single-masted 'round' ship, or cog, was replaced by two- and even three-masted ships with finer lines and a sharper bow, though still built high fore and aft. The two-masted ship began to appear in about 1420, the three-masted about 30 years later. The mainmast carried a topmast, and the topsail makes its appearance above the main course in about 1450. In another 20 years the foremast, too, carried a topmast and topsail. The mizen was almost invariably lateen-rigged.

The development of three masts and square rig on the two foremost masts gave the impetus towards a substantial increase in size, which in turn produced the opportunity of making considerably longer voyages. English ships, by the middle of the century, were trading through the Mediterranean to the Levant; by the end of the century they were venturing out into the Atlantic in search of the mythical Isle of Brasil. All round the English coasts the ports and harbours were busy, and the great forests of oak which covered most of southern England echoed to the sound of the axe to satisfy the demands of the shipbuilders.

Simultaneous with the development of the trading ships was that of the King's ships. Henry V built the *Jesus*, of 1,000 tons, in 1420, and other ships built by him, the *Holy Ghost, George, Christopher,* and *Trinity Royal,* were not much smaller. But, more important in the naval aspect, he was the first to mount large naval guns in his ships. He also has his champions who claim him as the father of the British Navy, and if one is doubtful about the claim, there can certainly be no doubt that he was the first English king to appreciate the true use of a navy. He used it during the wars in France to keep the English Channel clear of enemy warships, at other times to check the piracy which was rife in all the seas of the world.

If one has to sum up the Plantagenet navy as spasmodic, and limited almost entirely to the transport of troops in wartime, the story changes with the Tudor kings. With them, for the first time, we begin to get permanence. Henry VII built a number of ships, including one with four masts, the largest ship yet built in England. He had the first drydock in English history constructed at Portsmouth; he set up the nucleus of a royal dockyard in the Thames at Greenwich. Henry was a king who fully appreciated that the prosperity of England was bound up with the sea and that a flourishing ocean trade needed a flourishing navy behind it to protect the ships from piracy and illegal seizure. The permanence which he gave to his navy provided the basis of a proper career structure for its officers, and it is from the years of his reign that we can trace the evolving pattern which consolidated itself into the British Navy as we know it throughout the years of history.

In his efforts to promote and consolidate the seaborne trade of the nation, Henry's first parliament passed a Navigation Act under which the wine trade of Bordeaux was reserved for British bottoms. This first Navigation Act was followed by others, designed not only to provide increasing employment to English ships but also to foster the use of English, Welsh, and Irish crews. On this firm foundation he encouraged the building of larger ships by instituting cash bounties for the construction of ships of over 100 tons. And as the merchant ships grew larger, so too did the King's own ships.

Henry VII had not the whole answer; his ships were still designed and armed with the view of grappling an enemy and taking her by boarding. The guns carried in the *Regent,* the four-masted ship mentioned above, were mainly serpentines, an anti-personnel gun firing small shot. All guns carried were mounted on the upper deck.

It was left to his son, Henry VIII, to take the final step in the evolution of the fighting ship. Like his father, Henry VIII was fully alive to the importance of the sea in England's future prosperity. He inherited seven royal ships when he came to the throne, and during the next five years he built another 24. Throughout his reign of 38 years he continually added to his navy. But his main contribution in this particular field of ship construction was the introduction of the heavy gun. In his ships the guns were mounted on the lower deck and were fired through gunports cut in the ships' sides. The object of sea fighting was now no longer to grapple and board, but to destroy by gunfire at a distance. English cannon of this period, cast mainly in the Sussex iron foundries, were the best in the world, and the new model warship designed by Henry could more than hold its own with any other ship of any other nation. His largest ship was the *Henry Grace à Dieu,* better known perhaps as the *Great Harry,* a four-master of 1,500 tons.

Following in his father's footsteps in providing a permanent career for his officers, Henry drew up a set of regulations both for the management of his fleet in battle and for the discipline of the crews. An even greater contribution to the orderly growth of the Navy was his substitution of the Keeper of the King's Ships by a Navy Board. The Board was established by Letters Patent on 24th April 1546, and consisted of Commissioners charged with the superintendence of various civil aspects of administration, such as construction and repair, ordnance, victualling, etc. With the growth of the Navy from a few royal ships spasmodically maintained and employed into a permanent force of some dozens of ships, the administration was beyond the compass of a single man.

The operational control was still vested in the Lord High Admiral, still one of the Great Officers of State. He sent his instructions to the Navy Board and left it to them to put them into effect. It is in the conjunction of Lord High Admiral and Navy Board that we get the foundation of Admiralty as we know it today. The twin system existed, in fact, until 1832, although the office of Lord High Admiral had long since been put into commission and Lords Commissioners appointed to execute the office. When the two bodies came together in 1832, they formed the single entity known as the Admiralty.

A further move by Henry was the foundation, in 1513, of Trinity House. Its initial duties included the professional examination of officers and petty officers, and the supply of seamen to the royal ships as they were needed. It was only 50 years later that the duty of establishing lights, buoys, seamarks, etc., in coastal waters fell into their hands.

The final step in the evolution of the fighting ship came during the reign of Henry's daughter Elizabeth. The general pattern of all ships, irrespective of size, was what was known as 'high-charged', with towering forecastles and poops. This was a legacy of the days of grappling and boarding, the object of the high forecastle and aftercastle (or poop) being to enable defenders to fire down upon enemy boarders as they entered the ship in the waist. As her treasurer of the Navy Board Elizabeth appointed John Hawkins, a practical seaman who had made many trading voyages to Africa and the West Indies, mainly carrying slaves. Hawkins, from his own experience, knew that the high forecastle made sailing very difficult since it caught the wind and forced the ship down to leeward. In the ships he built for Elizabeth the 'castle' forward was swept away and a low bow substituted, though it still retained the old name of forecastle. The result was a vast improvement in the ship's sailing qualities, enabling her to sail closer to the wind and thus to make better ground to windward. The low bow also added a knot or two to her speed.

Here, then, was the final step in the development of the sailing man of war. For the next 300 years the only advances lay in the growth in tonnage and the evolution of a finer hull form, a more efficient sail plan, and a more powerful armament. Basically the ship of the line at Trafalgar in 1805 was no more than a developed version of Hawkins's ship of war of 1584, with the low bow and the high poop, though not built quite so high as in Elizabeth's day. The more powerful armament came not only from an increase in the size and efficiency of the guns but also from the incorporation in the design of additional gundecks.

How deeply an understanding of the importance of the sea to the growth and prosperity of England had spread through the country can be measured by the publication, in 1436 or 1437, of an anonymous treatise in verse under the title *De Politia Conservativa Maris*, but more familiarly known today as *The*

Sir John Hawkins, a portrait by an unknown artist. Hawkins, whom Queen Elizabeth appointed Treasurer of her Navy, made a considerable contribution to English expansion at sea by introducing the 'low-charged' ship, cutting down the previous high forecastle and making ships both faster and more manoeuvrable

Libel of English Policy from the wording of its prologue: 'Here beginneth the Prologue of the processe of the Libel of English policie, exhorting all England to keepe the sea, and namely the narrow sea: shewing what profite commeth thereof, and also what worship and salvation to England, and to all English-men.' The author is thought, with some reason, to be Bishop Adam de Moleyns, who was later murdered in Portsmouth in 1450.

The treatise is divided into an introduction and 12 chapters, each devoted to an analysis of the trade of the various European countries and demonstrating how dependent they all were on the freedom of sea passage through the English Channel (the 'narrowe sea'). But through each chapter runs the thread of the sea's particular importance to England, both as a regulator of European trade and as a defence against all enemies.

'Kepe then the sea that is the wall of England:
And then is England kept by Goddes hande.'

The importance of the *Libel* is that it set forth, in popular verse, not only what the Plantagenet kings knew and practised but also what the merchants of England were coming to believe. Its arguments on the importance of the sea to England's growing trade were unanswerable, and affected the merchants in their pockets. It is impossible to say what exact influence the *Libel* had on the setting up of the various companies of Merchant Adventurers in the great sea ports, but that it reflected their urges to increased trade is undeniable. It is equally impossible to say that the *Libel* had any direct connection with the voyages of discovery which were beginning to push out into the unknown, but that it focussed attention on the sea affair, which made the voyages possible, is equally undeniable.

For the next 50 years, trading voyages to Norway, the Baltic, Iceland, Spain and Portugal, and the Mediterranean, were common. Some of the ships, especially those engaged in the Spanish trade, must have been large, for in 1445 there is a record of two of them each carrying 200 passengers, as well as pilgrims to the shrine of Compostella. In one ship William Waldron, the Lord Mayor of London, shipped £24,000 worth of goods to the Levant. That there were many others, accounts of which have not survived, is certain; we can find brief references to them in the writings of such chroniclers as Botoler and Fabyan and Stow, but details are lacking. Even details of the second voyage to the west of John Cabot are lacking, though we do know about the first.

News of the discoveries of Columbus in 1492 caused little surprise in England, for there had been by that time quite a number of English voyages to the westward in search of the Isle of Brasil. The English were seamen enough, and experienced enough, to realise that success or failure depended on the latitude, and that a ship starting her voyage from Spain and running down the trade winds had a natural advantage over one which had to face the gales and high Atlantic seas of more northerly latitudes. But within four years of Columbus's triumph John Cabot had obtained letters patent from Henry VII

for a discovery to the westward, and in 1497, with a crew of 18 men in a ship of Bristol called the *Matthew*, had reached the coast of North America. There is some doubt about the exact point of first landfall, perhaps Newfoundland, perhaps Labrador, perhaps Cape Breton, but there is no doubt about the date, which was 24th June 1497. Within a very few years voyages to Newfoundland and Labrador were continuous and a settlement was established.

In 1530 William Hawkins of Plymouth, an experienced sea trader, fitted out a ship of 250 tons and made three voyages, calling first on the Guinea coast to load ivory, and thence to the coast of Brazil before returning home. His three voyages opened a regular trade to Guinea for ivory and gold, which proved to be a valuable school of seamanship and fighting for many of the men who commanded ships in the battle of the Spanish Armada. Many of these

Sebastian Cabot, the elder son of John Cabot, possibly accompanied his father on the three voyages of exploration between 1497 and 1498 which discovered Newfoundland or, more probably, Cape Breton. Sebastian, after working in the Spanish Hydrographic office, returned to England and was granted a pension by Edward VI. He was also made the first governor of the Company of Merchant Adventurers

English voyages were hotly contested by Portuguese ships, and captains and ships had often to fight their ships through.

Cathay, or China as we know it today, was always a magnet to the merchants, and in 1553 the Merchant Adventurers fitted out an expedition of three ships to open trade, carrying manufactured goods to be exchanged for silk and jewels. The route chosen was to the north-east and in command of the expedition was Sir Hugh Willoughby, with Richard Chancellor as second-in-command and Stephen Borough as master. Willoughby, in the *Bona Speranza* of 120 tons, reached Novaya Zemlya, where he and his whole crew perished. Chancellor, in the *Edward Bonaventure*, reached the White Sea, and from there journeyed to Moscow to open negotiations with the Russians. His voyage resulted in the formation of the Muscovy Company and the opening of a flourishing trade with Russia.

The careers of Stephen Borough, and of his younger brother William, are typical in representing the normal pattern of the interchangeability of mercantile and naval seafaring life, and of the depth of interest in the sea affair which permeated the nation at this time. There was nothing unusual in Stephen being chosen to accompany Willoughby's voyage of exploration; he was already an accomplished merchant seaman and fully aware of the need to pioneer new sea routes in order to foster the growth in trade. His interest went deeper than that, however, and realising that what the English seamen lacked was the scientific knowledge built up by the Spanish and Portuguese discoverers, his first act on returning from his voyage to the White Sea was to arrange for the translation into English of Cortes's *Arte de Navegar*, the Spanish standard textbook on navigation. It was at this stage that he entered naval service as Chief Pilot in the Medway, a post which brought him the duty of instructing and examining seamen in navigation.

His brother William's career followed on similar lines. He started as a merchant seaman with the Muscovy Company, and during the course of his voyages made many observations on the variation of the compass, on which subject he published a book in 1581. Two years later he became Comptroller of the Navy, and served at sea in command of naval ships with Drake at Cadiz in 1587 and with Howard of Effingham in the Spanish Armada battle of 1588.

This was very much a normal pattern. John Hawkins, the son of William Hawkins of Plymouth, began his seafaring career in the merchant navy, as did Francis Drake. Martin Frobisher was another. From normal trading voyages, in which they gained their initial experience of navigation and seamanship, they graduated into the great voyages of discovery of the period, and from those into naval service.

There was still no hard and fast line dividing the Navy and the merchant service, either in ships or personnel. In most of the voyages of discovery, which normally took with them the means of speculative trade, the Queen or one of her ministers took a financial share, even to the extent on occasions of contributing a royal ship. In war, the purely merchant ship became naval, fighting in the fleet under her own merchant captain and with her own merchant crew. On the edges of the amalgam, so to speak, were the hard core, long term career officers, purely naval or purely merchant throughout their serving lives, while in the centre lay the majority of men and ships which were mercantile in peace and naval in war.

The many voyages of trade and exploration made by English ships during the 30 years from about 1560 proved a rewarding trial of skill and courage which was to stand the Navy in good stead in the testing years to come. John Hawkins's three slaving voyages to Sierra Leone in Africa, across the Atlantic to the Spanish Main and Florida, and home to England in 1562, 1564, and 1567, set the pattern of many that were to follow. The first two were immensely profitable, with the Queen contributing her ship *Jesus of Lubeck*, of 700 tons, to the second. Nevertheless, the profit was not secured without a considerable show of force when the Spanish settlers on the Main refused to buy Hawkins's slaves, so that he had to persuade the Spaniards to take them at the point of the sword. His third voyage was a catastrophe, with the Queen losing her ship at the hands of the Spaniards. Nevertheless it is an important voyage in naval history, for the young Francis Drake accompanied his cousin John Hawkins as captain of the *Judith*, a barque of 50 tons. The treachery and treatment experienced at the hands of the Spaniards at Vera Cruz awoke in Drake a lifelong hatred of Spain and all things Spanish, a driving force which led him to those prodigious efforts which, in the end, sealed the fate of Spain as a maritime nation.

Opposite: Sir Francis Drake, the 'Jewel' portrait, painted in 1592 by an unknown artist. Drake's partnership with Hawkins in the privateering voyages to the West Indies, his great voyage of circumnavigation, and his raid on Vigo and the Canary Islands in 1587, were the first prickings of the bubble of Spanish invincibility at sea

This experience at Vera Cruz drove Hawkins into the Navy, where his skill and experience, gained in merchant voyaging, was placed for the rest of his life at the disposal of his country. It drove Drake to thoughts and acts of revenge, to another voyage to the West Indies in 1572 in which he held for a few hours the town of Nombre de Dios by force of arms while his crew loaded captured silver bars into the ships. He followed this up by ambushing the Spanish mule train laden with the year's treasure gathered in Peru and Chile as it made its way across the Isthmus of Darien. With this booty on board he made his way home to England.

The great voyage of circumnavigation followed, aimed as much against the Spanish maritime stranglehold on Pacific navigation as at the acquisition of booty. It was the rebellion of Drake, backed clandestinely by the Queen and her ministers, against that Papal Bull drawn by Pope Alexander VI which alloted to Spain dominion of all discoveries to the west, and to Portugal all discoveries to the east, of a line drawn through the Atlantic 300 leagues to the west of the Cape Verde Islands. The Reformation had, in any case, made Papal Bulls of no binding legality in English eyes, and the growing differences between England and Spain, so soon to break out into open warfare, gave to such a venture as Drake's voyage a national importance outweighing the mercenary basis on which it was planned and equipped.

There had, in the meantime, been other English voyages of discovery. Martin Frobisher had made two, in 1576 and 1577, in search of a north-west passage to China. John Davis followed him with three similar voyages in 1585, 1586, and 1587, spent some years in the Navy and commanded a ship in the attack on Cadiz in 1597, and then returned to trade, making three voyages to the East Indies. In 1583 Sir Humphrey Gilbert took a party of colonisers to Newfoundland, taking possession of the harbour of St. John and all land within 200 leagues of it in the name of the Queen of England. Thomas Cavendish repeated Drake's voyage of circumnavigation between 1586 and 1588, returning home with his ship loaded with treasure captured in the Pacific. Sir Walter Raleigh sent out at his own expense English colonists to a North American tract of land which he named Virginia in honour of the Queen, though the place of their landing is not in the state of Virginia as we know it today.

All this restless voyaging, this pushing out of English ships into all the far corners of the world, was certain to exacerbate still further the already bad relations existing with Spain. Spanish ships, encountered anywhere upon the face of the waters, were attacked and plundered, and though the Queen was ever ready to protest her personal innocence to the Spanish Ambassador in London, she was equally ready to overlook, when it came to her own subjects, the lawlessness of their depredations at sea. In the country at large these successful ventures against Spanish shipping and Spanish settlements in America were greeted with enthusiasm. Behind them all, hidden from the public's gaze by a curtain of mercantile interest, stood the Queen and her court, whose brains and capital were ideally matched by the courage and skill of the seamen.

As the years of the 1580s passed, war with Spain became a certainty. Elizabeth and her Council, fully aware of the danger to England if the Spanish occupation of the Netherlands should become permanent, did all in their power to nurture the Dutch resistance there. In the English Channel, the only ocean highway between Spain and the Netherlands, Spanish shipping was harried by a host of privateers of which the most numerous were English. In 1585, under a decree signed by Philip II of Spain, English corn ships in Spanish harbours were seized. The Queen sanctioned a retaliatory raid and commissioned Francis Drake to lead it, contributing two of her royal ships. Like those which had preceded it, it hid behind the curtain of a mercantile enterprise, with city merchants taking a two-thirds interest. Drake made the Spanish coast at Vigo and plundered the town, called at the Canary Islands and raided them, and crossed the Atlantic to the Spanish Main. He captured San Domingo and Cartagena and held them both to ransom for substantial sums.

The success of this rapidly planned and brilliantly executed raid struck Europe like a thunderbolt. It revealed that the god of Spain, upheld for so long by belief in her invincibility at sea, had feet of clay. The bubble of Spanish maritime dominance was being pricked.

The execution of Mary Queen of Scots in February 1587 was the final spark which ignited the flame of Philip's resolve to conquer England. There was more to it than the mutual animosities of the two

The *Ark Royal* was originally built for Sir Walter Raleigh and was named *Ark Raleigh*, her name being changed when she was purchased by Queen Elizabeth. In the Battle of the Spanish Armada she was the English fleet flagship, flying the flag of the Lord High Admiral. From a line drawing by Visscher

nations. Elizabeth of England stood, in the eyes of Europe, as the sole hope of the Protestant cause, Philip of Spain carried publicly the banner of Roman Catholicism. Unless Protestantism was eradicated from Europe, Spanish dominion of the Netherlands was a lost cause. While Mary lived there was always the hope that she might form the centre of a Roman Catholic revival in England and that Philip's ambition might be realised without fighting. Now that hope was no more. The 'Enterprise of England' became a reality in Philip's mind, and in the Spanish ports and harbours an army of labourers began to build and fit out ships to form the biggest fleet that the world had ever seen.

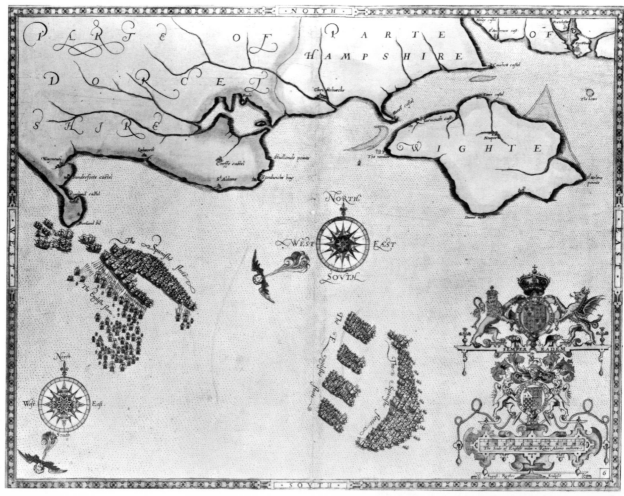

CHAPTER 2

*War with Spain – The Raid on Cadiz – Capture of the
San Felipe – The Battle of the Invincible Armada –
The Last Fight of the* Revenge *– Death of Hawkins and
Drake – The Capture of Cadiz*

CHRISTOPHER LLOYD

The vision of England's destiny as an empire founded on the seas is nowhere more finely expressed than in Richard Hakluyt's epic history of *The Principal Navigations, Voyages and Discoveries of the English Nation*, which was published the year after the Armada campaign.

Which of the kings of this land before her Majesty had their banners seen in the Caspian Sea? Which of them have dealt with the Emperor of Persia, as her Majesty hath done, and obtained for her merchants large and loving privileges? Who ever saw before this regiment an English Ligier (ambassador) in the stately porch of the Grand Signor at Constantinople? Who ever found English Consuls and Agents at Tripolis in Syria, at Aleppo, at Babylon, at Balsara, and which is more, who ever heard of an Englishmen at Goa, before now? What English ships did heretofore ever anchor in the mighty river of Plate? Pass and repass the unpassable (in former opinion) straits of Magellan, range along the coast of Chile, Peru, and all the backside of Nova Hispania, further than any Christian ever passed, traverse the mighty breadth of the South Sea, land upon the Luzones in despight of the enemy, enter into alliance, amity and traffic with the princes of the Moluccas and the Isle of Java, double the famous Cape of Bona Speranza, arrive at the Isle of Santa Helena, and last of all return home most richly laden with the commodities of China, as the subjects of this now most flourishing monarchy have done?

Such words could not have been written during the first half of Elizabeth's reign. Like the dramatists, the seamen of that age came into their own during the last quarter of the century. It was then that the prospect of riches to be won by invading the Spanish seas around central and south America tempted an average of over a hundred such voyages to be undertaken annually.

From a political point of view it was like dogs baiting a bull. Elizabeth herself had no illusions about the comparative strength of her realm and that of Philip II of Spain, so she had postponed the inevitable conflict as long as possible. Philip was not only King of Spain and Portugal but Lord of the Indies in the east as well as the west, King of the Two Sicilies (Naples and Sicily), and ruler of the Low Countries. Mary Queen of Scots had been his niece and he had been deeply involved in her plots to gain the throne of England. As His Most Catholic Majesty he enjoyed the special favour of the Pope. A war against such a power was not to be undertaken lightly; but when it combined the motives of a Protestant crusade with the prospects of unlimited gain, as it did in the case of Drake and many others, it had a formidable popular backing.

When Drake returned from his raid on the West Indies in 1586, incidentally bringing with him the first Virginia colonists who had given up the struggle, Philip's intention to invade England was already too obvious to be ignored. His original plan was to gather an armada (i.e., an armed fleet) from all the provinces of Spain at Cadiz, whence the Marquis of Santa Cruz would undertake the hazardous business of convoying a large body of transports to meet the Duke of Parma at Antwerp, where 17,000 of the best troops in Europe would embark to sail up the Thames and besiege London.

But Santa Cruz, who had had a long and distinguished career at sea, died before the plan could be put into execution and the command was transferred to the Duke of Medina Sidonia, a great noble-

Opposite above : One of a set of Armada charts, engraved by Augustine Ryther in 1590 from drawings by Robert Adams, showing the Armada off Plymouth; *Below :* Another of the Ryther charts showing the action fought off Portland Bill on 23rd July. A shift of wind gave Medina Sidonia the chance to cut off a portion of the English fleet under Frobisher which had stood too far to the eastward. Frobisher escaped, and with the wind again veering to the west, the Armada was shepherded up Channel, the Spanish ships 'going allwaies before the English like sheepe'

THE BIRTH OF SEA POWER

man but without experience of command at sea. But neither had Lord Howard of Effingham when he was put in command of the English fleet at Plymouth. The object in both cases was the same, because only a great nobleman could control unruly subordinates.

There was much discussion on how best to counter the Spanish threat. The Queen wanted her ships to ply up and down at the mouth of the Channel because she feared they might miss the Armada in the Bay of Biscay. Drake favoured what we should call a pre-emptive strike on the Spanish fleet before it put to sea. In 1587 he was given his chance in the operation known to history as 'the singeing of the King of Spain's beard', when he burned the shipping collected in Cadiz harbour. However brilliant the way this raid was handled, it was in fact premature because some of the provincial squadrons had not yet arrived, though Drake undoubtedly did great damage. The English ships hung about off Cape St. Vincent to intercept these squadrons, only to receive information of the arrival of a Portuguese carrack, the *San Felipe*, at the Azores on its return fully laden from the Spice Islands. The temptation to Drake to seize a prize reputed to be worth more than £2,000,000 was too great. She was sighted off Sao Miguel in the Azores and, after a token show of defence, surrendered to Drake. She was stuffed with spices, silks, ivories, and calicoes and carried in her strong room gold, silver, and some caskets of jewels.

On account of the Cadiz raid the sailing of the Armada was postponed until July, 1588. When it left Lisbon it consisted of 130 ships of all sizes and 27,000 men. Most of the vessels were poorly armed transports and most of the men were soldiers rather than sailors, a despised class in Spain. Four galleys sailed with them, but were forced to leave the fleet after encountering a gale in the Bay of Biscay. There were also two huge galleasses, a transitional type of ship powered by both oars and sail, which were stationed on either side of Sidonia's flagship, the *San Martin*. All but two of these ships reached Calais safely, partly because Sidonia obeyed his orders to reach Parma and not become engaged with the English on the way, but chiefly because an excellent formation was maintained in the fleet after it had entered the Channel. The English described this as a crescent or half-moon, but that was because they saw it from astern during the week-long chase up Channel. In reality it was shaped like an eagle, with the

Charles Howard, second Baron of Effingham and first Earl of Nottingham, Queen Elizabeth's Lord High Admiral at the time of the Spanish Armada battle. This portrait by Daniel Mytens, painted in 1619, shows him in his robes as a Knight of the Garter

flagship and the galleasses as the head, warship squadrons from Castile and Portugal on either wing, the vulnerable transports or urcas forming the body, and two protective squadrons bringing up the rear.

When on 19th July (according to the old English calendar, 31st July according to the new Spanish one) this vast concourse of shipping was sighted off the Lizard it must have looked most impressive. Spanish galleons were of the older type, with towering superstructures and brilliantly painted hulls. Their sails were emblazoned with pictures of the saints or decorative coats of arms, and from their masts streamed long pennons of varying colours. Spanish sailors left the business of fighting to the soldiers and the gunners who, after being buffeted by gales in the Bay, can have had little stomach for a hand-to-hand encounter. Moreover, since the rate of sailing was so slow, victuals and water were already nearly expended. Morale was so low that Sidonia begged the King to call off this 'Enterprise against England', but Philip insisted that his majestic Armada should continue its course towards Flanders.

The same victualling problems confronted the English, whose ships had been at Plymouth since May. 'My good lord,' wrote Howard to the Lord Treasurer, 'there is here the gallantest company of captains, soldiers and mariners that I think was ever seen in England. It was a pity they should lack meat, when they are so desirous to spend their lives in her Majesty's service.' The logistical aspect of the campaign was as faulty on the English side as on the Spanish: supplies of all sorts, ammunition as well as food and water, ran short or turned bad, with the inevitable consequence of widespread sickness. Five days before the enemy came in sight Howard was writing: 'God of his mercy keep us from sickness, for we fear that more than any hurt the Spaniards will do'.

The English, of course, had the immense advantage of proximity to their home bases, so that any ship suffering damage or running short of supplies could put into a friendly harbour. Their morale was greatly superior to that of the enemy because they were defending their homeland. Nor were they inferior in the number or tonnage of their ships – 102 ships (according to one estimate) at Plymouth, with a reserve of 50 more in the Thames under Lord Henry Seymour; 195, according to another estimate, with 14,384 seamen and 1,540 soldiers. In fire power and manoeuvrability they were certainly superior. On shore, regiments were formed; Raleigh and Grenville commanding in the west, with the main army at Tilbury, where the Queen visited it from her palace at Greenwich. Booms were laid across the Thames; beacons built on every hilltop to be fired as signals when the enemy came in sight, and all church bells ordered to be rung.

Captain Fleming was the first to see the Armada off the Lizard. He brought the news to Howard and Drake, whom he found playing bowls on Plymouth Hoe. The traditional story is probably correct, but Drake's supposed remark, 'There's time to finish the game and beat the Spaniard too' can only be traced to an 18th century source. There was certainly no time to be lost in getting to sea because the wind was blowing directly into the Sound. Only by consummate seamanship did the English ships take up station astern of the Armada as it passed the Eddy-stone rock. If Sidonia had not so strictly obeyed his orders to join Parma, he might have attacked the English as Drake had attacked his own ships at Cadiz the previous year.

Howard's fleet was in no distinct formation as it pursued the Armada up Channel, always keeping its distance but ready to snap up any ship which got into trouble. Thus on the first night, after Drake had been deputed to lead the fleet with a lantern at his masthead, the light suddenly vanished until he reappeared the next morning with the excuse that he had found the *Nuestra Señora del Rosario* disabled after a collision and had taken her into Dartmouth. She and the *San Salvador,* sent into Weymouth, were the only two galleons captured before they reached Calais.

The wind shifted slightly when the Armada was off Portland, and enabled Sidonia to take the offensive, but before he could cut off Frobisher's squadron it veered again to the west and the two fleets slowly continued on their way. Calais was reached on 6th August, but there Sidonia was informed that Parma was not ready and that the Dutch Sea Beggars (the naval part of the revolt of the Netherlands) blocked the mouth of the Scheldt. Sandbanks lined the coast eastward and there was an onshore wind. The narrow anchorage at Calais offered little security, so that unless Sidonia received prompt supplies of food and water his crews would be in a bad way.

With wind and tide in their favour, it was an ideal opportunity for the English to launch fireships loaded with barrels of tar and bundles of faggots down on to the Spanish ships at night. Fireships were far more dangerous than gunfire to ships huddled together with no sea room to manoeuvre. As these flaming combustibles drifted down upon them, every galleon's cable was cut in order to escape out to sea, even if it meant drifting blindly along the coast. Those which were caught in harbour were burned.

At sunrise the next morning the 'Invincible Armada' lay scattered along the coast towards Gravelines with an onshore wind driving them on the sandbanks and the English battering them with gunfire. Drake of course led the 'first charge', as he called it. Each ship in turn bore down before the wind to deliver a broadside, then turned as another swept down upon the stricken ships. Just when it looked as if all would be wrecked, the wind shifted to the south-west, so that the main body could straggle out towards the open sea. 'There was never anything pleased me better,' wrote Drake, 'than seeing the enemy flying to the northwards. I doubt it not but ere it be long so to handle the matter with the Duke of Sidonia as he shall wish himself at Cadiz among his orange trees.'

The weather did the rest. The English pursued as far as the Scottish border, but by then their ammunition and their victuals were expended. They returned in a very weak state to the Thames. The Spanish were forced to continue around the north of Scotland, driving before another gale, and galleon after galleon was wrecked on the western shores of Scotland and Ireland as they tried to weather those rockbound coasts.

When Queen Elizabeth ordered a medal to be struck to commemorate the first English victory by sea, it bore the words 'God blew with his winds and they were scattered.' But had it not been for the damage inflicted during the battle of Gravelines, and had not Sidonia been prevented from replenishing his supplies, most of his ships might have reached home safely. As it was, only 50 out of the original 130 returned.

The war with Spain continued until the death of the Queen 15 years later. The record of those years is something of an anticlimax. There were brilliant feats of arms, but there were also plenty of fiascos and disasters. Spain was too great a power to collapse suddenly, nor was there any consistent strategy on the part of her enemy. Such British navy as was emerging was still much in embryo, and the proper use of sea power had yet to be learned. There were more expeditions and raids, and many more privateers, but the only germ of naval strategy to be discerned was Hawkins's plan for a blockade based on the Azores. No treasure fleet was ever intercepted, because such fleets were now heavily escorted and also because ships were incapable of keeping the seas for more than a few months in the summer. There was no overseas base for supplying a fleet, so that sporadic cruises were alone feasible.

One episode in the Azores blockade has caught the imagination of posterity, largely because of the vivid way in which it was recounted by Raleigh. This was the last fight of the *Revenge* by Sir Richard Grenville in 1591. His ship was part of a fleet commanded by Lord Thomas Howard, but when the

Sir Richard Grenville commanded the *Revenge* in the famous fight against the Spanish fleet off the Azores in 1591. A portrait by an unknown artist

others hauled off in the face of a greatly superior force, Grenville determined to stand and fight. Some have called his action reckless, others have praised him for standing by to rescue those of his men who had been left on shore. In an age which prized glory above everything else, Grenville certainly won imperishable fame by pitting the *Revenge* against the whole Spanish fleet for 15 hours until, mortally wounded and with more than half his crew killed, he surrendered. The *Revenge* and the *Jesus of Lubeck* in 1568 were the only two royal galleons ever lost to Spain.

Drake's reputation declined after the disastrous failure of his expedition to Lisbon in 1589. He had been sent to destroy the remnants of the Armada, but the expedition he commanded was ill-organised and ill-disciplined. Only 2,000 of the 19,000 men who sailed ever returned: the rest died of drink and disease without accomplishing anything. The Queen blamed Drake for the fiasco, so that he remained in

Opposite: An engraving by John Pine of one of the tapestries formerly in the House of Lords, commissioned by Howard from Cornelius Vroom after the campaign. It shows the two fleets anchored off Calais and the attack by English fireships to force the Spaniards to sea again

disgrace for seven years. Quite rightly, she complained that her commanders sailed 'more for profit than for service.' Drake was not the only one tempted by what he genially called 'comfortable dew from heaven'. It was this lust for loot that ruined any consistent strategy. However brilliant the individuals, what was required was a permanent navy with professional standards of conduct.

Both Drake and Hawkins were brought out of retirement in 1595 for a last attack on the Indies. They were old men, and they no longer got on well together. And this time the Spanish defences in the Caribbean area had been greatly strengthened, so that a success such as that of 1585 was out of the question. Hawkins died off Puerto Rico; Drake died off Porto Bello on 7th January, 1596; and the fleet returned without accomplishing anything.

The brilliant capture of Cadiz later that year atoned for their failure. Since it was led by the flower of Elizabethan nobility, each of whom was determined to perform some outstanding feat of arms on his own account, it is something of a miracle that it succeeded. The Earl of Essex commanded the soldiers who landed and sacked the town. Howard of Effingham commanded the ships in the *Ark Royal*, with his cousin Lord Thomas Howard in the *Mere Honour* and Sir Walter Raleigh in the *Warspite*. Medina Sidonia had the misfortune to be governor of the city. When all was over he reported that 'neither ships, nor fleet, nor galleons, nor Cadiz is left.'

It was the last great exploit before the war petered out on the death of the Queen, and it illustrated the heroic qualities of an age of brilliant episodes but no consistent strategy. In naval as in colonial affairs it was an age of reconnaissance rather than of settlement, of adventure and discovery rather than lasting achievement. The first attempts to colonise Virginia failed; the first attempts to make contact with India only bore fruit in the next century. Splendid successes, such as the defeat of the Armada and the capture of Cadiz, must be set against dismal failures, such as the Lisbon expedition. The need now was for professional officers of long training, not a horde of brilliant amateurs. More ships designed specifically for battle, together with a corps of officers who put service to the state before private gain, were what were required.

Since it was an age of promise rather than achievement, it was a time when the future was unveiled to men of discernment. We have seen how Hakluyt boasted of the prospects of maritime empire. Francis Bacon, the wisest of the Elizabethans, could also point out the significance of the war with Spain in his essay *On the True Greatness of Kingdoms*:

To be master of the sea is an abridgement of monarchy. He that commands the sea is at great liberty, and may take as much and as little of the war as he will. Surely, at this day, with us of Europe, the vantage of strength at sea (which is one of the principal dowries of this Kingdom of Great Britain) is great.

CHAPTER 3

The Dutch Wars – Blake in the Mediterranean – The Four Days' Battle – The Birth of Naval Tactics – De Ruyter in the Medway – Battles of Barfleur and La Hougue

CHRISTOPHER LLOYD

The British Navy may have been small in Tudor times, but that of the first two Stuart Kings was even smaller and far less effective. By 1618 the navy had shrunk to 27 ships. Pirates from as far afield as the Mediterranean ranged the Channel at will, capturing ships and burning towns and villages. Corruption percolated from the top to the bottom of naval administration, and the record of those years is one of futile expeditions and miserable seamen.

During the same period, however, there was a marked expansion in the merchant marine. Overseas trade developed with the founding of the great chartered companies, such as the East India Company and the Hudson Bay Company, while colonial settlements and trading 'factories' or depots, took root overseas. The history of Virginia as a permanent English colony dates from 1607, in which year Surat also became a factory for the East India Company. The New England colonies followed in the west, as did the trading stations at Madras, Calcutta and Bombay in the east.

The development of the Dutch maritime empire was proceeding along the same lines at the same time. Already there were conflicts between the two nations in the Spice Islands, forcing the English to restrict their activities to India. The Dutch share of the carrying trade of Europe was increasing so rapidly that a situation was soon reached, as a blunt sea captain said, wherein 'the trade of the world is too little for us two, therefore one must down.' The three Dutch wars in the middle of the century were thus the inevitable climax of imperial and economic rivalry.

In the forge of those three wars a professional British Navy was created. Very gradually the age of the amateur, of gentleman captains, and even of privateers began to recede. In its place there dawned the age of great fleets of warships owned by the state and commanded by trained officers who adopted codes of tactics and professional standards of conduct under which the good of the Service took precedence over opportunities for self-enrichment. In place of temporary levies of ships there was the building of a permanent establishment of ships designed specifically for war. At last it had become obvious that a ship cannot carry a large number of guns as well as a cargo, and that if she is an expensive warship owned by the crown she must be fought and maintained by a permanent corps of officers. Thus the distinction between the warship and the merchant ship, and hence between the Royal Navy (as it was called from the time of Charles II) and the Merchant Service, became clear as soon as a functional fleet of warships commanded by permanent officers paid by the state came into existence.

The seamen who formed the ship's companies did not, however, make the navy their career. For another two centuries the state hired them (often by force) and discharged them as soon as the ship paid off, when in most cases they transferred themselves easily to a merchant vessel, since the skills still required in both types of ship did not materially differ.

The men responsible for the birth of a modern navy were Cromwell's three Generals-at-Sea – Robert Blake, Edward Popham, Robert Deane – and their successors after the Restoration, James, Duke of York, Prince Rupert, George Monck (who be-

Opposite: Robert Blake, one of the first three 'generals-at-sea' and England's principal admiral during the First Dutch War. 'Thy name was heard in thunder through th'affrighted shores of pale Iberia, of submissive Gaul, and Tagus trembling to his utmost source, O ever faithful, vigilant, and brave, thou bold asserter of Britannia's fame, unconquerable Blake'. So runs the legend under this picture after Thomas Preston

ROBERT BLAKE
General and Admiral of the FORCES
of ENGLAND. &c.
Denatus 17. Aug. 1657. Ætat. 59.

——————————— Thy Name.
Was heard in thunder through th' affrighted Shores
Of pale IBERIA, of Submissive GAUL,
And TAGUS trembling to his utmost source.
O ever faithfull, Vigilant, and brave,
Thou bold asserter of Britannia's FAME,
Unconquerable BLAKE!

Mr. Glover's London. p. 21.

Drawn from a Painting in the Possession of Mr. J. Ames. By Tho. Preston. and Dedicated to ye Citizens of LONDON.

Samuel Pepys, a portrait painted by Sir Godfrey Kneller. Pepys, both as Clerk of the Acts and as Secretary of the Admiralty, devoted his genius to the administration of the Navy and did much to eradicate many of the abuses of the Stuart period

came Duke of Albemarle after transferring his allegiance from one government to another); and above all, Samuel Pepys, the most famous and most efficient of all Secretaries of the Admiralty.

Pepys began his career as Clerk of the Acts on the Navy Board which, as we have seen, was responsible for building, maintaining and manning the ships. He ended as Secretary of the Admiralty, of which his patron, the Duke of York, was Lord High Admiral. When, under the Commonwealth, and again when James was driven from office because he was a Roman Catholic, this office was put into commission, the executive affairs of the navy were conducted by a Board of Commissioners appointed to execute the office of Lord High Admiral, commonly known as Lords Commissioners of the Board of Admiralty. During the Dutch wars it quickly became apparent that the business of victualling the fleet, as well as that of caring for the sick and wounded and for prisoners of war, was now on too big a scale to be handled by the old private contract method, so there

came into existence, at first on a temporary and then on a permanent basis, the Victualling Board and the Sick and Hurt Board.

The warship became distinct from the merchant ship when the number of guns she carried increased from one tier to two, and then to three. When Phineas Pett of Deptford built the *Prince Royal* in 1610 he produced what was virtually the first three-decker; but his son Peter's *Sovereign of the Seas* of 1637 is the real prototype of the first-rate line-of-battle ship with three masts, carrying 100 guns on three decks. She was 232 feet overall and 48 feet in the beam, with a displacement of 1,637 tons. Though much more ornate, with garlanded ports and a magnificently carved and gilded stern, she was basically the same type of ship as the *Victory* of 1765 which led the British fleet at Trafalgar. In her day ships were rated by the size of their complements – 800 men for a first-rate three-decker – but by the time of Pepys it became the practice to rate them according to the number of guns they carried.

From the same date the earliest scale models have survived. These were constructed to show the Navy Board and the Board of Admiralty the sort of ship it was intended to lay down, but the actual building was still done by eye, the knowledge of the best builders, according to Pepys, 'lying in their hands so confusedly that they were not able to render it intelligible to anybody else.' Nevertheless, the earliest treatises of naval architecture were written about this time.

Over 100 ships on either side participated in the battles of the Dutch wars, which occasionally lasted over several days and were fought over wide areas. To control these huge fleets a tactical code known as the *Fighting Instructions* was issued in 1653, to be expanded by later commanders-in-chief. Their scope was limited by the primitive method of signalling then in use. A gun was fired and a flag hoisted in a particular position to denote the manoeuvre required. Thus the line ahead formation, the most important tactical innovation because it made the maximum use of broadside fire power, was signalled as follows: 'When the Admiral would have the fleet drawn into line of battle he will hoist a union flag and a pennant at the mizen peak.' Line ahead tactics were first employed at the battle of the Gabbard in 1653, in accordance with Instruction No. 3. A new era in sea warfare had dawned when a squadron, or indeed a fleet, became the tactical unit instead of the single ship.

Just as the *Fighting Instructions* imposed some sort of order in the tactical handling of ships, so a disciplinary code for the conduct of men on board was essential. In Tudor times individual captains usually composed such orders, but in 1652 the first Articles of War were issued and court martial procedure was set up to try offenders. These rules were incorporated in the first Naval Discipline Act of 1661, in which 25 out of the 37 articles carried the death penalty. The preamble of that act contains the noble formula (borrowed from the Navigation Act) which still stands today with only minor alteration of the last four words. The change was made in the Act of 1749 of which the preamble read: 'For the regulating and better government of H.M. Navies, ships of war and forces by sea, wherein under the good Providence and protection of God, the Wealth, Safety and Strength of this Kingdom is so much concerned.'

When it was found necessary to build a special type of ship as a warship a professional type of naval officer was required to command such an expensive piece of government property. But the tradition of the amateur lingered until the middle of the century. Even Robert Blake, the greatest admiral of the age, was such a one. Almost nothing is known about his early career, until he suddenly appeared as a successful general in Cromwell's New Model Army. When the Civil War was over and a New Model Navy was created, he was appointed the first of the Generals-at-Sea. The word 'general' still meant 'commander-in-chief', the word 'admiral' denoting his ship, but the convention was changing so that before the end of that war 'admiral' meant a man and not a ship, just as the word 'seaman' or 'sailor' was replacing the older word 'mariner'.

Blake learned what was required of him in his

A scale model of HMS *Dreadnought*, a 60–gun third-rate of 1692, with the lower strakes removed to show the construction of the ribs. The *Dreadnought* fought at Barfleur in the Blue Squadron commanded by Sir George Rooke

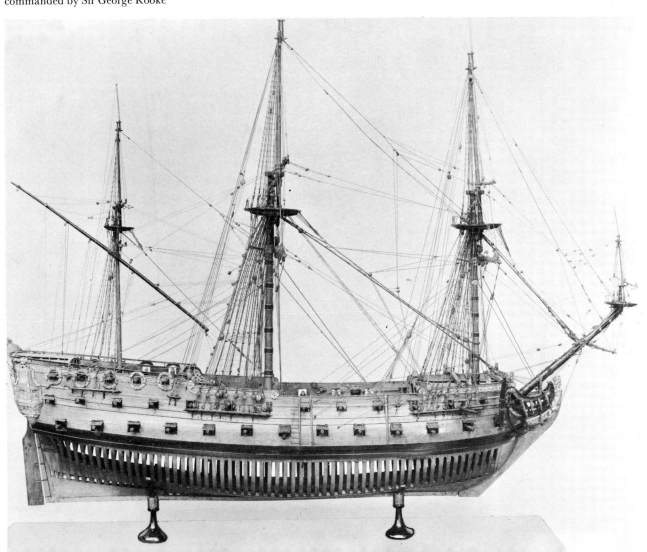

new element in an astonishingly short space of time. As the royalist historian Clarendon said, in a noble tribute paid him on his death,

He made it manifest that the science might be attained in less time than was imagined, and despised those rules which had long been in practice, to keep his ships and men out of danger ... He was the first that infused that proportion of courage into the seamen, by making them see by experience what mighty things they could do, if they were resolved; and though he hath been very well imitated and followed, he was the first that drew the copy of naval courage, and bold and resolute achievement.

After the death of Cromwell and the restoration of Charles II as king there were fewer of the distinguished amateurs of the old style, often called gentleman captains to distinguish them from the tarpaulin captains promoted from the lower deck. It was the work of Samuel Pepys to combine what was best of two distinct social classes into what we should call a naval officer. It was not a task which could be completed in a single generation, but the key reform which made it impossible for a mere courtier to command a king's ship without knowing his business at sea was the institution of an examination for lieutenants in 1677. Following up the ideas of the Duke of York, who had encouraged young gentlemen to make the sea their profession by entering the navy as what were known as King's Letter Boys with the pay of midshipmen (hitherto a warrant officer's post), Pepys laid it down that no one could become a lieutenant unless he passed an examination in seamanship and navigation. As he wrote soon afterwards, 'I thank God we have not half the throng of that bastard breed (i.e. gentlemen who were not trained officers) pressing for employment which we heretofore used to be troubled with, they being conscious of their inability to pass this examination.'

The concept of a hierarchy of rank inevitably followed. The better an officer's qualifications, the longer he had served at sea, the higher was his pay. By the end of the century it was possible to compile the first *List of Sea Officers*, or *Navy List*, giving the seniority of admirals, captains, lieutenants, and masters (still a post for warrant officers responsible for the navigation of the ship). In this way a corps of professional officers who made the Navy their career came into existence.

Such was not the case with the seamen who composed the ship's company. The Navy was never popular because the discipline was stricter and the pay lower than that offered by merchant skippers, especially in wartime. Early in the century the practice of paying men by wage ticket had been introduced for the sensible reason that it was unwise to carry much cash on board in those days. But when a ship was paid off, the seaman who expected hard cash for his pains was as often as not given a ticket which, when he presented it at the Navy Pay Office on Tower Hill in London, was seldom honoured in full value. Cromwell had increased the monthly pay of an able seaman (that is to say a seaman who could reef, hand, and steer) to 22s. 6d., and that of an ordinary seaman to 19s. (at which figure it remained until 1797, the longest wage freeze in history). But as long as Parliament quarrelled with the King over financial matters, there was seldom enough cash to pay the men punctually.

What exacerbated the situation was the increasing demand for men as the Royal Navy expanded and its responsibilities widened. By the end of the century wars were no longer fought only in the Channel and the North Sea (as were the Dutch Wars), but in the Mediterranean, across the Atlantic, and in the Indian Ocean. Whereas 16,000 men had been enough to man the fleet in 1653, 42,000 were required in 1688 to man the 173 ships in commission. About the same number were required for the merchant marine, and even more for the armies of the Duke of Marlborough. Since the total population of England and Wales was still under six million, the strain on available manpower necessitated recourse to unpopular methods of impressment, which in turn made service in the Navy still more disliked.

Pressing, that is to say conscription or drafting by force, was an ancient feudal obligation. It did not bear hardly on the population as long as the Navy was small and there were plenty of vagrants to be picked up. But by the end of the Dutch Wars press gangs were common, and in the Anglo-French wars which followed they became the principal means of recruitment. Bounties were offered to volunteers, but over half the Navy consisted of pressed men who took every opportunity to desert.

By the time Pepys left the Admiralty, when his patron James II lost his throne at the Revolution of 1688, a Royal Navy in the sense of a professional force employed on board ships specifically designed for war had come into existence. It was during the period of the three Dutch Wars between 1652 and 1674 that this fundamental change occurred.

We have seen why these wars were inevitable. By mid-century the Dutch were outstripping the English in the race for maritime empire. Their fishing fleets were far more numerous than the British, and when their shipwrights developed the fluyt as a general cargo ship, they were able to dominate the carrying trade of Europe. During Holland's golden age the Dutch not only built the best ships and published the best marine charts, but they produced the best marine painters of all time in the Van de Veldes, father and son. None the less Holland suffered from two fatal weaknesses which ultimately brought about her downfall. Since there were no fewer than five admiralties in the federation of the United Provinces, it is something of a miracle that any Dutch fleet could be fitted out. What was more serious was the fact that the main artery of her trade was the English Channel. If the great trading fleets from her empire in the East Indies or those from the Baltic could be prevented from reaching home, grass would indeed grow in the streets of Amsterdam. Such therefore was the main strategic objective of the English when war broke out.

The English claim to a salute at sea in the Channel was regarded as derisory by foreign powers until Cromwell decided to enforce it. This was known as the sovereignty of the seas, by which was meant the Narrow Seas, for long claimed by a succession of English kings. At the same time the maritime rivalry between the two countries was exacerbated by the English Navigation Acts of 1651 and 1661, in order to safeguard English shipping by what we should today call flag discrimination.

The consequence of this enforcement of the salute was the First Dutch War of 1652 to 1654. It began with a brush between Blake and Martin Tromp off Dover, when the latter refused to lower his topsails by way of salute. It continued with battles off the Kentish Knock, at the mouth of the Thames, and off Dungeness, in the Downs, where Blake was worsted by Tromp in a battle from which originated the story that Tromp lashed a broom to his masthead to show that he had swept the English off the seas. The next year the two met again when Tromp conducted a masterly rearguard action all the way from Portland to the mouth of the Texel in order to save the

George Monck, first Duke of Albermarle, began his career in the Army but became one of Cromwell's 'generals-at-sea' during the Commonwealth (1649–60). Largely instrumental in the restoration of Charles II as king in 1660, he became Commander-in-Chief of the English fleet and led it in many battles of the Dutch wars. A portrait painted by Sir Peter Lely

Dutch East Indies fleet. The English fleet, under Monck and Deane, had the best of the fighting in the battle of the Gabbard and won a definite victory off Scheveningen, when the Dutch coast was blockaded and Tromp lost his life. Peace came early in 1654, but the underlying reasons for a war in which sea battles had been fought on an unprecedented scale remained unresolved.

Meanwhile Cromwell turned his attention to the old scourge of the Barbary pirates by sending Blake to chastise them in the Mediterranean. A short but successful war with Spain on Elizabethan lines then developed. Admiral William Penn (the father of the Quaker founder of Pennsylvania) was sent to capture Hispaniola in the Drake tradition. When he and General Venables found it too well defended, they turned aside to take possession of the almost uninhabited island of Jamaica in 1655. This was the first English naval base overseas, but Cromwell was not impressed: he threw both Penn and Venables into the Tower of London for failing to carry out their instructions.

Meanwhile off the coast of Spain Blake and Admiral Richard Stayner did what no Elizabethan seaman had been able to do; they captured a treasure fleet and maintained a blockade of Cadiz throughout the winter. In 1657 Blake stretched across to Santa Cruz at Teneriffe in the Canaries to intercept another well-protected treasure fleet. There he fought a successful battle against a fleet at anchor protected by forts, a feat which had no equal until Nelson's battle of Copenhagen nearly two and a half centuries later. Blake received his death wound in this fight, dying at sea within sight of Plymouth on his return.

The Second Dutch War (1664–7) was a continuation of the same policy in less glorious fashion, partly because it coincided with the disasters of the Plague and the Fire, partly because it showed up the defects of Charles's administration of the Navy contrasted with that of Cromwell. But it must be borne in mind that although Cromwell built a large fleet, he did not pay for it, saddling Charles II's Navy with a debt of over £1,000,000. It was no wonder that neither the seamen's wages could be paid nor the ships fitted out in time to meet the Dutch.

The Dutch were now at the height of their power, and also in alliance with France. Admiral Mihiel de Ruyter had succeeded Martin Tromp as one of the finest admirals of the age, and Cornelis Tromp continued the fighting tradition of his father. Yet the English took the offensive with attacks on Dutch possessions in West Africa and North America, where New Amsterdam was captured and renamed New York in honour of the Lord High Admiral, James, Duke of York.

In the first battle off Lowestoft the Duke of York and Penn, now Sir William, defeated Opdam when the latter's flagship blew up and he lost his life. But the longest and hardest fought of these contests, in which over a hundred ships on either side were often engaged, was the Four Days' Battle of 1st–4th June, 1666, so called because, beginning off the Dutch coast and ending at the mouth of the Thames, it lasted for four days. The English had made the mistake of dividing their fleet when a report reached them that the French were coming up Channel to assist their allies. A squadron under the command of Prince Rupert had been sent to stop them. Monck (now the Duke of Albemarle), with only two-thirds of the English fleet, stumbled upon the Dutch fleet in thick weather near Dunkirk. Cornelis Tromp and de Ruyter attacked him and forced him out to sea

in heavy fighting which continued until nightfall, when Albemarle withdrew to the north-westward for such repairs as were possible. During the night he called a Council of War of his captains and to them made a famous speech which put great heart into them for the next day's fighting.

'If we had dreaded the number of the enemy,' he said, 'we should have fled; but though we are inferior to them in ships, we are in all things else superior. Force gives them courage. Let us, if we need it, borrow resolution from what we have formerly performed. Let the enemy feel that though our fleet be divided, our spirit is entire. At the worst it will be more honourable to die bravely here on our own element than be made spectacles to the Dutch. To be overcome is the fortune of war; but to fly is the fashion of cowards. So let us teach the world that Englishmen would rather be acquainted with death than fear'.

On the second day Monck returned to the battle with such of his ships as he had left, 44 all told. The Dutch still had 80, but some of these had been badly damaged by the English broadsides of the previous day. The second day's fighting was heavy, with Tromp's squadron becoming separated from the remainder of the Dutch fleet and being attacked by Albemarle to such an extent that twice Tromp was forced to shift his flag into another ship. But by the end of the day de Ruyter was reinforced by 16 fresh ships from Holland, and Albemarle knew that retreat was the only possible course if the fleet was to be saved from annihilation. He drew away to the north-westward towards the shelter of English shores, hotly pursued by the Dutch throughout the night.

Albemarle's retreat was continued throughout the third day. The badly damaged ships were sent ahead and behind them Albemarle gathered his sounder ships, now reduced to 16, as a protective screen. The Dutch attacked continuously, but so dogged and furious was the English reply that never once were the Dutch able to break through to the damaged ships ahead in spite of their great superiority in numbers.

Only one tragedy marred this remarkable day's fighting. In the early afternoon Admiral Ayscue's flagship, the *Royal Prince*, ran ashore on the Galloper Sand. She was surrounded by Tromp's squadron and set on fire, Ayscue and all her ship's company being taken prisoner. The *Royal Prince* was one of the largest and latest of the English men of war, and her loss was a sad blow for Albemarle.

Opposite: The launch of the English fireships against the Spanish Armada off Calais in 1588, an attack which caused the Spanish ships to cut their cables and run. A painting by an unknown artist; *Overleaf:* The painting by Abraham Storck of the Four Days' Battle, fought between the English and Dutch fleets in 1666. Incidents from all four days appear in this picture, including the capture of the *Swiftsure* by the Dutch (left), de Ruyter's flagship, *Zeven Provincien*, in action (centre) and the *Royal James*, Prince Rupert's flagship, losing her main topmast (centre right)

A typical warship of the Dutch wars, showing the rigging plan. Although this drawing is of a
Dutch ship, they were almost identical with English sailing warships except for the design of the stern galleries

In the late afternoon a squadron of 25 sail was sighted approaching from the west. It could have been the French, having evaded Prince Rupert in the Channel, or it could be Rupert. It was an hour before Albemarle could be certain that it was indeed Rupert, bringing new hope for the morrow.

Albemarle returned to the offensive on the fourth day. The wind had freshened and the English fleet came up to the Dutch 'with all sails set, the trumpets sounding, and drums beating in every ship, the seamen waving in defiance their hats and the officers their plumed beavers'. Soon the English were engaged all along the line of battle, and for two hours they fought as hotly as ever. By the fury of his attack Albemarle broke through the Dutch line of battle, only to find a second line still to windward of him. Virtually surrounded, the English ships fought on. A Dutch observer in de Ruyter's flagship wrote:

At this moment the look-out was extraordinary, for all were separated, the English as well as we ... Our admiral had with him thirty-five or forty ships of his own and of other squadrons, for the squadrons were scattered and order much lost. The rest of the Dutch ships had left him ... Thus in less than no time we found ourselves in the

Opposite: The attack by the Dutch fleet in the river Medway in 1667, from the painting by Jan Peeters. The ship in the foreground is the *Royal Charles*, which was captured and taken back to Holland. Six other large English ships were set on fire

midst of the English who, being attacked on both sides, were thrown into confusion and saw their whole order destroyed, as well by dint of the action as by the strong wind that was blowing. This was the hottest of the fight. We saw the high admiral of England separated from his fleet, followed only by one fireship, with which he gained to windward, and passing through the North Holland squadron, placed himself again at the head of fifteen or twenty ships that rallied to him.

The fighting was, mercifully both for Dutch and English, brought to an end by a thick fog which came down a little before 7 p.m. The casualties on both sides were exceptionally heavy. The Dutch withdrew to seaward, Albemarle and Rupert limped slowly home, their ships sadly shattered. 'This', wrote Campbell in his history of the Royal Navy, 'was the most terrible battle fought in this, or perhaps in any other war, as the Dutch admirals themselves say'.

It was an English defeat, but even in this adversity the conduct of Albemarle and his men could draw a tribute from the Dutch Grand Pensionary, de Witte, in conversation with the English ambassador:

'If the English were beaten, their conduct did them more honour than all their former victories. Our own fleet could never have been brought on after the first day's fight, and I believe that none but their's could; and all that the Dutch had discovered was, that Englishmen might be killed and English ships be burned, but that English courage was invincible'.

The Four Days' Battle was a landmark in English naval history for it marked quite clearly the final transition from the crude tactics of former battles to the formal line of battle which was to be such a feature of naval actions for the next hundred years. Among the witnesses of the battle in the Dutch fleet was the French naval historian de Guiche.

'Nothing', he wrote, 'equals the beautiful order of the English at sea. Never was a line drawn straighter than that formed by their ships; thus they bring all their fire to bear upon those who draw near them … They fight like a line of cavalry which is handled according to rule, and applies itself solely to force back those who oppose; whereas the Dutch advance like cavalry whose squadrons leave their ranks and come separately to the charge'.

Two months later the English fleet had been repaired and was at sea again. It met the Dutch fleet off the North Foreland on St. James' Day, 25th July. Once again, Albemarle and Prince Rupert forced the pace, and de Ruyter was thrown into complete confusion by the accuracy of the English gunnery. Cornelis Tromp, 'who fought like a madman rather than a wise commander', had once again, as in the Four Days' battle, got his squadron separated from the main Dutch fleet and was soon in trouble. De Ruyter was unable to come to his assistance for he was too hotly engaged by Albemarle and Rupert, his line of battle was breaking up, and some of his captains, irresolute in face of the English attack, were stealing away and making their separate ways back to Holland. Soon the whole Dutch fleet was in flight with the English in full cry in pursuit. Before midnight of the 26th the Dutch were back in their harbours, with over 20 fewer vessels and 7,000 fewer men than when they had sailed, and the English fleet was anchored off the Dutch coast.

For a week the ships remained in Dutch waters, burning and destroying. A fleet of just on 170 merchant ships lying at anchor in the Vlie river was destroyed by fire and the chief villages on the island of Terschelling were sacked and put to the torch. These operations were under the command of Sir Robert Holmes, and for many years were known as 'Sir Robert Holmes, his bonefire'. The damage caused to the Dutch was estimated at £1,200,000, a prodigious sum in those days.

But lack of money to supply the fleet, together with the disasters of the Great Plague and the Fire of London, forced the king to delay fitting out his fleet in 1667. It was a calculated gamble, for there were talks of peace with the Dutch. But they came to nothing, with the English ships still laid up at their winter moorings in the Medway river. Here de Ruyter found them, piloted to Chatham by English deserters in the Dutch ships who cried, 'We did heretofore fight for tickets, now we fight for dollars.' The chain stretched across the river was broken by Dutch ships, the forts silenced by fire, and many of the English vessels at anchor were burned. The *Royal Charles* was taken and towed back to Amsterdam, where her magnificent gilded stern may still be seen. After such a catastrophe it is perhaps surprising that the English were allowed to retain New York under the terms of the treaty of Breda which was

Prince Rupert of the Rhine, a portrait by Sir Peter Lely. Rupert, one of the more dashing of the English admirals during the wars against the Dutch, arrived in the nick of time in the Four Days' Battle in 1666 to save the English from severe defeat

signed the following year.

Holland was finally defeated in the Third Dutch War (1672–4) chiefly because Louis XIV of France had changed sides and invaded the country with his armies. For the Dutch it was a war of survival against superior forces by land and sea. De Ruyter fought defensive actions by making clever use of the shoal waters around the Dutch coast, where the heavier draught of English warships made it difficult for them to follow. The French squadrons which now fought on the English side proved as useless as they had been when fighting on the Dutch side in the previous war. Moreover, the war was unpopular in England, where it was now seen that the real enemy was Catholic France, not Protestant Holland. After both sides had engaged in hard-fought battles in the Schooneveld and the Texel, peace was signed early in 1674, the Dutch conceding the English claim to sovereignty in the Narrow Seas.

After the great exertions of these wars the Royal Navy declined in the latter part of the reign of Charles II, chiefly for political reasons connected with the Test Act and the Popish Plot scare. The

Opposite: An incident on the fourth day of the Four Days' Battle showing Prince Rupert's flagship, the *Royal James*, losing her main topmast. The mizen is already over the side. Part of a painting by Van de Velde the Younger

39

Duke of York was removed from his office as Lord High Admiral because he was a Roman Catholic, and even Pepys was confined to the Tower in 1679 because he employed a Catholic musician. Both of them returned when the Duke ascended the throne as James II, so that Pepys was able to repair some of the administrative damage done in his absence.

Samuel Pepys had proved himself a brilliant administrator and a sturdy champion of all that was best in the Royal Navy. He was justified in claiming that 'the Navy of England will never be found to have been in the good condition I have had the leaving of it twice, viz. in 1679 and 1688.' More than any other man, he had put the Navy on a permanent footing. Ships had been built to increase the fleet from 156 in 1660 to 173 in 1688. An officer corps with professional qualifications had been formed. Important advances in the art of navigation had been made by the founding of the Royal Observatory at Greenwich in 1674, and by the commissioning of Captain Greenville Collins to survey the seas surrounding Britain. His charts replaced those of the Dutch, at the time the most expert cartographers in Europe, and were published under the title of *Britain's Coasting Pilot*, the first truly English marine atlas carried out under the auspices of the Admiralty. Their accuracy was a considerable improvement on that of the Dutch, and their publication perhaps foreshadowed the subsequent fame of the Admiralty chart.

In 1688 the Revolution in England swept James II from his throne because of his Roman Catholicism. It swept, too, Pepys from his commanding position as Secretary of the Admiralty. James, who for all his faults as prince and king, had, as Lord High Admiral, done much to lift the Navy out of the depths into which it had fallen under the first two Stuart kings, was succeeded by William of Orange, who came to England as King William III. But James never gave up his claim to the English throne. Befriended by Louis XIV of France, he tried to regain his kingdom by a landing with French troops in support on the Catholic shores of Ireland. Driven out from there by the immediate response of William in command of an English army, he and Louis turned to thoughts of direct invasion across the English Channel. A large French army was assembled at La Hougue with transports in readiness, and a French fleet was in the Channel under the command of the Comte de Tourville.

The decisive battle was fought off Barfleur in May 1692. Tourville, heavily outnumbered, fought his ships gallantly but they could not stand up to the superior weight of the English gunfire. His line of battle began to crumble and his fleet was forced away to the westward. Three French ships went ashore on the rocky coast near Cherbourg where they were set on fire and destroyed by the British; others, risking the dangerous passage of the Alderney Race, reached St. Malo in safety. Twelve of the larger ships, unwilling to face the rockbound channels around Alderney, worked their way into the bay of La Hougue.

Here they were attacked by the English under the command of Sir George Rooke. On the flood tide of the evening of 23rd May, 200 boats from the fleet swept in towards the shore. The guns of the forts opened fire but their noise was drowned by the cheers of the sailors. They made for six French three-deckers which were anchored under the guns of Fort Lisset. Driving the French crews out of their ships, the seamen lashed them together in pairs and put them to the torch. 'They dropped out of the bay', wrote a subsequent historian, 'with the ebb tide, leaving La Hougue one sheet of fire. During all the night the great ships blazed, and the explosion was heard from time to time of their loaded cannon as the fire reached them, till six culminating crashes announced that the flames had reached their magazines, and then sea and sky became sheeted with burning brands'.

The other six French ships were anchored under the fort of St. Vaast. Rooke returned to the attack on the morning tide of the 24th. Again the boats of the fleet raced in, this time into water so shallow that French cavalry were ordered to assist in repelling them. They were pulled off their horses by the seamen with boathooks. The French ships were boarded, their crews routed, and the ships' guns turned against the fort ashore, silencing it while the seamen set about their work of destruction.

James, who was there, saw his hopes of regaining the throne of England dissolve in the flames of the French ships. Yet he could not restrain a surge of pride in the actions of the British seamen. 'Ah,' he said to the Duke of Berwick who was standing alongside him, 'none but my brave English tars could have performed so gallant an action'.

The Battle of Barfleur, fought against the French in 1692, from the painting by L. Bakhuizen. The victory at Barfleur was followed four days later by the two boat attacks at La Hougue in which twelve French ships of the line were set on fire

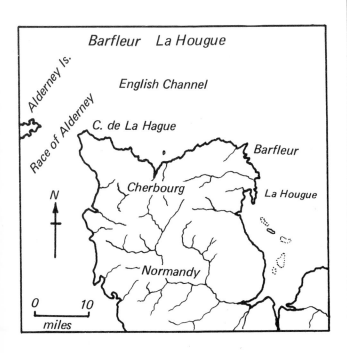

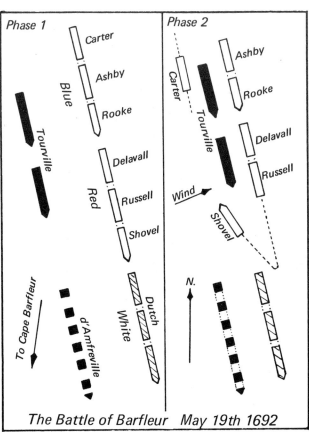

CHAPTER 4

*War of the Spanish Succession – British ships in the
Mediterranean – Capture of Gibraltar and the Battle of
Malaga – The Attack on Toulon – Capture of Minorca –
Operations across the Atlantic*

BRYAN RANFT

Although Louis XIV's navy had largely dissolved into ashes in the bay of La Hougue, he was still the possessor of the finest army in Europe. With it he planned to make France unsurpassable in power in Europe by filling the vacant throne of Spain with a French prince. The implications for Britain were too obvious to be ignored. A France predominant in Europe to this extent would have the use of ports in the Spanish Netherlands (modern Belgium) ideal for the invasion of Britain. British trade would be barred from the Netherlands, from Spain itself, and perhaps from the whole of the Mediterranean. Finally it would frustrate Britain's long ambition to acquire possessions and trade in Spain's crumbling West Indian empire.

The complexity of the threat determined the nature of the war and the Navy's contribution to it. France's strength centred on her armies, which Britain by herself could never equal. So the first essential was to organise a continental military alliance which Britain would have to support with men and money. The main aim of the alliance would be to keep France out of the Low Countries, and towards this the British Fleet could make little direct contribution. The battles would have to be fought on land, far away from the sea. But armies had to be paid and supplied, and the Navy's task of protecting the seaborne trade, which was the basis of Britain's wealth, was essential to this.

The Mediterranean was a different matter. Geography and the complex relations of the countries around its shores made it ideal for a maritime strategy. Naval power rightly used could make a direct contribution to the land fighting as well as

exercising diplomatic pressure to win allies and to influence neutrals. Both William III and the Duke of Marlborough, who directed Britain's strategy after the king's death in 1702, realised this to the full. As the war progressed they evolved a Mediterranean strategy based on the permanent presence of a strong British fleet, a strategy which was to be a constant feature of all Britain's future wars with France until the defeat of Napoleon.

For a British fleet to maintain control of the Mediterranean, it had to have a secure base. Without one it was impossible not only to maintain an effective blockade of the main French naval port of Toulon, but also to keep an effective fleet in the Mediterranean at all throughout the autumn and winter. Without facilities for refitting there, the ships of the line had to be sent back to Britain in time to avoid the dangers of the October and November storms in the western approaches. At the beginning of the war Britain, with her ally Holland, had a considerable naval superiority over France, with her ally Spain, and was thus in a strong position to launch a naval offensive to capture the essential base.

Cadiz had obvious advantages. It provided an extensive and safe anchorage and the facilities of an established port. Moreover, if Britain did not strike first, the French could seize it and establish control of the entrance to the Mediterranean. Such an action would make it impossible for the British to prevent the junction of the Toulon and Brest fleets which both sides regarded as an essential preliminary to a French invasion of Britain.

The invasion force under Sir George Rooke cleared the Channel on 25th July 1702. Including a

Opposite: Admiral of the Fleet Sir George Rooke, painted by Michael Dahl, commanded the
English fleet at the capture of Gibraltar, the Battle of Malaga, and at Barfleur and La Hougue.
He had learned the art of war under Prince Rupert and Monck in the battles of the Dutch wars

Opposite: The Battle of Vigo Bay, 1702, from the picture by Ludolf Bakhuizen. The French and Spanish ships in Vigo were all burned or taken, and although some of the treasure from the West Indian galleons which the fleet had escorted had already been landed, it was estimated that gold, silver, and other cargo to the value of 13 million pieces of eight fell into the hands of the victors

Dutch contingent, it numbered 50 ships of the line, 30 lesser warships, and 50 transports carrying troops. Although Rooke's orders laid down Cadiz as the primary objective, they also gave him discretion, should he find Cadiz too strong, to attack Gibraltar or any smaller Spanish ports such as Vigo or Corunna. As Rooke neared Cadiz he learned that it was strongly defended, but the Duke of Ormonde, in command of the troops, insisted on attacking. It was not an impossible task but, like so many 18th century amphibious operations, failed through lack of unified command and the failure of the military to advance rapidly after the initial landings. Rooke himself did little to help the soldiers. He had been against the attack from the first and claimed that ill health kept

him in his bed during most of the fighting. His chief concern was in getting his big ships home before the bad weather set in. The one naval contribution which might have brought success, a bombardment of the port, was never made on the grounds that it would antagonise the inhabitants against future co-operation. After three weeks of desultory land fighting, the attempt was abandoned. Rooke resisted pressures by Ormonde and the Dutch admiral to attempt any of the alternatives which his orders allowed, pleading the lateness of the season. However, an opportunity which not even Rooke could ignore prevented a completely ignominious return home. On 11th September the French admiral Chateaurenault, evading the watching British cruisers, had

Mediterranean Sea

The Western Mediterranean

arrived at Vigo with the immensely valuable Spanish treasure fleet from the West Indies. After some hesitation Rooke decided to attack but, still being confined to bed, left the execution of the operation to his second-in-command, Thomas Hopsonn. The treasure fleet and its escort were in a strong position, at the far end of a gulf protected by a boom and shore batteries. Troops were landed to deal with the batteries while Hopsonn and his Dutch consorts broke through the boom and attacked the French escorts. At the end of an afternoon's close cannonading the French squadron was annihilated. The flagship and six others were burnt and the rest either captured or driven ashore. The treasure galleons were similarly treated, but only a part of their cargo was captured as most of it had already been taken inland for safety.

The political fruits of sea power were again gathered in 1703, when the presence of a strong fleet under Sir Cloudesley Shovel in the Mediterranean persuaded the Duke of Savoy to abandon the French alliance and join that of Britain and the Dutch. Thus, in 1704 when Marlborough was fighting his great campaign in central Europe, diversionary attacks could be launched from Savoy to draw off some of the enemy's strength. Marlborough's strategic vision, however, went far beyond minor diversions, and he easily grasped the great strategic freedom which could be gained by the capture of France's centre of naval power in the Mediterranean, Toulon. With this in mind, Rooke was sent out with a combined Anglo-Dutch fleet of 40 of the line. Shovel, in command in the Channel, was instructed that if the French from Brest eluded him and sailed towards the Mediterranean, he was to detach a force strong enough to enable Rooke to hold his own. This flexibility, based on an understanding of the strategic unity of the Channel and Mediterranean theatres, showed a highly developed conception of the use of sea power. But the Duke of Savoy refused to join in an attack on Toulon, and so another use for Rooke's forces had to be found. He was instructed to assist the Hapsburg prince, who claimed the Spanish throne against Louis XIV's nominee, to establish himself on Spanish soil. The new claimant, however, found little local support and in July Rooke judged it more profitable to turn his forces against Gibraltar, a fortress which had attracted English governments since the days of Oliver Cromwell. The time was now opportune. Rooke had a strong fleet and 2,000 marines, and his intelligence suggested that Gibraltar was weakly fortified and garrisoned. In fact it was held by under 100 regular soldiers and 50 local militia. The attack began on 21st July when the marines landed to cut off the fortress from the Spanish mainland. On the following day a naval bombardment lasting six hours was followed by an assault landing of seamen to silence the few batteries still firing. A cease-fire and surrender soon followed. The gate to the Mediterranean had thus been easily gained, but Rooke found himself in a hazardous position when he discovered that the French fleet had sailed from Toulon and was in a position to attack his ships as they lay off the Rock. The one major naval battle of the war was about to be joined, and the victor would hold Gibraltar.

The French, under the Comte de Toulouse, had 51 ships of the line and some 20 oared galleys. Rooke had 41 English and 12 Dutch of the line, but they were inferior to the French in weight of broadside

45

and, moreover, short of powder and shot after the long bombardment of Gibraltar. In addition he had nothing to counter the galleys which, on a day of little wind, could give the French valuable tactical mobility in attack and could save crippled ships by towing them out of the battle. The issue was clear. The French wished to retake Gibraltar, but to do so they must first destroy Rooke's fleet or drive it from the scene. Rooke had to maintain his fleet in such strength and situation as to make it impossible for the French to land and lay siege to the Rock.

The two fleets met off Malaga. In preliminary manoeuvrings on 12th August Toulouse gained a tactical advantage by getting his force between Rooke and Gibraltar, but this was balanced to some extent by Rooke's having the advantage of the wind which, on the 13th, enabled him to launch an attack. As the British bore down on the French a gap appeared in their line of battle and the enemy tried to break through. Skilful handling of their ships by

Rooke and his second-in-command, Shovel, prevented this and the two fleets, arrayed in two lines, ship facing ship, began a close-range battering duel. Shovel, in the van, after four hours of this close action, succeeded in breaking the French line and forced the scattered ships to leeward. But Rooke in the centre was hard pressed. He faced the heavier French ships and was particularly short of ammunition. Shovel, appreciating Rooke's predicament, fell back to support his chief just in time to stop the French breaking through. The Dutch in the rear equalled Shovel's earlier success and broke through the French line opposite them.

Both sides spent the night trying to repair the heavy damage they had received. At dawn the wind changed in favour of the French and the British fleet prepared to receive their attack. But none came, and Rooke determined that on the next day he would break through the French line, which still lay between the British ships and Gibraltar, and make for

The Battle of Malaga, fought immediately after the capture of Gibraltar in 1704, a line engraving by N. Visscher. It shows the general area of operations of the English fleet under Rooke and Shovel, and the French fleet under the Count of Toulouse

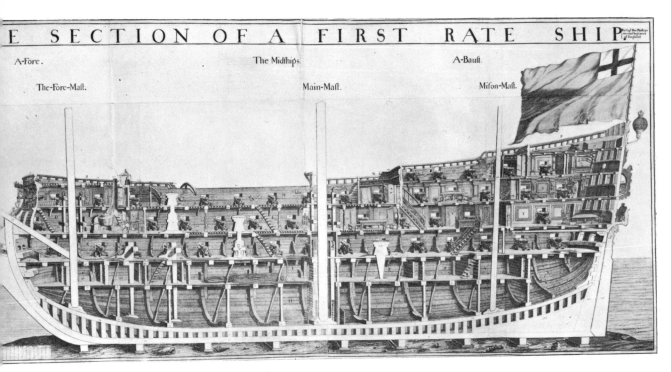

E SECTION OF A FIRST RATE SHIP

A-Fore.   The Midfhips.   A-Bauft.

The-Fore-Maft.   Main-Maft.   Mifon-Maft.

A sectional drawing of a British first-rate ship of the line of the early 18th century. The average length of a first-rate was 146 feet, her beam 47 feet, and her displacement about 1,750 tons. She carried a crew of 780 men and was armed with 100 guns, 26 of which were cannon (42-pounders), 28 culverins (18-pounders), 44 sakers (6-pounders) and two falcons (3-pounders)

the Rock. Absence of wind on the 14th made such an attack impossible, and at dawn on the 15th, as Rooke made ready to make his breakthrough, he saw that the French had vanished from the scene. Toulouse, very much aware of his battered ships, had come to the conclusion that they could not endure another pounding. The British were still between him and his base at Toulon, so he had taken advantage of the favourable wind to slip around them in the night.

Such was the battle off Malaga. Tactically indecisive, it was a strategic victory for Rooke. Not only was Gibraltar saved, but never again during the war did the French seek a major engagement to gain control of the Mediterranean. They did make two further attempts to retake Gibraltar but on each occasion were driven off by the timely arrival of a squadron from Lisbon under Sir John Leake. Yet valuable though Gibraltar was, it was not as yet a satisfactory naval base. It had no safe anchorage, and the inadequacy of its water supply severely limited its use by a large fleet.

From 1704 to 1706 Marlborough was fighting the great continental campaigns which destroyed the offensive capability of France's armies. At Blenheim he defeated the French and Bavarian armies in central Europe, and at Ramillies his victory assured the safety of the Spanish Netherlands. The Navy's contribution to these victories was to ensure that the enemy got no reinforcements from the Mediterranean by sea, and to draw off and disperse his strength by amphibious operations. In the summer of 1705, supported by a strong fleet under Shovel, the Earl of Peterborough captured Barcelona after a short siege. Not only was this Spain's chief commercial centre, but it also provided a base for Britain's Hapsburg ally, now crowned Charles III of Spain, from which he could expand his power and thus provide further distraction for France. In 1706 an attempt was made to retake the city. The fortifications were in fact breached, but on 26th April just as the French were prepared to storm the walls, an approaching allied fleet was sighted. Immediately the French naval covering force withdrew to Toulon,

Admiral John Benbow, a portrait painted by Sir Godfrey
Kneller. The hero of the Battle of Santa Marta, 1702, when,
deserted by other English captains, he fought a small French
fleet virtually single-handed for five days. Benbow died of
wounds received in the action; of the captains who deserted him
two were shot, one died in prison, and a fourth died before he
could be brought before a court-martial

as long as there was a strong French fleet at Toulon,
the fortunes of a single battle could bring strategic
disaster. If Toulon itself could be taken not only
would this danger be removed, but a way would be
opened for the invasion of France itself. Marlborough
had long intended to make the attempt and, in 1707,
planned one of the most ambitious amphibious
operations in history. France's chief naval arsenal,
Toulon, was virtually undefended on the landward
side, and Marlborough's plan envisaged a major
attack by the Austrian and Savoyan armies from the
north, supported by a simultaneous attack from the
sea under Sir Cloudesley Shovel. Unfortunately,
the Imperial commander, the great Prince Eugene,
was never enthusiastic about the project and made
his approach too slowly. The French were able to
reinforce the garrison, and this increased strength
forced the allies to abandon the siege. But before he
withdrew, Shovel moved in his bomb-ketches and
heavily bombarded the French fleet in the dockyard.
To save their ships from complete destruction the
French scuttled them in shallow water. Thus,
though the great design had failed and no base had
been secured, the direct threat to the British fleet
was removed for the remainder of the war.

On the voyage home in October 1707 Shovel
encountered the stormy weather in the approaches
to the Channel which had always haunted English
admirals during operations in the Mediterranean.
Four of his ships went ashore in the Scilly Islands in a
famous shipwreck, others were badly damaged, and
Shovel himself lost his life. The need for a winter
base in the Mediterranean could not have been more
drastically demonstrated.

In 1708 the need was met with the capture of
Minorca. The fleet under Sir John Leake and a
military force under the Earl of Stanhope met with
little resistance on land and the French fleet was
powerless to intervene. Not only did this capture give
Britain the splendid anchorage at Port Mahon for a
winter refuge but the new base was ideally situated
for masking Toulon and controlling the trade passing
through the Mediterranean. With Minorca and
Gibraltar in her hands, Britain was established as the
predominant naval power in the Mediterranean.

There were minor maritime operations in other
theatres of war. Colonial operations across the
Atlantic were on a small scale and usually undertaken to protect specific local interests. In 1710 a

leaving the way open for Leake to sail in with troop
reinforcements sufficient to force the French Army
to raise the siege. In the taking and holding of
Gibraltar and Barcelona, and with the launching of
powerful attacks on the enemy's flanks, Britain
demonstrated all the flexibility and offensive capability provided by skilfully used sea power.

Even so, her control of the Mediterranean was not
secure. As long as Britain had no adequate base, and

well-planned combined operation captured Port Royal, the capital of France's Nova Scotia, while naval forces attacked shipping and settlements along the Newfoundland coast. But the limitations of Britain's military planning were revealed in 1711. A larger expedition, including 5,000 troops, commanded by Admiral Sir Hovenden Walker completely failed to take Quebec. Shortage of provisions and bad pilots who wrecked many of the transports in the St. Lawrence river rang the expedition's final knell.

With her main fleets hemmed in by the British Navy, France mounted an increasingly dangerous attack on seaborne trade, especially in home waters. After the battle of Malaga, the swarms of privateers from the Channel and Biscay ports were reinforced by small squadrons of warships. Serious losses were inflicted on the trade which was necessary for the prosecution of the war. Single ships were the most frequent victims, but weakly protected convoys could fall victim to a surprise concentration of cruisers. The losses, although serious, were not decisive and the government showed its determination to give adequate naval protection to merchant shipping by the Cruisers and Convoys Act of 1708, which included a provision that a minimum of 43 ships would be made available for the protection of trade.

In spite of the exhaustion of France and growing war weariness among Britain and her allies, peace did not come until 1713. The Treaty of Utrecht left no doubt where victory lay, or about what was important to Britain. France and Spain were never to be united and the Netherlands should be ruled by Austria, not France. Gibraltar and Minorca were to remain British, and the privateer base at Dunkirk was to be demolished. Hudson's Bay, Newfoundland, and Nova Scotia were all to go to Britain, which was also given the monopoly of the rich slave trade with Spain's colonies in the New World. Thus Britain was now both an Atlantic and a Mediterranean power. Her mercantile and naval strength had grown as that of France had declined. Such were the fruits of an overall strategy in which sea power, added to Marlborough's military genius, had given to Britain a decisive capability of attacking her enemies at places and times of her own choosing.

Sir Cloudesley Shovel, second-in-command of the English fleet at the capture of Gibraltar and the Battle of Malaga. In 1707, when returning to England from the Mediterranean where he had been Commander-in-Chief, four ships struck upon the 'Bishop and Clerks' rocks in the Scilly Islands. One of them was Shovel's flagship, the *Association*, and the admiral was drowned with 900 of his men

CHAPTER 5

War of the Austrian Succession – Vernon at Porto Bello
and Cartagena – Anson's Voyage of Circumnavigation –
The two battles of Cape Finisterre

BRYAN RANFT

The colonial gains of the War of the Spanish Succession, which had made Britain the predominant maritime power in the Mediterranean and the Atlantic, brought with them a vivid awareness in Britain of the trade advantages which lay in the development of the 'New World'. Colonial rivalry, particularly in the West Indies, led to the outbreak of fighting in 1739, and the war only later developed into a dynastic struggle concerned with the balance of power in Europe. Because of its colonial origins the war produced world-wide naval fighting in the Caribbean, the Pacific, and the East Indies. Although none of these campaigns was decisive, they did demonstrate that Britain could now exercise sea power throughout the world and were a foretaste of the great colonial war of 1756–1763.

The first clash came in the Caribbean between the expanding economy of Britain and the moribund empire of Spain struggling to maintain its monopoly of the rich trade of the New World. British merchants and seamen did not confine themselves to the limited trade with the Spanish colonies permitted by the Treaty of Utrecht and, on their side, the Spanish coastguards were not over-gentle with the British interlopers. It was the rough treatment of one of these, Captain Jenkins, which aroused so great a popular clamour in England that the peace-loving prime minister, Sir Robert Walpole, was compelled to declare war against Spain. There were two views on how it should be fought. Some thought in terms of a limited war against Spain's shipping, especially the treasure fleets from South America, combined with destructive raids on her colonial

ports. Others, led by Walpole's political opponents, wanted the conquest of some of the Spanish colonies, of which Cuba was their favourite example. The government veered from one to the other; but when Admiral Edward Vernon sailed with five ships of the line in July 1739 to reinforce the squadron already in the West Indies, it had made up its mind. His primary task was defined as capturing the galleons which brought the main South American trade to Spain each October and the destruction of as much other Spanish shipping as possible. His orders contained nothing about capturing territory.

Vernon arrived at his base, Port Royal in Jamaica, in October 1739. There he established that the galleons had not yet arrived in their port of assembly, Havana, and instead decided to attack Porto Bello. He knew that he would find some shipping there, perhaps indeed some of the galleons, and considered that the destruction of its fortifications would make it useless in future as a trading port or point of assembly. In spite of the violence of his speech and letters, Vernon was professionally most cautious, and rejected the temptation to attack the richer port of Cartagena as being too strongly defended.

The fortifications of Porto Bello consisted of three main works, one, the Iron Castle, at the harbour entrance, the other two inside the harbour. Vernon knew that the only way for a naval force to succeed against land fortifications was by a bombardment at point-blank range followed up by landing parties while the defenders were still demoralised. When he mounted his attack on 21st November his ships advanced to within 200 yards before opening fire, towing their boats already filled with soldiers ready

Opposite: Anson's final exploit was the capture, off the Philippine Islands, of the annual
Spanish treasure galleon on its way to America. This picture by Samuel Scott shows the action
between the *Centurion* and the treasure ship, the *Nuestra Señora de Covadonga*. The treasure amounted to 1,313,843 dollars and 35,682 ounces of silver

to land as soon as Vernon gave the signal. Although a change of wind prevented Vernon's skilful plan for a simultaneous attack on all three forts, the initial bombardment and storming of the Iron Castle destroyed the never very strong spirit of resistance of the governor and garrison. On the next day the port was surrendered. After destroying all the fortifications and taking possession of the shipping in the harbour, which included two frigates, Vernon returned to Jamaica. Although the attack on Porto Bello was well planned and boldly executed, it was nevertheless a relatively minor affair. Yet such was the desire in England for revenge against Spain that when the news reached London, Vernon became a popular hero overnight.

Vernon was unable to attempt another operation until March 1740. With his ships refitted after the winter storms which were so great a hazard in the West Indies, and reinforced by bomb-vessels and fireships from England, he sailed to bombard the port and shipping at Cartagena. The capture of the place, with its strong fortifications and garrison, was still beyond Vernon's resources. The bomb-vessels kept the harbour under fire for three days but did no significant damage. More disappointingly, they failed to achieve Vernon's larger objective, which was to compel the Spanish naval force of five ships of the line and five galleons, more than double his own force, to come out and fight. On 10th March he had to withdraw, but he had gained a most accurate knowledge of the approaches and fortifications and had formed, perhaps, too low an opinion of the fighting qualities of the garrison.

Vernon's later failure to intercept ships from Spain bringing troop reinforcements to Cartagena was another obstacle to success when eventually he felt himself strong enough to make a full scale attack. For this he had to wait for large reinforcements from England. In the interval he achieved another small but wildly popular success. At the end of March he attacked Chagres, the headquarters of the hated Spanish coastguards. After a seven hour bombardment of the castle, the port surrendered and its fortifications were totally destroyed.

By now Vernon was becoming very apprehensive of the arrival of substantial Spanish naval reinforcements, and a possible entry of France into the war. He would far rather have had additions to his fleet than the large military expedition upon which the

British government had decided. Encouraged by Vernon's success at Porto Bello and Chagres, the Cabinet now hoped for the capture of Cartagena and Cuba. Vernon, with his knowledge of the threat of storms to shipping and even more of the wastage which disease would cause in land operations, was sceptical from the first, but could only await the arrival of the new force. Numbering some 8,000 troops and 20 ships of the line, under Sir Challenor Ogle, it did not arrive in Jamaica until January 1741. Most unfortunately for any hope of success, the military commander, Lord Cathcart, had died on the voyage and was succeeded by Major-General Thomas Wentworth, with whom Vernon could never co-operate. They did agree that Cartagena

Admiral Edward Vernon, who with six ships captured the Spanish port of Porto Bello in the West Indies in 1739. A subsequent combined operation against Cartagena in 1741 was a failure, as was an attempt to take Santiago da Cuba in the following year. In 1745 he was responsible for the naval operations around Britain which prevented French supplies and support reaching the Young Pretender in Scotland

should be their first objective and on 4th March 1741 the great expedition of 29 ships of the line, 24 smaller ships, and 85 transports and storeships arrived off the port.

The only possible way of attack was by penetrating the inner harbour through a narrow passage, the Boca Chica. This was heavily defended by four forts and a fascine battery of 18 guns. On 9th March Vernon's carefully prepared plan was put into action. The two outer forts were silenced by heavy close range bombardment and soldiers were landed to attack the main fort, St. Louis, which had 68 guns. It was then that Wentworth's lack of boldness, which was to cause a deepening gulf between him and the admiral, first became apparent. Both Vernon and Ogle had urged him to attack immediately on landing so as to take advantage of surprise and to preserve the health and morale of his troops. But the general was apprehensive of heavy casualties if he attacked the fort before it had been weakened by bombardment. Vernon knew that his ships could not get close enough to St. Louis to silence its guns, but reluctantly agreed to a bombardment on the 23rd. His forebodings were justified. Little serious damage was done to the fort but the ships and their crews suffered heavy damage and loss of life.

Two days later Wentworth launched his attack and, as Vernon had predicted, the garrison surrendered without resistance. This must have been wounding to Wentworth's pride, already irritated by the series of increasingly critical letters from Vernon which he had received since he landed. Vernon lost no opportunity of pointing out the activity and success of the sailors, who had captured the fascine battery, in comparison with the dilatory behaviour of the army which had unnecessarily delayed before Fort St. Louis.

The fall of this castle made it possible for the fleet to move into the inner harbour. Vernon was so confident that a bold attack would capture the town that he rashly sent off dispatches to England announcing its fall. But he had reckoned without Wentworth, who refused to attack without a naval bombardment of the remaining castle. Vernon flatly refused. He knew that the ships could not get within effective range and judged that the garrison, like the others, would offer little resistance. It was not until 9th April that Wentworth attacked, and was

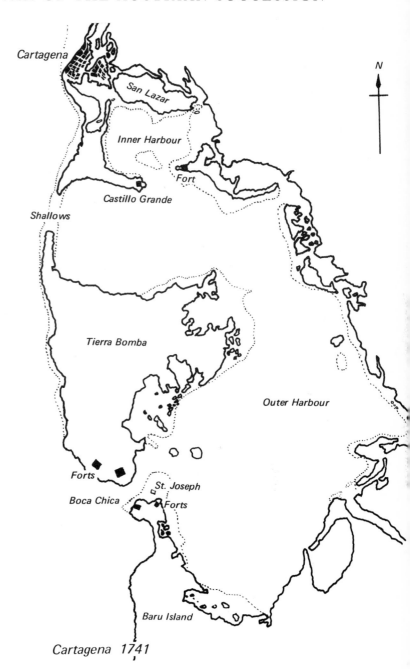

Cartagena 1741

George Anson, from the portrait by Sir Joshua Reynolds. Anson sprang into naval prominence after his successful voyage of circumnavigation in 1740–44, being made a Lord Commissioner of the Admiralty on his return. He was First Lord of the Admiralty during most of the Seven Years' War, a great naval administrator and a fine seaman

repulsed with the loss of 43 officers and 600 men. In the following week he told Vernon that of his original 8,000 men only 3,500 were now effective. He would need another two weeks to build a battery to support a second attack on the fort, and that within that time sickness, which was now widespread, would reduce his strength further. In the face of this weakness the expedition was abandoned. After destroying the captured fortifications it returned to Jamaica.

An attack against St. Iago de Cuba in July 1741 failed for exactly similar reasons, the losses from sickness among the troops being particularly heavy. Vernon and Wentworth were now so estranged that they could communicate only by letter. Hitherto Vernon had enjoyed a general naval superiority in those waters and had been able to attack where he wished, but this strategic freedom ended in March 1742 with the arrival from Spain of a fresh squadron

of ships. A design to attack Panama was abandoned and Vernon was unable to accomplish anything more before his return to England in October 1742. The whole expedition had shown that until more was known of the causes and treatment of tropical diseases, land operations in the West Indies were doomed to failure. Even more had it made clear that any combined operations would fail unless there was unity of purpose and method between the naval and military commanders.

If the immediate causes of the failures to capture Cartagena and St. Iago lay with the commanders on the spot, there were also serious weaknesses in the direction of the war by the government at home. Lack of secrecy in planning, muddled and even self-contradictory orders to commanders, and general neglect of the administrative measures necessary to ensure the fighting fitness of the expeditions it sent out, all characterised the conduct of Walpole's government. Nowhere was this more apparent than in the events which led to Commodore Anson's voyage round the world in 1740–4. It originated in grandiose schemes to overthrow Spain's empire in South America and the Philippines and so open up the Pacific to British trade and possible conquest. These schemes all foundered in the chronic weakness which beset the Royal Navy at this time, the shortage of manpower. Even if enough men had been found for a powerful expedition, it is unlikely that it would have been more successful than that of Vernon and Wentworth. Scurvy at sea and tropical diseases ashore, far more than battle casualties, decided the fate of such enterprises.

The force which finally sailed in September 1740 consisted of Anson's flagship, the *Centurion*, of 60 guns, five smaller warships and two supply ships. Only the *Centurion* was to see England again. Of the 1,500 men who set out, more than 1,300 were to die of scurvy. The quality of the land forces destined to destroy Spanish ports in the Pacific, which was the limited land aim finally given to Anson, was appalling even by the standards of the time. Instead of the promised regiment of regular soldiers he received 500 decrepit Chelsea pensioners and 200 raw marines, most of whom had never fired a musket or set foot aboard ship.

Such were the delays and lack of secrecy in the preparations for the expedition that the Spaniards were able to send out a superior force, under the

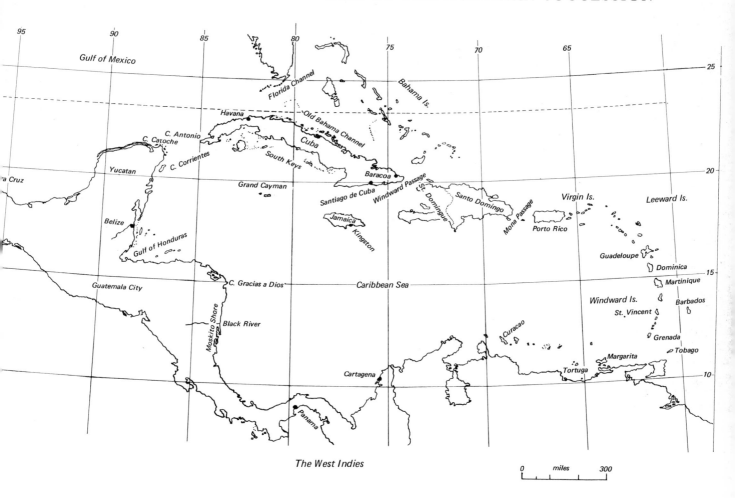

The West Indies

0   miles   300

command of Don Jose Pizarro, to intercept it. The two squadrons in fact never met, but the wild weather off Cape Horn did more damage to Anson than the Spaniards were ever likely to do. Only the *Centurion* and two other ships arrived at the rendezvous at Juan Fernandez. They had lost more than 600 of their ships' companies, mainly from scurvy. With this depleted force Anson could only carry out raids on local Spanish shipping and against the smaller ports. His first attempt at a greater prize – the capture of the galleon which sailed annually from Acapulco to Manila with a rich cargo of silver coin and plate – was a failure for the Spaniards, aware of his presence, kept the ship safely in port.

His force now reduced to two ships, Anson started on his long voyage across the Pacific to Macao. Scurvy struck the crews again, the *Gloucester* had to be abandoned for lack of men to work her, and

Anson arrived in China in November 1742 with only the *Centurion* and 200 men. After a five month stay, refitting the ship and bringing her crew back to health, Anson set sail to try to redeem his failure by capturing the Acapulco galleon on his voyage home. On 20th June 1743 he sighted the *Nuestra Señora de Covadonga* off the Philippines, and after a 90-minute close range action, forced her to surrender. The Spaniard was smaller and more lightly armed than the *Centurion*, so this was no David and Goliath victory. But it was a reward for the extraordinary powers of leadership and determination shown by Anson in being able to fight an action at all after so long and hazardous a voyage. When Anson arrived home in the summer of 1744 with treasure from the galleon worth over £1,000,000, it was fitting that he should be received with great acclaim. But the price of his success had been high. More than 1,300 of his men had died of disease, only four by enemy action.

After 1740 the war which had begun in the West Indies developed into a European struggle for the throne of Austria, in which Britain was faced by France as well as Spain. The conflict further grew into a struggle for predominance in North America and India between the colonies of the protagonists. Although the British capture of Louisburg, the key to the St. Lawrence, in 1745 was significant for the future destiny of Canada, the main naval interest of the wider war lay in the Mediterranean and in British home waters.

In the Mediterranean the Spanish and French fleets were a threat to Austria's possessions in Italy. A decisive victory was necessary to remove this threat, but the opportunity was lost at the battle fought off Toulon in February 1744. Owing to the rigidity of the *Fighting Instructions* which governed British fleets in action, and the lack of co-operation between the various flag-officers, the action was indecisive. Worse than this, the commander-in-chief, Thomas Mathews, abandoned the pursuit of the retreating enemy, for which he was court-martialled and cashiered.

The fruits of this failure to reduce enemy strength in European waters were seen in 1745 when the French, having established themselves in Flanders, prepared a cross-Channel invasion in support of the Stuart pretender to the British throne, Prince Charles. The Prince, evading the watching frigates, had landed in Scotland in August and had rapidly become master of the country. He marched into England and by December had reached Derby, appearing to be threatening London itself. The landing of a French force at this time would have been decisive, and it was only by the skilful dispositions made by Vernon, in command in the Channel, that it was prevented.

The hinge of his strategy was a strong squadron in the western approaches to the Channel, where it could intercept any French force coming from Brest, with smaller ships in the Channel itself. This preparedness, which was to remain the pattern of Britain's naval defence against French invasion throughout the days of sail, supplemented by offensive raids against the invasion vessels in the cross-Channel ports, compelled the enemy to call off the invasion. Prince Charles found little support in England, and was forced to withdraw to Scotland and to final defeat.

After his return from his great voyage, Anson had been made a member of the Board of Admiralty where he was largely responsible for the improvements in administration and strategic direction which characterised the remaining years of the war. It was a fitting reward for his labours that in 1747 he won one of the two decisive naval battles of the war. In May he engaged a French squadron of nine of the line off Cape Finisterre. Since he had taken command of the Western Squadron he had followed Vernon's example in practising more flexible and aggressive tactics, and the result of this was seen when, as the French ships tried to avoid action, he hoisted the signal for 'General Chase'. This gave freedom to each English captain to bring to action the first enemy ship he could catch up with, and resulted in the capture of six. This victory prevented reinforcements reaching France's colonies and was a sign of England's returning naval predominance.

Admiral Sir Edward Hawke, who succeeded to Anson's command, repeated his predecessor's feat in October. Again off Finisterre he intercepted a French squadron, this time escorting a great convoy to the West Indies. Handling his force of 14 of the line with great flexibility and abandoning the concept of maintaining the formal line of battle for that of 'General Chase', Hawke achieved a decisive victory. As each British ship came into action with an opponent it poured in a broadside and then passed on in pursuit of another enemy to leave its first opponent to a following British ship. Six of the eight French ships of the line suffered such damage and casualties that they surrendered after an action lasting from 11 o'clcock in the morning until nightfall. Hawke's own ships were too battered to pursue the convoy but he had the foresight to send off a sloop to the Windward Islands to warn the admiral there of the convoy's coming. This resulted in the convoy being intercepted and most of its ships being captured when it arrived in the West Indies.

The heavy losses in ships and men suffered by France in these two actions not only secured Britain's colonies against further attack but also weakened the enemy's ability to attack her trade. For Hawke himself, the action off Finisterre was a rehearsal for the even greater victories of 1759. In the war as a whole, although France was militarily successful on the Continent, her losses at sea and the growing threat to her colonies presented by Britain's power at sea made her ready to agree to peace in 1748. Britain herself was economically weakened by the long struggle, and because of France's strategically threatening gains in the Low Countries, was not in a strong bargaining position. To free this area from French control, even Louisburg had to be handed back. As for the original cause of the war, the conduct of the Spanish coastguards in the West Indies, it was not even mentioned in the peace treaty signed at Aix-la-Chapelle. So indecisive a result of a long war between a France and a Britain whose interests clashed in Europe, North America, India, and the Caribbean, was not likely to lead to a lasting peace. In under eight years, the struggle was to begin afresh.

After replenishing and recovering at Juan Fernandez, Anson took his much reduced squadron to cruise against the Spaniards on the South American coast. After capturing the town of Payta and removing the bullion and treasure found there, the town was put to the torch, only the churches being spared. From the painting by Samuel Scott.

CHAPTER 6

The Challenge from France, 1756-62 – The Seven Years'
War – William Pitt's Strategical Design – Capture of
Quebec and Conquest of Canada – Lagos and Quiberon Bay –
Campaigns in East and West Indies

PETER KEMP

The Treaty of Aix-la-Chapelle, which had brought to an end the War of the Austrian Succession in 1748, left most of the problems unsettled. This was particularly the case in North America, where the failure to draw any agreed boundaries between the French in Canada and the British colonies along the Atlantic seaboard held all the seeds of future conflict. These British colonies were comprised of restless and enterprising men already pushing out westward into the vast back country, developing and expanding as they went.

The French, settled along the banks of the St. Lawrence River, dreamed their dream of empire too late. It originated in the mind of Admiral Galisonnière, Governor of Canada, who saw in the French settlement of New Orleans and French ownership of the basin of the Mississippi River, based on a claim of prior navigation, a chance to cut off all British expansion to the west. The weak link in his argument lay in the gap between the southern shore of Lake Erie, which France could claim as the southernmost boundary of her Canadian colony, and the head waters of the Ohio River which, by extension, could conceivably be held to be the northern extremity of the Mississippi basin. It was into this gap that the British colonists were advancing in their restless search for new trade.

In 1753 the Marquis Duquesne relieved Galisonnière as Governor of Canada and began to build a chain of forts across the gap. He clashed with British traders in the area and, alarmed, the Governor of Virginia sent a force to build an English fort at the head of the Ohio River, at the site where Pittsburg now stands. The British force was surprised by a superior French expedition, which promptly completed the building and named it Fort Duquesne. The gap was closed, and to open it the Governors of Virginia and Maryland sent Colonel George Washington at the head of a force of colonists to drive off the French. The attack on Fort Dusquesne was a failure, Washington was beaten off and later forced to surrender. Although it was to be another year before serious fighting broke out, the Seven Years' War had in fact begun.

Britain's position was a difficult one. If she were to start a European war, the French were well placed to seize the advantage. Allied as France was to Austria, the British king's possession of Hanover could not be defended, and the loss of Hanover would mean French control of the Dutch ports and a French fleet in the North Sea. Whatever was attempted, therefore, must not be considered the cause of a general war but must be directed solely against those points of French aggression which went beyond the accepted limits. Such a point was the chain of forts in America planned by Galisonnière and built by Duquesne. To attack and liquidate these forts Britain sent in 1755 a small naval squadron under Commodore Keppel to operate in American waters, and a small military force of two battalions under General Braddock to combine with colonial soldiers and drive out the French.

The French ambassador in London, by judicious bribery, obtained a copy of Braddock's orders. As soon as it was received in Paris, orders were given to assemble a force of six battalions and a squadron of 18 ships for Canada. The French plans were quickly learned in London and, to stop the troops reaching

Opposite: Sir Edward Hawke, Commander-in-Chief at Quiberon Bay, one of the great British admirals of the Seven Years' War. He had made his name as an admiral at the second Battle of Ushant in 1747; he crowned his career with the brilliant victory at Quiberon twelve years later

Augustus Keppel, later an admiral, seen in this portrait by Sir Joshua Reynolds as a captain. He commanded HMS *Torbay* at Quiberon Bay, the second ship to enter the dangerous waters of the bay. She was engaging the French 74-gun ship *Thesée* when the latter sank after being flooded through her gunports

irreparable harm was done; if he intercepted the whole squadron, the blow to French hopes in North America would be so considerable that the risk of war could be accepted, and indeed might not come about if the rest of Europe could be persuaded that the act was only in response to an illegal claim by France.

What the British government failed to reckon with was the prevalence of fog off the Newfoundland coast. Boscawen's fleet failed to make contact for the French squadron had lost cohesion in the fog, and Boscawen only managed to cut off a couple of stragglers. The remainder were not sighted in the fog and reached Louisburg, where the reinforcements were landed.

The now inevitable war was declared in the summer of 1756, though much was still to happen before the actual declaration was made. French reinforcements from Brest avoided Admiral Hawke's blockading fleet and reached Canada. Braddock and his British-Colonial force had already been disastrously defeated in a French ambush. With their Indian allies the French ravaged in Pennsylvania, Virginia, and Maryland, and the British-held port of Oswego on Lake Ontario was captured and razed to the ground.

As a distraction to force the Royal Navy to divide its forces, another French force was assembled at Toulon. It was directed against Minorca. Indecision in the Admiralty, coupled with the need to keep the Western Squadron strong, left it too late to beat off the French expedition to Minorca. Boscawen, now blockading the French Biscay ports, was strengthened with ships beyond his immediate need; Hawke was despatched to round up the French seaborne trade; and with what ships were left, ten of the line, Vice-Admiral John Byng was sent to the Mediterranean to guard Minorca. He picked up three more ships at Gibraltar, delayed there rather longer than he need have done, and arrived off Minorca on 17th May 1756 to discover that the French troops had invested Port Mahon, the last British stronghold on the island. Contact with the French fleet was made on the 19th, but it was not until the following day that action was joined, the wind being too light for the fleets to be brought together.

The battle was indecisive, and for four days afterwards Byng remained in the area, undecided what to do. On the 24th he called a Council of War, put to it

their destination, a strong British squadron was assembled at Plymouth under the command of Admiral Edward Boscawen, ready to sail as soon as the French put to sea. In fact he sailed earlier, for the French ambassador presented an ultimatum to the British government claiming the whole of the disputed territory in North America for France. Six days after Boscawen sailed from Plymouth, the French reinforcement put to sea from Brest.

Boscawen's orders included the following clause: 'If you fall in with any French ships of war or other vessels having on board troops or warlike stores, you will do your best to take possession of them. In case resistance should be made, you will employ the means at your disposal to capture and destroy them.' The whole point of this order was all or nothing; if Boscawen missed the French completely, no

some leading questions, and received the answers that he wanted, that it was impossible for the fleet to relieve Port Mahon and that Gibraltar would be endangered if he did not return with his fleet to guard it. He withdrew to Gibraltar and left Minorca to its fate. The British flag was hauled down in surrender on 28th June.

The tragedy had not been Byng's indecisive battle with the French fleet, it had been his complete lack of strategic appreciation. His object was not defeat of the French fleet; it was the defeat of the French expedition to Minorca – a seaborne expedition dependent on the sea for its supplies and communications. Byng had only to remain at sea off Minorca, prevent the arrival of supplies and reinforcements to sustain the French troops who had been landed, and the whole attempt must inevitably have withered on the bough. But Byng was not the man for such a command; nothing in his previous career had indicated that he possessed the brand of resolution required for such a task. He failed as, being Byng, he was bound to fail, and he paid the penalty. An infuriated nation demanded his blood, the administration in London needed a scapegoat on whom to shift the blame for their earlier neglect, and Byng was court-martialled, sentenced to death, and shot upon the quarter-deck of H.M.S. *Monarque*.

Hawke was sent to the Mediterranean to take over Byng's command but he arrived too late to retrieve the disaster of Minorca. There was in fact little that he could do in the face of French inactivity. The official declaration of war had been made when it was learned in London that the French had landed in Minorca, but this made no difference to the actions of the French fleet in Toulon. Hawke trailed his coat a few times before the port, but the French ships were not tempted. Dispirited by the lack of action, Hawke returned home in 1757.

But politically, in England, things were astir. The failure of the Duke of Newcastle's government to provide successes, allied to popular demand for a change, forced King George II to call in William Pitt to office late in 1756. The king disliked Pitt, the great Whig families mistrusted him; and Parliament was not ready to give him the backing he needed to prosecute the war in the way he thought it should go. In the following spring George II dismissed Pitt, but it soon became obvious that there was no one else in Britain who could take his place. Three months

Admiral John Byng was in command of the fleet sent into the Mediterranean in 1756 to relieve Minorca, at the time invested by the French. Failing to achieve success, he was sent back to England, court-martialled, and sentenced to death. He was shot on the quarter-deck of HMS *Monarque*

later he was back in office as Principal Secretary of State, with Newcastle as the titular head of the government, and it was this oddly assorted couple that, for the next four years, steered Britain to a series of unparalleled and world-shaking victories. 'Pitt does everything,' wrote Horace Walpole, 'the Duke of Newcastle *gives* everything. As long as they can agree in this partition, they may do what they will.'

Pitt 'did' everything; as Principal Secretary he was in supreme control of Navy, Army, and Foreign Affairs. He was a first-class administrator, and to this was added a strategical brilliance which could see clearly the necessities of the immediate war situation and the moves and campaigns which were to follow. As a start he brought back to the Admiralty, as his First Lord, Admiral Lord Anson, who had in fact fallen from office when the previous administration had been dismissed. It was a shrewd appointment, for Anson himself was a brilliant administrator, and under Pitt's direction could be guaranteed to have the Navy ready for any task which Pitt should give it.

Even in 1757 little went well for Britain at sea. It was too late in the year when Pitt came to power for naval operations to be planned and launched with any hope of success. A combined operation designed to capture Louisburg had in fact been planned in the spring, but the lack of drive and urgency with which it was mounted ensured its arrival in Canada too late in the season to be sure of success. Moreover, three separate French squadrons had been able to give the slip to the British blockading forces in Europe, and each had reached Canada without interception. When the British ships and soldiers assembled in Halifax for their proposed assault on Louisburg, they discovered that French naval strength there was superior to anything the British Navy could muster in those waters, and in the face of so much naval power an operation so hazardous as a seaborne landing against a defended fortress was too great a risk to contemplate. All that could be done was to call off the attempt.

With William Pitt firmly in the saddle, a new drive became quickly apparent. Instead of a series of un-linked operations, poorly planned, and designed more to satisfy a public demand for action than to prosecute the war, Pitt decided the main lines of his strategy and subordinated all naval and military operations to its execution. He realised that a land war in Europe would drain away British strength into the most unproductive field, and that the best chances of British success lay in the use of her in-comparable Navy to attack France in her weakest spots. His main strategy was therefore to fight as far as possible a holding war in Europe and to con-centrate the main British pressure on the periphery of France's overseas empire where, faced with the realities of British sea power, it would be most difficult for her to reinforce her colonial garrisons. The points on the periphery where the main attacks were to be made were Canada, the West Indies, and India.

For the holding war in Europe Pitt relied on a series of financial subsidies to equip and pay for allied troops to face the French armies and to hold them out of Hanover and the western German and Dutch states. At the same time he drew a substantial number of French troops westward away from the main European battlefield by a series of amphibious attacks against targets on the Biscay and Channel coasts. This was the classic use of superior sea power directed against a stronger land power, exploiting the element of surprise to its maximum and holding down a substantial force to guard a coastline which might be attacked at any point along its hundreds of miles of length.

The main amphibious raids were carried out at Rochefort, St. Malo, and Cherbourg, with smaller descents elsewhere on the Brittany coast. The Rochefort raid was in fact a failure due to irresolute leadership by General Mordaunt in command of the troops, but even in its lack of military success it proved a substantial diversion. In the other two major operations a vast amount of material damage was done through the burning of ships and stores and the spiking of guns, and it was estimated that at least 50,000 French troops were tied down in coast-guard duties instead of assisting the military campaign in Europe.

While these raids were in progress, Pitt never for a moment diverted his eyes from the main operations of the war. As virtually supreme commander he planned and wrote the orders himself. Canada was his first objective, and his plan for 1758 included land attacks on Fort Duquesne and the Ohio valley, and the line of the Great Lakes, and the most important of all, the capture of Louisburg as a preliminary move to open the St. Lawrence River for an attack on Quebec. No detail was too small for Pitt's atten-tion; he selected the bases from which the attack was to be sustained, collected the necessary stores and despatched them in convoys to arrive well in advance of the operations, detailed the troops to be used, both home-based and colonial, and saw that suffi-cient transports were collected at the various bases in readiness for the final assault. Finally he chose the commanders. For the naval command he selected Boscawen, 'my favourite admiral', and to lead the military his choice fell on General Amherst, with James Wolfe as one of his brigadiers. As Boscawen sailed from England with his fleet, Hawke descended on the Basque Roads and destroyed a French squadron preparing to take out reinforcements and stores to Canada. Farther south, in the Mediterranean, Admirals Osborne and Saunders broke up a French concentration from Toulon which had sailed with the same object. In this operation was captured the Marquis Duquesne, together with the French flagship *Foudroyant*, a psychological blow which cast French hopes into the pit. Duquesne, as Governor of Canada in 1754, had built that chain of forts which connected the Great Lakes with the Ohio Valley. In doing so he had been building on the plan of his predecessor, Admiral Galisonnière, who later had commanded against Byng at Minorca. Galisonnière's flagship on that occasion had been the same *Foudroyant* which was now flying the flag of Britain instead of that of France. The point was not missed in Paris.

Boscawen arrived with his fleet at Halifax on 9th May, very much later than he had hoped. He had

met calms and contrary winds throughout his passage, which had taken 11 weeks instead of the more usual four. Within a week the ships were replenished and watered, and after battling against adverse winds, arrived off Louisburg at the end of the month. It was 7th June before the weather was calm enough to attempt a landing in the Bay of Gabarus, to the westward of Louisburg, a somewhat obvious frontal attack which had been substituted by Amherst from Wolfe's original plan of three separate landings to disguise the main line of attack. The boats of the fleet put the soldiers ashore against a heavy defensive fire, and it was fortunate that, at the last moment, a small rocky cove was discovered which was masked from the French fire. Wolfe made a dash for it and managed to get enough men ashore to withstand a French counter-attack, though many men were

The capture of the French 84-gun ship *Foudroyant* by the *Monmouth*, of 64 guns, on 28th February 1758. The *Foudroyant* was captured after a long chase throughout the night in which the captain of the *Monmouth* was killed and the ship commanded by her First Lieutenant

drowned and many boats smashed on the rocks as they went in.

With the army ashore the fate of Louisburg was sealed. It was to take some weeks yet before the fortress fell, for there were difficulties in landing the siege train and advancing it to the walls of the town. Boscawen spared neither seamen nor guns in his eagerness to help the army in its task. There were five French ships of the line in Louisburg harbour, but on 21st July three of them were set on fire by British batteries bombarding the town. Boscawen waited no longer. On the night of the 25th the boats of the fleet under Captains Laforey and Balfour, with 600 seamen on board, crept into the harbour under cover of darkness and seized the two remaining ships. One, the *Bienfaisant*, took the ground as soon as her cable was cut and was set on fire. The other, the *Prudent*, was towed by the boats across the harbour and anchored under Wolfe's batteries. It was the final blow to the French, and within a day or two the capitulation was signed. With Louisburg, the whole of Cape Breton Island and Prince Edward Island fell into British hands.

The Hon. Edward Boscawen, Admiral of the Blue, painted by Sir Joshua Reynolds. He commanded the fleet in the operations which led to the capture of Louisburg in 1758, and in 1759 was Commander-in-Chief in the Mediterranean and victor in the Battle of Lagos

Louisburg was recognised by both British and French as the key to Canada, but the many delays which had built up, starting with Boscawen's laborious passage across the Atlantic and augmented by the slowness of the military advance after the landing in Gabarus Bay, made it late in the season to contemplate an immediate advance up the St. Lawrence. While the admiral and general were discussing the possibility, news came in of the disastrous defeat of the British military attack on Fort Ticonderoga at the foot of Lake Champlain in the attempt to clear the line of the Great Lakes. To Boscawen and Amherst it looked as though New York might be in danger from a French attack, and they decided to send six battalions of soldiers to reinforce General Abercromby in his retreat from Ticonderoga. The attack on Quebec would have to wait until the following summer.

Leaving a force of 10 ships of the line under Admiral Durell to winter in Halifax and prevent any French reinforcements reaching Quebec when the ice broke in the following spring, Boscawen returned home. There were various minor encounters with French ships during his voyage home, mainly with a French squadron which had escaped from Quebec and given Durell the slip, but the weather was too boisterous for any full-scale action. One of the French ships, the *Belliqueux*, was captured by Captain Saumarez in the *Antelope*, but that was the full extent of British success.

On the whole, Pitt was reasonably well satisfied with the progress of his grand design. Just as Boscawen was leaving for England, news was coming in of British military successes which more than made up for the diasaster at Fort Ticonderoga. The British advance into the Ohio head-waters had ended with the capture of Fort Duquesne by forces led by General Forbes. On the site of the French fort he raised a new one which, in honour of the British Prime Minister, he named Pittsburg. And even the setback at Ticonderoga was, in the end, retrieved by a greater success. Abercromby, on his retreat, was persuaded by the great colonial leader Colonel Bradstreet to let him lead an attack on the French fort at Frontenac, on the southern tip of Lake Ontario. Bradstreet reached the lake at Oswego and launched his little force of 3,000 men in bateaux and whaleboats against Frontenac. He moved with such speed that he found the fort virtually unguarded. It

Admiral Sir Charles Saunders, the portrait by Sir Joshua Reynolds. Saunders commanded the fleet which navigated the St Lawrence River in 1759 and assisted at the capture of Quebec. Until this feat of navigation, no ship larger than a frigate had managed to proceed so far up river

fell almost at once. Frontenac was the headquarters of the French naval force which dominated the inland waters, and the entire French squadron of nine ships fell into Bradstreet's hands. They were all either carried off or burnt, and the fort itself was razed to the ground. With this one stroke the British regained naval control of the Lakes and virtually cut off Quebec and Montreal from the rest of Upper Canada and the Ohio River. If the fall of Louisburg presented to Britain the key of the front door to Canada, the destruction of Frontenac and the capture of the Lakes flotilla made certain that the back door was also open.

The new year dawned with Pitt's plans for the continuation of the operations in Canada fully made. Wolfe was to command the army in place of Amherst, who had succeeded the luckless Abercromby in command on the mainland. Boscawen was no longer available to command the naval side; his success at Louisburg had entitled him to a larger command and he had been sent out as commander-in-chief in the Mediterranean. Hawke, too, was not available as he was needed in the Channel. Anson's choice was Charles Saunders, who had been with him in his great voyage of circumnavigation, a man whom the First Lord could recommend to Pitt as a brilliant seaman. Saunders was specially promoted to the rank of vice-admiral for the task ahead.

Saunders and Wolfe reached Halifax at the end of April, only to find Durell and the ships which had been left in Canada through the winter still at anchor there. They should have been off the entrance to the St. Lawrence River to prevent any French supplies and reinforcements reaching Quebec. Durell however had considered the ice was still too thick for French ships to get through and so had remained inactive. Saunders ordered him out at once, but by the time he reached the St. Lawrence it was too late. The ice had in fact broken early and a French replenishment convoy had made the passage up in safety. Saunders and Wolfe arrived in the river at the end of June to receive the news which they had so dreaded, that in spite of all the detailed planning and the orders to Durell, the vital French convoy had got through.

In the French view the safety of Quebec lay in the difficulties of navigation in the St. Lawrence. Small ships could get up without much risk but the tortuous channel, the perennially adverse winds, and the currents of the great river were held to be an insuperable bar to the passage of large ships. Wolfe himself had expected the Navy to be content with the completion of its task in transporting the army up the river as far as the Ile de Bic, some 120 miles below Quebec, perhaps supporting him with three or four small craft above that point for the actual assault on Quebec itself. But Saunders had different ideas. French hearts sank as they saw the whole of Saunders's fleet perform what they considered an impossible feat. In three divisions, accompanied by all the transports, the whole of Saunders's battle fleet navigated the river in perfect safety, all ships reaching the Ile de Coudres, 60 miles below Quebec, without mishap.

Above the Ile de Coudres occurred the infamous Traverse passage, supposedly impassable to any ship above the size of a frigate. It was a passage dreaded by big ship captains. But Saunders still had no doubts. Mark boats were moored on either side of the tortuous channel, and French pilots, captured by Durell, were placed on board the British ships. They were ignored by the masters of the transports who, standing on the forecastles of their ships, navigated through the rapids by the look of the water. Saunders left his heaviest ships at the Ile de Coudres under the command of Durell, but with four of the smaller ships of the line, and all the frigates, he made the passage and anchored his ships just below the Quebec basin. As a feat of pure seamanship it was unparalleled, and the defenders of Quebec, as they saw British ships of the line anchoring just below their citadel, must have felt the first chill wind of defeat.

But Quebec was not to fall so easily as that. Standing on its rocky promontory at the confluence of the St. Lawrence and St. Charles rivers, it was impregnable to frontal attack. The long reconnaissance to find a means of landing troops to take Quebec in the rear is too well known a feature of the operation to need description here; but it was a period of frequent naval movements both to deceive the French and to give Wolfe every assistance possible. Naval ships made the passage of the river past the city, so that the whole river above and below Quebec was firmly in British hands. And having proved that the Traverse passage held no dangers for British ships, Saunders ordered up the remainder of his fleet, leaving only two ships of the line at the Ile de Coudres. With the fleet now at his disposal in Quebec waters, Saunders was able greatly to intensify his pressure on the French forces. Keeping Quebec under a heavy bombardment, he sent Admiral Holmes with a squadron of cruisers above Quebec where they were able to dominate the river and destroy many of the French supplies which, for the sake of safety, had been moved up river to Deschambault. Even more important was the effect of the ships on the French defensive movements, for by threatening many points they were able to keep the French troops on the move and to exhaust them.

It was in these conditions of perpetual threat that Wolfe was at last able to find the way out of his difficulties. All attempts to take the city from below had failed against the rock-like defence of the French commander Montcalm, but the continual threats of landings above Quebec were beginning to cause him alarm, to the extent where he began to divide his forces. On the morning of 9th September Wolfe, on a reconnaissance above the river, made out from the opposite bank a possible path up the cliffs about 200 yards to the right of the Anse du Foulon, and at the top, on the Plains of Abraham, there were no French defenders. He decided to make the attempt on the night of the 12th.

The transporting of the troops to the foot of the Anse was, of course, the task of the Navy, and it was a task which filled Admiral Holmes with disquiet. On a pitch dark night, and with a racing tide under the boats, he was expected to bring a force of 1,700 men down river in the ships' boats a distance of 15 miles under the noses of the French sentries. But if his mind was filled with disquiet at the incredible difficulties in the way of fulfilment of his task, there was no lack of resolution. In command of the boats he placed Captain Chads. At two o'clock in the morning of a pitch black night, the boats of the fleet, carrying 1,700 soldiers, began their 15-mile journey. Half an hour later Holmes weighed anchor and, with the transports carrying the second wave of troops, dropped down river to the Anse du Foulon so silently that the French sentries on the river bank neither saw nor heard any sign of the movement.

Captain Chads, meanwhile, was racing down river. In the blackness of the night he had nothing to guide him to the appointed landing place. At the precise time stipulated in his orders he and the boats arrived at the foot of the path, and within minutes the first of the light infantry to land were scaling the steep cliff which would lead them on to the Plains of Abraham above. With all the men of the first wave ashore, Captain Chads took his boats out to meet Holmes and the transports, which had just arrived, and ferried the second wave of 1,900 men ashore. They then crossed the river, picked up the remainder of the military from the opposite bank, and landed them at the same spot. By nine o'clock in the morning some 4,800 soldiers were drawn up in line of battle on the Plains of Abraham between Montcalm and the city he was defending.

This was by no means the end of the naval task. Long before the land battle began the seamen began work on the guns. These, like the soldiers, had to be brought ashore in the boats and then hauled by hand up the steep cliff. For hour after hour the seamen toiled at their task, ungrudging in their efforts to help their military comrades in the hour of decision. And even when the battle was over, and

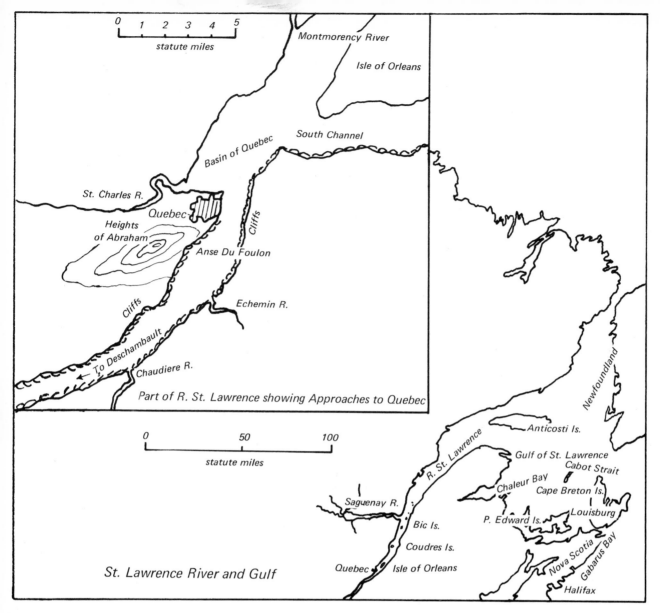

Part of R. St. Lawrence showing Approaches to Quebec

St. Lawrence River and Gulf

Montcalm defeated, the task was not done. All the siege artillery had to be landed by the same route, for the city itself had still not surrendered. Again the Navy took a hand. Saunders concentrated his ships of the line in the Quebec basin, where their broadsides could bear on the lower town of Quebec itself. With the upper town also under fire from the siege guns of the Army, Quebec surrendered on the 28th.

The fall of Quebec, however, did not yet mean the fall of all Canada. It was to take one more campaigning season before Pitt could see his great dream come to full fruition. British troops were left in Quebec to garrison it throughout the winter, and Saunders landed from the fleet all the supplies and provisions he could spare to keep them going until a relief expedition could arrive from Britain in the spring. If Quebec were to be held, and if Canada were to be won, there would need to be no repetition of Durell's mistake in allowing a French convoy to reach the St. Lawrence when the winter ice broke.

The winter in Quebec was severe, and more than half the British garrison succumbed to starvation and scurvy. In the early spring the French troops were on the move, and this time it was a British force that was under siege in Quebec. Two convoys set out from Europe, one British and one French. On 9th May the watchers on the battlements of Quebec saw the topsails of a frigate standing up-river. As she anchored in the Basin, the watchers ashore saw a flag creep up to her masthead and break out. It was the Union. The frigate was the *Lowestoft*, forerunner of a British squadron which reached Quebec a few days later, bringing with it storeships and transports with fresh troops. Quebec was saved, the French siege raised, and the final campaign began.

67

The Battle of Lagos, in which Boscawen defeated de la Clue in 1759, painted by Thomas Luny. In the picture the ship in the centre is Boscawen's flagship, the *Namur*, having lost her mizenmast after a fierce engagement with the *Ocean*. In the right foreground is the French ship *Centaure*, which fought most gallantly and greatly held up the British pursuit

The convoy from France arrived in the entrance of the St. Lawrence on the day when the *Lowestoft* anchored off Quebec. Learning that it had been fore-stalled, it put into La Chaleur Bay where, a few days later, it was discovered by two small British squadrons and destroyed.

While Saunders and Wolfe had been investing Quebec, France had revived once again her old scheme of bringing the war to a successful end by an invasion of Britain. The new plan differed from its predecessors in that the decisive landing was to be on the Essex coast by 20,000 men based on Ostend, masked by a preliminary landing in the Firth of Clyde by another army of 20,000 men based in Brittany, and further disguised by a diversionary raid on Ireland, under the privateer commander Thurot. This it was hoped would disperse the defences. Necessary control of the sea was to be achieved by the Toulon fleet escaping from the Mediterranean and joining hands with the Brest

fleet. Together they would escort the Brittany army and land it in the Clyde, then would sail round the north of Scotland to Ostend to bring over the final 20,000 men and put them ashore in the Blackwater Estuary. The French had hoped to persuade Russia, Sweden, Denmark, and Holland to add their ships to the French to cover the invasion, but this was a hope that Pitt's diplomacy very quickly nipped in the bud. Success therefore depended on French ships alone, and the necessary prerequisite was the junction of the two fleets from Toulon and Brest.

Watching the French ships in Toulon was Boscawen with the Mediterranean Fleet. Following the loss of Minorca, his nearest base for repairs and provisions was Gibraltar, and thither he sent two or three ships at a time for rest and refit. In August, following an unsuccessful attempt to force the French admiral, de la Clue, to put to sea by attack-ing two French frigates lying outside Toulon, Boscawen withdrew his whole fleet to Gibraltar. All his ships by now needed cleaning and refitting, and victuals and fresh water were running low.

His withdrawal to Gibraltar gave de la Clue his chance. He slipped out of Toulon and made for the Straits of Gibraltar, hoping to get through while the British ships were under repair. He was sighted by a British frigate stationed off the Rock, and Boscawen at once gave the order to put to sea notwithstanding that some of his ships had their sails unbent and their yards struck. By superhuman efforts in the dockyard Boscawen's ships were at sea within two hours with the signal for a general chase flying, the ships to engage as they came up without waiting to form a line of battle.

In the running fight which developed Boscawen's flagship, the *Namur*, lost her mizen mast and both topsail yards and began to fall astern. The admiral had his boat hoisted out and made for the *Newark*, to hoist his flag in her and continue the battle. On the way the boat was holed by a French shot, but Boscawen, plucking off his wig, stuffed it into the hole and reached his new flagship unscathed.

The rear ship of the French line, the *Centaure*, put up a magnificent defence and for three hours held the British at bay almost single-handed. She struck her colours only when she was shattered beyond further fighting and her captain and more than half her crew had been killed. By the time of her surrender darkness was falling on the Straits, and fighting for the day had come to an end.

Boscawen pursued the French throughout the night and was rewarded at daybreak by the sight of four ships of the line standing in towards the coast of Portugal. Two others had broken away in the night and were making for Cadiz unknown to their admiral. The four French ships entered Lagos Bay and de la Clue's flagship, the *Océan*, ran herself ashore with all her sails set so that all three masts

Hawke's flagship at Quiberon Bay, HMS *Royal George*. She was a first-rate of 100 guns, launched in 1756, and finally foundered at Spithead in 1782. This painting of her is by Dominic Serres

went by the board and fell over the bows. The other three anchored under the guns of a Portuguese shore battery.

Boscawen, eager to get among the enemy, was not one to let any questions of neutrality hinder him. He followed the French in, set fire to the *Océan* and the *Redoutable*, and towed out the *Téméraire* and *Modeste* as prizes. 'I flatter myself,' he wrote to Pitt, 'that my conduct in this affair will be approved by you. It is easier to satisfy that Court [i.e. Portugal] than for the French to build four men-of-war.'

The destruction of the Toulon fleet forced the French now to rely upon the fleet in Brest to cover the projected invasion, and orders were sent to the French admiral there, Conflans, to escort the troop transports with all the ships he could muster. But to seaward of the harbour lay Hawke with the Western Squadron of 17 ships of the line, with an inshore squadron of frigates under Commodore Duff keeping a close watch on all French movements. Throughout the summer and autumn Hawke lay waiting with his ships, supported by a constant stream of victualling ships from Plymouth bringing fresh meat, vegetables, beer, and fresh water to keep the inevitable scurvy at bay, and to maintain his seamen in health. Under the watchful eye of the British ships Conflans could make no move.

Autumn gave way to winter, and with it came the gales and wild seas of Biscay. Hawke warned the Admiralty that there would be occasions when he would have to withdraw from his station off Brest and shelter in Torbay. But a westerly, onshore gale which would drive him to shelter would equally prevent the French from getting out from Brest, and an easterly wind which would bring Conflans out would just as surely carry the Western Squadron to Biscay.

Early in November Hawke was driven off his station by a westerly gale. The same gale brought into Brest a French squadron from the West Indies, and its safe arrival revealed to Conflans that the British blockade had been temporarily lifted. On 13th November the gale backed into the south-east and Conflans was able to get his ships to sea on the following day, the same day that Hawke sailed from Torbay and stood down Channel. Conflans steered to the southward to Morbihan to pick up the transports assembled there; Hawke south-westward to round Ushant and rejoin his station.

An easterly gale on the 16th held up Conflans and he was forced to heave-to. The same gale sped Hawke's ships westward. On this day a victualler returning from Duff's inshore squadron spied Hawke at sea and reported sighting the French fleet on its way southward from Brest to Morbihan. Hawke needed no urging. 'I have carried a press of sail all night,' he reported in a despatch to the Admiralty on the 17th, 'with a hard gale at south-south-east, in pursuit of the enemy, and make no doubt of coming up with them at sea or in Quiberon Bay.'

Early in the morning of the 20th one of Hawke's frigates made the signal for a fleet in sight. Hawke immediately made the signal to form a line of battle abreast. An hour later the fleet in sight was identified as French. Conflans made for Quiberon Bay, thinking that inside the bay he could take up a stronger defensive position to hold off the inevitable attack.

The southern entrance to Quiberon Bay lies between the Cardinal Rocks on the one hand and the Four Shoal, a dangerous rocky bank, on the other. Conflans passed the Cardinals at about 2.30 p.m., but his hopes of taking up a strong defensive position within the bay were dashed by the headlong speed of Hawke's pursuit. Setting every sail the ships could carry, oblivious of the gale, the heavy rain squalls which blotted out sight of the land, and the dangerous, rock-strewn waters, the British ships swept on. The months spent on watch outside Brest were telling their story of magnificently trained and hardy seamen and an overwhelming superiority in pure seamanship. As the rear division of the French fleet was

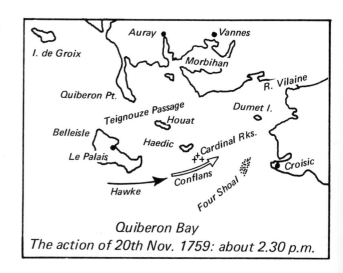

Quiberon Bay
The action of 20th Nov. 1759: about 2.30 p.m.

rounding the Cardinals, the British van division was in action with it.

The wind rose in the afternoon. It threw the French line into disorder; it enabled the British ships to come the sooner into action. Inside the bay the battle developed largely into single ship actions as the British ships came up within range, each selecting an opponent in the gloom and gathering darkness of the November afternoon. Hawke himself, in his flagship the *Royal George*, rounded the Cardinals shortly before four o'clock, meeting the *Soleil Royal*, with Conflans on board, trying to lead his ships out of the bay and back to sea. Hawke ordered the master to lay his ship alongside the enemy, and when the latter protested, in view of the rocks and shoals of these narrow waters, is reported to have said: 'You have done your duty in this remonstrance; now obey my orders and lay me alongside the French Admiral.' The two ships engaged broadside to broadside, and the *Soleil Royal* was driven so far to leeward that she could not weather the Four Shoal. She was forced to wear and

retrace her course into Quiberon Bay.

By five o'clock it was getting dark. The ebb tide was running out against the westerly gale and a tremendous sea raged in the Bay. All round, the sea broke and thundered on the rock-bound coast and the Four Shoal. As the short winter day closed in darkness, the British ships anchored to await the morning light and a resumption of the battle.

Although Hawke could not yet know it, he had already won a considerable victory. The French *Formidable*, flagship of Rear-Admiral du Verger, had been so battered by British broadsides that she had struck her colours to the *Resolution*. The *Thésée*, a new 74-gun ship, had heeled over and sank after having been in action with the *Torbay*. The *Héros*, raked by the *Magnanime*, had lost every officer and 400 of her crew, and surrendered to the *Chatham*. The *Superbe* foundered in the wild sea after receiving two broadsides from the *Royal George*. And the French vice-admiral, with seven ships tacking to keep clear of the rocks and shoals, had got himself embayed in the estuary of the Vilaine river and could not get out.

The French ship of the line *Thésée* sinking during the Battle of Quiberon Bay. Engaged by the *Torbay*, her middle-deck gun ports were submerged in the tempestuous sea and she filled and sank. From the painting by Richard Paton

THE SEVEN YEARS WAR

As yet no British ship had been lost, but at ten o'clock that night, while attempting to rejoin the fleet, the *Resolution* ran aground on the Four Shoal. In spite of all the efforts of her crew she was unable to get off. Some of the French ships, under cover of the darkness, managed to get out to sea and made for the shelter of the Basque Roads. One of them, the *Juste*, ran ashore in the mouth of the Loire and broke her back.

The scene which met Hawke's eyes as the dawn broke was indescribable. The French flagship, in the darkness of the night, had anchored in the midst of the British fleet. She cut her cable and ran ashore on the southern shore of the Bay. The *Héros*, which had struck her colours the previous day – it had been too rough to put a prize crew on board – also cut her cable and ran ashore. The *Essex*, ordered by Hawke to engage them, was wrecked on the Four Shoal. The *Soleil Royal* was set on fire by her own crew and the *Héros* was burned by the British. Boats of the fleet took off the crews of the *Resolution* and *Essex* as they lay wrecked on the Four Shoal.

There remained the seven French ships in the estuary of the Vilaine. By jettisoning all their guns, they managed to get across the bar into the river in a desperate attempt to escape from the fury of Hawke's attack. Hawke had ideas of trying to destroy them

Many painters have been attracted to the Battle of Quiberon Bay as a subject, among them Thomas Luny whose picture is shown above. Like others before him, he has taken the sinking of the French *Thésée* as his central theme while the main battle rages in the background

The scene in Quiberon Bay on the morning after the battle. In the foreground is the British *Resolution*, wrecked on the Four Shoal during the night. Beyond her, also aground on the shoal, is HMS *Essex*. In the background, ashore and in flames, are the French flagship *Soleil Royal* and the *Héros*. From the painting by Richard Wright

73

with fireships, but the scheme was impracticable. In the event, four of them later broke their backs in the shallow waters of the river.

The victory at Quiberon Bay not only shattered French plans for the invasion of Britain; it also swept away the naval power of France. She now had little left to fight with at sea, and French possessions all over the world were at the mercy of the British Navy. Three great victories in a single year, Lagos, Quebec, Quiberon Bay, all of them adding up to the total defeat of France at sea, was a glorious vindication of Pitt's strategy. Not for nothing could Horace Walpole write: 'Our bells are worn threadbare with ringing for victories'; not for nothing could David Garrick, in his pantomime *Harlequin's Invasion*, write his stirring verse 'Heart of Oak', to be set to music by William Boyce, in celebration of the wonderful year.

*   *   *

It was not only in Canada and in the waters around Europe that the Navy had been active. In the West Indies the problem at first had been the protection of seaborne trade against naval attack from the two French bases of Martinique and Haiti. By 1759 Pitt had come to the conclusion that the British superiority at sea had reached so marked a pitch that a major expedition could be spared to attack the French islands. Martinique was too strongly held as yet, but the French island of Guadaloupe was captured by a force of 6,000 troops supported by ten ships of the line and several frigates. When the end came in Canada and North America, troops from there were available to add their weight to the British expeditionary force, and in 1761 Dominica was captured. Martinique fell the following year, and with it was broken all French power in the Caribbean Sea. British seaborne trade flowed freely, protected by the Royal Navy, and one by one the remaining islands still in French possession fell to British arms.

One last dying effort by France to stave off the inevitable defeat came in 1761 when the new king of Spain, Charles III, joined France under the terms of what was known as the 'family compact'. Though it added the Spanish Fleet to that of the French, the tight grip held by the British Navy along the whole coastline of France and Spain down to Gibraltar effectively prevented the movement of any enemy ships. A reinforcement of ships was sent to Saunders

in the Mediterranean, and no enemy movement was possible there either. And in the meantime the overwhelming British strength at sea made it possible to strike at Spain in her possessions overseas. Havana, capital city of the Spanish colony in the West Indies, was an obvious choice, for it was the port from which the defence of the annual treasure fleets from America to Spain was organised. The city fell to a joint naval and military attack in August 1762, and with its loss was lost also a squadron of Spanish warships and more than a hundred merchant ships, captured. More important still, it was a crippling blow to Spanish financial resources, for it was on the safe and punctual arrival of the treasure fleets that the Spanish economy depended.

As in the West Indies, so also in India and the East Indies. Again the problem at first was commerce protection against attack by the French. A small naval squadron under Rear-Admiral Watson, reinforced by four ships to bring it up to approximate parity with French naval forces in the area, operated in conjunction with the military under Robert Clive, supporting with its gunfire the shore attacks which, by 1757, had recaptured Calcutta, driven the French out of Chandernagore, and brought the whole of Bengal under British control.

The whole future of France in India now depended on control of the sea around the Indian coasts. The French admiral, the Comte d'Aché, had he used his fleet vigorously, could well have achieved a position of commanding strength, for his ships outnumbered those of Watson, and later of Rear-Admiral Pocock who took over the command when Watson died of fever. But d'Aché was a cautious admiral who never sought battle against the British squadron. Three indecisive actions between Pocock and d'Aché were fought at sea, the last, in 1760, ending more in favour of the British than the French. D'Aché retired with his squadron to Mauritius, and with the British now in undisputed control of the sea, the end for France in India was near. In January 1761 Pondicherry, the central bastion of French power in India, surrendered to the Army under Eyre Coote and to the Navy under Rear-Admiral Steevens, who had succeeded Pocock in command at the end of 1760.

There remained one more action to complete the story. It was again aimed at Spain when she entered the war on the side of France in 1761. As Havana

One of a series of 12 plates illustrating the attack on, and capture of, Havana in 1762. This was a combined naval and military operation under the joint command of Admiral Sir George Pocock and General Lord Albemarle. This view shows the city under bombardment

A water-colour sketch, painted on the spot by Phillip Orsbridge, of the attack on French vessels at the mouth of the Senegal River in April 1758. The French fort, twelve miles up river, was captured. The expedition, reinforced from Britain, went on to capture Gorée later in the year

had been the key to Spanish wealth in the West Indies, so was Manila the key in the East. In October 1762 the town was captured by a combined naval and military force commanded by Rear-Admiral Cornish and Colonel Draper, and the whole of the Philippine Islands surrendered soon after. The loss of this source of wealth was as grievous a blow to the Spanish economy as the loss of Havana. Never, perhaps, had so short a war cost any country so dear as did the 10 months of her hostilities cost Spain.

At the peace, signed in 1763, many of the conquests around the world were handed back to their original owners, for it was no part of the British design to try to reign supreme on the world stage. But Canada, so hardly won in three years of campaigning, was retained in British hands for fear of a renewed attempt to check the westward march of the American colonists, which had in fact been the prime cause of all the fighting. Soon, indeed, these colonies were to gain their freedom in as bitter a war as had ever been fought, but their development of the vast lands to the westward had been made possible for all time by the defeat by Britain of the French attempt to divide the country along the line of the Mississippi and Ohio valleys.

CHAPTER 7

*Opening the Oceans 1764-1800 – The Golden Age of
Discovery – Byron, Wallis, Cook, Vancouver, and Flinders –
Institution of the Hydrographic Department of the
British Admiralty*

PETER KEMP

Supreme upon the sea as a result of the Seven Years' War, the British Admiralty took its duties seriously. Discovery, it was decided, was a function of sea power; nor was the art of navigation to be neglected. Accordingly, within a year of the signature of the peace treaty, two ships were fitted out to proceed on a voyage of discovery around the world. They were placed under the command of Captain the Hon. John Byron, who had been a midshipman in Anson's squadron of circumnavigation but had been wrecked after rounding Cape Horn. 'Nothing,' wrote Their Lordships when drawing up Byron's orders, 'can redound more to the honour of this nation as a maritime power, to the dignity of the Crown of Great Britain, and to the advancement of the trade and navigation thereof, than to make discoveries of countries hitherto unknown.'

Byron's voyage around the world was notable only for his almost incredible feat of sailing across the Pacific without making a single discovery. His lack of success, however, was no discouragement to the British Admiralty, and within three months of his return another voyage of discovery was under way, commanded this time by Captain Samuel Wallis and Captain Philip Cartaret. Their two ships became separated after navigating the Magellan Strait and Wallis struck out into the Pacific. After seven weeks he sighted mountainous land ahead, and anchored the next day off a large island to which he gave the name George III Island, better known to-day as Tahiti. Having refreshed his crew, he made the best of his way to Tinian, discovering one or two small islands to which he gave names, and from there returned home round the Cape of Good Hope.

Cartaret, separated from Wallis and in a small ship with very few stores, steered for Juan Fernandez Island for wood and fresh water, confident that, as in Anson's day, it was still uninhabited. He reached it to find a Spanish fort and garrison installed. Denied access for water, he sailed on to Masafuera, managed with great difficulty to water his ship, and in his turn set out to cross the Pacific. Six weeks later an island was seen and was given the name of the midshipman who first sighted it from the masthead, Pitcairn. With his crew suffering from scurvy, he finally reached the island of New Britain, first discovered by William Dampier some 60 years earlier. He made the discovery that this was in fact two islands, and named the second New Ireland. He finally reached England ten months after Wallis had returned.

There followed the three great voyages of James Cook, a man whom one can look upon as the real founder of modern surveying at sea. After serving in North Sea colliers he volunteered to join the Navy as an able seaman in H.M.S. *Eagle*. Here he came under the notice of Captain Hugh Palliser, who in 1759 managed to get him appointed as master (the equivalent of navigator) of H.M.S. *Mercury*. He was in that ship during the expedition against Quebec and his part in discovering and buoying the deep water channel of the St. Lawrence river helped Saunders's fleet to perform its great feat of navigation in penetrating up to the Quebec basin. He spent the rest of the war in surveying the coast of Newfoundland.

When a new voyage to the Pacific was planned at the urging of the Royal Society to observe the transit of Venus across the face of the sun in 1769, the

Opposite: Captain James Cook, the great navigator, was one of the few seamen of the 18th century who rose from the lower deck to become a post-captain. His survey of the St Lawrence River was partly instrumental in enabling the British fleet to reach Quebec in 1759, and his three great voyages of circumnavigation (he was killed during the third) opened up much of the unknown world. This portrait of Cook is by Nathaniel Dance

name of James Cook was put forward. His work on the Newfoundland coast had already been very highly esteemed by the British Admiralty, and they decided that he should command the expedition, giving him a commission as a lieutenant in the Royal Navy for the purpose. Cook selected for the voyage a strongly built ship of 370 tons, based on the lines of a North Sea collier. She was named *Endeavour,* and in July 1768 she sailed from Plymouth bound for Tahiti from which place, on the recommendation of Captain Wallis, the transit of Venus was to be observed.

Cook was charged by the Admiralty, in addition to observing the transit, to investigate the report of the existence of a vast southern continent which many geographers were convinced must lie to the south of the Pacific and Indian Oceans. On leaving Tahiti after successfully observing the transit, Cook sailed westward and discovered a group of islands which he named the Society Islands, in honour of the Royal Society. These were surveyed, and the accuracy of Cook's work was such that many of his observations are to be found in the charts of the islands of today.

From these islands he sailed south, as far as the latitude of 40°S., but found no continent. Stormy weather drove him to the northward again, and in October he sighted land. It was the North Island of New Zealand, and for the next six months Cook carried out a survey of the coast with the same extreme accuracy as he had achieved at the Society Islands.

Leaving New Zealand he steered westward and on 29th April anchored in Botany Bay, on the east coast of Australia. The *Endeavour* went ashore on the Great Barrier Reef in June, but was refloated and brought safely into the mouth of a river, named Endeavour after the ship, where she was refitted. Cook surveyed much of the coast of New South Wales, and passing through the Torres Strait, also examined the coast of New Guinea. From there he sailed to Batavia to refit, and thence around the Cape of Good Hope, reaching England after a voyage of 35 months.

This first circumnavigation by Cook is important not alone for his discovery of New Zealand and Australia, but also because it was achieved without the loss of any man from scurvy. Forty men were lost from dysentery and fever contracted during the visit to Batavia, but whereas scurvy had been the great killer in all previous voyages of long duration, on this occasion no one succumbed to the disease. Cook attributed his immunity from scurvy to a daily ration of wort, made from malt, and *sourkraut,* or pickled cabbage; compulsory daily washing by all men in cold water; and the ship kept dry between decks in all weathers. He more probably owed his immunity to his insistence in gathering green vegetables on every possible occasion, even extending this insistence to wild celery gathered from Tierra del Fuego when off the Horn. It is a sad commentary on the lack of medical knowledge of the time that Cook's success in keeping scurvy at bay held back the introduction of the true specific into the Navy by a quarter of a century. It is an even sadder commentary on the naval administration of the time that Surgeon James Lind had discovered the real cure 15 years earlier, but his writings on the subject had never been followed up by the British Admiralty.

Within three months of his return, Cook was promoted commander and appointed to lead a second voyage of discovery. Once again the main object of the voyage was to prove or disprove the existence of the great southern continent so beloved by geographers. Two Whitby colliers were purchased, refitted for the voyage, and given the names *Resolution* and *Adventure.* They left Plymouth in July 1772 and, after calling at the Cape of Good Hope, Cook sailed to the southward. Meeting the ice, the two ships sailed along the edge and eventually reached the latitude of 67°15′S. The whole area of sea between South Africa and New Zealand was searched for the unknown continent, and Cook eventually anchored in Dusky Bay, New Zealand, confident that no southern continent existed in the Antarctic between Good Hope and New Zealand.

From New Zealand the *Resolution* and *Adventure* revisited Tahiti and the Society Islands, and then returned to New Zealand, where the *Adventure* lost company in thick weather and never made contact again. She returned to England around Cape Horn, reaching home in July 1774. Cook, in the absence of his consort, once again sailed south in search of the mythical continent. He reached a south latitude of 71° but was stopped by a vast ice field from proceeding any farther. With his crew still remarkably healthy, he determined on making further dis-

William Bligh, better known as the hot-blooded captain of HMS *Bounty* at the time of the famous mutiny, was Cook's sailing master during the third voyage of circumnavigation. He was no mean navigator himself, and successfully sailed a small boat with the survivors of the mutiny a distance of 1700 miles to Timor. He commanded ships at the battles of Camperdown and Copenhagen

coveries in the Pacific, and as a start decided to confirm the existence of Easter Island, reported by Roggewein in a previous voyage. Cook reached and made a survey of the island, and sailing on to the Marquesas group, discovered a new island in the group to which the name Hood Island was given after the name of the midshipman who first sighted it from the *Resolution's* masthead. Other new Pacific islands were discovered on the way to the Friendly Islands, and a complete and accurate survey of the New Hebrides group was made before the *Resolution* retraced her passage once more to New Zealand to refit. She then returned to England around Cape Horn, reaching Plymouth almost exactly three years after her departure.

Shortly after his return, Cook was promoted to captain and appointed to command a third voyage of exploration, again with two ships, the *Resolution* and *Discovery*. His instructions this time were to proceed to the Pacific and sail up the west coast of North America as far as possible to discover any passage leading from the Pacific to the Atlantic around the north of Canada, and beyond the

Behring Strait. This was the old search for a north-west passage, but from the reverse direction, revived after a period of some 200 years when a westward sea route to China had been the spur.

Cook used his voyage northwards in the Pacific to discover and survey yet more new islands, including the Sandwich group, and finally reached the west coast of America in the vicinity of what is now known as San Francisco, first visited by Drake in his voyage around the world two centuries earlier. Cook made his way northward to Nootka Sound, naming the land to the west of the sound after one of his midshipmen, George Vancouver. He continued to the northward to reach the latitude of 70°N, but everywhere his way was blocked by solid ice. Satisfied that no navigable way through to the Atlantic existed, he turned back to rest and refit in the Sandwich Islands where the two ships anchored in Karakakoa Bay on the west coast of Hawaii.

A few days later Cook was killed by the natives after an altercation ashore. Under the command now of Captain Clerke, the two ships sailed north again to make yet another attempt to find a way

Matthew Flinders, who was a midshipman in the relief expedition to Australia in 1795, remained to carry out extensive surveying work in those waters. On his return to England he was appointed to command a survey of the entire Australian coast. On completion of his task, and on his way home to England, he was made a prisoner of war by the French governor of Mauritius. He was held in captivity there for nearly seven years

through the ice beyond the Behring Strait, but no passage was found. Returning to the Cape of Good Hope the expedition returned to Britain, reaching the Nore in October 1780.

The occupation by the Spaniards of Nootka Sound in 1789 was the occasion of a new voyage which was to lead to yet more discoveries. George Vancouver, who had been a midshipman with Cook in his second and third voyages and was now a commander, was appointed to lead a small expedition of two ships, the *Discovery* and the *Chatham*, to receive the surrender of Nootka Sound, to which the Spanish Government had agreed, and at the same time to survey the coast. Vancouver first made for the Australian coast, discovering King George's Sound, and then proceeded to Dusky Bay in New Zealand. After a visit to the Sandwich Islands, the ships reached the North American coast and, surveying as they went, proceeded to Nootka Sound where Vancouver accepted the surrender of the Spanish commander. Surveying along the coast, he discovered that Vancouver, the land which had already been named after him by Cook, was in fact

an island. Continuing his survey, he sailed slowly south to the then virtually uninhabited San Francisco, which he described as containing 'a variety of as excellent harbours as the known world affords'. Vancouver also explored the surrounding countryside which he reported as being as beautiful as an English country park.

Vancouver continued to survey the coast as far north as 56°30′ and as far south as San Diego, interspersed with visits to the Sandwich Islands, on one occasion accepting from the king of Hawaii the cession of his island to King George of England. On his final visit to the American coast he fixed the position of Cape San Lucar, the southernmost point of the peninsula of California, and after a laborious passage down the coast of South America his two ships reached home after a voyage lasting four years and nine months.

In 1788, ten years after the death of James Cook, the first steps were taken to establish British communities in Australia and New Zealand. Captain Arthur Phillip, in the brig *Supply*, followed by Captain Hunter in the *Sirius*, with six transports and three supply ships, arrived at Botany Bay in that year. Nine miles to the northward they found a magnificent harbour which they named Port Jackson, the site of the present city of Sydney. The transports were filled with convicts from Britain, and it was from this first settlement that the eventual colonisation of Australia sprang.

In the relief expedition which reached Sydney in 1795 was a midshipman named Matthew Flinders, serving in H.M.S. *Reliance*. The surgeon of the same ship was named George Bass, and the two young men, discovering that the only chart of the coast was that made by Cook in his first voyage, were fired with the determination to carry Cook's survey further around the coast in both directions.

In spite of every discouragement and difficulty put in their way by the authorities, the two men acquired and equipped a small boat eight feet long which they named *Tom Thumb*. With one boy as their crew, they set out to chart the coast of New South Wales. In her they extended the knowledge of the coast, and three years later their work was rewarded by the gift of a whale boat with a crew of five convicts to assist them. In this small boat Bass charted 600 miles of coast, and proceeded as far as the entrance of the Strait which divides Australia from Tasmania and which now bears his name. As a result of these discoveries, the Governor of New South Wales gave to Flinders and Bass the use of a 25-ton sloop named *Norfolk* with a view to completing the survey of the Bass Strait. To them belongs the discovery that Tasmania was an island.

Flinders returned home to England in 1800 to find that, as a result of these recent discoveries, a plan had been approved by the British government to chart all the coasts of Australia. Flinders was appointed to command H.M.S. *Investigator*, and in January 1802 began a journey along the whole southern coast of Australia, charting the coastline with extreme accuracy throughout its length. There followed an equally accurate survey of the eastern and northern coasts of the continent as far as Melville Bay, taking in the Great Barrier Reef on the way. At Melville Bay the *Investigator* was found to be so rotten as to be unseaworthy, and Flinders returned in her to Sydney.

After a disastrous shipwreck on the way home to England, Flinders was made a prisoner of war by the French during a forced call at Mauritius when his small ship sprang a leak. He was held there for seven years and finally reached England in 1810. It was he who first suggested the name Australia for the new continent.

Hand in hand with these voyages of discovery went the perfection of the means of establishing longitude. It had long been recognised that the determination of longitude could be achieved by measuring the difference of time between the meridian altitude of the sun at the required place and its meridian altitude at Greenwich, which in England was known as the prime meridian. In 1714, at the instigation of the British Admiralty, a Board of Longitude had been set up and a reward of £20,000 was offered to anyone who could construct a chronometer of sufficient accuracy to enable longitude to be established. The challenge was taken up by John Harrison, who in all built four chronometers, each more accurate than its predecessor. Some of them were carried in many of these voyages of discovery, including Cook's second and third voyages, and when with his fourth chronometer he achieved the required degree of accuracy he was, eventually and rather grudgingly, given the £20,000 reward. One of the greatest stumbling blocks to accurate navigation had been overcome.

It was as a result of James Cook's three great voyages and the wealth of new discovery that they produced that in 1795 the British Admiralty decided to appoint an official Hydrographer to the Navy, to be responsible for the production of charts, the furtherance of the science of navigation, and the publication of nautical almanacs, tide tables, sailing directions and the like. The man chosen to fill the position was Mr Alexander Dalrymple, who had translated into English many of the accounts of voyages made by foreign seamen and who was one of the great experts in the geography of the world. It was from his first appointment that the great British Hydrographic Office grew, with its world-wide coverage of charts and sailing directions and its constant work in the surveying of ports and harbours, coasts and estuaries, and seas and oceans.

It is not for nothing that the second half of the 18th century is today known as the golden age of discovery. The whole world was being opened up by gifted men in their search for knowledge, with Britain contributing perhaps the most distinguished part in this restless search for navigational knowledge.

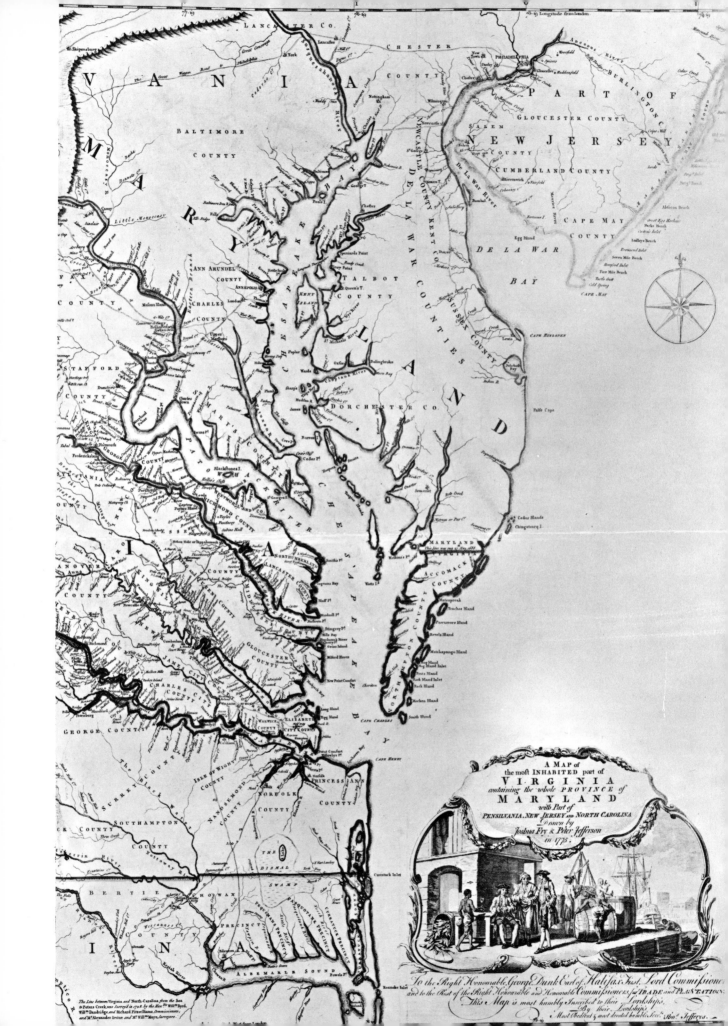

A MAP of
the most INHABITED part of
VIRGINIA
containing the whole PROVINCE of
MARYLAND
with Part of
PENSILVANIA, NEW JERSEY AND NORTH CAROLINA
Drawn by
Joshua Fry & Peter Jefferson
in 1775.

To the Right Honourable George Dunk Earl of Halifax, first Lord Commissioner
and to the Rest of the Right Honourable and Honourable Commissioners, for TRADE and PLANTATIONS,
This Map is most humbly Inscribed to their Lordships,
By their Lordships,
Most Obedient & most devoted humble Servt. Thos. Jefferys.

CHAPTER 8

*War of American Independence – French and Spanish Fleets
in the Channel – Rodney and Hood in the West Indies –
Battle of Chesapeake Bay – Battle of The Saints*

DONALD MACINTYRE

The Treaty of Paris, which brought the Seven Years' War to a conclusion, had hardly been signed before the British Government found itself at loggerheads with its American colonies.

Regulations which restricted the colonies to trading only with the mother country, and others designed to prevent commercial competition, had for a long time been a source of irritation to the Americans. The removal of any exterior threat by the successful outcome of what to them had been the 'French-Indian War' and of dependence on British arms for defence now emboldened the colonists openly to object.

It is fair to say, however, that the open rift in 1765 came over a matter of principle dear to the hearts of democrats on both sides of the Atlantic – that of 'No taxation without representation'. When Parliament imposed a stamp duty to raise money to support a colonial defence force it led to impassioned protests in colonial Assemblies, memorials of protest sent to London, and rioting with attacks on property. Though the Stamp Act was repealed, the British Government reaffirmed in a Declaratory Act its right to impose taxes on the colonies and proceeded to exact duty on a number of commodities entering them.

Active resistance by the colonists steadily grew, culminating in the famous 'Boston Tea Party' in 1773, the closing of the port of Boston, and the Declaration of Rights by the first Congress in the following year. In 1775 the first shots of rebellion were fired at Lexington.

The desultory war which followed during the next two years was, for the Royal Navy, an affair of minor expeditions in support of army operations, the most interesting of which were the two campaigns on Lake Champlain in 1776 and 1777. In the first of these Captain Charles Douglas of H.M.S. *Isis*, having relieved beleaguered Quebec in the nick of time in May and forced the besieging rebel force under Benedict Arnold to retreat to Crown Point at the southern end of Lake Champlain, proceeded to construct a flotilla at the other end of the lake from material brought overland or in boats with which to oppose a similar force gathered by Arnold.

When the two flotillas met in October, Douglas's possession of the *Inflexible*, mounting eighteen 12-pounders, the construction of which was a remarkable feat, dominated the fighting. After three days Arnold's force was practically wiped out, but the delay he had imposed prevented any further advance of the British Army that year. By the time it was resumed in July 1777 under General Burgoyne, Douglas had added the 26-gun *Royal George* to his flotilla which played a vital part in the advance to the southern end of the lake.

Burgoyne's campaign ended in capitulation at Saratoga in October 1777, however, an event which convinced the French that the opportunity was ripe for exacting revenge for the humiliations of the Seven Years' War. In March 1778 they informed the British Government that they had signed an alliance with the United States of America, and the war at once assumed the shape of a widespread oceanic conflict. The two navies which faced one another were, at the outset, very different from those which had met in battle fifteen years earlier.

The lesson of the previous war, that sea power

A composite picture made of two sheets of an American atlas published in 1776 showing the states of Maryland and Virginia and enclosing the area of Chesapeake Bay, off which was fought in 1781 the decisive naval battle of the War of American Independence

alone was the key to the defeat of Britain and to a restoration of the colonial empire, had been well absorbed by the French. Under the inspired hand of the Duc de Choiseul the French fleet had been re-built and revitalised and, after a pause following Choiseul's dismissal in 1770, the work had been resumed by M. de Sartine who became Minister of Marine in 1776. At the outbreak of war 73 ships of the line of 64 guns or more were in commission, many of them new and of a design benefiting from the application of the latest techniques evolved by a school of naval architecture.

In the Royal Navy, on the other hand, the splen-did fleet built up under the administration of Anson had calamitously deteriorated in both quality and quantity. The age was notorious in Britain for political jobbery and corruption in every walk of life. So far as the Navy was concerned, this man-ifested itself in widespread misappropriation of funds and falsification of accounts, leading not only to indifferently built ships to replace the large num-ber struck off the list, many of which might have been repaired, but also to empty storehouses and decay-ing dockyards. Another reason for a shortage of sea-worthy ships was that owing to exhaustion of supplies of home-grown oak, many built in the last fifteen years had made use of timber imported from the continent which proved to have a life barely a quarter of that of English oak.

As for personnel, in the absence of conscription which the Englishman with his passionate belief in the freedom of the subject would not accept, mann-ing the fleet depended, paradoxically, upon the haphazard and often cruel working of impressment which might send a ship to sea in the early stages of a war with a crew made up largely of landsmen. In the long run, however, the advantage in quality of men on the lower deck rested with the British who had a larger maritime population than the French upon which to draw when the requirement arose for replacements of skilled topmen and petty officers as a result of losses in action or from disease.

One thing that both navies had in common was a rigid belief in the maintenance of the line in the closest possible order during the approach to battle; but while the French carried this principle on to cover all stages of a battle, with captains forbidden to leave the line under any pretext without permission from the admiral to do so, the British *Fighting*

A 32-pounder British naval gun of the period. This particular gun was mounted in the *Royal George* and recovered from the seabed after the ship sank at her moorings in Spithead in 1782. The block of oak in front of the carriage is part of the *Royal George*

Instructions wisely left captains free to exercise their own judgment as to how they fought their ships once action was joined.

The most crucial difference between the two navies, however, was in their strategic principles. To the British, destruction of the enemy's fleet in close, decisive action was a prime object, from the achievement of which all the fruits of sea power would inevitably fall into their hands. The French, in contrast, invariably sent their fleet to sea to achieve some other object; battle with an equal or superior force was to be avoided if possible and in any case to be broken off at the earliest opportunity.

The difference of strategic thought expressed itself in fighting methods such as gunnery, in which the British aim was to smash the enemy's hull, inflict the maximum casualties, and pin the enemy down to a fight to the finish, whereas the French aimed pri-marily to cripple their opponents' rigging.

Such were the characteristics of the two navies that were now, once again, to strive for supremacy. The difference between their material state became immediately apparent. For whereas the French Toulon squadron of 12 ships of the line and five frigates, under the Comte d'Estaing, was able to sail unopposed to North America on 13th April 1778, at Portsmouth Admiral Keppel, appointed to command a Channel Fleet of 20 of the line, found only six fit for sea and they gave 'no pleasure to his

Opposite: A view of Gibraltar, from an engraving by F. Hegi after a painting by Alexandre Noel. Gibraltar, first captured by Rooke in 1704, has had to withstand many sieges and attempts at recapture, the most famous siege being that of 1781–2, finally relieved by Rodney and Howe. *Overleaf*: The death of Captain James Cook at the hands of natives at Karakakoa Bay, on the west coast of Hawaii. From the painting by T. Zoffany

seaman's eye'. Before the remainder were ready there came the news of d'Estaing's departure. Keppel, like other admirals of the Whig persuasion, had only agreed to serve against a 'continental' enemy, and was therefore ordered to give up ten of his ships to make up a squadron of 13 which Vice-Admiral Byron was to take to reinforce Lord Howe's squadron of six of the line in American waters.

Sailing on 9th June, Byron's squadron was beset by persistent foul weather and did not finally assemble at Sandy Hook, much damaged, until 26th September, when he took over command of the station from Howe who refused to serve any longer under a Tory administration. Fortunately, in the meantime Howe had so cleverly outmanoeuvred the greatly superior force under d'Estaing as to prevent him from bringing the aid eagerly awaited by General Washington.

At the first news of Byron's presence, d'Estaing retired into Boston harbour where his squadron remained until, with the approach of winter bringing operations in the north to an end, he sailed on 4th November for Martinique to operate against British possessions in the West Indies.

On the same day a British squadron of five ships of the line under Commodore Hotham, escorting a troop convoy carrying 5,000 troops, also sailed south from New York and arrived at Barbados on 10th December, the day after d'Estaing reached Martinique. The latter planned to attack the British islands, beginning with Barbados, but was forestalled by the British commanders on the station, Vice-Admiral Samuel Barrington and Major-General Grant, who wasted not a moment in launching their own expedition to capture St. Lucia where troops were landed on the 13th.

When d'Estaing appeared on the 15th, his fleet of 12 of the line was repulsed by Barrington and Hotham's seven, anchored in a defensive line across the mouth of a narrow inlet. Instead of persisting with his attack which, if resolutely pursued, must have destroyed the British squadron and left him master of the situation, d'Estaing, a soldier by profession, landed at the head of 5,000 troops and attacked the 1,300 British who had taken up a defensive position covered by their artillery. The French were thrown back with heavy losses, whereupon d'Estaing abandoned his efforts and returned to Martinique, leaving in British hands for the rest

of the war an easily defended and good harbour within thirty miles of the main French base at Fort Royal.

In European waters, meanwhile, neither the French nor the British fleets could congratulate themselves on their first encounter. This was the Battle of Ushant, fought on 23rd July 1778. The Brest squadron of 32 of the line under the Comte d'Orvilliers, meeting Keppel's Channel Fleet of 30, disabled some of the British ships, after which d'Orvilliers was content to break off the engagement and return to harbour. On the British side Keppel's second-in-command, Vice-Admiral Sir Hugh Palliser, a Tory and thus a political opponent, failed, either by intent or incompetence, to support his chief at a crucial moment of the battle. Though Keppel made no criticism in his despatch, the story reached the newspapers and Palliser responded by demanding and securing Keppel's court-martial on charges of mismanagement of the battle.

The trial which followed in January 1779 was held in a blaze of publicity. Keppel's acquittal was greeted with wild enthusiasm by the mob both in Portsmouth and London and he became a public hero. Nevertheless he requested to be relieved of his command, feeling unable to serve 'under the direction and authority of those whose approbation in the execution of his duty and support afterwards, experience had taught him he could not depend on.'

One particular thorn in the British flesh in 1778 and 1779 was the activities of the American Captain John Paul Jones. Based in France, he made two cruises in British home waters during these years, first in the sloop *Ranger* and then in the frigate *Bonhomme Richard*, raiding the coast and spreading much alarm. His greatest exploit was in September 1779 when, with three other American ships in company, he fought and finally captured the British frigate *Serapis* and the armed ship *Countess of Scarborough*. The two British ships were escorting a homeward bound convoy of 44 ships from the Baltic, and realising that his primary duty was the safety of his convoy, Captain Pearson of the *Serapis* placed his two ships in the path of the American squadron while the convoy reversed its course and steered towards safety. After a three-hour engagement between the *Serapis* and the *Bonhomme Richard*, in the course of which both crews more than once attempted to carry the other ship by boarding, a fire in the

Opposite: The capture of Porto Bello, from the painting by Samuel Scott. The attack was launched against the 'Iron Castle', seen in the picture under bombardment by Vernon's flagship, the 70-gun *Burford*. The castle was quickly captured, and Porto Bello then surrendered without further attack

89

magazine forced Pearson to strike the colours of the *Serapis*. The whole of the convoy succeeded in reaching safety. One odd result of this frigate action was that the fire in the *Serapis* was successfully subdued and the ship survived, while in spite of all efforts to save her, the *Bonhomme Richard* sank two days after the action from the damage she had received.

With both Howe and Keppel – and Barrington since his return from the West Indies – refusing to serve, the Government were at their wits' end to find a suitable successor. Sir George Rodney, who was eventually to emerge as the leading naval figure in the war, was ineligible on account of his financial straits, a circumstance sufficient to bar his appointment to any post in which opportunities for peculation existed. To command the Grand Fleet the veteran Sir Charles Hardy was brought out of retirement. Fortunately, fleet operations in home waters virtually ceased until June 1779, when Spain entered the war and d'Orvilliers sailed with 30 ships of the line to combine with a fleet of 36 Spanish ships, designed to cover a grandiose scheme of invasion.

With only 35 ships available to form the British Grand Fleet, the situation appeared perilous in the extreme. But d'Orvilliers' combined Franco-Spanish fleet was little more than a 'paper tiger'. Too unwieldy to manoeuvre, its crews ravaged by sickness and dying at a frightening rate, short of water and provisions, and lacking pilots with a knowledge of the English Channel, it cruised aimlessly in the Channel for six weeks. Though it demonstrated off Plymouth and chased Hardy up Channel at the end of August, it achieved nothing. By 14th September it was back at Brest where the Spanish Fleet parted company to return to its own ports.

This painful experience caused the Franco-Spanish alliance to abandon any idea of mounting an invasion of England. The Spanish now concentrated on the siege of Gibraltar while the French prepared to send a strong naval reinforcement to the West Indies where d'Estaing had defeated Byron in July 1779 and had captured St. Vincent and Grenada. Vengeance on Britain for past humiliations was a more potent lure than aid to the rebellious colonists. Only when the onset of the hurricane season brought operations in the islands to a halt would the desperate calls by Washington for naval aid be answered.

Admiral Lord Rodney, victor of the Battle of the Saints in 1782, painted by Sir Joshua Reynolds. He proved himself to be the leading naval commander of the War of American Independence, and it was his victory in 1782 which enabled a satisfactory peace treaty to be signed.

Nevertheless, the centre of the naval war was clearly shifting across the Atlantic.

To command in the West Indies, where the main clash was certain to occur, Sir George Rodney was at last selected, having liquidated his debts. He was a gouty, irascible, and haughty aristocrat of 61, of no strong party allegiance, who set his face against the political squabbles which had been undermining discipline. His first task, in command of a squadron composed of 15 ships of the line of the Channel Fleet and five more destined for the West Indies, was to escort a fleet of transports for the relief of Gibraltar and a convoy for the East Indies. In the course of this mission he first captured a valuable convoy of

Spanish storeships for their fleet at Cadiz and then annihilated a Spanish squadron of 11 ships in the Moonlight Battle off Cape St. Vincent on 16th January 1780.

The relief of Gibraltar accomplished and the East Indian convoy sent on its way, Rodney sailed for the West Indies with four ships of the line, reaching Barbados on 17th March 1780. His arrival coincided with that of the Comte de Guichen, also with reinforcements of four of the line and a large troop convoy, at Martinique. A period of move and counter-move ensued with de Guichen, with 23 ships of the line, coming out from Fort Royal bent on attacking Barbados, and Rodney, with 21, trying to bring his unwilling opponent to decisive action. It culminated in the controversial Battle of Martinique on 17th April 1780. In this action Rodney attempted to seize the opportunity presented by a disarray of the French fleet to concentrate his whole force on the enemy's rear. Unfortunately this effort to break out of the shackles of the *Fighting Instructions,* with their unimaginative insistence on engagement with the entire enemy line, was frustrated by the inadequacies of the British signal system of the day and a consequent lack of comprehension of the Admiral's intentions by a number of his captains.

The usual drawn battle left both sides largely crippled. When, after temporary repairs, they again met Rodney once again tried in vain to force de Guichen to fight, both fleets finally withdrawing to their main bases of Fort Royal and Barbados to refit. The arrival of a Spanish fleet of 12 ships of the line tilted the balance considerably in favour of de Guichen and forced Rodney to adopt the defensive; but the Spaniards refused to co-operate in any joint enterprise. De Guichen, six years older than Rodney, worn out and disheartened, and ignoring the appeals of Washington and Lafayette to come north to their assistance, returned home at the onset of the hurricane season in August. Rodney, hearing of the arrival of a French squadron of seven of the line at Rhode Island, which they occupied, sailed north to New York, taking charge of the desultory operations on the American coast until the middle of November.

John Paul Jones, the American privateer, engaging the British *Serapis* off Flamborough Head in 1779 during a cruise with the *Bonhomme Richard* in British waters. The *Serapis* was finally forced to surrender, but the convoy she was escorting made good its escape

He then returned to the West Indies to find the islands devastated by a hurricane. Of the ships he had left there, a number had been destroyed and the remainder dismasted; what was worse was that no stores for their repair were available.

Reinforcements from England were soon on their way, however, where naval affairs were now showing great improvements as a result of the labours of Sir Charles Middleton, Controller of the Navy since 1778, who was to be better known to history as Lord Barham. In January 1781 the reinforcements arrived, eight ships of the line, four frigates, and more than 100 merchantmen bringing the urgently needed stores. In command came Rear-Admiral Sir Samuel Hood, an old friend and comrade-in-arms of Rodney, specially promoted when his career was almost at an end as a consequence of the continued refusal of so many flag officers to serve.

The old friendship, alas, was not long to survive Rodney's haughty rejection of a junior's advice and Hood's intolerant criticism of the shortcomings of his elderly and often ailing chief. The first friction arose as a result of Rodney's absorption with the immense booty of the Dutch West Indian island of St. Eustatius, captured without a fight on Holland's entry into the war on the side of France.

When intelligence of French reinforcements on their way reached Rodney, Hood was ordered to sea with the majority of the fleet to intercept. With no sign of the enemy after a month, Hood proposed that his ships, in which scurvy had appeared, should be allowed to return to harbour to refit and refresh until further news should be received. Rodney ordered him instead not only to remain at sea but to station himself off Fort Royal. Hood's insistence that only by keeping to windward of Martinique could the enemy be effectively intercepted, was also rejected. The consequence was that when a French fleet of 20 ships of the line under the Comte de Grasse appeared on 28th April, Hood was unable from his leeward position to force an engagement. De Grasse entered Fort Royal virtually unscathed, his junction with the four ships already there giving him a superiority of five ships of the line over Rodney, many of whose ships were damaged and their crews ravaged by sickness.

Except for the capture of Tobago, however, de Grasse achieved nothing before, with the hurricane season approaching, he sailed with 28 of the line to escort the season's convoy clear of the islands and was lost to sight. Rodney correctly judged that the French would concentrate against the isolated British army under Lord Cornwallis operating in Virginia, and that Chesapeake Bay would be de Grasse's destination. He sent urgent warning to Admiral Graves, commanding on that station, and ordered Hood with 14 ships of the line to join him. Rodney himself, worn out by sickness, sailed for home with the trade convoy to recuperate.

Hood reached Sandy Hook on 16th August, bringing Graves's strength up to 19 of the line. A day earlier de Grasse had anchored in Chesapeake Bay and disembarked 3,000 troops to join the Franco-American army investing Cornwallis at Yorktown. Graves knew nothing of this and it was only when, following a French squadron of eight of the line under de Barras which sailed south on the 25th, he arrived off the Virginia Capes on 5th September to descry a forest of masts in the bay, that he realised what a concentration he faced.

Nevertheless a splendid opportunity was now offered to him. De Grasse put to sea to cover the junction with de Barras and was forced to beat to and fro to weather Cape Henry, with the result that his van squadron was clear of the cape before the remainder. Had Graves acted promptly, de Grasse's van must have been overwhelmed. But Graves hesitated, and meanwhile solemnly formed his line of battle. Even when de Grasse had worked his way out of the bay unhindered, Graves manoeuvred his ships to close the enemy in a converging line ahead so that the van ships came into action one by one while the rear squadron under Hood was still far out of gun shot. Though Graves now made the signal to bear down and engage, he kept the signal for the line flying – the sacred line which a captain quitted at his peril – and so made the order to engage impossible to carry out. Even Hood, a bitter critic of Graves's failure to bring a concentration on de Grasse's van, never considered leaving the line so long as the signal for it flew, and was shocked when Graves sent a memorandum round the fleet the day after the battle indicating that the signal for the line could be overridden by that for battle. Hood, commanding the rear division, hardly got into action at all and, in commenting on Graves's lamentable performance, showed how a concentration on the enemy's van could have been brought about, either

Two wash drawings made by an unidentified artist showing two stages of the Battle of Chesapeake Bay. The first shows the British fleet approaching the bay, with the French fleet (left) coming out. The second drawing shows the British van attacking the enemy while the rear remains unengaged. The cause of this was the British admiral's decision to keep the signal for the line of battle flying while at the same time hoisting the signal to bear down and engage. The signal for line of battle was considered to override all others in the British Fighting Instructions

The Navy in the East Indies, a picture painted by Auguste Louis de Rossel de Cerci of the final
battle in the campaign fought between a British fleet commanded by Rear-Admiral Sir Edward
Hughes and a French fleet by the Bailli de Suffren. This was the action off Cuddalore,
fought in 1783.

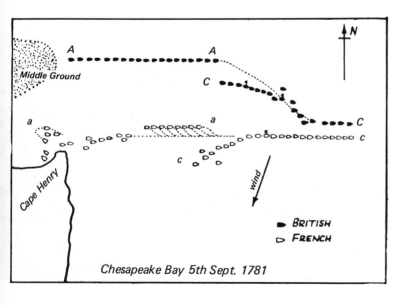

by the signal for the line being hauled down or, even
if the signal had been left displayed, 'the commander-
in-chief had set the example for close action'. The
latter would have entailed the commander-in-chief
being the first to break out of the line, however, and
Graves had neither the independence of thought nor
the moral courage to do so.

The upshot was yet another indecisive skirmish.
Yet even now Graves might have retrieved the situation if he had made at once for the Chesapeake
anchorage, either to rob de Grasse of it or to force
him to fight to regain it, as Hood proposed. Again
Graves hesitated, so that when at last he made for
the anchorage on the 11th he found de Grasse already there, his strength increased by de Barras's
reinforcements. Graves now had no alternative but
to sail away, leaving Chesapeake Bay to de Grasse,

and the fate of the British army was sealed. A month later Cornwallis was forced to capitulate, and the last chance of a successful outcome of the war with the colonists had gone.

While these widespread operations, decisive in respect of the war with the colonies but ineffectual in aiding France's main objective of humbling Britain were taking place across the Atlantic, the French and Spanish, whose combined strength in European waters far outweighed anything that Britain could muster, were totally failing to take advantage of the situation there.

In the spring of 1781 the British Grand Fleet of 28 of the line under Admiral George Darby sailed to relieve Gibraltar with a large convoy and, though France and Spain could have mustered a combined fleet of 50 to oppose Darby, they did nothing to prevent the expedition. Not until June did the two fleets combine under the supreme command of the Spanish Admiral Don Luis de Cordova to cover a convoy of troop transports to open the siege of Minorca. When, on completion of this, they appeared in the western approaches to the Channel in August, Cordova with 49 of the line would not risk attacking Darby's 22 ships as they lay at anchor in Torbay; soon afterwards the French and Spanish squadrons separated and returned to their own ports, having accomplished nothing. Between September and November Darby, at sea with 25 ships of the line to cover the home-coming convoys, was left unmolested.

Only in the North Sea had fleets met in battle, small British and Dutch squadrons, each covering Baltic convoys, engaging in a mutually destructive fight while their convoys proceeded in safety. Though yet another separate naval campaign was about to open in Indian waters in which small British and French squadrons, under Sir Edward Hughes and the Bailli de Suffren respectively, were to engage in a series of fiercely fought actions, the storm centre for the rest of the war was to be the West Indies where the capture of Jamaica was to be the main French objective. Rodney, reappointed to the command, left England on 14th January 1782 with 12 ships of the line and in spite of tempestuous weather reached Barbados on 19th Febuary.

In the interval Hood had been in command since returning from the American coast on 5th December.

A picture by Nicholas Pocock of Hood's repulse of the French in Frigate Bay in 1782. Hood's tight line of anchored ships withstood all attacks by the superior French fleet and successfully defended the island of St Kitts against recapture by the enemy

The scene during the Battle of the Saints as the British ships broke through the French line, depicted by Thomas Luny. In this action the French flagship, the *Ville de Paris*, was captured, and the French Commander-in-Chief, the Count de Grasse, taken prisoner.

With a fleet of 22 ships of the line, many of them in a crazy state and barely seaworthy, he was opposed by de Grasse with more than 30. He was thus unable to prevent the loss of St. Kitts to a French expedition supported by de Grasse with 25 of the line, though in the course of the operations he was able to display the great qualities which were later to earn Nelson's adulation as 'the greatest sea officer I ever knew … equally great in all situations which an admiral can be placed in.'

In particular he inaugurated a custom previously unheard of in the rigidly rank-conscious British Navy of taking his captains and junior officers into his confidence and explaining his intentions to them. As a result he was able brilliantly to outmanoeuvre his opponent, first luring him to sea from his anchorage at Frigate Bay, St. Kitts, where he was supporting the operations on land, and then seizing the anchorage for himself, from which de Grasse was unable to dislodge him. Finally when news of Rodney's return reached him, he gave his greatly superior enemy the slip by taking the fleet to sea in

the night, totally darkened, getting clear away to join his chief on 25th February off Antigua.

The two fleets, now at roughly the same strength, retired to their respective bases, Fort Royal and Gros Islet Bay, St. Lucia, to refit and prepare. De Grasse's intention, as soon as his ships were ready, was to sail with a troop convoy, join up with the Spanish squadron lying at Havana, and attack Jamaica. Following the usual line of French strategic thought he hoped to achieve this without having first to fight the British fleet. From Gros Islet Bay, Rodney watched and waited, determined to foil this plan by bringing de Grasse to decisive action. And on the evening of 7th April 1782 he received the long awaited news from his scouting frigates that the French fleet was getting under way. By noon the next day the British fleet, 36 sail of the line, was clear of harbour and the same evening sighted de Grasse's 33 on the northern horizon. During the night both fleets were working their way through the calms in the lee of Dominica into the channel between that island and the little group of

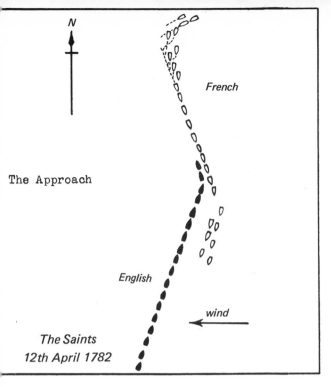

The Approach

The Saints
12th April 1782

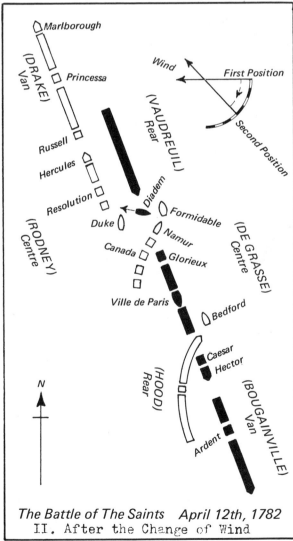

The Battle of The Saints   April 12th, 1782
II. After the Change of Wind

islets called Les Saintes, where a steadier wind was blowing.

Fourteen French ships of the van under the Marquis de Vaudreuil and eight of the British van under Hood had got clear by the following morning, offering the former a splendid opportunity to destroy the smaller force before support could reach them. De Vaudreuil, however, true to the current French doctrine of avoidance of close action, and influenced by a healthy respect for the short-range carronades, known as 'smashers', newly mounted in British ships at that time, held off and achieved little before being recalled by de Grasse when Rodney's centre and rear won clear of Dominica.

De Grasse had by this time sent his convoy away to shelter under the guns of the shore batteries round Basseterre Bay. The fallacy underlying the concept that he could cover its onward passage merely by holding off the enemy fleet must have been evident to him by this time. Nevertheless he continued to attempt to avoid action and might have succeeded but for the ill-luck that dogged him, ill-luck which centred on one of his rear ships, the 74-gun *Zélé*. She had already narrowly escaped being cut off and captured through falling away to leeward during the night of the 9th. Now, during the night of the 10th, she collided with another 74-gun ship and, losing her topmast, again dropped away to leeward, forcing de Grasse to bear down to cover her.

Even so Rodney was still well to leeward on the evening of the 11th and, though he beat through the night under a press of sail, would have had little hope of coming up with the better sailing French ships had not the luckless *Zélé* once again transformed the situation by colliding during the night with none other than the fleet flagship, the *Ville de Paris*. This time she lost her foremast and bowsprit and at daylight was far to leeward in tow of a frigate.

When Rodney ordered away four ships in chase, de Grasse concentrated his scattered force and bore down to the rescue. Rodney saw a chance of seizing the windward position by steering close-hauled to the east-north-east. De Grasse at once saw the danger and formed his line, also close-hauled, on the opposite tack. Thus the two lines were following converging courses. The first to reach the point of intersection would gain the windward gage. A slight shift of the wind gave the race to the French, Rodney's leading ship reaching the French line at its

Above: Another view of the Battle of the Saints, painted by Nicholas Pocock. The British carronades, a new type of gun mounted on the upper decks of the British ships, did tremendous execution amongst the French fleet and completely demoralised some of the crews to an extent that one or two ships surrendered almost before firing a shot

Below: On 11th September 1782 Lord Howe sailed to relieve Gibraltar, under siege by a combined French and Spanish force, including 48 ships of the line. Before Howe could arrive Gibraltar was attacked from the sea on 14th September by heavily protected Spanish floating batteries. All were set on fire and destroyed by the garrison.

ninth ship from the van.

It seemed as though yet another sea battle was to be fought by two parallel lines of ships, a situation likely to be fatal to British hopes of forcing a decision even though, as the ships glided slowly by on opposite courses at less than pistol shot, the superior British gunnery and the devastating fire of their carronades wreaked havoc. But following the French custom, by the time the two lines had passed one another the British ships were just as likely to be so crippled aloft that they would be unable to renew the action.

But now, just as the British van was drawing clear of the French rear, the wind, ever fickle and shifting amongst the islands, veered again, taking the close-hauled French ships aback while permitting the British ships to luff. Gaps appeared in the French line, through which the British flagship *Formidable* led six ships of the centre while the rear squadron, led by the *Bedford*, passed through another gap. Ahead of the *Formidable* the 90-gun three-decker *Duke* similarly sailed through to windward. As they filed past the enemy ships lying on either side with their sails aback, they poured broadsides into their hulls, inflicting frightful casualties and reducing them to utmost confusion.

The British manoeuvre left the way clear for the shattered French ships to flee to leeward, and this they now proceeded to do, ignoring de Grasse's frantic signals for them to reform. A number, however, including de Grasse's once splendid flagship, the 104-gun *Ville de Paris,* had suffered too heavily even to flee. By sunset she had struck to Hood's flagship *Barfleur*, and de Grasse was a prisoner on board the *Formidable.* Four other French ships of the line had been captured. A most notable victory had been won – 'the greatest victory, *if it had been followed up,* that our country ever saw', as Nelson was to write later.

But to Hood's intense chagrin, no signal for General Chase was hoisted when the enemy fled, a signal which, Hood insisted, would have led to the capture of at least 20 of their ships, though this is arguable to say the least. Nor did Rodney order Hood away with 10 of the line to intercept the flying enemy until five days after the battle. Hood made straight for the Mona Passage between Dominica and Puerto Rico where he captured two 64-gun ships of the line and two frigates, from whom

he learned with bitter disgust that the main portion of the shattered French fleet had sailed through only the day before.

The bizarre sequel to the victory of The Saints provides one of history's more farcical chapters. A Whig administration had come into power in March and decided to supersede Rodney in his command. His relief, Sir Hugh Pigot, sailed from Plymouth on 17th May, the day on which the frigate *Andromache* arrived with Rodney's triumphant despatches. Too late, efforts to recall Pigot were made, and on 10th July he arrived at Port Royal, Jamaica. Rodney returned home to find himself a great national hero, with the Government seeking to amend its blunder by pouring honours on his head.

Whether Hood's criticisms of Rodney's conduct after the Battle of The Saints were justified or not, his appreciation that only annihilation could enable the fruits of naval victory to be gathered was an advance in naval strategic thought and one which, together with his tactical ideas for a concentration on a part of the enemy's line, he undoubtedly passed on to his protégé and admirer, Horatio Nelson, who was in his time to exploit them so brilliantly.

Rodney's victory by no means brought naval operations to an end. The Combined French and Spanish fleet in the West Indies was still a formidable force and continued to pose a serious threat to Jamaica, to British trade convoys, and, during the hurricane season when a French squadron went north, to the British army at New York.

In European waters the French and Spanish could still muster a fleet superior to that of Britain. But the memory of The Saints had conferred a moral advantage on the Royal Navy over the French that was to continue to the end of the age of sail. No further encounters occurred in the west. In European waters, when a British fleet under Lord Howe, returning at the end of 1782 from relieving Gibraltar, was intercepted by a Franco-Spanish fleet with a superiority of 10 ships of the line and lay-to for a whole day inviting attack, the enemy contented himself with a distant cannonade before making off.

Thus the material advantages built up for the French Navy under the administration of Choiseul, Sartine, and de Castries were set at naught by a faulty strategic concept of naval warfare. The Peace Treaty in 1783 brought France none of the restorations of her colonial empire for which she had gone to war.

The Midshipman's Mess, from the painting by A. Earle

'Divine Service as it is usually performed on board a British frigate at sea', a painting by
A. Earle. The woman sitting amongst the marines would be the wife of one of the men on
board, a privilege extended only to a few reliable men

CHAPTER 9

Life at Sea in Nelson's Day – Recruitment – Victuals –
Punishment – Pay – Disease and Hygiene – Women in the
Fleet – The Great Mutinies of 1797

CHRISTOPHER LLOYD

The Royal Navy reached its maximum strength under sail in the year 1810, when there were 625 ships in commission, 102 of them line-of-battle ships, and 142,098 seamen and marines in pay. There were also 23,455 Sea Fencibles (a sort of naval militia), some 20,000 privateersmen exempt from impressment, and an expanding merchant marine. There was also an army of some 200,000 men. All this was out of a total population of England and Wales of little more than 8,000,000.

There was no difficulty about the supply of officers because the Navy was an honourable career, comparatively well paid, and with the possibility of making a fortune out of prize money. For a long time past it had attracted the sons of the aristocracy (even Prince William Henry was sent to sea as a boy), as well as those from the middle classes (Nelson was a parson's son). If an officer reached the rank of admiral he was assured of a substantial sum from his share of all the prizes taken on his station. Frigate captains could do almost as well after a successful cruise as commerce raiders; hence the greater popularity of frigate service compared with the tedious business of blockade in a ship of the line.

A boy destined to become a naval officer entered about the age of 12 or 13 as a Captain's Servant (renamed Volunteer First Class in 1794). He was a 'follower' of a relation or an acquaintance, just as an apprentice was indentured to a master on shore. He was accommodated in the gunroom until he became a midshipman, when he moved to the midshipmen's berth in the cockpit below the waterline on the orlop deck. After six years at sea, if he was over the age of 20, he might 'pass for lieutenant'. If he failed in this examination, he remained a midshipman and was called an 'oldster' to distinguish him from the 'youngsters' on their way up the naval ladder. Such passed-over midshipmen remained in the berth, but a fork stuck in a beam after dinner was the signal for the youngsters to retire and leave the oldsters to their long and deep potations.

Once he had become a lieutenant, an officer's future promotion to captain or admiral depended partly on 'interest' or influence, partly on opportunity. Long wars provided plenty of the latter, but in peacetime the Navy List became clogged with those who could only be promoted by a strict rule of seniority; hence the excuse for the old naval toast, 'A bloody war or a sickly season'. The rank of commander became substantive in 1827 in order to provide some incentive to the inflated numbers of lieutenants after the Napoleonic wars were over.

Between the executive sea officer, who was commissioned by the Board of Admiralty which was responsible for the operational side of naval affairs, and the civilian officers – chaplain, purser, and surgeon – who were appointed by warrant from the Navy Board (which was responsible for building and manning the ships) there was a great gulf until 1843. Such officers did not wear distinctive uniforms (though surgeons did after 1805), and they were badly paid in comparison with their equivalents in the Army. Moreover, the purser (pronounced 'pusser') was not a 'gentleman'. He might be described as a grocer at sea who found many ways in which to supplement his meagre salary, such as the regulation that he was allowed one-eighth of every measure of food and drink issued, nominally to cover wastage.

Another type of officer who stood a reasonable chance of promotion to quarterdeck rank was the master. He was a warrant officer responsible for the navigation of the ship, and since he was usually an intelligent and able man, like James Cook, he often began as a master's mate and ended as a captain. Apart from this narrow channel, promotion from the lower deck was exceptional.

The warrant officers on whose broad shoulders lay the business of running the ship were the gunner, boatswain, master-at-arms, and carpenter, to all of which ranks an able seaman, as distinct from an ordinary seaman or a landsman, could aspire. In addition there were innumerable petty officers such as the sailmaker, clerk, steward, cooper, barber, loblolly boy (surgeon's assistant), or the cook, a post reserved for men handicapped by a wound. All these and their mates were called idlers because they did not stand a watch.

The remaining two-thirds of the ship's company, generally called 'the people', were composed of able and ordinary seamen, landsmen, and boys. They were recruited either as volunteers attracted by the generous bounties offered in wartime, or as pressed

'Manning the Navy', a late 18th century print after Samuel Collings showing a press gang in operation on Tower Hill, London. Though the brutality of this method of manning the Royal Navy is often stressed, in fact it was only conscription, or national service in war, under more rough and ready methods. Pressing was only used in wartime, and produced perhaps one-third of the complements of ships

men who had been rounded up by a press gang, taken to a local tavern called a 'rendezvous' or 'rondy', and from this recruiting centre sent to a receiving ship, whence they were distributed around the fleet.

By this date the impressment service was well organised both by land and sea, where pressing tenders cruised in the Channel to take men off returning merchant ships, those outward bound being exempt. At the beginning of the Revolutionary War, Quota Acts were passed specifying the number of men to be contributed by each borough and county. In order to provide this quota, magistrates often drafted petty criminals or vagrants. Only *bona fide* fishermen, apprentices, or householders were granted a 'protection' or passport which exempted the bearer from impressment, and even this valuable document was of little use once a man had been forcibly taken to sea.

The type of man serving on board a warship in Nelson's day therefore varied enormously. He might be white or black, a true British tar or a foreigner of any nationality. About half of them were pressed into a Service which they detested and for which they were ill suited. Only iron discipline judiciously applied could weld them into an efficient crew, but it was this same discipline which forced them to desert in their thousands. Captains of ships at sea were authorised to search neutral vessels for such deserters. Since the United States had the biggest neutral merchant marine, Americans suffered most. It was very difficult to tell an Englishman from an American when they both spoke the same language and when forged citizenship papers were cheap. The high-handed methods of recruitment for a Navy desperate for men was therefore the chief reason for the quarrel between Britain and the United States which led to the war of 1812–14.

When a ship was commissioned, those joining her were divided into two watches, the starboard and the larboard (the word 'port' not officially replacing the latter until 1844). They were rated according to their ability as seamen, quartered to their guns, and divided into messes of four or six men, the mess tables being hooked up to a beam when hammocks were slung or the guns run out of their ports. When the ports were closed on account of bad weather, the atmosphere on those overcrowded decks must have been nauseating, as well as positively dangerous to the health of the men.

Opposite: A naval recruiting poster of *circa* 1770

All True-Blue
BRITISH HEARTS OF OAK

Who are able, and no doubt willing, to ferve their Good

KING and COUNTRY

ON BOARD OF

His Majefty's SHIPS,

Are hereby invited to repair to the Roundabout Tavern, near New Crane, Wapping, where they will find

Lieut. JAMES AYSCOUGH,

Of the BELLONA,

Who ftill keeps open his right real Senior, General and Royal,

Portfmouth Rendezvous,

For the Entertainment and Reception of fuch

Gallant SEAMEN

Who are proud to ferve on board of the Ships now lying at

Portfmouth, Plymouth, Chatham and Sheernefs,

Under the COMMAND of

Vice-Admiral Geary, Rear-Admiral George Lord Edgcumbe, and Commodore Hill; viz. The

Centaur	74	Prince of Wales	74	Bell-Ifle	70	Portland	54
St. Antonio	74	Defence	74	Buckingham	64	Minerva	32
Bellona	74	Temeraire	74	Achilles	ditto	Rainbow	44
Ajax	74	Fame	—	Yarmouth	—	Cerberus	28
Arrogant	74	Prudent	74	Rippon	—	Mercury	20
Hero	74	Ramallies	ditto	Firm	64	Garland	24
Cornwall	ditto	Albion	—	Augufta	—	King's Fifher,	16

With a Number of Frigates and Sloops at the above Ports.

Lieut. Ayfcough will be damn'd happy to fhake Hands with any of his old Ship-mates in particular, or their jolly Friends in general.—Keep it up, my Boys!---Twenty may play as well as one.

Able Seamen will receive Three Pounds Bounty, and Ordinary Seamen Two Pounds, with Conduct-Money, and their Chefts, Bedding, &c. fent Carriage free.

N. B. For the Encouragement of DISCOVERING Seamen, that they may be impreffed, a REWARD of Two POUNDS will be given for Able, and THIRTY SHILLINGS for Ordinary Seamen.

Succefs to His Majefty's NAVY! With Health and Limbs to the Jolly Tars of Old England---JAMES AYSCOUGH

GOD SAVE THE KING.

Printed by R. HILTON, in WELLCLOSE-SQUARE

Able seamen were classified as forecastle or top-men, the others, less skilful or older, being called the afterguard or the waisters. All stood a watch. A watch bill for a typical first-rate line-of-battle ship with a complement of 839 men shows 548 men watched and 291 officers, servants or idlers, who were not watched.

Because each ship was almost a kingdom to herself, her captain possessing very extensive powers especially on a foreign station, it is difficult to generalise about conditions at sea. The official *Regulations and Instructions* were too often ignored, and the modern reader too easily forgets that the age of Nelson was a brutal age, on shore as much as at sea. The savage penalties of the penal code and the near-starvation of so many members of the poorer classes must be borne in mind when we consider how such men were treated at sea.

According to the official victualling scale, they were better fed than on land, where meat was rarely eaten. At sea each man received 1 lb. biscuit and 1 gallon of beer daily, 4 lb. of salt beef and 2 lb. pork a week, with weekly rations of 2 pints of dried pease, 3 of oatmeal, $\frac{1}{2}$ lb. butter, and 1lb. of cheese. But it was the quality not the quantity of food which mattered. The biscuit, known as bread, was often infested with weevils, the beer turned sour after a few weeks at sea, the cheese was so hard it could be fashioned into buttons. The introduction of canned meat and vegetables in 1813 was a major step in the improvement of the health, and therefore of the efficiency of the fleet.

The one issue which was universally popular was grog, introduced in 1740 by Admiral Vernon in the form of half a pint of rum diluted with a quarter of a pint of water and issued twice daily. The word 'groggy' describes the effect of this potent mixture on many empty stomachs, and since drunkenness had always been one of the commoner vices of sailors, it was the cause of half the punishments.

Discipline was maintained either by official floggings, when a man was seized up to a grating to be lashed with a cat-o'-nine-tails, or by unofficial beatings, known as 'starting a man', with a rope's end or cane wielded by brawny bo'suns and their mates. According to the regulations, a captain could only inflict a dozen lashes without a court martial, but the ships' logs are evidence that few captains felt bound by this limitation. Floggings of one to four

dozen lashes were frequent. The worst punishment was a flogging round the fleet, when a man received a dozen lashes alongside each ship. It was an ordeal which few survived. In the decade after Trafalgar a more humane attitude prevailed: 'starting' was abolished and flogging restricted to more serious offences. It was never officially abolished, but was suspended in 1879 when the last recorded case occurred. Only in the worst ships were such methods of punishment complained of, because the men realised that with such a heterogeneous crew on board they had to be protected against each other.

Up to 1797 the most general grievance was the rate of pay – 24s. a month for an able seaman, from which were deducted 6d. for the Royal Hospital at Greenwich, 4d. for the chaplain, and 2d. for the surgeon. The rate had remained unchanged since 1653; nor was this pittance given until a ship was paid off, often after years of service in foreign parts. Even then it might be in the form of a wage ticket which was often encashed at far below its face value. As we shall see, pay was the principal cause of the great mutinies.

Since disease killed ten times as many men who fell in action, and since the losses due to this cause increased the difficulty of manning the fleet, it is important to realise that the seamen of Nelson's day were better off than their predecessors. This was because the suggestions of Dr. James Lind, the father of nautical medicine, made half a century earlier were at last being implemented. It is true that his suggestion that a uniform be provided for the men was not acted upon until 1857, a hundred years after he had suggested it; meanwhile they existed in the rags in which they had been pressed, or in clothes bought from the purser's slop chest. But Lind's advice on hygiene and ventilation, above all his recommendation of lemon juice as a cure for scurvy, was adopted by his disciple Sir Gilbert Blane when Commissioner for Sick and Wounded early in the war against France.

The chief diseases to which seamen were prone in those days were typhus (due to dirty clothing), scurvy (due to lack of fresh vegetables), and tuberculosis (due to the fetid atmosphere below decks). Scurvy, the curse of the sea in the 17th and 18th centuries, was almost eradicated by a regulation of 1795 for the issue of lemon juice after six weeks at sea on salt provisions; in later years lime juice was substituted for it. The worst epidemics occurred in the

Top: A view of the Royal Hospital for Seamen at Greenwich, from an engraving by Rigaud in 1786. Founded in 1694, Greenwich Hospital provided a home and a pension for wounded seamen of the Royal Navy

Above: The middle deck of HMS *Hector* in 1782, drawn by Thomas Rowlandson during a visit he made to Portsmouth to view the wreck of the *Royal George*. When in harbour, British warships were normally 'out of discipline' and families were allowed to live on board. In practice, 'families' was held to include women of all descriptions

Left: Tom Allen, a seaman who became Nelson's trusted servant, painted by T. Burnet. He finished his days as a pensioner at Greenwich

105

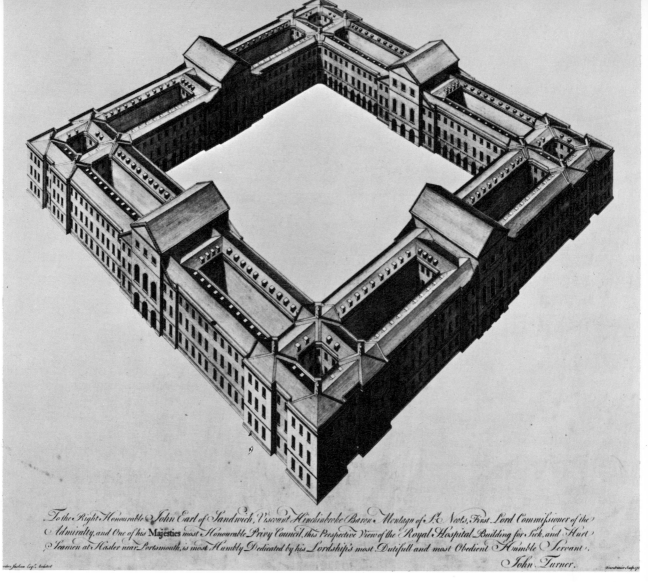

To the Right Honourable John Earl of Sandwich, Viscount Hinchinbroke Baron Montagu of St. Neots, First Lord Commissioner of the Admiralty, and One of his Majesties most Honourable Privy Council, this Perspective View of the Royal Hospital Building for Sick and Hurt Seamen at Haslar near Portsmouth, is most Humbly Dedicated by his Lordship's most Dutifull and most Obedient Humble Servant. John Turner.

The naval hospital at Haslar, of which this 'perspective view' is dated 1750, was in its time the largest brick building in Europe. It is still the main hospital for the Royal Navy

West Indies, where men died by hundreds from malaria, yellow fever, or dysentery. No cure for these existed, only a recourse to bleeding on a formidable scale, or draughts of an infusion of Peruvian bark, the predecessor of quinine. In surgical operations carried out under the most primitive conditions in the cockpit, the chief danger was always gangrene. The only skill possessed by the average naval surgeon was the rapidity with which he carried out his bloody task.

A grievance which must arouse sympathy today was the lack of shore leave. It was prohibited on account of the temptation it offered to desert. The consequence was that every type of vice flourished on board, and disgusting scenes took place when boat-loads of prostitutes were allowed on board ships in harbour. Officers frequently took their wives with them on board, but officially no women were permitted to remain when a ship put to sea. There were exceptions for short passages for sailors' wives.

The best summary of the complaints of sailors is to be found in the petitions sent by the seamen of the Channel Fleet to the Admiralty during the mutiny at Spithead in 1797. They complain that their wages are so low they cannot support their families on shore. They object to the short measure due to deductions in favour of pursers, and of the quality of the food provided. They protest at the prohibition of shore leave. Only in the matter of pay were they successful. A recalcitrant Admiralty was compelled to pass through a frightened Parliament an Act raising naval pay by 5s. 6d. a month. A further increase in 1806 brought the monthly pay of an able seaman to 33s. 6d., that of an ordinary seaman to 25s. 6d., and that of a landsman to 22s. 6d.

The fleet mutinies at Spithead and the Nore in the summer of 1797 were unique in their occurrence and in their drama. As Herman Melville wrote in *Billy Budd*, 'To the British Empire the Nore mutiny was what a strike in the fire brigade would be to London threatened by general arson.' They occurred at the height of the war, between the victory off Cape St. Vincent and Duncan's victory off Camperdown. As the petitions show, they were essentially strikes for better living conditions. At Spithead, where the first outbreak took place on Easter Sunday, 16th April, when the Channel Fleet refused to put to sea, the mutiny was conducted with extraordinary restraint. Officers were firmly put on shore and plain speaking to the Admiralty resulted in the Act increasing the pay, as well as obtaining a royal pardon.

The mutineers had gained their object, so far as this was possible, before the movement spread to the fleet at the Nore at the mouth of the Thames and the North Sea Fleet at Yarmouth. This was a far more sinister affair, the moving spirit being Richard Parker, who called himself President of the Floating Republic. London was virtually blockaded by its own ships and the watch on the Dutch fleet had to be maintained by the only two loyal ships in Duncan's fleet. But one by one the ships deserted the cause, so that Parker was forced to surrender on 13th June. He and 28 other ringleaders were hanged, but unusual humanity was shown by the frightened authorities when all was over.

There were other sporadic outbreaks as long as the war lasted, but these minor mutinies were due either to tyrannical captains or to an unusually recalcitrant crew. That there were no more fleet mutinies considering the hard conditions which continued to prevail at sea, particularly in the big ships engaged on the dull and interminable business of blockading Brest and Toulon, can only be explained by two reasons. In the first place the nation held the seamen who protected it and won such a notable series of victories in high esteem. Secondly, there was a remarkable combination of rigid discipline and good leadership on board most ships in Nelson's navy. Out of the heterogeneous and unpromising material provided by the press gangs and the Quota Acts, the most efficient fighting machine ever seen in the age of sail was thereby created. When the war was over, a smaller navy, manned by volunteers, provided an opportunity for many reforms in living conditions at sea.

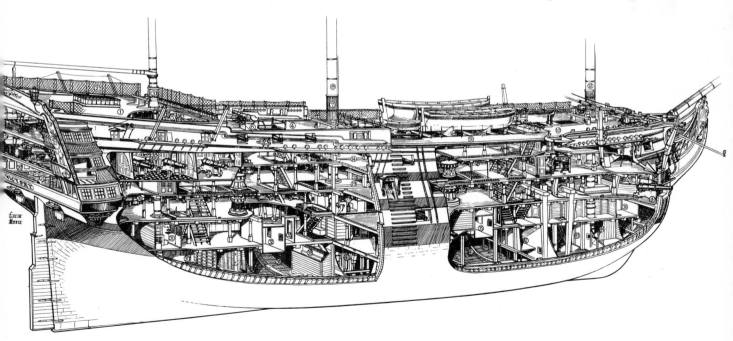

A cross-section of HMS *Victory*. Now preserved at Portsmouth Dockyard as a national monument, she was laid down at Chatham in 1759 to the design of Sir Thomas Slade and launched in 1765. She was a first-rate of 100 guns and in her day was the fastest sailing ship of the line

An incident in the Battle of Camperdown, showing one of the Dutch ships dismasted by the fury of the British attack. Admiral Duncan led his ships in without waiting to form a line of battle, and by this means gained an overwhelming victory. From the painting by P. J. de Loutherbourg

CHAPTER 10

The Revolutionary War with France – Mediterranean
Operations – Capture of Toulon – Nelson in Corsica –
Atlantic Operations – Withdrawal from the Mediterranean –
Battle of Cape St. Vincent – Attempts at Invasion –
Mutiny in the Fleet – Battle of Camperdown

OLIVER WARNER

Although Great Britain had tasted defeat when, in 1783, her representatives signed the Treaty of Versailles, confirming the loss of those American Colonies to retain which she had endured an eight-year war, yet defeat may be salutary. It was so in this case, for by the end of the struggle the Royal Navy was as seasoned as any sea or land armament in the world, while among the captains was a constellation of officers who would show their quality in that protracted war with Revolutionary and Napoleonic France which was to come. This began in 1793 and continued over more than two decades.

The French Revolution, which had been set on its way by the summoning of the Estates General in May 1789, gathered such momentum that three years later, when the French opened the River Scheldt in violation of treaties, threatening to make Antwerp a rival to London as a port and focus of international trade, a clash of arms became certain. Within a few days of the execution of Louis XVI on 21st January 1793, France declared war on Britain and on Holland, soon to become her satellite.

The London Government mobilised two principal fleets for the protection of country, trade, and possessions overseas. For once, the Navy was not only ready but of reasonable size. A scare in 1790 of war with Spain had ensured that officers had had up-to-date experience of service afloat, and there would not be the scramble with which too many wars of the past had begun.

Commands-in-chief were entrusted to veterans – the Atlantic Fleet was assigned to Admiral Lord Howe, who was 68, and the Mediterranean Fleet to Admiral Lord Hood, who was close upon 70. Howe's own view was that an admiral was unlikely to serve successfully at sea in time of war at over 60, but his opinion, naturally enough, was not shared by the elderly officers who made up the bulk of the flag-list, or even by George III, who never felt more confidence than when Howe had charge of the navy in home waters. Hood, a more arrogant and far less successful man than Howe, had no reservations about his own age or abilities, and it was he who had the first opportunity to take the initiative. This was in a strange place, Toulon.

In August 1793 Royalist elements in the French port and arsenal admitted Hood's ships. It was a gesture he was swift to exploit, for if he were able to secure a base there, control of the western Mediterranean would follow automatically. Unfortunately, Hood had insufficient troops to support the advantage, and the forces with which Spain, Sardinia and Naples supplemented his efforts were of little use. The alliances with which the war had begun in fact stood no strain, and it was not long before Spain changed sides.

Hood's brief occupation of Toulon ended disastrously. The port was soon ringed round by hostile forces, among whose officers was a young artilleryman, Napoleon Bonaparte, whose dispositions did much to make Hood's anchorages untenable. Such allied troops as were not driven into the sea were withdrawn, and Hood's priceless opportunity, to destroy or remove the entire French Mediterranean Fleet before he left the remaining Royalists to the mercy of their compatriots, was not taken with the necessary vigour and efficiency.

The Navy then had need to find a base elsewhere.

The French *Vengeur du Peuple* sinking in the Battle of the Glorious First of June, Lord Howe's
victory of 1794, in which she had been engaged by the British *Brunswick*. From the painting
by Robert Dodd

Hood's idea was that it should be in Corsica. The patriot, Pascal Paoli, well known and much admired in Britain, supported an insurrection against the French garrisons, and British sailors, mainly by their own efforts, at length took the fortress positions of Bastia and Calvi. Once the island was rid of the French the Corsicans offered sovereignty to George III, who appointed a Viceroy, Sir Gilbert Elliot.

Among his captains Hood had a rising young officer, Horatio Nelson, who was forward in the defeat of the French in Corsica. His resource was endless, but it was at the siege of Calvi, in July 1794, that he was wounded in the right eye, losing the sight of it though not the eye itself. By the end of the summer Corsica was as secure as the Navy could make it, while on the other side of the world, amphibious operations resulted in the capture of the French West Indian islands of Martinique, St. Lucia, and Guadeloupe, naval responsibility for which had rested upon Admiral Sir John Jervis, the future Earl of St. Vincent.

Hood was soon recalled from the Mediterranean, never again to be employed afloat. In the Atlantic, after a barren initial cruise, Howe won the first decisive tactical victory over the main fleet of Revolutionary France at the battle in 1794 which became known as the 'Glorious First of June'. Howe was at sea with threefold purpose: to safeguard Britain's outward bound trade; to prevent an immensely important convoy of grain from America from reaching France, where the harvest had failed; and to defeat the enemy fleet under Villaret-Joyeuse if he had the good fortune to meet with it. In the first and third of these tasks he succeeded, but the French Government considered that the defeat of their admiral, with the loss of seven ships of the line, six captured and one sunk, was a small price to pay to ensure the arrival of the grain.

Howe was a master of his profession, to which he devoted his energy with single-minded purpose. With such a large and untried fleet as he commanded, his methods were of necessity those of strict

control. He, and such earlier students of tactics as Admiral Richard Kempenfelt, had improved the system of signalling beyond recognition, and his battle, which was the culmination of a series of manoeuvres and engagements far out at sea in the latitude of Brest, during which he gained the wind gage, was a triumph of experience and skill. The captains of his 26 ships of the line, when they closed with their opponents on the morning of what was indeed a glorious day, were intended to break through the French at all points, continuing to engage from the leeward position. Howe's prophecy that he would capture or destroy an enemy ship for every successful attack of the kind he proposed was fulfilled exactly.

There were two criticisms of Howe's tactics and strategy, both of them answerable. The first concerned the escape of the French convoy: but this could not have been captured or destroyed without either a victory over, or evasion of, the French fleet, and Howe had in fact ordered Admiral Montagu, with a detached force, to search for the merchant-men. Montagu failed, partly by ill-luck. The second criticism was one which professional sea officers have made after many limited victories – that success was not followed up. Sometimes, notably perhaps after Rodney's victory over de Grasse at The Saints in 1782, such criticism could be justified, but not in Howe's case for, as he pointed out, those ships which had done best in the battle were in no condition for a close pursuit, and how could he have depended on the comparatively undamaged ships doing better in a general chase than they had done in close action under the admiral's eye?

Howe's victory was important in its effects upon the spirits of Navy and nation alike. The opening fleet engagement of the War of the American Revolution, fought in 1778 between Keppel and d'Orvilliers, had not only been indecisive, but had led to such dissension, political and personal, as to split the Navy into inimical factions. The 'Glorious First of June' was a tonic, fortified by a personal visit of the king and queen to the fleet on its return to Spithead. George III crowned the occasion by awarding gold medals to flag officers and captains,

Opposite: Samuel Hood, later Viscount Hood, painted by John Hoppner. He was second-in-command to Rodney at the Battle of the Saints, and was Commander-in-Chief in the Mediterranean in the early part of the Revolutionary war with France. Like his brother Alexander, he had a long career in the Navy, serving for 54 years. Nelson always claimed that he learned his naval tactics from Hood

Admiral of the Fleet Earl Howe, Commander-in-Chief of the Channel Fleet at the Battle of the Glorious First of June. This portrait by John Copley shows him in the undress uniform of an admiral

and although in this particular instance the choice was invidious, the practice itself was continued.

The king and his Government had some reason to celebrate such success as they enjoyed at sea, for on land the French were carrying all before them. The threat of foreign invasion, which had come initially from Austria and Prussia, united France in patriotic fervour, and the Battle of Fleurus, following hard as it did on the heels of the saving of the grain convoy, proved that the enemy was as likely to be successful on land as were the British in sea fighting. Fleurus, where an Austrian army was defeated by Jean-Baptiste Jourdan, caused the withdrawal of the allies from the Austrian Netherlands – the modern Belgium and Luxembourg – and safeguarded France's land frontiers.

In July 1795 Spain concluded a treaty with France, and in the following month she declared war on Britain, thus putting her ships and bases at the disposal of the country which was becoming the most menacing land power in Europe. Against this success, Britain could only count the seizure of

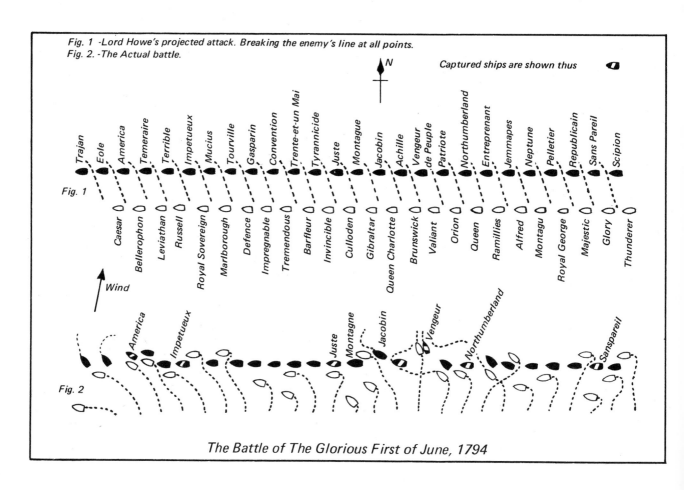

The Battle of The Glorious First of June, 1794

Dutch overseas possessions, the Cape of Good Hope, Malacca, and the greater part of Ceylon. She had indeed entered into a formal alliance with Austria and Russia, in the hope that pressure would continue to be exercised upon France on the continent, but Russia remained inactive, and Austrian generals were unsuccessful.

The year 1796 brought no comfort whatever. Ireland was in a state of unrest, and as the United Irish party had sent their representative, Wolfe Tone, to ask help of the French Republic, an attempt at invasion became increasingly probable, and was in fact made in the final months. By that time Hood's younger brother Alexander, now Lord Bridport, had succeeded Howe in operational, though not yet nominal, command of the Channel Fleet, but it was more the stormy weather than the Admiral's vigilance which brought ruin on the enemy's scheme.

In the Mediterranean, the British withdrew from Corsica, and the French armies were so successful in Italy, where Bonaparte first made his name as a general, that even Jervis's determination could not make Britain's position tenable in the area of the Middle Sea, with nowhere east of Gibraltar for ships to provision and repair. Nelson and other enterprising officers might harry as they would in the Ligurian Sea and elsewhere, but could do nothing to prevent a succession of Italian states, Piedmont, Genoa, Milan, Parma, Modena, Tuscany and the Papal Territories, from coming directly under French influence, or under immediate threat.

Nelson's own last sad duty before he left the Mediterranean was to withdraw British troops and stores from Elba. Early in February 1797 he rejoined Jervis off Cape St. Vincent, just in time to take a leading part in a victory which was to rejoice a country where the gloom was such that it was accounted 'the darkest hour in English history'.

Jervis's base was then at Lisbon, the capital city of Britain's oldest ally. His purpose was to prevent a Franco-Spanish combination of fleets proceeding northwards to Brest in preparation for an invasion of England or Ireland. On paper Jervis was always heavily outnumbered, but he had brought his officers and men to such a pitch of training that one of the best of his captains, Collingwood, remarked: 'Should we not be grateful to him who had such confidence in his fleet that he thought no force too great for them?'

On 1st February the Spanish naval commander-in-chief, Juan de Cordova, sailed from Cartagena with a big fleet – 28 of the line, including the *Santissima Trinidad* of 132 guns, the largest man-of-war afloat, and six three-deckers. He had two objects. The first was to take his ships to Cadiz, as a first step towards combination with the French. The second was to cover the passage of a consignment of mercury from the mines at Almaden, north of Malaga. Large supplies were required for amalgamating the silver ore from the New World, on which the Spanish economy depended. De Cordova's business was to see the laden merchantmen safely past Gibraltar and into Cadiz.

Easterly winds blew de Cordova far into the Atlantic, and this gave Jervis his chance, sheltering as he was in the lee of Cape St. Vincent, to intercept the Spaniards as they beat back towards the land. With him, he had only 15 ships of the line, six of them newly arrived from home, but he had no doubts whatever about the capabilities of those he commanded and, as he remarked with perfect truth, 'a victory is very necessary to England at this moment.'

Jervis led his close-hauled line between the scattered formations of the enemy, and then, reversing course, attacked the larger body, which was to windward. Soon after the leading British ship, the *Culloden*, had turned as signalled, Nelson, in the *Captain*, which was the third ship from the rear, realised that if he did not act at once and independently, the enemy might escape before the rear ships could play an effective part in the action. He wore

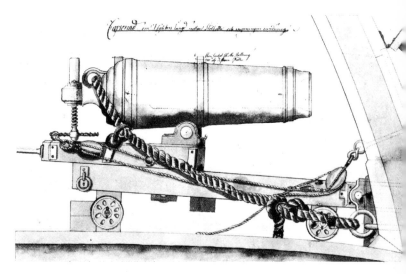

The carronade, a short, light carriage gun making use of a small propellant charge to fire a relatively heavy shot for a limited range, was introduced into the Royal Navy in about 1779, and was later copied by other navies.

The Battle of St Vincent, fought in 1797 between a British fleet under the command of Sir John Jervis and a Spanish fleet commanded by Don José de Cordova. Four Spanish ships were taken in prize. From the painting by Thomas Luny

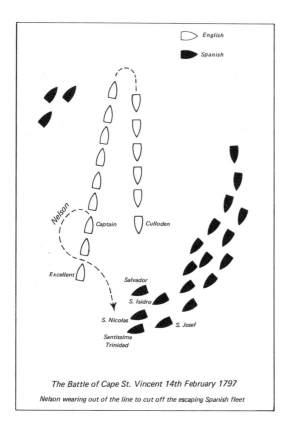

The Battle of Cape St. Vincent 14th February 1797

Nelson wearing out of the line to cut off the escaping Spanish fleet

the 74-gun ship in which he flew a commodore's pendant out of the line and headed straight for the enemy. He was soon supported by Collingwood and others, and it was largely his bold move which ensured that Jervis reaped the benefit of his tactics. Four Spanish ships were taken, including two of the first rate, and at one stage the *Santissima Trinidad* herself surrendered to Saumarez in the *Orion*, though in the confusion of the fighting she got away, badly crippled. She was lucky ever to reach the safety of Cadiz, but at length she did so, with her bad news and her sad tale of casualties.

Jervis had been right. Training told, and so did constant exercise of the great guns at sea in all weathers. It was as good a tonic to the fleet as Howe's victory of 1794, and the achievement was against great numerical odds. Jervis's earldom was well won, and so were the gold medals which were awarded, without exception, to all admirals and captains of the ships of the line. The way was not yet open for a return to the Mediterranean, but any serious ideas of invasion by the enemy were postponed. In fact, in the very month that the battle was fought, the French made a landing in Pembrokeshire but the ships did not even wait to see the fate of the soldiers. The men surrendered – a thousand of the so-called Black Legion, half of them convicts – to the local Fencibles under Lord Cawdor, without firing a shot.

This lightening of the clouds, by a remarkable victory and a farcical enemy failure, was short-lived, for the general gloom had reason behind it. Regarded widely, the war was going as badly as possible, and commercial distress was such that the Bank of England suspended cash payments. In April, as if to emphasise misfortune, mutiny occurred in the Channel Fleet, where the seamen concluded, rightly, that their conditions were intolerable. Anonymous petitions reached Lord Howe, who was recuperating at Bath, and the Admiralty, but they were disregarded until too late. It was not altogether without design that the complaints occurred when the French were comparatively inactive, as regards their main fleet, or that they were addressed not to Lord Bridport but to Lord Howe, still the nominal Commander-in-Chief, and known for his regard for his men.

Once it had occurred, mutiny was widespread, effective and well organised, but for most of the summer months only the fleet under St. Vincent, active and of high morale, was free from it. At Spithead, the trouble subsided after concessions had been wrung from authority, and Howe, in spite of his age and infirmities, had redeemed his earlier disregard by visiting all ships. At the Nore, to which the trouble spread, it was even more serious, for in Richard Parker the seamen found a demagogue so well able to influence his audiences that for a time most of the traffic of the Port of London was brought to a standstill.

Events at the Nore, Great Yarmouth, and elsewhere fell hardest on Admiral Duncan's ill-assorted force, whose duty was to watch the Dutch. He had at best a scratch fleet, which at one stage was reduced to two effective ships, one of which was his own. But in October, not only did the seamen redeem their honour by valour in action, but Duncan himself gained one of the hardest fought victories in the history of the sailing Navy.

Admiral Sir John Jervis, who took the title of Earl of St Vincent after the battle of the same name in which he commanded the British fleet. A portrait painted by Sir William Beechey

Alexander Hood, later Lord Bridport, succeeded Lord Howe as Commander-in-Chief of the Channel Fleet. He was the younger brother of Samuel Hood, later Lord Hood, and of his 87 years, 59 were spent in the Royal Navy. This portrait was painted by Lemuel Abbott

THE FRENCH REVOLUTIONARY WAR

In the early autumn the Dutch admiral, de Winter, was ordered to sea, for no very good reason except to exercise his ships with a view to a future scheme of invasion. The original strategic plan had been for an attempt on England by French and Spanish fleets, this to occur simultaneously with an invasion of Ireland mounted from Holland. St. Vincent's success over de Cordova had spoilt the main scheme, and the project as it would affect the Dutch had never been organised with skill. It was true that Wolfe Tone, who had taken part in the fiasco of Bantry Bay in the previous winter, was appointed to the staff of General Daendels, who commanded the Dutch army, but from his surviving diary it is clear that he expected little – and he was not disappointed.

Duncan, who had had warning of enemy movements, summoned every available vessel, and with 16 of the line, two of them inferior in armament, he engaged his opponent off the coast of Holland on 12th October. He approached de Winter in irregular columns, his idea being to 'break the enemy line and engage them to leeward, each ship her opposite', which was an echo of Howe's methods at the 'Glorious First of June'. The Dutch fought hard, as they had done in the many stubborn fights of the previous century, but once again sea experience told, and at the end of the day, Duncan found himself in possession of 11 battered prizes. His was a great feat, all the sweeter after the months of trial and anxieties which he had endured during the earlier part of the year.

Duncan's triumph came through the impetuosity of his attack. Many of his captains had had no chance to exercise together, while as for the efficiency of his communications, the story is told of Captain Inglis of the *Belliqueux*, who like Duncan was a Scot, that he threw down his signal book on the deck with the words: 'Damme! Up wi' the hel-lem and gang into the middle o' it.'

After the battle, and his own surrender, de Winter said to the victor: 'Your not waiting to form line ruined me: if I had got nearer the shore and you had attacked, I should probably have drawn both fleets on it, and it would have been a victory to me, being on my own coast.'

Duncan was 66 at the time of Camperdown, and if the war at sea had until then proved nothing else, it had at least shown the quality of veteran leaders. The French had yielded to Howe, the Spaniards to Jervis, the Dutch to Duncan – yet the struggle had so far brought little comfort to the nation, apart from the assurance that her seamen were equal to anything.

Three times, in March and October 1796, and again in the following year, Pitt made overtures for peace with France. Each time they came to nothing, for the Republic remained not only in a position of strength but had well kept plans for still further expansion. It was the execution of these plans which eventually led to a return of the British fleet to the Mediterranean. It also led to a renewed hope that the Navy upon which Britain depended would not only continue to keep her shores inviolate but would be the means by which, in some way not then clearly discernible, war could be brought home to the enemy on 'the extended scale', to quote a phrase of Nelson's, 'to bring Bonaparte to his marrow-bones'.

The hope was justified. In a series of operations which for scope and drama have rarely been equalled, the two men of war who came to symbolise for their respective countries all that was most dynamic in leadership, drew close to one another. Bonaparte by land, and Nelson by sea, displayed their respective geniuses, and the quality of their imagination.

Adam Duncan, the British admiral at Camperdown, was made a viscount after the battle. His fleet was immobilised by mutiny shortly before the battle was fought, but his firm action with the ringleaders, and the collapse of the mutiny at the Nore, enabled him to get to sea with all his ships in time for the action. From the portrait after Raeburn

The turning point in the Battle of St Vincent. Seeing that some of the Spanish fleet would escape if not cut off, Nelson wore his ship out of the line of battle and sailed her into the path of the escaping Spaniards. His ship, the *Captain*, is here seen capturing the Spanish *San Josef*, having already taken the *San Nicolas*. From the painting by Nicholas Pocock

The Battle of Camperdown, fought in 1797 against a Dutch fleet, painted by Thomas Whitcombe. Camperdown was one of the most bitter battles of the war, fought in the shoal waters off the Dutch coast, and resulted in the total capture or destruction of the Dutch fleet

CHAPTER 11

*Return to the Mediterranean – Battle of the Nile –
Effects of the battle in Italy and elsewhere – Failure of
attempts to relieve the French Army in Egypt*

OLIVER WARNER

By the year 1798 nothing seemed beyond possibility to the Government of the French Republic except immediate mastery at sea. Bonaparte was sent to Dunkirk and the coast of Flanders to report on the prospects of invasion of Great Britain. 'The people of Paris do not remember anything', he said to his secretary, Bourriene, referring to the fact that wonder at his campaign in Italy seemed to have diminished. 'My glory has already disappeared. This little Europe does not supply enough of it for me. I must seek it in the East: all great fame comes from that quarter ... If the success of a descent upon England appears doubtful, as I suspect it will, the Army of England shall become the Army of the East, and I go to Egypt.'

His visit over, Bonaparte reported as follows:

Whatever efforts we make, we shall not for some years gain the naval supremacy. To invade England without that supremacy is the most daring and difficult task ever undertaken ... If, having regard to the present organisation of our navy, it seems impossible to gain the necessary promptness of execution, then we must really give up the execution, *be satisfied with keeping up the pretence of it*, and concentrate all our attention and resources on the Rhine, in order to try to deprive England of Hanover and Hamburg ... or else undertake an Eastern Expedition which would menace her trade with the Indies ...

Bonaparte's idea of an Eastern venture met with such enthusiasm that every available port on the Mediterranean seaboard was soon bustling with preparation. In London, the authorities became aware that something big was in train, but the ultimate aim of what would clearly be a considerable armada was a secret well kept, and with no ships on watch beyond Gibraltar there was no means of gaining firmer information. The first counter-measure, so the Admiralty decided, was to reinforce St. Vincent, and to order him to detach a strong squadron to take what measures it could to disrupt the French plan, whatever it should be.

Nelson was picked upon as leader, and although his selection was supported both by Spencer, the First Lord of the Admiralty, and by St. Vincent, the Commander-in-Chief, it caused great jealousy. Nelson was young, not yet 40, and although he had done brilliantly in the Atlantic battle of the previous year and been made a Knight of the Bath, he was a very junior rear-admiral, and he had recently had a spell on shore recovering from the loss of his right arm, a wound sustained in an unsuccessful attack on Teneriffe the previous summer.

St. Vincent cared nothing except to choose the right man. Nelson's reappearance at the end of April 1798 had, so he wrote, given him new life. He despatched the *Vanguard* on reconnaissance even before his expected reinforcements arrived, promising Nelson some 'choice fellows of the inshore squadron' the moment topsails from home came in sight, and he was as good as his word. Nelson's original force consisted of three 74-gun ships, his own *Vanguard*, Captain Berry, the *Orion*, commanded by Sir James Saumarez, the *Alexander*, Captain Ball, two frigates and a sloop. On 19th May, the *Mutine* brig joined Nelson with the news that the 11 additional ships which were to join would be in charge of Thomas Troubridge, an old friend and shipmate of Nelson and a favourite with the Commander-in-Chief.

A model of an English frigate of the Nelson era. Too small to lie in the line of battle, there was a
mutual understanding between opponents in battle that frigates were not engaged by ships of
the line. Their duties in action were to serve as signal repeating ships. On detached service their
chief employment was in operations against enemy trade

Then came the first of a succession of misfortunes
which marked the earlier stages of Nelson's mission.
On 20th May, when his ships were off Sardinia,
there blew such a gale that the *Vanguard* was dismasted and nearly driven ashore. She was saved by
the skill and seamanship of Ball, and was repaired
with the help of Ball and Saumarez, but to Nelson's
chagrin his frigates and sloop disappeared in the
heavy weather. They feared that the *Vanguard* was
lost or would need the immediate services of a dockyard, so they never rejoined. But the 'choice fellows'
arrived on 7th June. Ships and captains make up a
roll of honour as being perhaps the finest squadron
ever assembled, even in the classic era of sail. There
was Troubridge in the *Culloden,* Darby in the

Bellerophon, Louis in the *Minotaur,* Peyton in the
Defence, Samuel Hood – a relative of Lord Hood – in
the *Zealous,* Gould in the *Audacious,* Foley in the
Goliath, Ben Hallowell in the *Swiftsure,* Westcott in
the *Majestic,* Miller in the *Theseus,* and Thompson in
the *Leander.* The *Leander* was a 50-gun ship, all the rest
being of 74 guns. The weakness in the squadron was
that the little *Mutine,* commanded by Thomas
Masterman Hardy, was the only ship available for
observation.

This lack of frigates for observation was the reason
why Bonaparte and his army, and Brueys with the
accompanying fleet – in all, 13 ships of the line,
including the huge flagship *L'Orient* of 120 guns,
seven frigates, numerous gunboats, and nearly 300

transports of varying sizes – were able to assemble at sea from their respective ports early in May and to sail to Malta. The French arrived off that island on 9th June, two days after Nelson's force was collected. The Grand Master of the Knights of St. John surrendered with no more than a token resistance. Bonaparte spent a week reorganising the affairs of the island, left a garrison behind him under the command of General Vaubois, and then sailed away eastwards, entirely unmolested. The aim of his expedition, as defined by a secret decree of 12th April, included the occupation of Egypt and the exclusion of the British 'from all their possessions in the East to which the General can come'. The ultimate objective included India, her share in the control of which sub-continent Britain had steadily extended throughout the 18th century, almost entirely at the expense of France.

Nelson was in the Bay of Naples by 17th June but could get no news of the whereabouts of the French, whom he suspected were destined for Alexandria. Four days later, when south-east of Sicily, he learnt from a Genoese captain of the surrender of the Knights of Malta. After consulting his senior captains, who took the same view of the enemy's aim as he did himself, the squadron made for Alexandria at its best speed. Nelson sighted the ancient Pharos, or what remained of it, on 29th June, but there was no sign of the enemy. With a heavy heart, he ordered a return to Sicily. '*No frigates*', he wrote despairingly to Sir William Hamilton, the British Minister at Naples, 'to which has been, and may be again, attributed the loss of the French fleet.' He added later, 'the Devil's children have the Devil's luck.'

In fact, the two fleets at one stage passed close to one another, but it was during the hours of darkness. The British made twice the speed of the French, and no contact ensued, though at one point certain French officers believed they heard Nelson's signal guns. By 2nd July Bonaparte was in possession of Alexandria. Less than three weeks later he defeated the Mameluke army, which defended Egypt on behalf of the Sultan of Turkey, at the Battle of the Pyramids, and became master of the country. The harbour at Alexandria was not then suitable for the entrance of a fleet of men-of-war, so Brueys anchored in a strong position in Aboukir Bay, near the Rosetta mouth of the Nile.

Nelson meanwhile beat back to Sicily, where his ships obtained fresh water and other supplies, an amenity connived at by the local Governor, who in fact had no choice in the matter. His disheartening cruise had one effect which was to be of immense consequence. His captains had been enabled to learn his methods, to know his plans in whatever circumstances the enemy were met with. They knew, moreover, that they would be trusted: they were free, within reasonable limits, to use their own initiative. In Nelson's own words, they were 'a band of brothers'. United in disappointment, would they not also be united if their luck changed?

Learning nothing in Sicily, Nelson returned once more to Alexandria, and in Egyptian waters, on 1st August, he was given news which electrified every officer and man in the squadron. Brueys was in sight. His ships of the line, with attendant frigates, lay snug in their bay, protected by shoal water and with a shore battery sited on Aboukir Island. The French admiral could feel satisfied. He had done his duty; the army was established ashore and advancing. He himself was well disposed for defence. Against the approach of most admirals he would have been secure, but no one was ever safe against Nelson.

Captain Henry d'Esterre Darby, who commanded HMS *Bellerophon* at the Battle of the Nile. He took her alongside the 120-gun French flagship *L'Orient* and engaged her for an hour. From a mezzotint after Sir William Beechey

For the first time in weeks Nelson felt relief. Speculation was over and action imminent. Every captain knew his duty. He ordered them to prepare for action, and then sat down to dinner. Such were the conditions of the days of sail that while battle was bloody and protracted, a test of nerves which few welcomed, the preliminaries, with wind the source of motion, were often leisurely.

On the evening of 1st August the wind blew Nelson towards Aboukir Bay at just the right pace for him to make the best dispositions. When Brueys, perhaps half unbelieving, saw that the British meant business that day, his satisfaction would have had its first jolt. Admirals were usually more circumspect than Nelson ever was; a long-range cannonade was the most Brueys would have expected. That would have been his own procedure, his gunners aiming high with the idea of shattering masts and spars.

Nelson, on the other hand, intended to sail straight in and settle Brueys there and then. The French could not escape, and Nelson, confident as he was in the quality of his officers and men, could not get at him fast enough. He meant to set a new standard in victory, to make the utmost of an astounding opportunity against an enemy embayed.

Captain Foley, in the *Goliath*, had the honour of leading the attack, and in so doing he showed initiative worthy of Nelson at St. Vincent. He led *inside* the French anchored line, which meant negotiating shoal water in light which would fade soon after battle was joined. It was a great risk which came off triumphantly. The French were unprepared for any attack from the landward side, and as Foley was followed by Hood in the *Zealous*, Gould in the *Audacious*, Saumarez in the *Orion*, and Miller in the *Theseus*, the destruction of the French ships nearest Aboukir island, on which the unlucky Troubridge stuck fast in the *Culloden*, soon became a matter of certainty. They would be between two fires, and with not the remotest possibility of making sail to try to escape.

The flagship was actually the first of the British line to range herself on the seaward side of the French. She was followed, in succession, by the rest. Two late arrivals, the *Alexander* and the *Swiftsure*, came into action only with the darkness, being saved from the fate of the *Culloden* by Troubridge's signalled warning.

The battle was as dramatic as any in history, the

Captain Sir Edward Berry, Nelson's flag captain in the *Vanguard* at the Battle of the Nile. The *Vanguard* anchored opposite the third ship in the French line, the *Spartiate*, which surrendered after an exchange of broadsides. This portrait was painted by John Copley

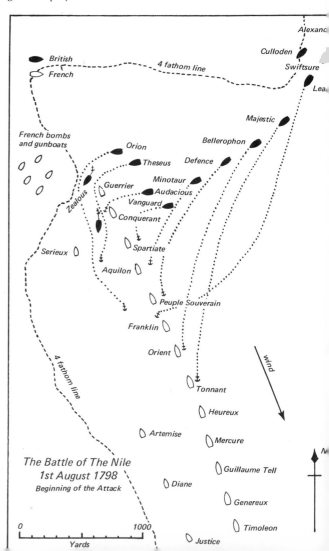

The Battle of The Nile
1st August 1798
Beginning of the Attack

A French painting of the Battle of the Nile by Durand Brager, showing the *Tonnant* engaged with HMS *Majestic*. The *Tonnant* was anchored next astern of *L'Orient*, which can be seen blowing up in the background

climax being the burning and explosion of *L'Orient*, involving the loss of Admiral Brueys, of Commodore Casabianca and his son, who was to become famed in the song – 'The boy stood on the burning deck', – and most of the ship's company. This was an event so tremendous, morally and as a spectacle, that it caused an appreciable lull, as if the combatants on both sides were temporarily stunned. Then the struggle continued, until there were only two French ships of the line fit to beat out of the bay. In the early hours of the following morning they sailed past the dismasted but still unconquerable *Bellerophon*, where all officers were dead or wounded, and the vessel herself barely saved by the efforts of John Hindmarsh, who was not yet commissioned.

In one of the escaping ships was Admiral Villeneuve. Napoleon held that he was 'lucky', which was a great asset in the eyes of the Corsican. In an immediate sense this was so, but it was also true that the idea of Nelson in victorious action haunted

Villeneuve for the rest of his life, and was to have its influence on the future war at sea.

Nelson himself was wounded during the action. He received a gash on the forehead immediately above his sightless eye. A flap of skin came down over the good one, and he was temporarily 'stone blind', as he wrote later to Lord Howe. At first he thought his wound was mortal, but the surgeon soon reassured him, and he was back on deck, bandaged, to see *L'Orient* blow up. When morning came, and the damage could be assessed, Nelson said that victory was not a word strong enough for such a scene as was around him. He had achieved the annihilation of the French squadron as a fighting force in what was one of the masterpieces of war.

The admiral's immediate thought was how his achievement would affect the wider scene of conflict. Two or three facts were soon apparent. The French army, whatever its exploits might be in Egypt, was marooned. India was safe. Nelson sent

The scene at about 10.00 p.m. in the Battle of the Nile when the French flagship *L'Orient* blew
up. The French Commander-in-Chief, Admiral Brueys, perished in the explosion, as also did his
flag-captain, M. Casabianca, who had taken his small son on board with him. This was the
origin of Mrs Heman's poem: 'The boy stood on the burning deck.' From the picture by
Thomas Whitcombe

word at once, by the hand of a reliable officer, to the authorities in the sub-continent, thus relieving them of a load of anxiety and saving great expenditure on defence. Sicily was safe. Malta with its garrison could be blockaded. And once the home authorities had been made aware of the completeness of the victory, and of the fact that the British would again dominate the Mediterranean, who knew what successful new coalition of nations pledged to the downfall of Napoleon might be brought about?

The immediate impact of the Nile was on morale. England, naturally enough, was jubilant. When the First Lord of the Admiralty first had the news, he fell flat on the floor outside his room, so great had been his suppressed anxiety. As for Naples, the Italian kingdom which had been in most danger from the French expedition, the rejoicing knew no bounds.

It was to Naples, where he knew himself certain of refreshment, welcome, and diplomatic help from Sir William Hamilton, that Nelson took a substantial part of his squadron. Saumarez could be trusted to shepherd the prizes safely to Gibraltar, and to give Lord St. Vincent an account of what had been done and of his admiral's immediate intentions. It was Nelson's way to exploit victory to the utmost, and if in the event he proceeded too far and too fast, the fault was in the instruments employed.

Hamilton, although by then a man of 68, long past his brilliant best, had been a guardsman in his youth, and he was for immediate action against the French on land. He persuaded the King of Naples that, with sea communications safe in the hands of Nelson, his army could advance against the Papal States, which were in French occupation, and that he himself could become Ferdinand the Victorious. 'Advance,' urged Minister and Admiral, 'trusting to God for his blessings in a just cause … or remain quiet and be kicked out of your dominions.'

The king, who was no soldier, took the advice and marched on Rome, which he entered in triumph. But the French, though at first unprepared, reacted quickly, and by virtue of threats rather than through serious fighting, they soon had the Neapolitans, and their Austrian general, Mack, in headlong retreat. If Nelson's sea battle had won him a peerage and a shower of adulation, its immediate result was the loss of Naples, followed by the need to ensure the withdrawal of king, court, and treasure to the comparative safety of Sicily, which would become the base of the British squadron.

It was all unfortunate, even ignominious, and Nelson's position was not made easier by the fact that he was becoming enslaved by Lady Hamilton, an association which was to endure for the rest of his life. The Christmas season of the year of the Battle of the Nile was one of the gloomiest of Nelson's life, and he had no one to blame but himself, for as early as his days in the *Agamemnon* he had had bitter experience of how Italian troops were likely to fare at the hands of the French. Caution and patience would have served Naples, and the allied cause in general, much better.

Although he could not know it at Palermo for some time, Nelson's success had in fact greatly strengthened Pitt's hand in reviving an active coalition of Britain, Russia, and Austria, while, away in India, a long series of wars against the rulers of Mysore were at last concluded by the capture of Seringapatam. The Russians and Austrians enjoyed a series of successes in Italy and on the Rhine, while Bonaparte, in attempting to subjugate Syria, met resistance and eventual repulse from the Turks at the siege of Acre. The Turkish troops had the support of British ships under the orders of Sir Sidney Smith, an officer who, though difficult as a subordinate, shone on detached service and in partisan operations.

During the summer even Naples was briefly recovered, and Nelson received the Sicilian dukedom of Brontë. Good as the news seemed, there was one cloud which nothing could dissipate. Bonaparte, leaving his troops in Egypt, evaded the watching British in a fast Venetian-built vessel. He landed safely at Fréjus on 9th October 1799 and in a month was master of France, his status that of First Consul. Incidentally, he had had one of the luckiest escapes of his life, for his ship, *Le Muiron*, was sighted on 7th October by a fleet under Admiral Lord Keith. But dusk had fallen, and the British look-outs took *Le Muiron* to be one of their own frigates.

Four events in the Mediterranean remain to be described, in only two of which Nelson was concerned. The least important, though not the least satisfactory, was that the two French ships of the line to escape the fate of the rest at Aboukir were captured, Nelson being present on one of these occasions. The next was the only serious attempt by the French Government to restore the general situation at sea in an area vital to their interests, and relieve their Army of the East.

In March 1799, Bruix, then Minister of Marine, was ordered to hoist his flag at Brest, and to bring out the French Atlantic fleet. Bruix evaded Bridport, which was seldom difficult; Collingwood, who was then under Bridport, described the escape as 'horrible bungling work'. And from April to October an enemy force was in constant motion. Although in strength, and in consequence a ceaseless threat, the French never sought battle. In the end they were entirely unsuccessful in what they sought to do.

Bruix's first intention was to join up with a Spanish squadron at Cadiz, but he was foiled by Keith, and his later movements kept both friend and foe guessing. St. Vincent, who was in failing health and about to hand over chief command to Keith, was set upon defending Minorca, and there was nothing strong or fast enough to stop Bruix from entering the Mediterranean from the wastes of the Atlantic, and making Port Mahon his goal. This, however, he did not do. At first he made for Toulon: then, since the news from Italy was bad, he was diverted to Genoa. From Genoa he went back to Toulon, and then proceeded to Cartagena.

At Cartagena lay Admiral Mazareddo, with 19 Spanish sail of the line. Had they combined, Bruix and Mazareddo could have been able to obtain the ascendancy in the Mediterranean, could have ensured the relief of the French army in Egypt, and given it support. But Spain's interests were westwards. Mazareddo was not willing to risk his ships on behalf of a French expedition at the other end of the Mediterranean. He was ordered to make for Ferrol, while Bruix, loath to sail east without Spanish support, chose to return to Brest. He was chased for weeks, without success, by the unlucky Keith.

At the outset of Bruix's cruise, Nelson received orders to send his ships to defend Minorca. He disobeyed. Many of his crews were on detached service on the Neapolitan mainland: he himself was preoccupied with the affairs of Naples and Sicily. He did not believe – and in this he was right – that Minorca was seriously threatened. Not unnaturally, his attitude brought upon him the displeasure both of the Admiralty and of Keith, now St. Vincent's official successor. Nelson was instructed to return to England, which he did overland, in company with the Hamiltons. He was fêted everywhere he went in a

Europe which seldom had the chance of making much of a leader who had won an outright victory against the French.

It was under Keith's regime that the garrison at Malta surrendered. This was in 1800, after one of the most remarkable defences in the history of the island. The French commander, Vaubois, deserves remembrance for his feat, and as he lived to be nearly a hundred he had many years in which to enjoy his fame. Malta itself was to play an increasingly important part in the war, for reasons which were not, at the time, readily apparent.

It also fell to Keith to convoy a British army to Egypt. This he did in March 1801, when the French had been established in the country nearly three years, and where they left a lasting impression. At the head of the troops was Sir Ralph Abercromby, who was mortally wounded in the first engagement; but his successor, Hely-Hutchinson, beat the French decisively at Marabout, the very place where Bonaparte had first landed. It then became a matter of agreeing terms under which the French should return home. In the event, these were generous. They sailed with all the honours of war.

The events which led to the Nile, and to its chequered aftermath, had reaffirmed the 'combat supremacy', to use an expressive phrase of Mahan's, of the Royal Navy. It had also illustrated the flexibility of sea power. Victories gained elsewhere had enabled the British to re-enter the Mediterranean in strength, even though their lack of bases remained unremedied. Bases were in fact less essential to a sailing fleet than to a powered one. It was sometimes years between the visits of ships to ports, and, so long as water and supplies could be brought by transport, the other ingredient essential for operations, human endurance, could always be depended upon to the perpetual wonder of less maritime nations.

The protracted but abortive foray by Bruix had shown that a sailing fleet could be at large for months, sometimes undetected, sometimes ineffectively pursued, always a cause for anxiety. Bruix's only possible chance of success lay in willingness to face opponents in battle, whatever their strength, and this he was never prepared to do.

By the turn of the 19th century, the Mediterranean had become as secure as British sea power, unsupported ashore, could make it. Although this was a gain, the time had not yet arrived when it could be

Lemuel Abbott's famous portrait of Lord Nelson, painted in 1797 when he was in London recovering from the loss of his arm at Santa Cruz. Lady Nelson, writing at the time of the Battle of the Nile, gave as her opinion: 'The likeness is great, I am well satisfied with Abbott'

exploited. Yet it was all the more valuable because of a threat from a new quarter. This was the Baltic, trade to and from which was important to Britain, particularly in masts, hemp, flax, and tar, so vital for her fleet. It was therefore to the Baltic, so different and so remote from the sunlit and fabled Mediterranean, that Nelson was next sent.

CHAPTER 12

*The Armed Neutrality of the Baltic Powers – Nelson at
Copenhagen – The Grand Army at Boulogne –
The Peace of Amiens*

OLIVER WARNER

The threat to Great Britain from the Baltic was a complicated story in which, though it may have seemed unlikely, Malta played a part. The Tsar of Russia, Paul I, although in alliance with Britain, was not merely a half-hearted supporter but ripe for the diplomatic wiles of the French. He had got himself appointed Grand Master of the Knights of Malta and he coveted the island as providing a base in the Mediterranean. Britain, which had borne the burden of siege and blockade, had no intention of yielding Malta to anyone, least of all to Russia. The King of Naples had a better claim, and even he was not considered.

Exclusion from Malta offended Paul. French promises flattered him, and his first step towards open rupture with Britain was to revive the old idea of a Maritime Confederacy of the North or, as it had been known in earlier days, an Armed Neutrality. As formulated during the War of American Independence by Russia, Sweden, and Denmark, the ideas behind the association were first, that neutral ships might trade without molestation even along belligerent coasts; second, that the flag covered all goods except contraband of war; third, that a blockade, to be respected, must be efficient.

Denmark, a kingdom which then included Norway, held the key to the Baltic, as she continued to do until the loss of her southern territory later in the century and the cutting of the Kiel Canal. At Elsinore her kings had collected Sound Dues for centuries, and if her fleet were strong enough, she could close the Sound to traffic altogether. Although the Danish royal house was related to that of Britain, she had suffered most, among the northern coun-

tries, from interference with her trade, and she listened to Paul's ideas with attention. Sweden's attitude, which was affected by her sovereign's dislike of Bonaparte as well as by his fear of Russia, was half-hearted, while Prussia's role at sea was small enough to be disregarded. It was the matter of Denmark which needed to be settled first, and relations with that kingdom were soon in a delicate state.

In July 1800 a Danish frigate, the *Freja*, was captured in the English Channel after a smart action. She was brought in, together with the six merchantmen she was escorting, by the British force which had been ordered to search the convoy. The Danes demanded immediate restoration of their ships, and prompt satisfaction for what they deemed to be a signal insult to the honour of their flag. Britain's answer was to send Lord Whitworth to Copenhagen, while a squadron under Admiral Dixon entered the Sound, to make it clear beyond doubt that business was intended.

For a time moderate counsels prevailed, and late in August a convention was arranged whereby Britain restored the ships, but Denmark, for her part, agreed to suspend the right of convoy. Neither side was satisfied, and the incident of the *Freja*, when reported to St. Petersburg, together with the news that Dixon was in the Sound, led Paul to sequestrate all British ships and property within his dominions. This was tantamount to an act of war.

Bonaparte certainly held it to be so, and attributed any delay in a formal treaty with France merely to the distance which separated Paris and the Russian capital. Whatever his other shortcomings, which were considerable and included mental instability,

Opposite above: The Battle of Copenhagen, a painting depicting the height of the action with the line of British ships under Nelson attacking the Danish fleet which was drawn up at anchor in defence of the city. The action, fought on 2nd April, 1801, resulted in the capture of most of the Danish ships. *Below:* A Danish view of the Battle of Copenhagen, with the Royal Dockyard in the foreground. HMS *Elephant*, flying Nelson's flag, is in the centre of the drawing, just above the small windmill

the Tsar was not far behind Bonaparte in the stretch of his imagination. He asked the First Consul to use his good offices with Spain to obtain the accession of the United States and Portugal to the Armed Neutrality, an idea which Bonaparte took up with more enthusiasm than success. He himself toyed once again with the idea of an invasion of India.

The Baltic winter gave Britain the chance to organise counter-measures, the first of them being the assembly of a fleet to act in northern waters. Command was given to Admiral Sir Hyde Parker, with Nelson as his second. The combination of tactical brilliance with age and irresolution – Parker was 62 and notoriously easy-going – was on the face of it odd, and could have been disastrous, since it took Parker a long time not merely to decide on any plan but even to take Nelson into his confidence. Once he did so, the situation became transformed.

Parker duly sailed for Denmark, not without spurring from the Admiralty, on 12th March 1801. Before the month was out, Denmark had placed an embargo on all British vessels in her ports. Simultaneously, her forces from Holstein entered Hamburg and declared the Elbe closed to British merchantmen. Later still the Danes took possession of Lübeck as part of the process of interfering with British trade. Already the Armed Neutrality had shown itself to be much more than that, and all was set for a clash. As London saw it, Danish-Russian action was direct aid to France. It ranged still more forces against an island which was fighting for survival, and which could afford to pull no punches.

Service in the Baltic was not popular. No fleet action had been fought there by Great Britain and the prospects of prize money were negligible. Nelson, after years in the Mediterranean, did not relish the prospect of northern weather, but he had a firm grasp of the importance of Parker's mission and from the outset tried to infect his chief with a proper sense of urgency.

By 24th March, when the fleet was not far from Elsinore and Parker still uncertain what to do, messages came from Copenhagen making it clear that Denmark would not climb down. To Parker Nelson wrote:

'... the more I have reflected the more I am confirmed in opinion, that not a moment should be lost in attacking the Enemy: they will every day and hour be stronger; we shall never be so good a match for them as at this moment ... I am of the opinion the boldest measures are the safest; and our Country needs a most vigorous exertion of her force, directed with judgement. In supporting you, my dear Sir Hyde, through the arduous and important task you have undertaken, no exertion of head or heart shall be wanting from your most obedient and faithful servant, *Nelson and Brontë*'

Parker deliberated whether to proceed by way of the Belt, where the dangers to navigation were considerable, or that of the Sound, which involved facing the batteries mounted near Kronborg Castle. The admiral was informed that the Governor of Kronborg would dispute the passage, but when Parker decided to defy his threat, the Danish guns did little harm. Keeping his ships well away from the Danish shore, the British noted with satisfaction, and some surprise, that batteries on the Swedish side of the Sound were silent. This was in fact significant, not only then but for later stages of the war with France. Sweden was sometimes forced to act against Britain. She never did so willingly since her rulers considered, over the years and in the long run, that the interests of the two nations were more likely to coincide.

The seaward approach to Copenhagen was guarded by the formidable Trekroner batteries, named after the ancient crowns of Denmark, Sweden, and Norway. An attack necessitated the passage of the Outer Deep, between the island of Amager, on which part of Copenhagen is built, and that of Saltholm. When that had been achieved, a change of wind was necessary if the inshore defences were to be invested. The operation was rendered difficult by the presence of a shoal, called the Middle Ground, which was between Amager and the Outer Deep.

If the natural hazards were considerable, the Danes had made sure – for they had been given plenty of warning – that protection of their capital city was reinforced by moored ships of varying sizes, and by floating batteries, heavily gunned. Behind, grounded on shaols, were armed xebecs, and on the shore itself were gun emplacements, all this backed by the resources of a famous dockyard.

Having surveyed his task, which was far more formidable than Nelson's had been at Aboukir Bay, Parker summoned a Council of War. Nelson disliked such assemblies. As he wrote later, and out of long experience: 'If a man consults whether he is to fight, when he has the power in his own hands, *it is*

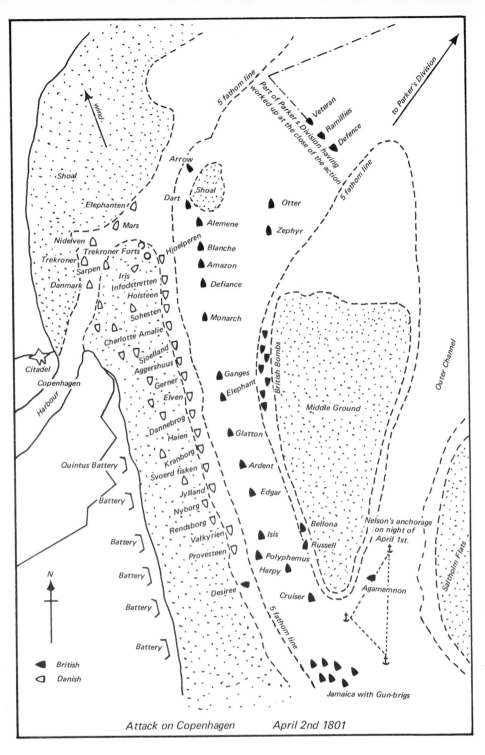

wind

5 fathom line

Part of Parker's Division having worked up at the close of the action

Veteran
Ramillies
Defence

to Parker's Division

5 fathom line

Arrow
Shoal
Shoal
Dart
Otter
Elephanten
Mars
Alemene
Zephyr
Nidelven
Blanche
Trekroner Forts
Hjoelperen
Trekroner
Amazon
Sarpen
Iris
Danmark
Infodstretten
Defiance
Holsteen
Sohesten
Monarch
Charlotte Amalie
Sjoelland
British Bombs
Aggershuus
Ganges
Gerner
Elephant
Elven
Middle Ground
Citadel
Dannebrog
Copenhagen
Haien
Glatton
Harbour
Kranborg
Svoerd fisken
Ardent
Quintus Battery
Jylland
Edgar
Battery
Nyborg
Rendsborg
Bellona
Nelson's anchorage on night of April 1st.
Valkyrien
Russell
Battery
Provesteen
Isis
Polyphemus
Battery
Harpy
Saltholm Flats
Battery
Desiree
Cruiser
Agamemnon
Battery

Outer Channel

N

British
Danish

Jamaica with Gun-brigs

Attack on Copenhagen   April 2nd 1801

certain that his opinion is against fighting.' (The italics were his.) On board the flagship he devoted all his powers of persuasion to stiffening Parker and his fellow officers. He had already decided that, although the defences looked daunting 'to those who are children at war', it was his view that 'with ten sail of the line I think I can annihilate them; at all events, I hope to be allowed to try.' Parker agreed, giving him 12 ships of the line, with auxiliaries, for the close attack. The Commander-in-Chief, with the

heavier units, which were likely to ground in shoal waters, would threaten from a deep-sea channel which led past the Trekroner, and would be ready to deal with any Danish force which might venture out of the harbour.

The fleet anchored on 1st April 1801 on the side of the Middle Ground furthest from the Danish batteries. During the night Nelson, who flew his flag on board the 74-gun ship *Elephant*, dictated orders for his squadron, which were sent off by boat to all concerned. The wind, as those with local knowledge thought it would, duly changed, and in the early morning Nelson sailed on what he later held to be the stiffest task of his life. In negotiating the King's Channel to take station opposite the enemy at their various moorings, his leading ships would be exposed to the fire of the entire line. At the end of this, and to be faced before ships could rejoin the units under Parker, was the powerful Trekroner.

From the outset there were such setbacks as many admirals would have looked upon as disasters. First, Nelson's old ship, the *Agamemnon,* went ashore, far out of range and on the wrong side of the Middle Ground. The pilots employed, for the most part drawn from the merchant service, had so little confidence that in many cases captains had to con their ships themselves. Before final positions were taken up, and action became general, two more ships of the line grounded, the *Bellona* and the *Russell,* only the *Bellona* being in a position to take any appreciable share in the battle. In the redispositions which these mishaps made necessary, five frigates – nothing larger than that – found themselves most exposed to the guns of the Trekroner.

At 1.30 p.m. when action had been in full fury for over three hours, there occurred one of the more extraordinary incidents in the history of warfare. Parker hoisted the signal to discontinue the engagement. 'The fire is too hot for Nelson to oppose', he said to his Captain of the Fleet – from a distance of four miles!

The signal was noted by Captain Riou of the *Amazon,* and led directly to his death. He obeyed, and was killed in trying to withdraw his ship. This was one of the saddest losses of the battle, for Riou had been an outstanding frigate captain. As for Nelson, his disobedience has passed into legend. 'Leave off action!' he said to Foley, his flag-captain, the same man who had led the line at the Nile, ' ... now, damn me if I do ... You know, Foley, I have only one eye. I have a right to be blind sometimes, and I really do not see the signal!'

Soon after he had spoken, the Danish fire began to slacken. Many of the floating batteries had broken adrift and were ablaze between the lines; while the flagship, the *Dannebrog,* was drifting helplessly before the wind. Nelson ceased fire and, under a flag of truce, sent a note ashore which he sealed with careful deliberation. This was given to the Prince Royal,

who was acting for his father, Christian VII, and it was headed: 'To the Brothers of Englishmen, the Danes.' It read:

Lord Nelson has directions to spare Denmark, when no longer resisting; but if firing is continued on the part of Denmark, Lord Nelson will be obliged to set on fire all the Floating-batteries he has taken, without having the power of saving the brave Danes who have defended them ...

A truce was agreed and, after a further exchange of messages, firing ceased. 'This', said Captain Fremantle of the *Ganges,* another Mediterranean comrade-in-arms of Nelson, 'was certainly as convenient for *us* as for the Enemy, as we had several ships on shore, and most of the ships engaged crippled so completely that it was with difficulty they could sail out.'

Nelson's reception by Parker after the battle was as cordial as were the congratulations after the fight off St. Vincent. But there was an immense difference between Parker and the then Sir John Jervis, for Nelson, an already weary man who had faced the dangers and responsibility of a day in which casualties were desolating, knew that he must continue to depend upon his own and not Parker's exertions if all advantage were not to be lost. So much was this true that Parker actually delegated to Nelson the negotiations with the Danish Prince Royal which were to follow next day. During the course of an astonishing interview, conducted in English which, fortunately, the Prince spoke, the truce was extended for fourteen weeks and Denmark agreed to suspend her participation in the Northern Confederacy.

Sweden and Russia still remained to be dealt with, and Nelson lost no time in probing Swedish intentions by means of a sortie. They were not belligerent, and no immediate danger was to threaten from that quarter. As for Russia, which Nelson described as 'the trunk' of the whole Confederacy, an event had occurred at St. Petersburg which, had it been known in Copenhagen on 2nd April, would have rendered the battle unneccessary and spared many gallant lives. On the night of 24th March, while the British squadron was still at the entrance to the Sound, Tsar Paul was strangled by one of his own people. By the time the news became generally known his son and successor, Alexander, was in process of reversing some of the more misguided decisions of the murdered man. Among them was to be abeyance of the activities of the Confederacy which had brought

Parker and Nelson to the north.

As there was nothing further useful Nelson could do he was allowed to return to England for a short spell of leave. It had now become almost axiomatic with the Admiralty that he should be sent to the area of greatest stress at sea. This was obviously the Channel coast. On the opposite shore of the Channel, visible on a clear day through telescopes, a great army lay encamped, as it had been for a long time, ready for an invasion at the first chance of a successful crossing. Nelson's new task was to reorganise the inshore defences of the east and south-east coasts of England, and for a time he flew his flag in a frigate whose usual station was the Downs.

It was his way to act and, like Drake before him, he was fondest of what he called a 'home stroke' — attacking the enemy on his own coast and not tamely waiting for him to take the initiative. The French invasion centre was Boulogne and it was there, on 21st August 1801, that Nelson hoped to destroy the flotillas which were preparing for one of Bonaparte's darling projects. The French, who had been warned by bombardments of other parts of the coast and who were well aware of the nature of their opponent, were

Captain Edward Riou, in command of HMS *Amazon* at Copenhagen, was killed while in action against the Trekroner Battery. Riou was one of the most brilliant frigate captains in the Royal Navy

fully prepared, and the attempt failed with heavy loss. This was due to the enemy ships, whose anchor cables were to have been cut, mooring with the new-fangled chain cables instead of the more usual rope. Even so, Nelson's orders to the captains of the vessels to be employed give as vivid an idea as he ever conveyed of his conception of how war should be waged at sea.

'... When any boats have taken one vessel,' he wrote, 'the business is not to be considered as finished, but a sufficient number being left to guard the prize, the others are immediately to pursue the object by proceeding on to the next, and so on until the whole of the Flotilla be either taken or totally annihilated, for there must not be the smallest cessation until their destruction is completely finished.'

Nelson had nothing to learn from Bonaparte about the meaning of total war and of following up success to the limit.

So far as the British Navy was concerned, the affair at Boulogne was one of the last acts of war before preliminaries to the brief Peace of Amiens were agreed. This was to mark a lull before an even fiercer renewal of the struggle. Bonaparte needed a breathing space in which to reorganise France for still greater exertions. Great Britain had such hopes of future peace that masses of English tourists flocked to the continent.

Under the Treaty of Amiens Britain restored all her conquests overseas except for Ceylon and Trinidad, and agreed to return Malta to the Knights of St. John, though in fact she failed to do so. France withdrew from Neapolitan territory and from the Papal States, and undertook to restore Egypt to Turkey, a matter over which, since the landing of a British army, she had no choice. From Britain's point of view, it was an indifferent peace; from France's, a good one. Britain would have done well to employ her respite in building and repairing ships while officers and men enjoyed a long-hoped-for rest ashore. She did nothing of the kind. Lord St. Vincent, who had been given charge at the Admiralty, was set upon reform of the dockyards and was determined to institute economies wherever he could. His motives were good, but his methods and their effects were unfortunate. When the war was resumed in May 1803, the cry of shortages went up from every naval command. Indeed it was months, and in some cases years, before they were all made good.

CHAPTER 13

The War reopens – Nelson watches Toulon –
Bonaparte's plan and the movement of Villeneuve to the
West Indies – Nelson's pursuit – Calder's Action off
Finisterre – Dispositions before Trafalgar – The
Battle and its effects

OLIVER WARNER

The struggle between Britain and France reopened in an ominous way. Bonaparte deliberately lost his temper in public with the British Ambassador, and when Paris declared the war renewed, he swept all Englishmen in France into captivity, an unprecedentedly severe and unjustified procedure. He most certainly was planning new campaigns, and although he probably knew that Britain was as little eager for hostilities as any nation in Europe – if otherwise, why were so many Englishmen in France? – he made much of the fact that no effort had been made to withdraw from Malta.

The great encampments on the French side of the Channel remained. Now, once again, they filled with men and training for invasion proceeded. Agents had informed Bonaparte of a fact of which he hoped to make the fullest use; the dire results of St. Vincent's probing of the dockyards. France had in fact won an advantage without striking a blow, and the promise of a successful invasion never seemed better. For while St. Vincent had been nosing, Bonaparte had been building; and both France and Spain, as their enemies were the first to admit, built fine ships.

St. Vincent once said that the Mediterranean command required 'an officer of splendour'. To this post Nelson was appointed, his flag in H.M.S. *Victory*. Important as the Mediterranean was, and always would be, the Channel Fleet or Western Squadron was Great Britain's principal bulwark. The charge of this was given to Admiral Cornwallis, familiarly known as 'Billy Blue'. He was respected by every officer and man in the Navy, Nelson included. Cornwallis had seen much service during

his life and was a perfect master of close and distant blockade. With Cornwallis and Nelson at the head of the two main fleets, England could feel secure. The fate of the pair was oddly different. Cornwallis remained, for the French, the great deterrent, but he was never destined to engage in another major action. Nelson's, as so often, was to be the more dramatic role.

Yet, for more than two long years there was a pause at sea. Nelson, in the *Victory*, kept distant watch on Toulon, wearing away his life and energy in trying to guess French intentions, eager to fight the enemy fleet whenever it left port. It was a lonely, dedicated life of duty, hard on a sociable and volatile man yet willingly accepted in the service of his beloved country. At first Nelson had to make do with few ships, many of them in need of overhaul. By 1804, when the Spaniards once more threw in their lot with France, he was still in not much better case, except that month by month, keeping the sea in all weathers, watering sometimes off Sardinia but never himself putting foot ashore, he grew more and more confident of the quality of those he commanded.

By the year 1805, with Spanish naval resources mobilised, with French ports filled with shipping and his army of invasion ready, Bonaparte unfolded to those nearest to him his large-scale plan for victory. In essence it was simple, but it depended for success on so many uncertain factors that it could never have been conceived by a sailor. All the main squadrons, French and Spanish, were to evade the British watch and cross the Atlantic to a rendezvous in the West Indies. Once assembled, the huge fleet, the

Opposite: Admiral Sir Charles Middleton, who as Lord Barham was First Lord of the Admiralty throughout the Trafalgar campaign and was the strategical brain behind it

135

main elements drawn from Toulon, Cartagena, Cadiz, Ferrol, Rochefort, and Brest, were to return to Europe, under Villeneuve's command, make a diversion in Ireland where, as ever, there were 'troubles', defeat or sweep aside Cornwallis, and gain control of the Channel for long enough for the flotillas from Boulogne and elsewhere to cross. Once ashore, on English beaches, Bonaparte had no doubt that his army could advance, capture London, and end the war in a way which he, the Emperor of the French, would dictate. It was a scheme worthy of the man who, seven years earlier, had conquered Egypt and who had then believed himself on the way to India.

Part at least of his idea seemed at one time to hold promise. In the early months of the year Villeneuve, the Emperor's 'lucky' admiral, twice escaped from Toulon, when frigates on inshore watch had been driven to seaward by stress of weather or the attentions of a superior force. In the first instance touch was soon regained and Villeneuve's movements reported, but high seas proved too much for his seamen, confined to port as they had been for so long, and he was forced to return with ships damaged and himself somewhat shaken by the incompetence of his captains.

Once the French were out, Nelson's idea, for want of firm information, was that their intention was either another 'Eastern expedition' on the lines of that of 1798, or that they had designs on Naples and Sicily, which were his special care. After each of Villeneuve's escapes, Nelson made a long cast to the eastward. The time and effort were wasted, yet had he not acted thus he would have felt himself guilty of neglect. If Villeneuve made for the Atlantic, his ships could not pass Gibraltar without, in due course, alerting all the watchers off the Spanish and French Atlantic seaboard. Nelson alone was responsible for what happened in the Middle Sea.

The second time Villeneuve got away, during the last days of March 1805, Bonaparte's plan was really set in motion and his hopes rose accordingly. Yet it was not as a potential conqueror that Villeneuve emerged, and he was so apprehensive of being overtaken by Nelson that he allowed insufficient time for the Spanish admiral in charge at Cartagena to join forces with him. Even when off Cadiz, when his movements had become known to Cornwallis's cruisers, he allowed the barest minimum of time for

such Spanish ships as were ready, to join him. The rest were ordered to follow as soon as they could.

When Villeneuve's departure from the Mediterranean at last became clear to Nelson, he was so delayed in his pursuit by head winds that it was not until early May that he was clear of Gibraltar. Off the coast of Portugal he detached a three-decked ship, the *Royal Sovereign*, to ensure the safe passage of troops under General Craig which were destined for Sicily. Then, with his squadron of ten seasoned ships of the line and three frigates, though with the *Superb* dreadfully slow owing to the foulness of her bottom, he headed across the Atlantic to the West Indies, to that 'station of honour', as he called it, with which he had been familiar since a youth.

Nelson reached Barbados in June and his instinct told him to head north at once for Martinique, where he felt sure he would come upon the combined Franco-Spanish fleet, and perhaps have the good fortune of Rodney in April 1782 when he met and defeated de Grasse off The Saints. Nelson's numbers were far inferior to Villeneuve's, but this never troubled him, so sure was he that he could give his opponent such a mauling that he would be in no fit state to recross the Atlantic with the prospect of a meeting with Cornwallis at the end of it.

Villeneuve was indeed where Nelson supposed him to be, cruising off the Leeward Islands, doing a certain amount of damage to British trade, and waiting for the reinforcements his Emperor had told him to expect. Only driblets came, for Admiral Ganteaume, preparing for his great sortie from Brest, had been punched back by the Western Squadron, leaving Villeneuve on his own. Nelson meanwhile, misled by information which from the first he suspected though it came from a military officer whom in the past he had found to be reliable, had gone to Trinidad. For a few hours he had dreams of coming upon the French embayed in much the same state as Brueys had been at the Nile, but the anchorages were empty. Still worse, the moment Villeneuve had news that Nelson was on his trail, he was up and away, heading stright back to Europe.

Nelson's own command being the Mediterranean, it was his duty to return thereto, and he shaped course for Gibraltar where, in July, he set foot ashore for the first time for nearly two years. He was tired and disappointed, but not disheartened. Sooner or later, so he believed, he and Villeneuve

would meet again. Unbeknown to him the brig *Curieux*, which he had sent on ahead to try to find the enemy, had succeeded admirably. Having observed Villeneuve's course, which indicated a Biscay port rather than the Mediterranean, the captain sped away for England, giving the Admiralty time to dispose a force to ensure the enemy a warm reception.

The Franco-Spanish fleet did not indeed return to Europe unmolested, for Cornwallis detached a strong squadron under Sir Robert Calder to cruise off Finisterre, and on 22nd July 1805 Calder and Villeneuve sighted one another and fought an engagement in misty weather. Calder mistook his duty, which was so to maul Villeneuve at any cost to himself – as Nelson would certainly have done – as to prevent any possibility of his doing further mischief. Calder, who was in inferior strength to the enemy, thought he had done very well indeed in capturing two Spanish ships of the line, and relished the prospect of praise (and almost certainly honours) from home. He was due for one of the shocks of his

Sir William Cornwallis, known throughout the Royal Navy as 'Billy Blue', was in command of the fleet blockading Brest which prevented the escape of the French fleet based there. In Napoleon's invasion plan, this fleet was to have evaded the blockade and joined Villeneuve in the West Indies. From the portrait by D. Gardner

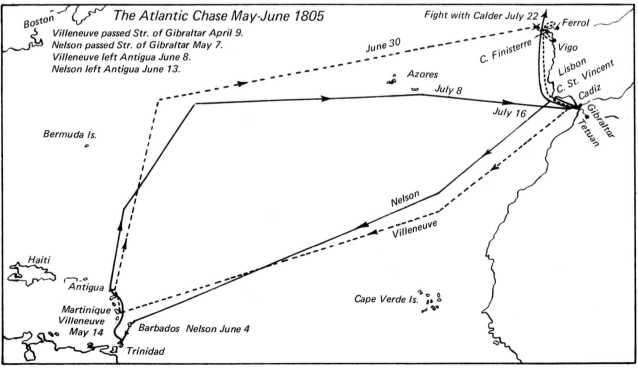

The Atlantic Chase May-June 1805

Villeneuve passed Str. of Gibraltar April 9.
Nelson passed Str. of Gibraltar May 7.
Villeneuve left Antigua June 8.
Nelson left Antigua June 13.

Fight with Calder July 22

Boston
Bermuda Is.
Haiti
Antigua
Martinique
Villeneuve
May 14
Barbados Nelson June 4
Trinidad
Cape Verde Is.
June 30
Azores
July 8
C. Finisterre
Ferrol
Vigo
Lisbon
C. St. Vincent
Cadiz
Gibraltar
Tettuan
July 16
Nelson
Villeneuve

life. St. Vincent, Duncan, and Nelson had set new standards in sea fighting, and Calder's action, which was not renewed though it possibly could have been next day, brought upon him censure, not approval. Calder was indignant at the public reaction to his encounter, though he had no business to be. He had been St. Vincent's chief of staff or First Captain on Valentine's Day 1797, and should have imbibed more tactical and strategic fire from his great leader. 'It is, as Mr. Pitt knows, annihilation that the country wants, and not merely a splendid victory, honourable to the parties concerned.' So wrote Nelson on another occasion; but it was true then. As a result of what he felt was unjust treatment, Calder demanded an enquiry. Once again he was unlucky. His wish was granted, but the enquiry took place after Trafalgar, by which time the new standards had not merely been set, but improved upon, and he was censured.

Villeneuve, after his action with Calder, put in to Vigo, and later made one more effort to complete his master's orders. He had not been long at sea when his courage failed him. He reversed his course and made for Cadiz, a port watched only by a very weak detachment under Collingwood. Collingwood very sensibly lifted his blockade of Cadiz to let Villeneuve enter, and then clamped down again with his close watch.

At Cadiz, Villeneuve was in a good position from which to make a sortie into either the Atlantic or the Mediterranean, as strategy indicated. He had not

Captain Henry Blackwood, of the frigate *Euryalus*, played an important part in the moves which led to Trafalgar. Lying off Cadiz, he reported the movements of the Franco-Spanish fleet, his signals being repeated by relaying ships to Nelson over the horizon. *Below:* The main deck of HMS *Victory*, showing a tier of guns on their carriages and the shot garlands for the stowage of balls for the guns. The *Victory* had three gundecks

been long in port before Bonaparte, despairing at last of his 'lucky' admiral, decided to relieve him. He also broke up the camps on the Channel, and turned his thoughts towards a military, not an amphibious enterprise. He would, so he decided, revert to military conquest, and would employ his fleet in the Mediterranean. He would renounce any direct attempt against a country which seemed more and more impossible to subdue.

It was some time before the switch of French direction became known in London. Even when it had become clear, there still remained the paramount task of watching, and if possible defeating, the principal enemy fleet. If this could not be used in the service of invasion, it could always threaten and preoccupy. Above all, detachments could disrupt that world-wide trade which, then as now, was the force which kept Britain alive and fighting.

After making dispositions to safeguard the Mediterranean, Nelson proceeded home, with only the *Superb*, the ship so long overdue for docking, in company. On the way he exchanged messages with two of his oldest friends – with Collingwood off Cadiz, who told him he still thought that the enemy objective might be Ireland, with Cornwallis off Ushant. The iron sense of duty of these admirals had been tried, ever since the reopening of the war, as hard as had Nelson's, but they had helped to save their country, and they would spend the last ounce of their strength in her service. Nelson told Collingwood he hoped soon to rejoin him. Villeneuve's immediate destination was not then known either to Nelson or Collingwood, for the Frenchman was still on his way south, but Nelson hoped that Collingwood would soon be given a respectable addition of force. Cornwallis, in fact, soon attended to this.

Nelson's return to England proved to be a mere interlude of 25 days, of greetings, plans, and farewells. He was the darling of the nation, and he loved its praise, though he felt that on this occasion he had done little to deserve it, since Villeneuve had eluded him. Old Lord Barham, then presiding at the Admiralty, was at first so uncertain of Nelson's strategic judgment that he took the step of sending to Spithead for the *Victory's* journals. He was soon reassured. Nelson's dispositions could not be faulted. His luck was another matter.

Meanwhile, if Nelson were willing to continue in his command, Their Lordships of the Admiralty would be gratified. Tired as he was, and longing for a protracted spell at home, Nelson at once assented. Barham then set about finding him as many additional ships as he could, and when Captain Henry Blackwood, of the frigate *Euryalus*, drove up early one morning to Merton with the news that the Combined Fleet was at Cadiz, Nelson knew that there was no time to lose if he, and not Collingwood, were to be at the head of the force which would meet the enemy at sea when they ventured out, as he believed they soon would.

Nelson had a plan. It was no secret. He would discuss it with fellow officers. He would explain it, in simpler terms, to statesmen. It even became known indirectly and in vague terms, to the enemy. Set as he was upon 'annihilation', Nelson knew that it was useless to contemplate any engagement which could become indecisive. There must be a full-scale *mêlée*, in which superior training and gunfire would tell to the full. He had already circulated a memorandum to his captains on the subject, and one of them, Keats of the *Superb*, was given a succinct idea of the matter as he walked with the admiral about his pleasure grounds.

'One day,' so Keats reported, 'talking on naval matters, he said to me: "No day can be long enough to arrange a couple of fleets and fight a decisive battle, according to the old system. When *we* meet them (I was to have been with him), for meet them we shall, I'll tell you how I shall fight them.

I shall form the Fleet into three Divisions in three Lines. One Division shall be composed of twelve or fourteen of the fastest two-decked ships, which I shall always keep to windward, or in a situation of advantage; and I shall put them under an Officer who, I am sure, will employ them in the manner I wish, if possible. I consider it will always be in my power to throw them into Battle in any part I may choose; but if circumstances prevent their being carried against the Enemy where I desire, I shall feel certain he will employ them effectually, and perhaps in a more advantageous manner than if he could have followed my orders.

With the remaining part of the Fleet formed in two lines, I shall go at them at once, if I can, about one-third of their line from their leading ship." He then said: "What do you think of it?" Such a question I felt required consideration. I paused. Seeing it, he said: "But I'll tell you what *I* think of it. I think it will surprise and confound the Enemy. They won't know what I am about. It will bring forward a pell-mell Battle, and that is what I want".'

According to Nelson, his admirals and captains, when he came to expound his ideas to them over the table of his great cabin, reacted very much less cautiously than Keats. They were surprised and delighted; 'some,' said Nelson, 'shed tears.' Their chief, so it seemed to them, had at last discovered a method of bringing about what none doubted would be a decisive victory by an attack in column, not in line, as the age-old *Fighting Instructions* usually enjoined. There would, all must have perceived, be an immense risk to the leading ships in each column, but anything was better than another action on the lines of the one which Calder had recently fought.

Nelson had already won two unorthodox victories at sea. There was no reason why the most resounding masterpiece of all should not be achieved in waters over which he, and many of his captains, had already fought so many times, and where they believed their moral ascendancy to be complete.

Nelson and the *Victory* sailed from England on 14th September, with Blackwood and the *Euryalus* in company. The ships represented the directing force and the eyes of the Mediterranean fleet.

'At half past Ten,' Nelson confided in his Diary, 'drove from dear, dear Merton, where I left all I hold dear in this world, to go to serve my King and Country. May the Great God whom I adore enable me to fulfill the expectations of my Country, and if it is His good pleasure that I should return, my thanks will never cease being offered up to the Throne of his Mercy. If it is His good providence to cut short my days upon Earth, I bow with the greatest submission, relying that He will protect those so dear to me, that I may leave behind. His Will be done: Amen, Amen, Amen.'

Nelson sent Blackwood on ahead to tell Collingwood that when the *Victory* joined the ships on watch, he wished for no formal salute, such as was given to a Commander-in-Chief when first rejoining his squadrons. He did not wish the enemy at Cadiz to learn of his arrival or of the fact that, besides the *Victory*, a number of other ships of the line, including his beloved old *Agamemnon*, were shortly to join him. Let Villeneuve continue to think the British to be in inferior force. It might help induce him to come out.

Villeneuve had, in fact, every reason for so doing. There were the Emperor's orders, for one thing, and the suspicion, soon to become a certainty, that he was losing favour. Quite as cogent as these reasons was the fact that the supplies available at Cadiz for

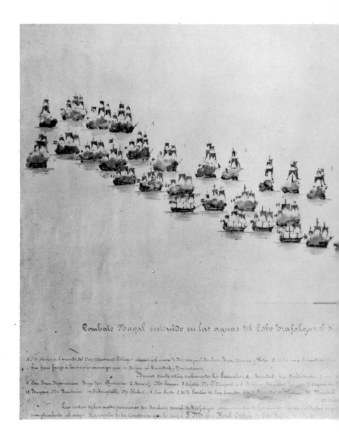

such a large fleet as his – 33 of the line, 18 French and 15 Spanish, with attendant frigates – were running short. There was also the lateness of the season. Far better, in the view of everyone but the Spaniards, to have a winter based at Toulon, and if Toulon could be reached without a serious fight, Villeneuve would consider himself fortunate. His fleet would be 'in being' and at the disposal of the Emperor to further his schemes for the south of Europe, and Villeneuve (superseded or not) would have escaped that dreaded further clash with the victor of the Nile.

When Nelson joined his fleet he found restless captains. Collingwood's discipline had been severe, and it was soon relaxed. Nelson's first business was to make friends with his officers, a high proportion of whom had not served with him before. Within a few days tension was reduced, ships were kept, for the most part, well out to sea, while Blackwood and his frigates reported, from close inshore, every movement of the enemy.

It was on 19th October that Blackwood first reported active preparations within the port of Cadiz. Villeneuve's original aim had been to drive off the inshore watch by a brief sortie, but he soon found himself committed with his whole fleet, and on 20th October his force was at sea and heading for the Straits of Gibraltar. The French had learned that Nelson had had to detach some of his ships to Gibraltar to water and provision, which was true enough, and a better chance of a successful passage to the Mediterranean by the Combined Fleet did not seem likely to occur.

Nelson was at pains not to show his full strength to the enemy until Villeneuve was on his way to Gibraltar, and for this purpose kept well out to sea and over the horizon. Reports from the frigates and their supporting ships of the line, such as the *Mars*, soon made it clear that Franco-Spanish seamanship and discipline left much to be desired. Their manoeuvring was ragged and every movement slow. Villeneuve's total numbers were 33 ships of the line against 27 under Nelson. Although the disparity did not worry Nelson in the slightest, it was clear that he would not have enough ships to form that fast, independent division of which he had spoken to Keats. Apart from that important reservation, his plan remained in force and he had had the opportunity, as in the anxious days which preceded the battle of the Nile, to assure himself that every captain understood not only the general scheme for

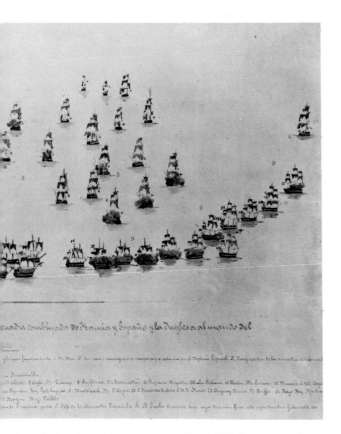

A wash drawing of the approach of the British fleet made after the battle by the flag captain of the Spanish Admiral Gravina. His view does not accord with the accepted version.

The entry in Nelson's journal, written in the morning of 21st October, 1805, included his well-known prayer before battle

The height of the battle, with the *Victory* breaking the line. This painting by George Chambers after Clarkson Stanfield also shows the French *Redoubtable* on the *Victory's* starboard side, with the *Temeraire* alongside her

engaging the French, but that it was a fixed principle with Nelson to allow individuals as much scope for initiative as possible. This was a rare trait in the Georgian navy, but it was one which, with such officers as he commanded, was abundantly justified. 'A band of brothers' he had described his Nile captains, quoting from his favourite play, *Henry V*. In far less time than he had been given in 1798, he had caused the same spirit to animate those 'cargoes of courage' which tossed about in the Atlantic off Cadiz.

Early on the day of battle, 21st October, Villeneuve's heart failed him, as Nelson felt sure it would, and he reversed course, hoping to regain the shelter of the batteries of the Spanish port before he was caught up in a *mêlée*. He was too late, for the weather did not help him. In the morning there were light airs, blowing towards the land, and a gradually increasing swell, though at first it had been almost a flat calm. Nelson foretold the coming of a gale before nightfall – the amputated stump of his right arm was, so he had long found, as reliable as any barometer – and he said to Hardy, his flag-captain, that he proposed to anchor after the battle. He could not have realised how few of his ships would be in any position to obey, so much would they suffer in their gear.

Nelson summoned Blackwood and the other frigate captains, giving them orders about repeating signals, directions to be passed on to slow-sailing ships, instructions regarding damaged ships and prizes, and other matters. He inspected each deck of the *Victory*, praising her good order. He drafted a will: and he wrote that prayer which has become part of the treasury of the English language.

'At daylight,' ran the last entry in his private diary, 'saw the Enemy's Combined Fleet from east to E.S.E.; bore away; made the signal for Order of Sailing and to Prepare for Battle. The Enemy with their heads to the southward. At seven the Enemy wearing in succession.'

Nelson, through his telescope, had observed Villeneuve's change of course, and he knew, if only the wind held and the Combined Fleet stood up to his attack, that nothing on earth could now prevent that battle of annihilation on which his mind was set. Then came the words:

'May the Great God whom I worship, grant to my Country, and for the benefit of Europe in general, a great and glorious Victory; and may no misconduct in anyone tarnish it; and may humanity after Victory be the predominant feature in the British Fleet. For myself individually, I commit my life to Him who made me, and may His blessing light upon my endeavours for serving my

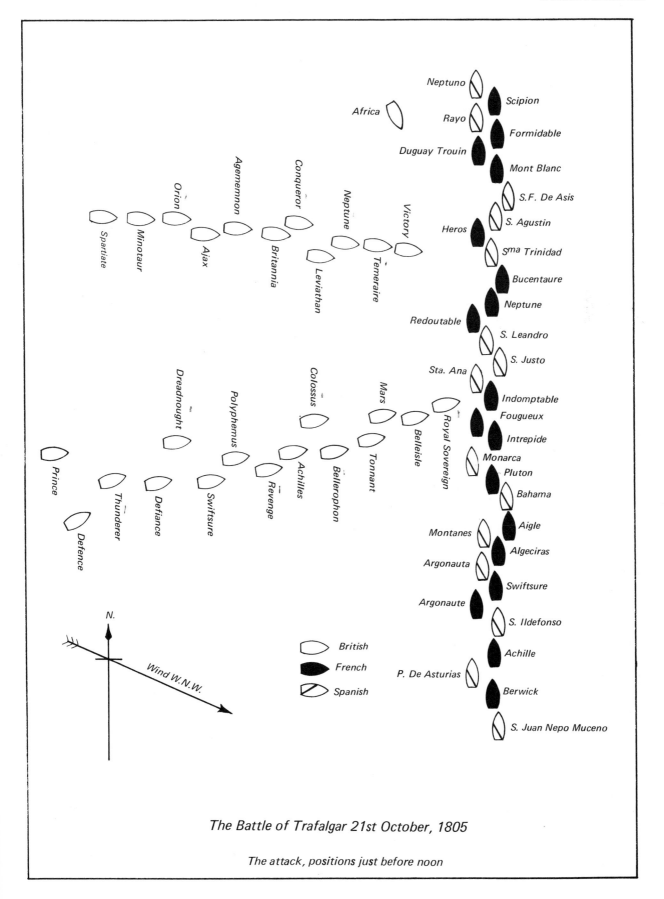

The Battle of Trafalgar 21st October, 1805

The attack, positions just before noon

Country faithfully. To Him I resign myself, and the just cause which is entrusted me to defend. Amen, Amen, Amen.'

One matter remained, a general signal to the Fleet. The admiral had wished to send the message: 'Nelson confides that every man will do his duty' which was warm, personal, and characteristic. But it involved a complicated hoist of flags, so Nelson agreed to the substitution of the much less intimate 'England expects …' for the first two words. Bonaparte, when the incident was reported to him, was impressed; not so Collingwood and others, who had already had their fill of signals and who were accustomed to doing their duty, in action or on watch, until their frames could stand no more.

Even more so than had been the case at the Nile, the light strength of the wind enforced a leisurely approach, but it was soon apparent that Villeneuve intended to make a fight of it, his line appearing to Collingwood, in the words of his despatch, to form 'a crescent convexing to leeward'. There was one notable feature of Nelson's approach: both his own, the 'weather' column, and Collingwood's, the 'lee', were led by the admirals in person, in their great three-deckers, the *Victory* and the newly-coppered *Royal Sovereign,* into which Collingwood had recently exchanged from the *Dreadnought*. The *Dreadnought* was a good ship but, being long absent from dock, was remarkable for her slow sailing.

By reason of the form of attack on which he had decided, Nelson's leading ships would of necessity be exposed to a high concentration of fire, and would be engaged, unsupported, long before the remainder of the British ships could reach them. In the circumstances Nelson was entreated either to fly his flag on board a frigate, or at the very least to allow the *Téméraire,* which was close astern, to get ahead of the *Victory*. Nelson appeared to agree to the latter suggestion, but when Captain Eliab Harvey was about to overtake him, the admiral picked up a speaking trumpet and told him he would thank him to keep in his proper station! What caused private amusement to some of the officers of the flagship were Nelson's repeated signals to ships in Collingwood's line to take station ahead of their admiral. This was contrary to his own expressed statement that, when contact with the enemy was once established, he would not interfere in the direction of the lee column; but that Collingwood should unnecessarily expose his person

was too much for Nelson to bear without protest.

As was only to have been expected from such an officer, Collingwood crowded on sail and his ship was in action for some time before the rest of the fleet. 'See how that noble fellow Collingwood carries his ship into action!' exclaimed Nelson, as he watched the oldest friend of his Service life begin that 'pell-mell battle' which he knew must be decisive. Soon, what the log of the *Mars* described as 'the din of war' increased to continuous flame and thunder, as both columns gradually came into action. It did not cease for over four hours.

As if nothing should be wanting to emphasise that this encounter off Cape Trafalgar was the greatest of all battles under sail, the *Victory* broke into the French line close astern of the *Bucentaure,* which wore Villeneuve's flag. The French van stood on unopposed, but it took so long for the ships to turn to go to the help of the centre that by the time they did so their appearance was useless. The battle had already been won and they made off, unscathed, to be snapped up later by Sir Richard Strachan in an appropriate pendant to the main action.

Succeeding British ships, in the words of one of their captains, 'scrambled into action as best they could', and always with effect, though it was the leading ships which did most of the damage, as well as suffering many casualties. Nelson, with sublime assurance, reckoned on the capture or destruction of 20 enemy ships, an unparalleled number in a major action fought between comparable fleets at sea. His hopes were exactly realised, though owing to general confusion after the action, to the difficulty of providing prize crews, to the great storm which arose later in the day just as Nelson had expected, and to the fact that certain enemy ships, including the great *Santissima Trinidad,* were sunk or ran ashore, only four prizes were brought into Gibraltar after the battle, none of them of the first rate. There was no British loss in ships, though two captains, Duff of the *Mars,* who particularly distinguished himself, and Cooke of the *Bellerophon,* the ship which had done so well and suffered so badly at the Nile, were killed in action.

The *Victory's* fire soon pulverised the *Bucentaure* into surrender, but Nelson then had to face the *Redoutable,* commanded by Captain Lucas, which was one of the few outstandingly well-trained ships in the Combined Fleet. Lucas's conduct was magnificent. Not only did he attempt to board the *Victory*, a far larger ship than his own, but it was from one of his fighting tops that the bullet was fired which struck Nelson down. The admiral was pacing the quarter-deck with Captain Hardy when he turned and fell, saying that they had done for him at last. He lived a few hours longer in the cockpit below, long enough to be told the full extent of his achievement, but when Hardy sent over a boat to the *Royal Sovereign* with news of Nelson's wound, Collingwood realised in an instant, from the expression on the messenger's face, that his chief would not survive the battle. The man he described as 'the glory of England' would within hours bequeath his command, with its huge responsibilities, to Collingwood.

Nelson could not have left it in better hands. There was only one other British flag-officer present at Trafalgar, the Earl of Northesk, but he was without the necessary experience and seniority to have taken up Nelson's burden successfully. Upon Collingwood fell the ordering of the fleet, the writing of the despatches, care of the prisoners, who included Villeneuve, and the furtherance of his Government's policy throughout the Mediterranean command, which then extended from the Atlantic coast of Spain to the Dardanelles.

No one ever summed up Trafalgar better than King George III in a letter which he caused to be written to Collingwood and which became the admiral's most treasured possession.

'Every tribute of praise appears to His Majesty due to Lord Nelson, whose loss he can never sufficiently regret,' so ran the message, 'but His Majesty considers it very fortunate that the command, under circumstances so critical, should have devolved upon an officer of such consummate valour, judgment and skill, as Admiral Collingwood has proved himself to be, every part of whose conduct he considers deserving his entire approbation and admiration.'

'It is there', wrote Collingwood to his wife when he read the letter, 'I feel the object of my life attained.' Between them, Nelson and Collingwood had not only achieved the greatest victory known to the classic days of sail but they had assured the predominance of the Royal Navy for the rest of the war. Ten further years of struggle remained, but it was Trafalgar that made all the future victories on land possible.

Cuthbert, Lord Collingwood, who as second-in-command at Trafalgar led the lee line into action, from the portrait by H. Howard. After the battle Collingwood remained for the rest of his life in the Mediterranean as Commander-in-Chief, dying on service in 1810

CHAPTER 14

*The Berlin Decrees and Orders in Council – The French
guerre de course – Duckworth at the Dardanelles –
Effects of the Treaty of Tilsit on Baltic Affairs – Second
Expedition to Copenhagen – Collingwood's aid to Spanish
revival – Successes in the West and East Indies – War
with the United States – Defeat of Bonaparte*

OLIVER WARNER

While it would be an overstatement to say that Bonaparte regarded his defeat at sea with equanimity, French newspapers scarcely mentioned the battle since they were full of resounding new achievements by the Emperor. By the autumn of 1805 Pitt had achieved yet another coalition – Britain, Austria, Russia, and Sweden – but it soon came to grief, for an Austrian army capitulated at Ulm and the Austrians and the Russians were beaten at Austerlitz. Pitt himself died, depressed and worn out, early in 1806, and he would not have been unduly elated by the principal naval success of that year, which was the recapture of the Cape of Good Hope. This was an invaluable staging post on the long voyage to India, where Britain's interests were becoming increasingly important, and where Arthur Wellesley, later to become Duke of Wellington, who returned home just before Trafalgar, had already begun to make a name as a general.

In November 1806 Bonaparte issued what became known as the Berlin Decrees, which stated that Britain was blockaded and forbade any trade with her by countries under French influence. In practice these decrees were every bit as futile as the plans which had led to Trafalgar, for as the Emperor's own brother Louis once remarked, 'you might just as well try to stop the skin from sweating as try to prevent trade.' Britain replied with reciprocal Orders in Council, the chief sufferers from which were the United States, which had done thriving business with continental countries ever since the war had opened.

At sea, since she could do nothing more extended, France engaged in a *guerre de course* – a war on merchantmen conducted by fast, single men-of-war, by small detachments of such, and by privateers. British watching cruisers could not be everywhere at all times, and during the remainder of the war this campaign, though unspectacular, had a considerable nuisance value. It entailed the continuance of the unpopular convoy system which led to unavoidable delays and frequent congestion at the ports, whilst there were still sufficient operational French and Spanish ships of the line to warrant the continuance of squadrons off Brest and Toulon.

The year 1807 was marked by increasing tension, which eventually led to open war, between Turkey and Russia. As Great Britain was formally allied with Russia, Collingwood was directed to send an expedition through the Dardanelles to Constantinople, both to further Russian interests and to intimidate the Turks, who were suspected of ill-will towards Britain. The admiral chosen to lead the expedition, Sir John Duckworth, met with no success, and his squadron suffered loss as it made its way back to the Aegean. The Russian admiral then in the Mediterranean had made no serious effort to join forces with the British, which caused Collingwood to write acidly to Sir Alexander Ball, who was then in charge at Malta: 'We are identifying ourselves at Constantinople with the Russians, an excess of friendship that I do not think they are disposed to show to us.'

Collingwood was correct in his deductions, and for a sinister reason, for Tsar Alexander I was shortly to come to terms with Bonaparte in much the same way as his father had done before him. He had reached the conclusion that, since he could not beat the French, it was better to be their friend and to share the world with Bonaparte. The two Emperors met on a raft moored in the middle of the River Neva at Tilsit, where the anti-French coalition was finally dissolved. It is a fair conclusion that if Duckworth had succeeded in intimidating the Turks, Alexander would have hesitated before making terms with Bonaparte; but Duckworth had no troops to support him and the navigational hazards of the Dardanelles and the Sea of Marmara in any case proved too much.

The ulterior aim of Bonaparte at Tilsit was the destruction of Britain. He was determined to extend his 'Continental System' to include all the countries of the Baltic. He aimed to secure the use of the Danish fleet which had been largely rebuilt since the Parker-Nelson sortie of 1801, and had designs upon the partitioning of Portugal, Britain's last remaining ally in the west. At the same time he had plans for the control of Spain.

Britain's immediate reaction to Tilsit was prompt and effective. An amphibious expedition was sent to intimidate Denmark a second time. Admiral Gambier was given charge of the fleet, Lord Cathcart of the Army, among whose generals was Wellington. Troops were put ashore in Zealand, and the Danish capital was bombarded from the landward side. Considerable fires were started and much damage done before the city surrendered. Terms were then agreed for the removal of the fleet, the principal units of which were towed back to England. Gambier had eliminated an immediate and serious threat, but Britain, by her two expeditions, had made a tenacious enemy. For the rest of the war Denmark identified herself with French interests, and as, with the timber resources of Norway and of her own countryside to draw upon she could build gunboats swiftly, she continued a menace to British interests in the north. Although on a small scale, sea warfare in the Baltic between 1808 and the end of the European struggle was continuous, intricate, and fierce.

So much was this so that the Admiralty decided on the organisation of a strong squadron to operate during the ice-free months when, in spite of Napoleon and his Berlin decrees, the trade flow to and from Britain was enormous. Command was given to Sir James Saumarez, with his flag in the *Victory*, and a better choice could not have been made. Saumarez had seen more operational service than any sea

Admiral Lord Gambier, in command of the British fleet at the second bombardment of Copenhagen in 1807. This was a joint naval and military operation, which resulted in the entire Danish fleet being surrendered to Britain for the remainder of the war. A mezzotint from the portrait by Sir William Beechey.

officer of his time – not excluding Nelson. As a tactician he was original and aggressive. Another virtue was that he was a fluent French speaker. As his role in the Baltic would largely be diplomatic, and as the language of the court of Britain's ally, Sweden, was French, this accomplishment was of great importance.

Saumarez's usual anchorage was at Wingo Sound, off Gothenberg, and one of his early measures was to seize the Danish island of Anholt, at which his ships could water, where he placed a small garrison of marines. Another invaluable seizure was the North Sea island of Heligoland, which served as an entrepôt of trade with Holland and Germany – for this was a great era of smuggling, which for both sides in the conflict had become, among the seafaring population, a principal, almost a patriotic, occupation. Delicacies from British possessions appeared regularly on the table of the Emperor of the French, and it was alleged that, in one campaign at least, French troops marched on British leather.

The year of Tilsit saw two invasions. Tsar Alexander sent an army into Finland which for centuries had been an integral part of the Swedish realm. The country was lost after sporadic resistance, heroic on the part of the Finns, ineptly led as they were by

Swedish officers who, in at least one instance, were suspected of treachery. This was over the matter of the loss of Sveaborg, one of the strongest sea fortresses of the Baltic. It surrendered with as little resistance as the Knights of Malta had offered to Napoleon in 1798. Concurrently, Bonaparte sent an army into Portugal, whose royal family fled to Brazil under the protection of the Royal Navy.

Of the two events, the occupation of Finland was more permanent, since it lasted until the present century when the country became independent. The invasion of Portugal, on the other hand, presented Britain with an opportunity for the exercise of sea power, and it was entirely characteristic of its flexibility that some of Saumarez's ships, the *Victory* included, after spending their summers in the Baltic, were sent during the winter months with troops and supplies for Portugal and Spain where, from the year 1808 when Bonaparte deposed the Spanish King and put his brother Joseph on the throne, national humiliation led to popular resistance. This gave Britain just the excuse she needed to open a front in the Iberian Peninsula, to which she sent her two best generals, Sir John Moore, who lost his life in a defensive victory at Corunna, and Wellington, who for six years, with the unfailing support of the Navy, made certain that the 'ulcer', which Bonaparte was one day to say helped to kill him, was kept in a condition of worrying eruption.

At the outset of the Peninsular War, Moore and Wellington had the immense advantage of the experience of Collingwood, who had held the Mediterranean command (including Cadiz) without a break ever since Trafalgar. Collingwood was regarded as a hero by the Spanish people. This was due to what they felt to be his noble conduct to their prisoners after Trafalgar, an attitude which they themselves had reciprocated in the case of the small parties of British prize crews and wounded who fell into their hands. When Spanish nationalism flowered, under Bonaparte's brutal assaults on a people's pride, Collingwood landed at Cadiz to assure the citizens of his support, and there he received a touching welcome.

The admiral's principal service during the five years after Trafalgar in which his bodily strength held out – he died at sea, utterly worn out, early in 1810 – beside his watch on Toulon and his support of Spanish resurgence, was to maintain the security of Malta and Sicily. The Navy had swept enemy trade from the Mediterranean except for inconsiderable coastal traffic, but it still flowed from the Levant, now in British hands, and the merchants of Malta had as a result grown wealthy. As for Sicily, while nothing Collingwood could do could prevent French military strength from occupying Naples, the maintenance of a British force in Sicily was considered essential by successive British governments. There it remained throughout the war, an effective bar to French schemes of conquest beyond the Italian mainland. And it was mainly from Sicily, on Collingwood's initiative, that an expedition was mounted in 1809 which seized the Ionian Islands from French occupation; it was one of his last services. Moreover, not only was the Mediterranean dominated by British sea power, it was the same story in the Adriatic, where Nelson's brilliant pupil, Sir William Hoste, won a miniature but clear-cut victory at Lissa in 1811.

Only once was Collingwood threatened during his years of power, and that was by a sortie which Ganteaume made from Toulon in 1808 to the Ionian Islands. The move failed dismally. Ganteaume's ships were scattered and did nothing; but Collingwood failed to intercept them though at one time, off the Gulf of Taranto, he was so near doing so that he issued a memorandum to his captains telling them exactly how he proposed to fight a fleet action. His method would have been a blend of Nelson's two-column approach, as at Trafalgar, and Howe's insistence on all captains breaking through the enemy line and engaging them from the leeward position to prevent escape. The memorandum had a certain rigidity for what Collingwood could never manage, and it was his only fault as a sea officer, was to delegate. Immensely able, ceaselessly thoughtful, strategically wise beyond the capacity of most naval officers, he insisted on doing everything himself, even to the extent of dispensing altogether with the services of a captain-of-the-fleet, who could have eased so much of his burden, and making his flag captains (in spite of his personal affection for some of them) mere cyphers.

Britain was fortunate in having such admirals as Collingwood and Saumarez in charge in two such key areas as the Mediterranean and the Baltic at so critical a time in the war, and it is hard to decide which of the two rendered services more important to their country. By the time Collingwood died, Wellington's army was well established in Portugal and Spain, and the work of the admiral's successors, first Cotton and then Pellew, became a matter of routine. Saumarez, on the other hand, faced a critical situation when Alexander and Bonaparte fell out, as they inevitably did, and when Napoleon, determined to emulate and exceed the ambitions of the hero-king, Charles XII of Sweden, attempted an invasion of Russia. If successful, this would have made him master of Europe from Moscow to Madrid.

Meanwhile, outside European waters, Britain was meeting with mixed fortune. Her predominance in the West Indies, and in the Far East, was not in question, but her resources were so extended that it was never absolute, particularly in the West Indies. In 1810 she took Mauritius from the French, and in the following year she defeated a Dutch force off Java, of which for a time she assumed control, just as she had done in the Philippines during the Seven Years War.

As against these successes a succession of unfortunate incidents involving the search of United States vessels for deserters from the British Navy brought about a war with America which could have been avoided with a little more tact and forbearance on the British side. At the outset, the Americans won a succession of frigate actions which gave a salutary shock to a Service which, since Trafalgar, had grown altogether too complacent.

The Americans also won control of a large part of the Great Lakes system of Canada and caused a considerable diversion of military forces which would have been better employed against the French. The war ended before the fate of Bonaparte was finally decided, but not before Washington had been burnt by British forces, or before a great deal of ill-feeling had been generated on both sides. Had a Collingwood or a Saumarez been given charge of the North American and West Indies Stations at the right time it seems certain, looking back on the period with the advantage of hindsight, that the war could have been avoided to the lasting benefit of Anglo-American relations.

Bonaparte's great march into Russia in 1812 turned into a disaster of the first order, and his discomfiture was increased by the fact that, throughout his campaign, Saumarez remained in control of the Baltic, including the furthest reaches of the Gulf of Finland. The effect of this fact, on Prussia particularly, can scarcely be over-emphasised though it is generally overlooked. Another event in the north of much significance was the deposition of Gustavus IV of Sweden as a direct result of the loss of Finland to Russia, and the strange choice of Bernadotte, a Marshal of France, as Crown Prince. Bernadotte, against all expectations, ultimately took an anti-French line in foreign politics and was known to have been impressed by the array of sea power which Saumarez was careful to arrange as the marshal was escorted across the Baltic from Germany to his new country.

In 1813, after Bonaparte's army, or what was left of it, had withdrawn from Russia, there came about the last of the anti-French coalitions – Britain, Russia, Austria, Prussia, and Sweden. The formal constituents were familiar but this time there was a difference, for Bonaparte's aggressive habits and rapacity had aroused the spirit of nationalism in Germany as well as in Spain and Portugal, and at what became known as the 'Battle of the Nations', fought at Leipsic in October 1813, he was utterly defeated. The way became open for the allies to march to Paris, which they entered the following year after Bonaparte's exile to Elba.

So far as the war at sea was concerned, the main events were now over, and it was for the diplomatists to secure what had been won by force of arms. Bonaparte's overthrow had been the result of the

Commodore Sir William Hoste, who commanded the British naval forces in the Adriatic towards the close of the Napoleonic War, where he fought the successful Battle of Lissa in 1811 which prevented the French from occupying the island

The action between the British frigate *Shannon* and the American frigate *Chesapeake*, fought off Boston on 1st June, 1813. This picture, one of a set of lithographs by Arthur Schetky, engraved by L. Haghe, shows the *Shannon* raking the *Chesapeake* with her broadside

pay for the aberration of one man, and it was fitting that when the Emperor, defeated in battle for the last time, and fleeing from a country which had suffered so much on his behalf, enquired about a passage to the United States, he should have been taken on board an English ship of the line off the coast of France. It was the *Bellerophon*, and a better choice could not have been contrived. The *Bellerophon*'s guns had thundered at the Glorious First of June. She had taken a major part in the attack on *L'Orient* at the Battle of the Nile. She had been in the very thick of it at Trafalgar. She was on service, in war and peace, for half a century.

Bonaparte was interested, as a technician of war, in all the ship's arrangements. He admired the discipline and neatness of her company. He charmed her officers and men, as was his way. When the ship anchored off Plymouth, as she eventually did, the great man was enabled to examine closely the coast of the island which, during all his years of power, had been his most implacable enemy. He even wrote to the Prince Regent suggesting sanctuary ashore, but the Regent and his Government had more sense than to listen to his plea. The island of Elba, scene of his first exile, had not been far enough from France. St. Helena, in the wastes of the South Atlantic, was fixed upon and it was highly appropriate. There Bonaparte could be kept confined. There he could be guarded by the Royal Navy. From there he was never likely to disturb again the peace of the world.

The long war had left the Royal Navy in so predominant a position that, over the ensuing decades, it was actually to suffer from it. The lessons of the sea campaign were never properly digested – so much so that the necessity for convoy and its military advantages in war became forgotten, while Nelson, from being the highly successful tactical commander such as he was thought of by all his contemporaries, became exalted into a patron saint.

Two matters were not perceived by the leaders of thought in the generations which followed those which had borne the burden of the war with France. The first was that Nelson's method was empirical. It was as misguided to try to extract any *general* lesson from the tactics employed at Trafalgar as it would have been to analyse those to be drawn from the battle of St. Vincent, which though on a smaller scale was also spectacularly successful. The second was the virtue of initiative, fostered within a general

effects of rising nationalism, of the immense land spaces and resources of Russia which could absorb and annihilate even the most intimidating invader, and the silent, ceaseless pressure of sea power. The first Treaty of Paris, the terms of which were in general confirmed after Bonaparte's return to France in 1815, gave Britain many overseas bases which became part of the foundation upon which she built an Empire which endured for more than a century. She kept Malta and Heligoland, those two well-placed islands, the second of which was relinquished in favour of Zanzibar towards the end of the century. She remained established at the Cape of Good Hope, in Mauritius, and in Ceylon. She added Tobago and St. Lucia to her West Indian possessions, and she assumed a Protectorate over the Ionian Islands. France was restricted to the boundaries of 1790, which was little enough to show for the loss of millions of lives and the expenditure of unreckonable treasure which Bonaparte had caused in his attempt to exalt himself. It was a stiff price to

Napoleon on board HMS *Bellerophon* after surrending to
Captain Maitland in 1815. This was the occasion on which he
is supposed to have said that wherever there was enough water
to sail a ship, there would be found an English ship of the line.
From the painting by Sir William Orchardson.

though not rigid framework of fleet instructions.
This point was in time lost sight of entirely, for the
naval authorities seemed to value initiative less and
less. The advent of steam, and later inventions such
as the improved breech-loading gun and the torpedo,
seemed merely to add confusion to rigidity.

Certainly the span between Howe and Collingwood had been an heroic age of naval endeavour,
one which would always be looked back upon with
justifiable pride. It was not only the succession of
victories but the proper understanding of the
flexibility and pressure of sea power which was so
remarkable. It extended to statesmen, and it is note-
worthy that Pitt, son of one of the greatest war
ministers Britain ever produced, was a particular
friend of Nelson, whose loss upset him more than
any other single event in his public life.

Experience in war is one of the best teachers, no
doubt the best of all. But the fees are high, and the
lessons themselves, however valuable, may soon

be forgotten. By 1815 the effects of British sea power
were felt throughout the world, and would continue
so for most of the following century. Yet stronger
opposition than the Navy ever met with must have
borne fruit in the trials which were to face it during
the two world wars of out own time. During their
course many matters had to be relearned. By far the
most important was the necessity to cultivate
initiative, already referred to, and the very serious
effect on the economy of an island realm which may
result from a determined, ruthless, and efficiently
conducted *guerre de course*.

Extravagant claims are sometimes made as to the
value of history. It is safe to say that if the Royal
Navy of the later 19th and early 20th century had
studied with close attention the unfolding of the
events of the struggle with Napoleon, and drawn the
more obvious conclusions, immense loss in life,
ships, and equipment would have been saved when
it faced its next large-scale and protracted tests.

Opposite: The battle of Martinique, fought in 1780 between a British fleet of 21 ships of the line commanded by
Lord Rodney and a French fleet of 23 under de Guichen. The action was indecisive, frustrated by the inadequacies
of the British signalling system. From the painting by Thomas Luny. *Overleaf:* The death of Nelson, by D. Dighton.
In the centre foreground is one of the midshipmen of the *Victory* firing at the mizen top of the *Redoubtable* from
which the fatal shot had come

CHAPTER 15

*The 'Pax Britannica' – Development of Steam Propulsion –
Guns and Armour – Torpedoes and Submarines –
Administrative Changes – Uniform and Pay*

DONALD MACINTYRE

When Napoleon Bonaparte's brilliant career and his imperial ambitions were finally halted in 1815 it was fitting that he should have surrendered to the captain of a British man-of-war, H.M.S. *Bellerophon.* For, more than any other factor, it was British supremacy at sea that had foiled him in his great ambitions. 'Wherever there is water to float a ship', he is said to have complained, 'we are sure to find you English in the way.' And in the course of the long struggle the Royal Navy had built up a prestige that was to be unchallenged for a century.

This was to enable it to ride supreme on the oceans of the world during the years which followed, its power and quality unquestioned, a state of affairs which was eventually to breed a dangerous complacency and mask a deterioration of fighting efficiency behind a façade of glittering splendour and impeccable ceremonial. The mask had slipped briefly during the American War of 1812 when American frigates repeatedly defeated their British equivalents where, too often, spit and polish had been applied at the expense of gunnery practice. The defeat of the U.S.S. *Chesapeake* by H.M.S. *Shannon* had both demonstrated this fact and, by restoring British reputation, caused it to be quickly forgotten again.

The establishment of a gunnery school in 1832 in H.M.S. *Excellent* at Portsmouth as a result of the persistent advocacy of the artillery expert, General Sir Howard Douglas, as well as that of Sir Philip Broke who had commanded the *Shannon,* went some way towards rectifying this state of affairs; nevertheless fighting efficiency continued to be subordinated to smartness of appearance and seamanship until the

reforms led by Admiral Sir Percy Scott at the beginning of the 20th century.

Another early though tentative step towards modernisation of training was the appropriation in 1836 of the Royal Naval College at Portsmouth as a centre for the instruction of half-pay naval officers of all ranks 'in the higher branches of science of their profession'.

Although the training and fighting efficiency of the personnel of the Royal Navy had begun to be insidiously eroded by the complacency bred of a long run of victorious sea fights in the Napoleonic War, materially the pre-eminence of the Navy was maintained, at least in the first half of the 19th century, by Britain's undoubted position in the forefront of the industrial revolution, and by the achievements of her engineers, particularly in the invention and development of the steam engine and its application to marine use. The first steamer to be put to practical use had been William Symington's paddle tug *Charlotte Dundas* in 1801. Although the Admiralty did not adopt steam propulsion until 1822 when it acquired its first paddle steamer, the *Comet,* this was to some extent because the paddle wheels and boxes occupied the space required for a ship's own broadside of cannon and were themselves very vulnerable to the gunfire of an enemy. The *Comet* and several similar ships completed in the next few years were employed as tugs or for other auxiliary functions; but over the next twenty years a number of steam paddle-driven sloops and frigates usually mounting single guns in the bow and stern were added to the Navy List, and continued to be so after the introduction of screw propulsion in 1836.

Opposite: Lord Howe, with drawn sword, standing on the quarter-deck of the *Queen Charlotte* at the Battle of the Glorious First of June, 1794. On the right, supported by his friends, is Captain Neville of the Queen's Regiment, who was mortally wounded in the action

A painting, by Louis Garneray, of the last battle fought under sail, the Battle of Navarino Bay
in 1827, in which a combined fleet of British, French, and Russian ships, under the command of
Admiral Sir Edward Codrington, defeated a Turkish fleet for the cause of Greek freedom

HMS *Agamemnon*. The first British steam-propelled ship-of-the-line to be built (1852) as such. The development of such ships, inaugurated in 1850 by the French *Napoléon*, devalued the Royal Navy's accumulated superiority in sailing ships-of-the-line and enabled her rival to achieve equality for the first time since Trafalgar

HMS *Warrior*. Britain's first iron-clad, laid down in May 1859. She and her sister-ship *Black Prince* were built in reply to the French Navy's first four ironclads, *Gloire*, *Invincible*, *Normandie* and *Couronne*. Both British ships had iron hulls with 4½ins. of wrought-iron armour on a backing of 18ins. of teak. The French ships had similar armour but, except for the *Couronne*, had wooden hulls

In a period of rapid colonial expansion, with minor affrays taking place all over the world in support of trading posts and in the suppression of the slave trade and of piracy, such vessels proved invaluable. Paddle gunboats played a vital part in the Opium War with China, 1841–42, though they belonged for the most part to the Honourable East India Company's fleet.

The war was basically a dispute over the right to trade with the Chinese in the face of opposition by the Imperial Chinese Government, though the origins were very complicated and are overshadowed by the discreditable nature of the trade itself, the illegal import of opium from India in exchange for Chinese tea, porcelain, and silks.

In 1841 a British squadron was despatched which eventually comprised four sailing ships of the line and a score of smaller men-of-war, including a paddle steamer sloop, covering a number of troopships and accompanied by a flotilla of the East India Company's steamers, some of them armed. It established a blockade of the Chinese coast, occupied the port of Chusan, and eventually, after destroying the forts at the Bocca Tigris which commanded the entrance to the Pearl River, forced its way up to Canton, destroyed the defences, and re-established the foreign trading 'factories' there. The port of Amoy was occupied and its defences dismantled, while in the north Tinghae and Chinhae were captured and occupied.

In the following year operations were renewed and it was not until Woosung, Shanghai and Chinkiang, far up the Yangtse-kiang river, had been captured that the Chinese Government agreed to negotiate for peace. The treaty signed at Nanking on 29th August 1842 opened the ports of Canton, Amoy, Foochow, Ningpo, and Shanghai to trade and ceded the island of Hong Kong to Britain in perpetuity.

Introduction of the screw propeller enabled steam propulsion to be applied to major units of the fleet, and in 1850 the 80-gun screw-propelled two-decker *Agamemnon* was launched. Her engine was essentially an auxiliary, primarily of use for entering and leaving harbour, and was viewed with disgust by the executive officers as coal dust and soot befouled her spotless deck. The reluctance to move out of the age of sail was to be found at all levels of the naval hierarchy, the Admiralty's main reason being that

steam could make its huge fleet of sailing ships of the line obsolete. The conservatism which was affecting progress in the Royal Navy can be gauged from the fact that the French Navy had two years earlier commissioned the 90-gun screw-driven ship of the line *Napoléon* which achieved a speed of nearly 14 knots and made successful long sea passages under steam alone. Both of these ships, with some other British and French screw ships of the line and a number of smaller British steamers, took part in operations in the Black Sea during the Crimean War in 1854 and, though no enemy fleet opposed them, effectively demonstrated by their mobility and independence of the wind that the age of sail in naval warfare was at an end.

In the Baltic, meanwhile, a large Anglo-French fleet which included 13 British and one French screw ships of the line bombarded and captured the fortress of Bomarsund in the Aland Islands during 1854. In the following year the allied fleet heavily bombarded Sweaborg but in this case the traditional superiority of forts over ships was confirmed and occupation of the fortress was not attempted.

The French, of course, had everything to gain from a revolution in naval material and it was they, under the influence of General Paixhans, who first supplied explosive shell to naval guns and gave their ships armour which such projectiles made necessary. The first sea-going armour-clad, the French *Gloire*, launched in 1859, was countered by the British *Warrior* in the following year which was armoured in addition to its iron construction. Though rated as steam frigates on account of their mounting only a single tier of guns, these were in fact the first capital ships of the age of steam. Both navies also introduced at this time the rifled, breech-loading gun, but whereas the French adopted the successful interrupted screw thread type, the Armstrong breech mechanism accepted by the Admiralty proved unreliable and unsafe. The Royal Navy then reverted to muzzle-loading for its larger guns until 1881.

At the same time advances in technology were enabling bigger guns to be manufactured. As the generally held concept of a sea fight was still that of two ships pounding each other at close range, a few large rifled pieces able to deliver massively destructive blows came to be preferred to the broadside tiers of numerous smaller cannon. To permit these fewer guns to cover a wide arc of fire, the old gun-carriages were replaced by pivot mountings. This in turn gave birth to the idea of enclosing the gun, or a pair of them, in armoured turrets revolving with the gun, leaving only the muzzles exposed. The proponent of the concept in France was the great ship designer, Dupuy de Lôme; in England it was Captain Cowper Coles.

It was John Ericsson, however, a Swedish engineer living in America, who had the first opportunity to develop the idea when in 1862 he built the *Monitor* for the Federal Government of the United States at the beginning of the American Civil War. The *Monitor* relied solely on her steam engines for propulsion, another innovation; but with a freeboard of barely one foot she could not be considered a sea-going ship.

The Royal Navy still gave their ships a full rig of sails as well as steam propulsion and were to continue to do so with some of them for another fifteen years. Cowper Coles's effort to combine this with a turret arrangement for the main armament ended in disaster when his ship, the *Captain*, capsized in 1871; while in the Admiralty's own version of such a ship, the *Monarch*, the rigging offered so much obstruction that the turrets, sited between the masts had no better a field of fire than normal broadside of individual guns.

The time to abandon sail rig had obviously come. This had already been accepted in the design of a number of coast defence ships, basically developments of the *Monitor* concept, such as the British *Glatton* and *Hotspur*. In 1873 the first battleship to rely solely on steam power, H.M.S. *Devastation*, joined the fleet, with twin turrets fore and aft and a solitary signal mast only. Meanwhile a ceaseless competition for dominance between iron armour protection and the gun was leading to an ever-increasing thickness of the one and of the calibre of the other, culminating in the *Inflexible*, launched in 1876 mounting two diagonally sited twin 16-inch turrets and protected by 24 inches of wrought iron armour.

The next development was that of steel armour plate by Schneider's of Le Creusot. As British steel manufacturers lacked the technique to emulate the French firm, the Admiralty was forced to accept 'compound' armour instead, in which a steel face was welded on to iron, which was to remain in use in the Royal Navy until 1892. At the same time impro-

HMS *Devastation*. Completed in 1873, she marked a revolution in capital ship design, being the first to dispense with any masts and yards for sail. Borrowing much from the monitor concept in her design, (her low freeboard, deliberately incorporated to effect a saving in armour, resulted in her running more or less awash in a seaway) she was at first universally condemned. She proved more successful than her detractors expected, however, and was the prototype for subsequent classes of battleship

HMS *Captain*. Built in 1873 to the design of Captain Cowper Coles R.N., an early enthusiast for the replacement of the broadside battery of numerous guns of moderate size by a few large guns on revolving, centre-line mountings housed in turrets, the *Captain* was an attempt to combine the turret arrangement with a full rig of sails. Her low freeboard proved fatal and she capsized in a squall, taking her designer and the majority of her company to the bottom with her

HMS *Victoria*. Completed in 1890, she and her sister ship *Sans Pareil*, were the last exemplars of the age of the 'monster' gun, mounting two 16.25-inch, 110-ton breech-loaders in an armoured turret forward. The design of subsequent British battleships favoured twin turrets of smaller (13.5-inch and, later, 12-inch) guns, one turret forward and one aft. The *Victoria* was lost in 1893 in collision with the *Camperdown* during close-order, precise manoeuvres

vements in the quality of gun propellants led on the one hand to increased muzzle velocity, on the other to the need for longer barrels. The former made smaller calibre guns acceptable, 12-inch or 13.5-inch being mounted in all but one of the *Admiral* class of battleships launched between 1882 and 1885 and, with two exceptions, 13.5-inches was to be the maximum calibre for the next 30 years. Longer barrels, making muzzle-loading of turret guns increasingly difficult, finally forced the Admiralty to revert to breech-loading, using an interrupted thread form of breech mechanism. This also permitted the mounting of the turret on top of a fixed armoured barbette inside which the ammunition was hoisted to be loaded into the breech, a form of mounting installed in the ultimate and, at last, homogeneous *Majestic* class of battleship, launched between 1895 and 1896.

By this time armour plate, too, had been greatly improved, first by the addition of nickel and chrome to the steel and then by methods of face-hardening, the first of which was invented by the American engineer H. A. Harvey in 1891 and adopted by the leading British steel manufacturers. Finally abandoning compound armour, the Admiralty were able to give the *Majestic* class an 8-inch belt of Harvey steel as compared with 18 inches of compound armour in the previous *Royal Sovereign* class.

Yet another development which had greatly affected battleship design had arisen out of the invention of the locomotive torpedo by Robert Whitehead in 1867. Though the Admiralty had been quick to appreciate the possibilities of the new weapon and had been the first to buy the rights of manufacture from the inventor, and though the British boat-building firms of Thornycroft and Yarrow had been the pioneers in production of fast steamboats to mount the explosive-headed spars which up to now had constituted the torpedo, it was the Russians and French who led the world in acquiring them and equipping them with locomotive torpedoes.

As with steam propulsion and, later, with the submarine, the British were far from enthusiastic about a development which threatened the ships on which their supremacy rested. When the traditional enemy, France, began to build up a numerous force of torpedo boats equipped with Whitehead's new weapon, it became necessary to provide the larger fleet units with a secondary anti-torpedo boat armament. The first to be so equipped were the *Admiral*-class in which the central citadel was elongated to enclose a battery of 6-inch guns of the new breech-loading type. From this time onwards the anti-torpedo boat secondary armament became a standard feature of battleships.

The requirement for a rapid rate of fire to combat attacks by torpedo boats encouraged the development of a quick-firing gun by Armstrongs in 1887 in which the interrupted screw breech block was opened or closed by a single motion of the breech lever. A rate of fire of 14 rounds a minute was achieved with the first 4.7-inch quick-firer as compared to two rounds a minute with the ordinary breech mechanism.

While these various developments in the make-up of the battleship had been taking place, its propulsion machinery had, of course, been advancing in power and complexity also. The engines had progressed from the early single-cylinder side-lever type through a variety of compound engines to the triple-expansion machinery which had been the standard since 1887 when H.M.S. *Victoria* became the first battleship to be so fitted. The pursuit of higher steam pressures, economy in fuel and reduction in weight had led to the development of the water-tube boiler as opposed to the earlier fire-tube type, and after a controversy over their respective merits lasting for more than a decade, the water-tube type finally superseded the other.

With the adoption of machinery of this type, the mounting of a main armament of four 12-inch breech-loading guns in two twin turret-barbettes, armour protection of Harvey (later Krupp) steel, and a secondary armament of quick-firers, as in the *Majestic* class, there came to an end the repeated innovations and changes in design which during the previous thirty years had provided a battle fleet of heterogeneous ships of widely varying armament and performance. No method of directing the fire of the guns had yet been devised and battle was still visualised as an affair of point-blank mutual bombardment although the guns were capable of accurate fire at a range of several miles. During the next ten years, when the Royal Navy began to expand in response to the German challenge, the additional units of the battle fleet were more or less standard ships not greatly dissimilar to the *Majestic*.

Such was the battle fleet maintained by the Royal Navy, at a strength equal to that of any two other major powers, as the ultimate weapon backing British foreign policy. Development of other types of steam men-of-war descended from the frigates, corvettes, and sloops of the age of sail had followed parallel lines. The steam sloops and gunboats, mostly paddle driven, which had comprised the earliest steam men-of-war have been discussed earlier. Soon after 1850, however, larger 'cruising ships' with displacements of between 1,500 and 5,700 tons for flag-showing and policing duties on foreign stations began to be built. Impetus towards construction of large cruisers with a fair turn of speed was given by the impressive performance of the U.S.S. *Wampanoag* completed in 1867 with the expressed function of commerce raiding, which achieved a speed of more than 17 knots. The immediate result was ships such as the *Inconstant* and *Shah* of some 6,000 tons armed with muzzle-loading

guns of 10-inch, 9-inch, 7-inch, and 6-inch calibres and equipped to launch the first Whitehead torpedoes. The shortcomings of such unarmoured, slow-shooting and ponderous ships was exposed when the *Shah* was unable to overcome the piratical Peruvian monitor *Huascar* during an engagement in 1877 and only escaped destruction herself through the poor shooting of her opponent.

The application of compound armour of sufficient thickness to be effective, however, resulted in even more unwieldy ships such as the *Shannon*, *Nelson*, and *Northampton* which were designated 2nd-class battleships. A solution to the problem was sought in the provision of a lower protective deck, only a few inches thick, but with sloping sides extending below the water line which, it was believed, would deflect a shell and prevent it penetrating to the vitals of the ship. The era of the protected cruiser really began with the construction of the *Esmeralda* by Armstrongs for the Chilean Navy in 1883 which had a speed of 18.3 knots and set the fashion by discarding sail rig, though this was not followed by the Royal Navy until 1890 when the *Blake* joined the fleet.

With the advent of the quick-firing gun, the 1st-class protected cruiser became a feature of all the major navies, growing steadily in size to culminate in the British *Powerful* and *Terrible* of 14,200 tons in 1895, while smaller 2nd- and 3rd-class protected cruisers also proliferated. As the effectiveness of high explosive shells increased, however, the protective deck came to be considered inadequate and when, with the development of Harvey, Schneider, and Krupp steel, it became possible to give them a protective belt, the armoured cruiser came to supersede the protected cruiser.

Their role in war, from the British point of view, was never clear, as they were too slow for scouting duties with the fleet and insufficiently armed to take their place in the line; it would seem that they were built solely in reply to similar ships of the French Navy who pioneered their design. In years to come they were to be castigated by Admiral Fisher as 'too weak to fight and too slow to run away', and would be replaced by, on the one hand battle-cruisers, on the other unarmoured, fast light cruisers.

As mentioned earlier torpedo boats had a more immediate appeal for other navies, and their chief impact on the Royal Navy was at first felt in the introduction of secondary batteries in battleships.

By the end of 1895, however, the number of such craft in other navies, particularly the French who led with 195 torpedo boats compared to the British total of 82, caused other antidotes to be sought. A type of craft known as a torpedo gunboat, or more colloquially torpedo 'catcher', was accordingly produced. They proved too slow and unwieldy to overhaul and engage the torpedo boats, whose speed was increasing year by year, and too conspicuous by night when the torpedo boats were intended to attack. The first of a new type, therefore, the torpedo-boat-destroyer, was ordered in 1893 and was launched as H.M.S. *Havock* in the autumn of that year by Yarrow's.

So successful was the *Havock* that a large number of others of a similar design was ordered from various yards, and each year a programme of some thirty or more further boats was authorised. These were driven by triple-expansion reciprocating engines and, though known familiarly as '30-knotters', few of them actually attained this speed in service. Meanwhile, however, the steam turbine, already in use to drive electric generators ashore, had been adapted for marine propulsion by the Hon. C. A. Parsons and had been spectacularly demonstrated in 1897 in his small craft, the *Turbinia*, at the Diamond Jubilee Review. Two years later similar engines were installed in the torpedo-boat destroyer *Viper* which attained the speed of 36 58 knots during her trials in 1900.

Another turbine-driven destroyer, the *Cobra*, was equally successful. Both these ships, however, were built with very light scantlings and when the *Cobra* broke her back in heavy weather and foundered, a somewhat illogical reaction set in against turbines and high speed, so that the next type of destroyer built for the Royal Navy was not only more strongly built but also reverted to reciprocating engines.

One more type of warship remained to be acquired by the Royal Navy to make the fleet complete prior to the advent of the aeroplane. This was the submarine. As long ago as 1776 the flagship of the British squadron in New York harbour during the War of American Independence had narrowly escaped destruction by David Bushnell's ingenious submersible craft, the *Turtle*. Twenty-eight years later Robert Fulton, another American, had offered his *Nautilus* to the Admiralty to have it rejected by Lord St. Vincent, at the time First Lord of the Admiralty, who considered that the Prime Minister

(Pitt) 'was the greatest fool that ever existed to encourage a mode of warfare which those who commanded the seas did not want and which, if successful, would deprive them of it'.

Although submersibles were built and operated with some success during the American Civil War and though experiments were made with varying success with submersibles in France, England, Spain, Sweden, and the United States in succeeding years, St. Vincent's attitude was maintained by the Admiralty until the launching in 1899 of Maxime Laubeuf's *Narval* at Cherbourg, a 200-ton ocean-going submarine, made it clear that such craft were practical propositions which could no longer be ignored. Relations with France being at that time far from cordial, it was to the United States, where a much less seaworthy submersible had been built after years of experimentation by Mr. John Holland, that the Admiralty turned and now signed a contract for five similar boats to be built by Vickers Sons and Maxim at Barrow-in-Furness. The Holland boat, though very small, had all the attributes necessary for development of a successful submarine except one – the double hull design of Laubeuf's *Narval* which gave it full buoyancy when on the surface and so made it properly sea-going as compared to the Holland type which proceeded 'awash' on the surface. British submarines continued to suffer from this weakness of design for the next decade, restricting them to a harbour-defence or, at best, a coastal role and concealing the true potential of such craft.

While the Royal Navy was undergoing the metamorphosis from a fleet of wooden sailing ships armed with the primitive muzzle-loading cannon not vastly different from those which had harried the Armada up the Channel in 1588, to one of steam-driven steel vessels mounting breech-loading, shell-firing guns worked by mechanical power, and locomotive torpedoes, changes in the organisation, administration and discipline also took place though not on the same scale as in material. Indeed, though the process of material modernisation which, in the main, began at the time of the Russian War in 1854, proceeded thereafter with such bewildering rapidity for the next forty years that ships and their equipment became obsolete almost before they were completed, the conditions of service for officers and men moved slowly and reluctantly into the new era.

The first major change in the administration of

HMS *Havock*. In 1892 torpedo-boats being built by the French attained speeds of over 27 knots. Rear Admiral J. A. Fisher, Third Sea Lord, appealed to Alfred Yarrow to produce a counter to these craft. The result was the first torpedo boat destroyer *Havock*, completed in 1893, mounting one 12-pdr and three 6-pdr guns and three 18-inch torpedo tubes and having a speed of 27 knots. Thornycroft, Yarrow and Laird each built two roughly similar boats. Their success led to 36 further boats being ordered in the following year.

the Navy took place in 1832, when the old system of divided control was ended by the abolition of the semi-independent Navy and Victualling Boards – the Civil Departments of the Navy – and the vesting of their powers in the Board of Admiralty. In place of the numerous Controllers and Commissioners of the Navy Board, of Victualling and of Transports, five separate and independent superintendents of departments were created under the Board of Admiralty collectively and the Lords of the Admiralty individually. The Admiralty Board itself was reconstructed at various times until in 1885 it assumed the shape it was to hold, with minor adjustments, for the next seventy-eight years and one which on the whole was to serve the Navy well.

The conclusion of the Napoleonic Wars resulted naturally in a huge reduction in the size of the Navy. Between 1813 and 1817 it was reduced from 99 ships of the line, 495 cruisers and 140,000 seamen and Royal Marines to 13, 89 and 19,000 respectively. So far as the lower deck personnel were concerned, the reduction in numbers was achieved by simple discharge. The resultant hardship and even destitution for many of the older ratings, a shameful consequence of the country's neglect of its servants, did not directly affect the Navy. Amongst the officers, however, where no regular scheme for retirement existed for post-captains and above, while even below this rank arrangements were very limited, the reduction of the fleet led to large numbers of all ranks unemployed on half-pay, choking the active lists and blocking promotion.

HMS *Powerful*. Built in 1895, she and her sister-ship *Terrible* were the largest (14,200 tons) 'protected' cruisers to be built, mounting two 9.2-inch and sixteen 6-inch quick-firing guns. Increased effectiveness of shells and development at this time of hardened steel armour led to the supersession of such ships by armoured cruisers

As a result Commanders-in-Chief were likely to be 75 years of age at least and sometimes were approaching 80. Lower ranks were proportionately equally too old for their appointments. A Royal Commission appointed in 1838 made a number of recommendations and a general scheme for retirement came into force in 1847. In 1851, an Order in Council further reduced the number of flag officers, captains, commanders, and lieutenants. Even so, the naval commanders in the Black Sea and the Baltic during the Crimean War were nearly 70 years old and the Navy's disappointing performance was attributed partly to the antiquity of the majority of its flag officers and captains.

The sub-division of the various ranks of flag officers into those of the Red, White, and Blue squadrons respectively was abolished in 1864 when admirals' flags as worn today were established and it was ordered that all H.M. Ships in commission should fly the White Ensign. Other changes in officers' ranks were the transformation in 1867 of the several grades of master into navigating lieutenants, sub-lieutenants, and midshipmen, the substitution of the title sub-lieutenant for that of mate in 1861, and the creation of the ranks of chief gunner, chief boatswain and chief carpenter in 1864. Officers' pay, which remained unchanged from the end of the Napoleonic Wars until the middle of the century, increased only very slightly between then and 1900. Officers' uniforms which in their general shape conformed to the fashion followed by the gentleman ashore, underwent frequent changes in those features which indicated the rank of the wearer, such as collar badges, buttons, cuff rings, and epaulettes. With the introduction of the monkey-jacket in 1889 and a general codification of the regulations two years later, however, a uniform approximating to that of today was finally introduced.

The recruitment, education, and training of naval officers received very little attention until 1854 when an old ship of the line, the *Illustrious*, was commissioned at Portsmouth as a stationary training ship for naval cadets. Up to this time cadets had gone straight to sea upon nomination to pick up their professional education as best they could from the naval instructors. The *Illustrious* was replaced on 1st January 1859 by the *Britannia*, an old 120-gun ship built in 1820 which was moved first to Portland and finally, in 1863, to moorings at Dartmouth. A second and larger *Britannia* which replaced the first in 1869 was to continue to function as the training establishment for officers for the remainder of the century, with sea-going training ships attached until, in 1885, a regular training squadron was established.

Technical training of officers in gunnery was conducted mainly in H.M.S. *Excellent*, mentioned earlier, until 1891, when the Gunnery School was established ashore on Whale Island, a piece of reclaimed land in Portsmouth Harbour. A second gunnery school housed afloat was established at Devonport in 1856, and subsequently another to serve the Chatham Division at Sheerness. Instruction in mining, in torpedo operation and maintenance, and in electrical engineering which was made the responsibility of torpedo specialists, was established afloat in H.M.S. *Vernon* at Portsmouth in 1876 and H.M.S. *Defiance* at Devonport in 1884. The R.N. College at Greenwich for the advanced training of officers in theoretical subjects was opened in 1873, while the training of naval engineers was moved from H.M.S. *Marlborough* to Keyham College in 1880.

Conditions of service for men on the lower deck retained the general pattern of Nelson's day for much of the 19th century. Lack of amenities for recreation in combination with the issue of a large daily ration of rum – half a pint until 1823, reduced then to a quarter of a pint when tea and cocoa were added to the naval dietary – was for a long while the cause of much drunkenness and consequent insubordination countered by the punishment of flogging, which was not finally suspended until 1879. A great improvement however, came about as a result of the further reduction of the rum ration to one-eighth of a pint in 1850. Although from 1825 onwards various uniform regulations were promulgated, they were little heeded and wide variations in the sailors' dress existed between ship and ship according to each captain's often eccentric whim, until 1857 when a uniform was finally established.

The first step towards modernising the career structure on the lower deck came in 1853 when, in place of the old system of signing on a crew for a commission and paying them off on completion, a system of continuous service was introduced under which a man engaged for ten years. The men's wages remained the same (£28 17s. 11d. a year for an able seaman), but extra pay for good conduct badges, for re-engagement, and the creation of numerous new and specially paid ratings improved the prospects for an ambitious and capable seaman. Even so it was to be a long time before an attractive career could be offered, and great difficulties were experienced in manning the fleet until widespread improvements in victualling, the free issue of kit and bedding, etc., were made as a result of recommendations made by a Royal Commission which reported in 1859, and the establishment of training ships for boys at Devonport, Portland, and Portsmouth between 1860 and 1862.

From this time onwards the quality of the naval personnel made steady progress and was to earn the admiration and affection of the British public for its conduct in the innumerable expeditions and affrays arising out of the period of colonial expansion and the imposition of the 'Pax Britannica' on large areas of the world. The exploits of naval brigades in Africa, in China, and during the Boer War, and the spectacular naval reviews staged at intervals at Spithead, allied to energetic and skilful propaganda by politically inclined naval officers such as Lord Charles Beresford, awoke a keen public interest in the Royal Navy leading to financial support by Parliament unprecedented in time of peace. Thus when British naval supremacy was challenged by the rising power of Germany at the turn of the century the means were at hand to meet the challenge both in quantity and in quality of men and material under the inspiring leadership of Admiral Sir John Fisher.

At the same time as the *Dreadnought* Fisher brought out the fast armoured cruiser, later called battlecruiser, of which the first to be laid down was HMS *Invincible*. Carrying eight 12-inch guns, these ships had a speed of $25\frac{1}{2}$ knots. The *Invincible* was Admiral Sturdee's flagship at the Battle of the Falkland Islands in 1914 and was sunk at Jutland two years later

CHAPTER 16

The German Challenge, 1900-14 – Fisher and the
Dreadnought – *The building race with Germany –*
A new concept of naval war – Fisher's legacy of a
revitalised Royal Navy

PETER KEMP

Sir John Arbuthnot Fisher, by the turn of the 19th century, had indeed become a towering figure in the councils of the Royal Navy. He had been a specialist in gunnery and torpedoes, and in the last years of the century had been Commander-in-Chief in the Mediterranean. These years had given the final proof of his qualities as a leader and innovator, and ensured his eventual climb to the top of the naval tree. Much that he saw around him in his post of Commander-in-Chief gave him grave disquiet, and when he left the Mediterranean at the end of his period of command in 1901, his head was full of plans for a new and vastly more efficient navy.

In the dying years of Queen Victoria's reign the European scene was darkened by the emergence of a new naval power. Germany, in 1898 and 1900, had passed two laws to provide herself with a fleet of considerable power, challenging even that of Britain. There could be no doubt against whom such a fleet was aimed; the Kruger telegram of 1896, the partition of the Portuguese colonies in Africa in 1898, the occupation of Samoa in 1899, and German anglophobia during the South African war were sufficient evidence that this was a threat aimed at Britain in her most vulnerable spot.

Fisher came to the Admiralty as Second Sea Lord in 1901, in which post his responsibilities lay with the personnel of the Navy. The new broom began to sweep clean. His first act was to improve the training of the 'young gentlemen' who were to become the future officers of his proposed new Navy. The normal age of entry was 14–15½ years, and cadets spent three terms (one year) in the wooden ships *Britannia* and *Hindustan,* moored permanently in Dartmouth river,

and one term in the training cruiser *Isis*. After that they went to sea as midshipmen in the fleet. Fisher remodelled the officer entry on public school lines. Two colleges were built, a junior at Osborne, in the Isle of Wight, and a senior at Dartmouth. The age of entry was reduced to 12½–13 years, which brought it into line with public school practice, and the two colleges provided four years of education, one-third technical and professional and two-thirds general. This was followed by two terms in the training cruiser, by which time both general and professional education was normally completed.

He made one other innovation. Formerly, all officers who were to become engineers or Royal Marines were separately entered and trained. This practice had tended to perpetuate the social gulf which had long existed in the British Navy between the executive branch and the engineers. Under Fisher's scheme all entered as cadets, were trained together, and only followed their chosen specialisation on completion of their midshipmen's time. In fact, the Royal Marines opted out of this scheme. It still took a good many years for the old prejudices against the engineers to die, but it was nevertheless a step in the right direction. Fisher's further belief, that this new scheme of combined training would make the specialisations interchangeable, never in fact got off the ground. It was asking too much to expect an officer to become an engineer for five or ten years and then return to executive duties, and vice-versa.

At the same time as reorganising the officer entry and training, Fisher gave his attention to lower deck methods of training. He swept away the insanitary

THE NAVY OF SIR JOHN FISHER

hulks in which boy seamen and artificers received their initial training and replaced them with new schools built ashore in the dockyard towns. The accommodation hulks in the three manning ports (Chatham, Portsmouth and Devonport) were similarly condemned and replaced by modern barracks. In the schools an enlightened syllabus replaced the old curriculum which, throughout the years, no one had had the inclination or energy to change.

These reforms aroused the concern and wrath of a number of the more conservative admirals, and there began to build up a distinct division of opinion within the Navy. Those who believed, with Fisher, that the Royal Navy was ripe for change and modernisation were said to be within the 'Fishpond'. Those who disagreed belonged, in the words of Fisher himself, to the 'Syndicate of Discontent', or the 'Yellow Admirals'. Much as one can now applaud Fisher and his great work in shaking out the apathy and the somnolence of the Victorian Navy, his share in the division of the Navy into two camps cast a heavy blot over the final years of his most distinguished career.

After a year as Commander-in-Chief at Portsmouth, following his spell as Second Sea Lord, Fisher returned to the Admiralty in October 1904 as First Sea Lord. His year at Portsmouth had been productive, and his restless brain had formulated an entirely new pattern of naval power designed to meet the threat which was building up against Britain on the other side of the North Sea. His main plan comprised four distinct schemes; the wholesale scrapping of obsolete warships, a radical reorganisation of the reserve fleet, the redistribution of fleets and squadrons to provide an interlocking system of reinforcement in any threatened area, and the introduction into the fleet of a completely new design of capital ship.

The first was a reasonably obvious provision. For too many years there had been a lack of any coherent strategical thought on the best types of ship with which to uphold Britain's imperial role at sea, resulting in a multiplicity of different classes of ship, many with different and mixed armaments which made the problem of stores and replacements difficult and costly. A great many of the ships themselves were completely unsuited to the roles for which they were designed.

In his memorandum on this subject to the First

Lord, Fisher wrote a little scenario:

Venus approaching her fleet at full speed.
Admiral signals: 'What have you seen?'
Venus replies: 'Four funnels hull down.'
Admiral: 'Well, what was behind?'
Venus replies: 'Cannot say; she must have four knots more speed than I had and would have caught me in three hours, so I had to close you at full speed.'
Admiral's logical reply: 'You had better pay off and turn over to something that is some good; you are simply a device for wasting 400 men.'

The final list of useless ships which Fisher produced amounted to a total of 154, of which 17 were battleships. Against the list he wrote in his large, bold hand: 'Scrap the lot.'

In 1904 the general pattern was to divide the reserve fleet into two classes, the fleet reserve and the dockyard reserve, the latter comprising ships under major refit or out of commission but with active service care-and-maintenance parties on board. Nominally the fleet reserve was made up of ships ready for active service, keeping on board a proportion, mainly engineers, of their normal complements. In emergencies, men were drafted from the barracks to bring them to full complement, and they were then supposed to be ready to take their place in the fighting line. But such experience as emerged from the annual manoeuvres demonstrated that the expectation was never realised. It was hardly surprising. Manned by men who had probably never been on board the ships before, it was only natural that each annual manoeuvres should produce a dismal tale of inefficiency and breakdown.

Fisher tackled this problem in his usual direct fashion. Sixty of the most ancient and useless ships in reserve were earmarked for scrapping. The dockyard reserve was handed over entirely to dockyard control and the care-and-maintenance crews withdrawn. With these men it then became possible to man the fleet reserve ships with nucleus crews of two-fifths of their full wartime complement of seamen and engine-room ratings, the whole of their turret crews, gun-layers, and sightsetters, and a captain with all the more important officers. With this nucleus of trained men permanently on board, operational efficiency was assured. At the same time, the reserve was reorganised into squadrons, each based on one of the home ports and each with a rear-admiral in command. No longer was there an unorganised collection of individual ships each more or less inefficient, but three homogeneous squadrons which exercised together and could provide useful and efficient reinforcement to any active fleet.

The new strategical disposition of fleets to meet the menace of growing German naval building was based on an interlocking system of mutual reinforcement. The Mediterranean Fleet, hitherto the largest and most important maintained by Britain, was reduced from 12 battleships to eight. A new Atlantic Fleet of eight battleships, based on Gibraltar, was created; its function to reinforce the Mediterranean or Channel Fleets as required. The ten most modern battleships formed the Channel Fleet, which was based on Dover. Independent squadrons of armoured cruisers operated in the Atlantic, East Indies, Australian, and Pacific sta-

tions, and they too were held available to reinforce the main fleets in emergency. All the foreign service squadrons of small second-class cruisers, which had formerly been stationed at various centres all over the world as part of the government's imperial policing policy, were recalled and scrapped. They were replaced by the introduction of naval coaling stations at strategic points so that no matter where a squadron might be required to operate in times of stress, it would find on arrival an adequate stock of steam coal, lubricating oil, and other essential stores.

The main purpose of this strategic reorganisation was to make certain that the main concentration of British sea power was always within easy steaming distance of the North Sea, although never so obviously concentrated as to give Germany any legitimate cause for alarm.

Admiral Sir John Fisher, at the time Commander-in-Chief in the Mediterranean, photographed in his day cabin in HMS *Renown* in 1900. He became First Sea Lord in 1904, and initiated the considerable reforms which transformed the Royal Navy into an efficient fighting force

A modification of this reorganisation was announced by the Admiralty in 1907 with the formation of a new Home Fleet. The three Reserve Fleet squadrons based at the Nore, Portsmouth, and Devonport were now brought together to form a single fleet under the command of one admiral, with the Nore division of six battleships kept fully manned, and the Portsmouth and Devonport divisions, totalling seven battleships, manned to three-fifths of full complement. To reach these numbers, the Channel, Atlantic, and Mediterranean Fleets were proportionately reduced. All new Dreadnoughts, as they left their builders' yards, went to the Chatham division of the Home Fleet, ostensibly because they were too modern to be able to exercise efficiently with the older battleships.

There was a good reason for this new Home Fleet. The Channel Fleet was recognised as an active fleet, and to strengthen it with the new construction battleships could prove an irritant to Germany which might force her to accelerate her building programme. But the new Home Fleet was well publicised as a reserve fleet, and its formation was thought unlikely to produce provocation on the other side of the North Sea.

This Admiralty reasoning could not, of course, be made public, and the official silence as to the reasons for the new organisation bore in it the seeds of the quarrel which was to develop and came to a head in late 1908 and early 1909 between the Commander-in-Chief of the Channel Fleet, Admiral Lord Charles Beresford, and the First Sea Lord. It was a quarrel which led finally to the forced retirement of both men from the Navy.

Fisher's final scheme was the crux of his whole major plan. In the summer of 1903 Fred Jane, founder and editor of *Jane's Fighting Ships*, had asked Colonel Cuniberti, the Italian ship designer, to write an article on the ideal battleship for Britain, to appear in *Jane's*. Cuniberti's proposed ship had an all-big-gun armament of ten 12-inch guns in place of the mixed armament of 12-inch and 9.2-inch which had hitherto been the practice in all navies in the world, armour protection to cover all magazine and engine and boiler rooms, and turbine machinery to give a speed of 20 knots. Fisher undoubtedly read the article while he was Commander-in-Chief at Portsmouth and was convinced by Cuniberti's arguments. Almost as he sat down for the first time in the First Sea Lord's chair, he issued a memorandum which read:

'The new navy, excepting a very few special local vessels, is to be absolutely restricted to four types of vessels, being all that modern fighting necessitates.
I. Battleships of 15,900 tons. 21 knots speed.
II. Armoured cruisers of 15,900 tons. $25\frac{1}{2}$ knots speed.
III. Destroyers of 900 tons and 4-inch guns. 36 knots speed.
IV. Submarines of 350 tons. 13 knots surface speed'.

This was a vast oversimplification, completely overlooking the smaller cruisers which served as scouts for the fleet and were at the same time the most economical type of ship for imperial policing and showing the flag. Nevertheless a reduction in types was a step in the right direction in the production of an efficient and homogeneous fleet. With the approval of the Board of Admiralty, Fisher referred his memorandum to a Committee of Designs which he had already packed with his own nominees.

This Committee's first act was to approve the design of a battleship which closely resembled Colonel Cuniberti's recommendation. This was the *Dreadnought*, the first battleship in the world to be driven by turbines, and an all-big-gun battleship mounting ten 12-inch guns in five turrets. She was completed in the record time of 11 months, and she proved to be a world-beater. Fisher was jubilant. 'A new name for the *Dreadnought*', he wrote in a typical outburst. 'The Hard-Boiled Egg. Why? Because she can't be beat!'

The appearance of the *Dreadnought* was the signal for an avalanche of criticism, and even abuse, from Fisher's 'Syndicate of Discontent'. While they had to admit that her merits, consisting in a marked increase in hitting power of her broadside compared with the previous mixed armament ships and a greater ease in tactical handling because of her high speed, were considerable, they lost no opportunity of pointing out that while she rendered every other foreign battleship obsolete, she performed the same service for every existing British battleship. Official arguments to the effect that it was impossible to hold back technological advance merely to retain a temporary advantage in obsolete ships were completely ignored. We know now that with this revolutionary ship Britain gained a two-year start on

Fisher's masterpiece, HMS *Dreadnought*, the first all-big-gun battleship in the world and the
first battleship to be fitted with turbines. She was launched in 1906, only 11 months after being
laid down, and carried ten 12-inch guns in five turrets

other nations in the modernisation of their navies, but this fact was not so apparent at the time.

Simultaneously with the *Dreadnought*, the Committee on Designs considered Fisher's requirement for the 15,900-ton armoured cruiser of $25\frac{1}{2}$ knots. The approved design was the *Invincible*, although in fact her sister ship, the *Indomitable*, was the first to be commissioned. The requirement for these ships, in Fisher's thesis, lay in their ability, through their heavy gun power and high speed, to force a recon-

naissance of the enemy's fleet. Smaller cruisers could be beaten off before coming in sight of an enemy's main fleet (the *Venus* scenario told the story), but the *Invincible* and her sisters carried eight 12-inch guns and could brush aside any outlying opposition. Another duty laid upon them by Fisher was to catch and annihilate the German 23-knot liners which, the Admiralty knew, all carried guns to be mounted on the outbreak of war for use in the destruction of commerce.

Submarine A.1 entering Portsmouth Harbour in 1906. Fisher was a man of remarkable vision
in regard to submarines and foresaw their offensive and strategic role in war at a time when
every other navy in the world considered them only as defensive weapons

It was only in 1912 that the nomenclature of these ships was changed from armoured cruiser to battlecruiser. It was an unfortunate choice of title for it gave, perhaps, some sort of implied licence for their use in a role for which Fisher had never designed them. They were never intended to lie in the line of battle although, subsidiary to their other duties, Fisher did indicate that they might be of value in a fleet action as a fast wing to reinforce the van or the rear of the main battle fleet.

Fisher's views on the use of submarines were extraordinarily advanced for the period. The universal concept in 1904 of the submarine's role was as a coastal defence vessel, and such exercises at sea in which they were used invariable stressed this role. In 1904 Fisher wrote a letter to the Third Sea Lord who, as Controller of the Navy, was responsible for naval building, setting out his views. The italics are his own:

'It's astounding to me, *perfectly astounding*, how the very best amongst us absolutely fail to realize the vast impending revolution in naval warfare and naval strategy that the submarine will accomplish. I have just written a paper on this, but it's so violent that I am keeping it! ... I have not disguised my opinion, in season and out of season, as to the essential, immediate, vital, pressing, urgent (I can't think of any more adjectives) necessity for more submarines at once, at the very least 25 in addition to those now ordered and building, and a hundred more as soon

as practicable, or we shall be caught with our breeches down. And then, my dear friend, you have the astounding audacity to say to me, "I presume you only think they (the submarines) can act on the *defensive*!" Why, my dear fellow, not take the offensive? Good Lord! if our Admiral is worth his salt, he will tow his submarines at 18 knots speed and put them into the hostile port (like ferrets after the rabbits!) before war is officially declared, just as the Japanese acted before the Russian naval officers knew that war was declared. In all seriousness, I don't think it is even *faintly* realised – *the immense impending revolution which the submarines will effect as offensive weapons of war*'.

These were prophetic words, and it is due to Fisher's belief in the submarine that, ten years after he wrote this letter, and when the testing time came, British submarines were able to operate in waters as far distant from their home bases as the Baltic Sea and the Sea of Marmara.

One other of Fisher's enthusiasms was for the substitution of oil for coal as the modern fuel for warships. He put up the suggestion to Lord Selborne, First Lord of the Admiralty, who minuted in the margin: 'The substitution of oil for coal is impossible because the oil does not exist in this world in sufficient quantities. It must be reckoned only as a most valuable adjunct!' But Fisher was not to be put off. Thirty-six torpedo boats built and launched in 1906–8 burned oil only in their boilers (they were known in the Royal Navy as the 'oily wads'); the destroyers built in 1906–7 (the *Tribal* class) and in 1909–10 (the *Acorn* class) were all oil-burners, and at the time of his depature from the Admiralty in 1910 the *Arethusa*-class cruisers were being designed to burn only oil.

The end of Fisher's reign as First Sea Lord came a little sadly. The formation of the Home Fleet has been mentioned above and it was through this reorganisation that the quarrel with the 'Syndicate of Discontent' came to a head.

In April 1907 Admiral Lord Charles Beresford was appointed Commander-in-Chief of the Channel Fleet and almost at once publicly denounced the formation of the Home Fleet as 'a fraud upon the public and a danger to the Empire'. In July he received a copy of the Admiralty's war orders, on the receipt of which he should have drawn up his own plans for approval by the Admiralty. He produced none at all in spite of periodic enquiries from the First Sea Lord. In November 1907 occurred the notorious 'paintwork' affair in which Rear-Admiral Percy Scott, then commanding the 1st Cruiser Squadron, sent a critical signal to one of his ships which had been ordered by Beresford to cancel her gunnery practice and return to harbour to paint ship in preparation for a visit of inspection by the German Kaiser. Beresford publicly reprimanded Scott on the quarter-deck of his flagship before the other officers of the ship and demanded his replacement. The Admiralty refused and confirmed Scott in his appointment. Finally, after much mutual recrimination, the Admiralty ordered Beresford to haul down his flag in 1909 after serving only two years in command instead of the more usual three.

The reason given was a decision to absorb the Channel Fleet in the new Home Fleet, a logical enough move in view of the fact that already the Home Fleet was the stronger of the two, and that the obvious threat to Britain's sea supremacy now lay in the North Sea and not the English Channel. But the decision rankled with Beresford, and his opportunity of revenge came with a scare about the rate of German naval building in 1909. This was the origin of the famous rallying cry which swept through the nation in that year: 'We want eight [battleships] and we won't wait!' Fisher came in for much criticism on the grounds that he had been caught napping by the speed of the German naval building. Beresford demanded an official inquiry, and in the state of

public disquiet the Prime Minister could not refuse. Although the Committee of Inquiry blamed Beresford for not acting in the spirit of the Board of Admiralty's paramount authority, they also blamed the Board for not taking Beresford sufficiently into their confidence.

But there was a sting in the tail of the Committee's report. They had, they declared, 'been impressed with the differences of opinion among officers of high rank and professional attainments regarding important principles of naval strategy and tactics, and they look forward with much confidence to the further development of a Naval War Staff from which the naval members of the Board and flag officers and their staffs at sea may be expected to derive common benefit.'

Fisher had always resisted any attempt to set up a Naval Staff in the Admiralty. In his philosophy the First Sea Lord was the fount of all naval knowledge and Naval Staffs could have no part in that. He had even committed his thoughts on the subject to paper. 'A Naval War Staff', he had written, 'is a very excellent organisation for cutting out and arranging foreign newspaper clippings. … So far as the Navy is concerned, the tendency of these "thinking establishments" on shore is to convert splendid sea officers into very indifferent clerks.'

Holding such strong views as this, Fisher of course had to go. His term of office was brought to a close in January 1910, but the five and a half years of his supreme naval power had been enough to sweep away the lethargy which had accumulated throughout the long years of Victoria's reign and to replace it with a navy both technologically more efficient and administratively more progressive. But the change had not been achieved without hurt, and the deep division of the Navy into two opposing camps had been a high price to pay. Fisher himself was a ruthless man who would break any officer who disagreed with him or stood in his path in his restless forcing of reform. And towards the end of his service he was suffering from a severe attack of *folie de grandeur*. Nevertheless, he was probably the only man who could have taken and shaken the old somnolent Navy and beaten it into a shape designed for modern war. It was his work, more than that of any other, which laid so surely the foundations of Britain's eventual victory in the war with Germany that was but just around the corner.

CHAPTER 17

*The First World War – Overseas Operations – Escape of
the* Goeben *and* Breslau *– The Dardanelles Campaign –
Coronel and the Falkland Islands – German cruiser warfare*

GEOFFREY BENNETT

Of all the reasons which led to the outbreak of the First World War, one is undisputed. Having unified Germany in 1871, Bismarck was content to dominate continental Europe with the armies of the Triple Alliance (Germany, Austria-Hungary, and Italy), and to rely on diplomacy to avoid a conflict with the British Empire. But the German Emperor Wilhelm II was determined to challenge Britain at sea, and so, too, was his Minister of Marine, Admiral von Tirpitz. The two Navy Laws of 1898 and 1900 which authorised the transformation of Germany's small coast defence force into a High Seas Fleet was a fact which Britain could only ignore at her peril.

Britain reacted to this challenge with an alliance with Japan (1902), with the *Entente Cordiale* with France (1904), and with a *rapprochement* with Russia (1907); and by laying down new battleships at twice the rate at which Germany could build them. As important were the reforms with which Admiral Fisher transformed a Royal Navy riddled with Victorian complacency into a 20th century fighting machine. By the summer of 1914 the British fleet was headed by 29 dreadnoughts and battlecruisers, with 20 more on the stocks, as compared with Germany's 20, with only seven building.

A British squadron was visiting Kiel for the opening of the enlarged canal when the heir to the Austro-Hungarian throne was assassinated on 28th June 1914 in Serbia. A harsh ultimatum from Vienna to Belgrade caused European nerves to flutter, but there was some optimism throughout Europe when Serbia responded with a conciliatory reply. But this optimism vanished when Austria rejected the reply on 24th July. Russia ordered general mobilisation

in Serbia's support, Tirpitz recalled the High Seas Fleet from its summer cruise, and the British First Sea Lord, Prince Louis of Battenberg, prevented the normal dispersion of the Reserve Fleet to its home ports after a test mobilisation exercise. The British Home Fleet was ordered to Scapa Flow, reaching there as the Kaiser answered the Tsar with a declaration of war, at the same time sending an ultimatum to her ally France. The advance of the German Army through the Ardennes in her war against France required Britain to fulfil her guarantee of upholding Belgium's neutrality, and she declared war against Germany on 4th August.

The naval situation in the Mediterranean was confused. France had been slow to build dreadnoughts, and by July 1914 she had only one at Toulon. Since Austria-Hungary and Italy, members with Germany of the Triple Alliance, each had three in the Mediterranean the Admiralty had deployed the battlecruisers *Inflexible*, *Indefatigable*, and *Indomitable* in this sea, together with four armoured cruisers and four light cruisers, all under the command of Admiral Sir Berkeley Milne. And to counter this fleet's influence on Turkey, in whom both Britain and Germany saw a potential ally, Germany was represented by the battlecruiser *Goeben* and the light cruiser *Breslau*, the two under the command of Admiral Souchon.

On 30th July Milne was told by the British Admiralty that his first task should be to aid the French in the transport of their African army. He was also told to shadow the *Goeben*, but not to allow himself to be brought to action against superior forces. Knowing that the German ships had coaled

Vice-Admiral Sir Doveton Sturdee, who was sent with the two battlecruisers *Invincible* and
Inflexible to the South Atlantic after the Battle of Coronel to prevent the return of von Spee's
squadron to Germany. On the day following their arrival at the Falkland Islands, the German
squadron came into sight

recently at Brindisi, he ordered the light cruiser *Chatham* to watch the Strait of Messina and sent the *Indomitable* and *Indefatigable* with the armoured cruisers to the Strait of Otranto, to ensure that the German ships did not join the Austrian fleet at Pola. But when the *Chatham* reported Messina empty, the Admiralty diverted the two battlecruisers to Gibraltar. Souchon was, indeed, heading west at high speed, but not for the Atlantic; at dawn on the 4th the *Goeben* appeared off Philippeville, the *Breslau* off Bone, each to carry out a short bombardment to disrupt the embarkation of the French Army. They returned the way they had come, having received a signal from Berlin that an alliance had been concluded with Turkey and that the two ships were to proceed to Constantinople. The *Indomitable* and *Indefatigable* sighted them heading east. The four ships, whose countries were not yet at war, passed each other at a distance of 8,000 yards, guns trained fore and aft. The British battlecruisers then settled down to shadow their likely opponents until the ultimatum to Germany should expire that night but were unable to hold their quarry and by nightfall Souchon's force had outstripped them. Captain

Kennedy of the *Indomitable* would have closed the northern entrance to Messina if Italy had not declared her neutrality; instead he joined Milne in the *Inflexible* to the west of Sicily to prevent Souchon making a further sortie against the French transports.

The British Admiral did not, however, ignore the possibility that the Germans might be less scrupulous in regard to neutral waters; the light cruiser *Gloucester*, Captain Howard Kelly, was ordered to watch Messina, where Souchon's ships arrived early on 5th August and were allowed to replenish their bunkers. Kelly reported them as soon as they sailed in the evening of the 6th. Because they steered first for the Adriatic, Admiral Troubridge, commanding the armoured cruisers, supposed they must be making for Pola in the Adriatic and went north to intercept. Not until midnight did he reverse course to the south, although Kelly reported that the *Goeben* and *Breslau* had altered course for Cape Matapan shortly after dark.

Milne ordered the light cruiser *Dublin*, Captain John Kelly, and two destroyers, which were en route from Malta to join Troubridge, to attack the *Goeben* during this moonlit night. Guided by his

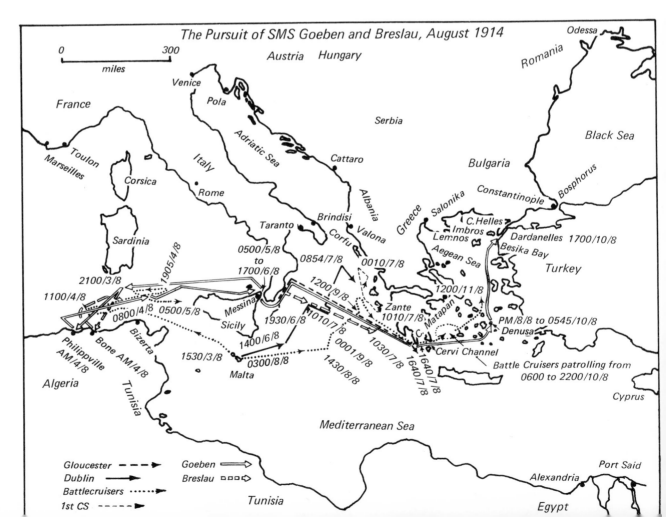

The Pursuit of SMS Goeben and Breslau, August 1914

brother Howard's reports, John led his puny force to a position on the enemy's bow. By 0330 he expected to sight them at any moment; but the *Breslau* glimpsed the *Dublin* without being sighted herself, allowing Souchon to turn his flagship away unseen. Events on board Troubridge's flagship, H.M.S. *Defence*, took a very different turn as the armoured cruisers headed to intercept the German vessels. At 0245, Captain Wray asked his Admiral whether he intended to engage the *Goeben*. 'Yes', answered Troubridge, and explained a decision that seemed to run counter to Admiralty orders not to engage a superior force, with: 'I cannot have the name of the Mediterranean Squadron stink'. Three-quarters of an hour later Wray said: 'The *Goeben* can circle round us within range of her guns but outside ours. It seems likely to be suicide for your squadron'. Troubridge replied: 'I cannot turn away now; think of my pride'. Wray countered with: 'Surely it is your country's welfare which is at stake' – and it was this argument that caused Troubridge reluctantly to abandon the chase.

Milne had, meantime, taken his battlecruisers into Malta for fuel, whence they sailed at 0030 on 8th August. Fourteen hours later, half-way to Cape Matapan, an Admiralty clerk made the mistake of sending a signal to 'Commence hostilities against Austria'. The C-in-C turned his battlecruisers north to support Troubridge in case of a sortie by the Austrian fleet. Not until 1230 next day did the Admiralty realise this and signal: 'Not at war with Austria. Continue chase of *Goeben*'. This loss of 24 hours made all the difference. On the afternoon of the 8th Souchon's ships stopped at Denusa to replenish their bunkers. If Milne had not delayed to coal his battlecruisers, or if there had been no false alarm over Austria, they could have caught the *Geoben* and *Breslau* as they left this Aegean island at 0545 on the 10th. As it was, Milne's ships were 40 miles north of Denusa by 1200 on the 11th when they learned that Souchon had entered the Dardanelles at 1700 the previous day. And when Turkey was reminded that belligerent vessels might remain in neutral waters for only 24 hours, the realities of German cunning were made clear: the *Goeben* and *Breslau* had been 'sold' to Turkey.

Both Milne and Troubridge suffered for allowing the German ships to elude them. Milne received no further employment throughout the war and

Troubridge was brought before a court-martial for failing to engage the *Goeben*. He was acquitted in view of the signals that he should not engage a superior force, but the verdict was not well received in the Admiralty. He was given various appointments during the war but never again employed at sea. This must have been the most bitter blow of all to a man who was the direct descendent of the Troubridge who had been one of Nelson's Band of Brothers.

'The curse descended irrevocably upon Turkey', wrote Winston Churchill, at the time First Lord of the Admiralty, after he had sent a signal to Admiral Carden: 'Assume command of squadron off Dardanelles. Your sole duty is to sink *Goeben* and *Breslau* if they come out'. But Souchon was after bigger fish. He helped General von Sanders to incite the Turks to anger at the Admiralty's requisition of their first two dreadnoughts which in August 1914 were nearing completion in British shipyards. Then he led a squadron into the Black Sea, ostensibly for exercises, in reality for a naked act of aggression. At dawn on 30th October the *Goeben* opened fire on Sevastopol, the *Breslau* on Novorossiisk, the Turkish cruiser *Hamidieh* on Odessa.

The British reacted to Turkey's entry into the war on Germany's side with what was later described as 'an act of sheer lunacy'. On 3rd November the outer forts protecting the Dardanelles were bombarded by the *Indefatigable*, *Indomitable*, and two French dreadnoughts. One fort was damaged, but the bombardment warned the Turks of the need to strengthen the Straits' defences. It also gave them time to do this, because not until Russia appealed for an allied 'demonstration' to relieve their armies in the Caucasus in January 1915, did Churchill signal Carden: 'Do you think it practicable to force the Dardanelles by ships alone?'.

The Admiral's plan, by which he expected to reach the Sea of Marmara in about a month, received Churchill's strong support. Admiral Fisher, who had been recalled as First Sea Lord, thought the operation needed troops ashore to back up the naval attack; nonetheless he added the new dreadnought *Queen Elizabeth* to the *Inflexible* and 16 French and British pre-dreadnoughts with which Carden engaged the outer forts on 19th February, almost without reply but also doing negligible damage. Bad weather then intervened until the 25th when the allied naval

British submarines operated in the Sea of Marmara during the Gallipoli campaign, running the gauntlet of several minefields in the Dardanelles to reach their destination where they harried the Turkish supply lines. This photograph shows the submarine E 11 returning from one of her periods of duty in the Marmara

gunfire was more effective; and on 1st March the destruction of the outer defences was completed by demolition parties from Carden's ships. But bombardments of the intermediate defences on the following days met considerable opposition from mobile howitzers; and when Carden began the next phase, the reduction of the defences of the Narrows, not even the *Queen Elizabeth's* guns could silence them. In consequence, the minesweeping trawlers could make little progress with clearing the Straits of their defensive minefields. On the 10th Churchill and Fisher ordered Carden to use all his force in 'a vigorous attempt to overwhelm the forts at decisive range'. He tried to do so, but again his minesweepers failed him and, near now to a nervous breakdown, he resigned his command.

His successor, Admiral de Robeck, quickly fixed the 18th for the 'big push'. At 1125 the *Queen Elizabeth, Inflexible,* and two pre-dreadnoughts began bombarding forts mounting 75 guns of from 6-inch to 14-inch calibre from six miles inside the Straits, whilst four more battleships engaged the mobile defences. By noon the latter were silent. Four French pre-dreadnoughts then fired on the forts with such effect that these were nearly silenced. Six

British battleships were moving up the Straits to continue this destructive fire when the retiring French battleship *Bouvet* was struck by a shell that detonated a magazine. In spite of this set-back, de Robeck ordered his trawlers to clear a way through the Kephez minefield. But, as with Carden, when these came under withering fire their fishermen crews slipped their gear and retired. More reverses followed. At 1611 the *Inflexible* was damaged by a mine in waters already swept; four minutes later the pre-dreadnought *Irresistible* was trapped in the same field; and when de Robeck ordered his ships to withdraw, the pre-dreadnought *Ocean* foundered.

For the price of six battleships and battlecruisers sunk or damaged, only two of the Turks' big guns had been destroyed. But with more pre-dreadnoughts on their way to restore his strength, de Robeck organised a minesweeping force of destroyers for another all-out attempt. Simultaneously, however, he learned that notwithstanding Fisher's growing opposition to the Dardanelles operation, Churchill had persuaded Kitchener to make 80,000 men available so that the allies could strike a blow that would force Turkey out of the war, remove the threat to the Suez Canal, and open a way for the supply of arms to

Russia. This changed de Robeck's mind. By 22nd March he was 'quite clear he could not get through without the help of troops' just when the Navy's attempt to force the Straits with ships alone was very near success. For by now the Turkish defenders were becoming demoralised and their ammunition nearly exhausted. If Carden's attacks had been more vigorous; if de Robeck had nerved himself to face further losses on the 19th, the forts and mobile defences might have been silenced by the 20th, when the British minesweepers would have had little difficulty in clearing a way into the Sea of Marmara. As it was, the allies were now committed to the Gallipoli campaign, for which their troops could not be ready until 25th April.

This further delay was as fatal as that between Carden's November bombardment and his first attempt to force the Straits. When de Robeck's fleet landed 29,000 men on five beaches around Cape Helles and Gaba Tepe, the Turkish defenders were ready for them. Neither then, nor in the eight months that followed, did allied troops gain more than a foothold on the peninsula. Three more pre-dreadnoughts were lost giving them bombardment support; the *Goliath* to a torpedo from a Turkish destroyer, the *Triumph* and *Majestic* to torpedoes from the German *U.21*. But the men of the British and Anzac divisions never advanced as far inland as Carden's small demolition parties had done in February. All through the summer their casualties mounted until it was clear that they could not overcome the Turks' fierce resistance. In November the British Government bowed to French pressure to open a new campaign in Salonika. In December the Royal Navy gave a final helping hand to its sister Service. On the night of the 18th the last troops were withdrawn from Suvla Bay and Anzac Cove, and three weeks later from the Helles beaches. That they did this without the loss of a single man was small consolation for a bloody defeat. Churchill had been right to press for an assault on the Dardanelles, for success there would have shortened the war. But neither the Admiralty nor the War Office was prepared for this master stroke, nor had Fisher or Kitchener much heart for it.

At the end of April 1915, the *Goeben* came into the Marmara to attack allied transports off Gallipoli, but on sighting the *Queen Elizabeth* quickly retired. Thenceforward Souchon was occupied in countering

the Russian fleet in the Black Sea, by whose mines the *Goeben* was damaged in December 1914, the *Breslau* in July 1915. Not until the Russian threat to Constantinople was removed in 1917 did his successor, Admiral von Rebeur-Paschwitz, attempt a sortie into the Mediterranean. On 19th January 1918 the *Goeben* and *Breslau* left the Bosphorus to bombard the allied base at Mudros. To gain secrecy, they ignored the mine danger, clearing Sedd-el-Bahr early on the 20th with only slight damage to the *Goeben*. At 0740 they surprised the monitor *Raglan* and the smaller *M28*, quickly sinking both. An hour later the *Breslau* struck a mine off Cape Kephalo; then, whilst manoeuvring to take her in tow, the *Goeben* struck another in the same British field. A few minutes later the drifting *Breslau* detonated four more mines, soon to sink. The *Goeben* headed back for the Straits, to strike a third mine at 0948. Listing heavily, she ran aground off Nagara Point, though she was towed off and back to safety off Constantinople before the nearest allied submarine could arrive from Corfu to attempt a torpedo attack. The *Goeben* was, nonethe-

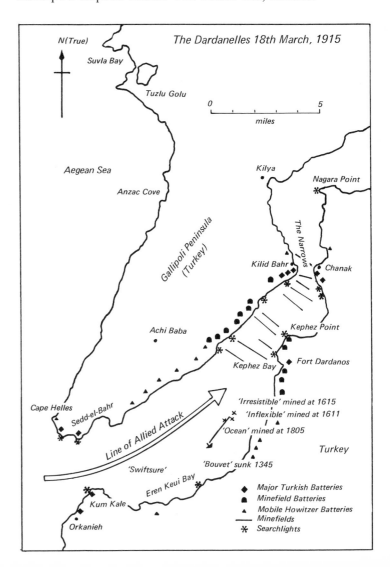

The Dardanelles 18th March, 1915

N(True)

Suvla Bay

Tuzlu Golu

0   5
miles

Aegean Sea

Anzac Cove

Kilya

Nagara Point

Gallipoli Peninsula (Turkey)

The Narrows

Kilid Bahr

Chanak

Achi Baba

Kephez Point

Kephez Bay

Fort Dardanos

Cape Helles

Sedd-el-Bahr

Line of Allied Attack

'Irresistible' mined at 1615
'Inflexible' mined at 1611
'Ocean' mined at 1805

'Swiftsure'

'Bouvet' sunk 1345

Turkey

Kum Kale

Eren Keui Bay

Orkanieh

♦   Major Turkish Batteries
▬   Minefield Batteries
▲   Mobile Howitzer Batteries
—   Minefields
✳   Searchlights

less, so severely damaged that her repairs could not be completed until November 1918.

The eight other German cruisers outside home waters on 4th August 1914 had much shorter lives. Five comprised Admiral von Spee's East Asiatic Squadron, the armoured cruisers *Scharnhorst* and *Gneisenau*, the light cruisers *Emden*, *Leipzig*, and *Nürnberg*. The others, also light cruisers, were the *Königsberg* off East Africa, and the *Dresden* and *Karlsruhe* in the Caribbean. All were so deployed because there were good reasons – colonies in Africa and the Pacific Islands, and substantial interests in China and Mexico – why Germany should be represented in peace by more than a handful of gunboats. And in war, reinforced by armed liners, they could carry on cruiser warfare against enemy merchant vessels, bombard military establishments, and destroy cable and wireless stations.

As a counter to the six cruisers east of Suez, Britain deployed three squadrons, which included the battlecruiser *Australia*, two pre-dreadnoughts, and 10 cruisers, supported by four French and Russian cruisers and, when Japan joined the allies on 23rd August, by her considerable fleet. If all these had made his destruction their first aim, von Spee's career must have been short. But Admiral Pierse's East Indies Squadron was required to protect trade against attacks by the *Königsberg*, and Admiral Patey's Australian squadron to support expeditions to capture Germany's Pacific Islands, whilst the Japanese fleet invested Tsingtao until it surrendered on 7th November. This left little more than Admiral Jerram's China Squadron to deal with von Spee's force which, at the beginning of August 1914, was widely dispersed, the *Scharnhorst* (flag), *Gneisenau*, and *Nürnberg* being at Ponape, the *Emden* at Tsingtao, and the *Leipzig* off the west coast of Mexico. And the British C-in-C was not helped by unwise Admiralty intervention; on 28th July he was ordered to concentrate at Hong Kong instead of watching Tsingtao, which allowed the *Emden* to escape and rejoin von Spee. When the German Admiral left the Mariana Islands on 14th August intending to attack allied trade off the west coast of South America, the *Emden* was detached to the Indian Ocean.

Captain von Müller struck with such effect in the Bay of Bengal and to the west of Ceylon that he drew every available allied warship in pursuit. Between 10th September and 28th October he sank or captured 23 merchant vessels. With singular audacity he bombarded the oil tanks at Madras and sank the Russian cruiser *Zemchug* at anchor off Penang. Not until 9th November was this 20th century Paul Jones's career ended. In the course of a dawn raid on the Cocos Island cable station he was surprised by the light cruiser *Sydney*. The *Emden* was soon reduced to a battered wreck which von Müller ran on a reef, then surrendered.

After futile raids on Apia and Tahiti, the *Scharnhorst*, *Gneisenau* and *Nürnberg* reached Easter Island on 12th October, where they were reinforced by the *Leipzig* from Mexico and the *Dresden*. The latter, after a brief period attacking trade off Pernambuco, had been driven through the Magellan Straits by the considerable force of cruisers which Britain and France deployed at the outbreak of war to protect their Atlantic trade. Admiral Cradock's West Indies Squadron located the *Karlsruhe* in the Bahamas as early as 6th August but an advantage in speed enabled her to escape.

News that both this ship and the *Dresden* were operating off Pernambuco drew Cradock south to where he believed they might be joined by von Spee's force. The Admiralty's reaction was belated and ineffective. When Cradock was ordered to cover the Magellan Straits, his armoured cruisers *Good Hope* and *Monmouth*, the light cruiser *Glasgow* and the armed merchant cruiser *Otranto* were reinforced by no more than the pre-dreadnought *Canopus*. The Admiralty intended Cradock to keep his force concentrated in the belief that the *Canopus'* 12-inch guns would suffice to deal with von Spee. Not until too late was it realised that because this pre-dreadnought had developed engine defects, Cradock's determination to locate an enemy of whom no definite news had been received for more than a month would impel him to go on without such a handicap. He had been ordered to protect British trade off the Chilean coast, and when he sailed north from Vallenar Roads on 30th October he left the battleship to follow as escort to his colliers.

Next day, while the *Glasgow* was paying a brief call at Coronel, the British force intercepted wireless transmissions from the *Leipzig*. Twenty-four hours later Cradock's four ships were spread 15 miles apart in the belief that they would soon encounter this single enemy vessel; and at 1620 her smoke was sighted on the *Glasgow's* starboard bow. Von Spee

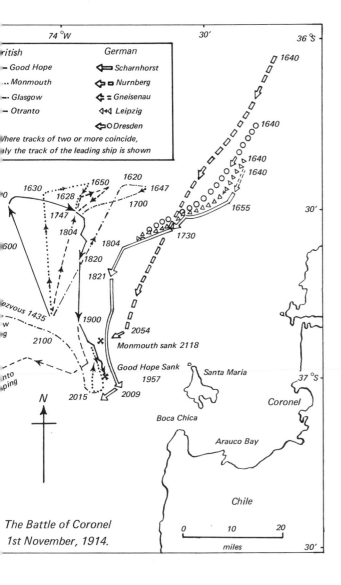

Map legend:

British	German
Good Hope	⇐ Scharnhorst
Monmouth	⇐◻ Nurnberg
Glasgow	⇐≡ Gneisenau
Otranto	◁◀◁ Leipzig
	⇐○ Dresden

Where tracks of two or more coincide,
only the track of the leading ship is shown

The Battle of Coronel
1st November, 1914.

0   10   20
miles

1640, 1620, 1650, 1630, 1628, 1647, 1700, 1655, 1747, 1804, 1730, 1804, 1820, 1821, Rendezvous 1435, 1900, 2054, 2100, Monmouth sank 2118, Good Hope Sank 1957, 2015, 2009, Santa Maria, Coronel, Boca Chica, Arauco Bay, Chile

N

74°W   30'   36°S   30'   37°S   30'

was under a like delusion. Having received no information of Cradock's squadron since leaving Easter Island until an agent reported the *Glasgow's* arrival at Coronel, his force was considerably dispersed when the *Leipzig* likewise sighted her.

Twenty minutes later Captain Luce of the *Glasgow* reported the *Scharnhorst* and *Gneisenau* in company with the *Leipzig*. With their slight advantage in speed the British might have escaped to the south; Cradock would have been complying with the Admiralty's instructions had he fallen back on the *Canopus*. But once he lost touch with von Spee, who could tell when he would be found again? Moreover, it was not essential to sink his ships; damage would compel them to seek internment in a neutral port.

Forty-five minutes later the *Good Hope, Monmouth, Glasgow,* and *Otranto* were in single line ahead on the south-easterly course that should bring them quickly within range of the enemy, although this headed them into a sea that made it impossible to fight their main deck guns. At 1818 Cradock radioed the *Canopus*: 'I am now going to attack the enemy'.

Von Spee had already identified his opponent and was in full pursuit; but not until 1900, when the sun dipped below the horizon and silhouetted Cradock's ships against the after-glow, did he allow them to close to 12,000 yards. The *Scharnhorst's* third salvo put the *Good Hope's* forward gun out of action, the *Gneisenau* set the *Monmouth* ablaze. By 1945, when it was quite dark, the *Good Hope* and *Monmouth* were in obvious distress. The *Monmouth* swung off to starboard burning furiously. At 1950 there was a tremendous explosion on board the *Good Hope*, after which she lay between the lines, a black hull lighted only by a dull glow. No one saw her go down; Captain Luce could only guess her fate. He turned his ship to succour the stricken *Monmouth*, but she could neither fight nor fly. So that he might divert the *Canopus* before she, too, was sunk, the *Glasgow* increased to full speed and left the enemy astern. The *Otranto* had been ordered to the south half an hour before.

Von Spee signalled to his light cruisers to search for the surviving British ships. They found the wreck of the *Monmouth* and, at 2118, sent her to the bottom, her flag still flying. As with the *Good Hope*, no attempt at rescue was possible; the sea was too rough for boats to be launched. The *Canopus*, achieving only a knot less than her designed speed, was still 200 miles from the scene when the *Glasgow's* wireless warned

The British squadron at Coronel was commanded by Rear-Admiral Sir Christopher Cradock, who was killed in the action together with the entire complements of the two British cruisers which were sunk

HMS *Good Hope*, Cradock's flagship at Coronel, which was sunk by von Spee's squadron, together with the *Monmouth*. Outgunned and manned largely by reservists, they had little chance against German ships with well-trained crews

The cruiser *Glasgow*, the only British ship to escape from the Battle of Coronel, rounded Cape Horn and joined Admiral Sturdee at the Falkland Islands in time to take her revenge for Coronel

her of Cradock's fate. Because the maximum range of her heavy guns was inside that of the German armoured cruisers, her captain decided she would be best employed covering the *Glasgow's* and *Otranto's* retirement to the Falkland Islands. And for fear of meeting this battleship, von Spee called off his pursuit and turned north, well content with a victory that gave him command of the south-west Pacific.

Of Cradock's defeat, Winston Churchill's successor as First Lord, Balfour, gave this verdict:

The German Admiral was far from any port where he could have refitted. If he suffered damage, even though he inflicted greater damage than he received, his power might suddenly be destroyed. He would be in great peril as long as his squadron remained inefficient, and if Admiral Cradock judged that he himself, and those under him, were well sacrificed if they destroyed the power of this hostile fleet, then there is no man but would say that he showed the highest courage. We shall never know his thoughts when it became evident that success was an impossibility. He and his gallant comrades lie far from the pleasant homes of England. Yet they have their reward; theirs is an immortal place in the great role of naval heroes.

Berlin reacted to the news of von Spee's victory with a warning that cruiser warfare now offered few prospects of success, and advised him to try to break through with all his ships and return home. The German Admiral agreed, but made two fatal mistakes. He delayed a full month before taking his five cruisers round Cape Horn and decided to interrupt his Atlantic voyage with a raid on the Falkland Islands.

The Admiralty responded to Cradock's defeat by sending strong reinforcements to every area to which von Spee might go. In particular, Churchill and Fisher sent the battlecruiser *Princess Royal* to the Caribbean in case von Spee should pass through the Panama Canal, and the *Invincible* and *Inflexible* to the South Atlantic. The latter ships sailed secretly from Devonport on 11th November under Admiral Sturdee's command. They reached the Falkland Islands on 7th December to form a squadron that included the armoured cruisers *Carnarvon*, flying the flag of Admiral Stoddart, *Kent*, and *Cornwall*, and the light cruisers *Glasgow* and *Bristol*.

Sturdee had intended to go through the Magellan Straits in search of von Spee off the Chilean coast as soon as his ships had coaled, leaving the *Canopus* to

defend the Falklands. But at 0800 on 8th December he received the startling news that the German squadron was approaching the Falklands. Unperturbed at being caught whilst coaling, he ordered his ships to raise steam for full speed. The *Kent* cleared the harbour at 0845 and most of the others an hour later. By 1000 the *Invincible* was at sea and flying the exhilarating signal, 'Chase!'

A 12-inch salvo from the *Canopus*, and a sighting report of two dreadnoughts in Stanley harbour, had decided von Spee to seek safety in a high speed flight to the south-east. Not until 1100 did he learn the fateful truth, that his squadron was being overhauled by two battlecruisers. At 1245 these great ships opened deliberate fire at a range of more than 16,000 yards. When they scored their first hit half an hour later, von Spee signalled his three light cruisers to leave the line and try to escape. In accordance with Sturdee's fighting instructions, the *Kent*, *Cornwall*, and *Glasgow* went in pursuit.

The battle was thus divided into a number of separate actions. That of the battlecruisers and the *Carnarvon* against von Spee's two armoured cruisers was prolonged by Sturdee's decision to avoid damage to his own vessels when they were so far from any dockyard. The *Scharnhorst* suffered repeated hits before going to the bottom at 1617 with all her crew. The *Gneisenau* survived until 1750 when the British ships, which had suffered virtually no damage, stopped to rescue 190 of her officers and men.

The *Kent* went after the *Nürnberg*, from which there were only seven survivors when she sank at 1926, two-and-a-half hours after first opening fire. The *Leipzig* was pursued by the *Glasgow* and *Cornwall* until 2030 when she, too, was sunk, darkness and icy seas preventing the rescue of more than eighteen of her crew. Only the *Dresden* eluded pursuit, to disappear round Cape Horn under the cover of darkness. And only one of von Spee's supply ships escaped destruction; the others were caught and sunk by the *Bristol*.

There was no doubting the magnitude of the British victory. By skilful tactics Sturdee had annihilated von Spee's squadron at negligible cost to his own force. Cradock's defeat had been decisively avenged.

The *Dresden* eluded searching British cruisers for nearly three months, but she did negligible damage to allied shipping. Then the Admiralty intercepted a

German survivors from the sunken *Gneisenau* being picked up after the battle. This photograph was taken by Sub-Lieutenant Duckworth from the quarter-deck of the *Invincible*, and shows HMS *Inflexible* in the background

signal disclosing her intention to rendezvous with a collier 300 miles west of Coronel. The *Kent* sighted her there on 7th March, but too late to catch her before dark. Prevented from coaling, the *Dresden* was compelled to anchor off Mas a Fuera. The *Kent* and *Glasgow* found her on the morning of the 9th. And in an action lasting less than five minutes she suffered enough damage for her captain to hoist a white flag, whereby he gained the time to scuttle his ship after her crew had reached the safety of a neutral shore.

The Admiralty had already solved the mystery of why they had received no reports of the *Karlsruhe* for so long. After capturing or sinking 76,500 tons of allied shipping by the end of October 1914, she had headed for Barbados to raid the island's defenceless capital. But fate, in the guise of unstable cordite, intervened. The *Karlsruhe* was rent by the spontaneous explosion of her magazines. Her two tenders rescued 140 of her officers and men and slipped

through the British blockade, reaching Germany early in December.

Since the few German armed merchant cruisers which escaped from neutral ports had now been sunk by allied warships, or been compelled to seek internment, only the light cruiser *Königsberg* remained to be accounted for. Deprived of her base by the cruiser *Astraea's* attack on Dar-es-Salaam at the outset of the war, she harried trade off Aden for a week, then found a haven in the delta of the Rufigi river, whence she emerged to sink the small cruiser *Pegasus* at Zanzibar on 20th September. But by the end of the month she had been located by the light cruisers *Dartmouth* and *Weymouth* and confined to her Rufigi hide-out until July 1915, when two shallow-draft monitors, the *Severn* and *Mersey*, arrived from Britain. These penetrated the mangrove swamps and soon reduced the *Königsberg* to a stranded wreck.

Her destruction brought down the curtain on the war in the far seas. No German warship was ordered out from Kiel or the Jade to raid the trade routes. A number of merchant ships were, however, armed with guns, torpedoes, and mines concealed beneath the trappings of their peacetime status, but very few achieved any success. The *Moewe* left Hamburg in December 1915, for a four months' cruise in the South Atlantic, which was followed by another in November 1916, from which she returned with a total bag of 34 allied merchant ships and the predreadnought *King Edward VII* sunk on a mine laid off Cape Wrath. Her record was, however, exceptional. The *Greif* was sunk in February 1916, two days after leaving Germany for her first cruise. The *Wolf* sailed in December 1916 to lay mines off the Cape of Good Hope and land ammunition that would enable General von Lettow-Vorbeck's beleaguered garrison to hold out in South-East Africa until the end of the war; but her subsequent cruise in the Indian Ocean brought her a bag of only 12 allied ships. The *Leopard* was sunk by the cruiser *Achilles* as she tried to break out of the North Sea in March 1917. The *Seeadler* passed the allied blockade under Norwegian colours, to operate first in the South Atlantic, then in the Pacific. But though she proved an armed sailing vessel's ability to avoid detection, she also showed how small were her chances of achieving much. She was wrecked in the Fiji Islands in August 1917 having sunk only ten allied ships.

Battle of the Falkland Islands December 8th, 1914.

CHAPTER 18

*Operations in Home Waters – Action in the Heligoland
Bight – The Dogger Bank battle – Battle of Jutland*

GEOFFREY BENNETT

From cruiser warfare to the opposing battle fleets, from the far seas back to home waters, where in August 1914 the British matched 27 dreadnoughts and battlecruisers to Germany's 18. Though the Grand Fleet, of which Admiral Jellicoe became Commander-in-Chief at the outbreak of war, was much the stronger, it could not adopt the traditional British strategy of close blockade; coal-fired boilers, mines, and submarines made this impossible. The Admiralty had therefore conceived the alternative of distant blockade; the High Seas Fleet was to be confined to the North Sea by a Grand Fleet based on Scapa Flow until it could be brought to action and destroyed. Again and again Jellicoe swept across the North Sea in the hope that the German battle fleet would come out, if only to try to prevent the British Expeditionary Force from crossing the Channel. But September came without Admiral von Ingenohl's dreadnoughts leaving their base in the River Jade. Persuaded that Paris would quickly fall to his Army, the Kaiser had ordained that his ships were to wage guerrilla warfare until such a weakening of the English fleet had been achieved that the two could meet on more or less equal terms.

Against German light craft which attempted to further this policy the Admiralty soon retaliated. Commodore Tyrwhitt's Harwich Force of two light cruisers, the *Arethusa* and *Fearless*, and 16 destroyers was ordered to raid the Heligoland Bight at dawn on 28th August. It was hoped that this would draw German ships out of the Jade to where seven submarines, controlled by Commodore Keyes, were waiting. Both forces were to be supported by Admiral Beatty's five battlecruisers and Commodore

Goodenough's six light cruisers. Tyrwhitt sighted patrolling enemy torpedo-boats shortly before 0700 and gave chase until he came within range of two light cruisers, the *Stettin* and *Frauenlob*, with whom the *Arethusa* and *Fearless* had a brief engagement. Tyrwhitt then swept westward to meet further torpedo-boats, which likewise fled after their leader had been sunk. At 1100 the *Arethusa* encountered the light cruiser *Strassburg* and drove her off into the mist. Next, the light cruiser *Mainz* was pursued to the north where she ran into Goodenough's squadron by whom she was sent to the bottom at 1310.

Before this, however, Tyrwhitt was again engaged by the *Strassburg*, supported by the light cruiser *Köln*. Both were driven off, but the appearance of yet three more light cruisers, the *Stralsund*, *Danzig*, and *Ariadne*, together with the *Stettin*, alerted the waiting Beatty to the possibility that Tyrwhitt's force, in which the *Arethusa* and two destroyers had suffered some damage, might be overwhelmed. 'Am I justified in going into that hornets' nest with these great ships?' he asked his Flag Captain. Captain Chatfield's advice was very different from that which Wray gave Troubridge: 'Surely we must go', he said. By 1135 the battlecruisers were heading at full speed to the rescue, and soon after 1230 their 13.5-inch salvoes sent the *Köln* and *Ariadne* to the bottom, only the mist saving the other German ships from a like fate. But though Beatty's boldness had achieved a decisive British victory, the raid had come too near disaster for the Admiralty to allow it to be repeated.

In November *U18* penetrated Scapa Flow. Though rammed and damaged by a trawler before

HMS *Lion*, flagship of Admiral Beatty's battlecruiser force at Jutland, in drydock. From a
collection of six drawings by Sir Muirhead Bone presented to the British Museum in 1917 by the
Admiralty

Scapa Flow, the Grand Fleet's base in the Orkney Islands. In the foreground is one of the 'Collingwood' class battleships at anchor, with cruisers beyond her. Scapa, one of the most desolate naval bases in the world, commands the northern exit from the North Sea into the Atlantic

she could find targets for her torpedoes, Jellicoe decided to move his base, first to Loch Ewe, then to Loch Swilly, until Scapa's defences could be strengthened. These harbours were so far away that the Grand Fleet had to remain at sea except when it needed coal, with its ships increasingly subject to defects through prolonged steaming. Though Jellicoe could now count 30 dreadnoughts and battlecruisers under his command, he had six away refitting, the *Audacious* had been sunk by a mine, and Cradock's defeat had brought Admiralty orders to detach three battlecruisers to the South Atlantic. For the time being the High Seas Fleet's 21 dreadnoughts and battlecruisers were numerically as strong. Equally important, Jellicoe knew the quality of the German dreadnoughts, that ship for ship they were better built than the British. In these circumstances he decided that he could only contemplate a fleet action in the northern half of the North Sea where the Germans could not rely on having submarines and minelayers to assist in a fleet action. Such caution might not accord with tradition, but destruction of the enemy was not to be sought without regard for the

consequences of failure, which would be the inability to maintain command of the sea by blockade. The Admiralty assured Jellicoe of their full confidence in his contemplated conduct of the fleet.

This caution, coupled with the Kaiser's restrictions on his ships, delayed a major clash between the two fleets for another eighteen months. Meantime, however, there were lesser engagements. On 3rd November Hipper's battlecruisers bombarded Yarmouth, which was too far south for the Grand Fleet to reach the scene in time. Copies of the German Navy's codes which had been salvaged from the wrecked cruiser *Magdeburg* enabled the Admiralty to decipher enough German radio signals to give warning of their future plans. Through them it was learned that von Ingenohl had ordered a further raid on the British east coast on 16th December, though it was not known that the raid was this time to be supported by the whole High Seas Fleet. British destroyers encountered von Ingenohl's advanced screen at dawn; and von Ingenohl, convinced that he was running into the whole Grand Fleet, hurried back to the Jade, leaving his bombarding battlecruisers to their fate. By the time the *Derfflinger* and *Von der Tann* had fired on Scarborough and Whitby, and the *Seydlitz*, *Moltke*, and *Blücher* had inflicted greater damage on Hartlepool, their escape routes through the east coast minefields had been cut. Admiral Hipper, commanding the German battlecruisers, chose the centre gap where an overwhelming British force of four battlecruisers under Beatty and eight dreadnoughts under Admiral Warrender was waiting. His advanced cruisers were sighted by Beatty's light cruiser screen under Commodore Goodenough, but an unfortunate signal by the *Lion*, Beatty's flagship, misled Goodenough into losing touch with the enemy. Hipper's force hauled away to the north before Admiral Warrender's powerful squadron could sight them.

On 23rd January 1915 Hipper again left the Jade with four battlecruisers to raid the British Dogger Bank patrol at dawn next day. The Admiralty had enough warning to order Beatty's five battlecruisers, now based on Rosyth, accompanied by Goodenough's light cruisers, to rendezvous with Tyrwhitt's force at 0700 on the 24th between Hipper and his base. Too late to reach the rendezvous in time, Jellicoe was ordered to bring his battle fleet south in support. As Beatty's ships met Tyrwhitt's north-east of the Dogger Bank, they sighted Hipper's which promptly turned for home. These were, however, steadily overhauled until, at 0900, the *Lion* opened fire on the *Blücher*. As the chase continued, Beatty's battlecruisers engaged their opposite numbers, and at 0930 the *Lion* scored a hit that was fateful in its consequences. A 13·5-inch shell pierced the armour of the *Seydlitz's* after turret. The flash passed down the trunk to the magazine into the adjacent turret, killing the crews of both. Only the prompt flooding of these magazines saved the ships from destruction.

By 0950 the *Blücher* was badly battered, whereas the British ships went unscathed until shortly after 1000, when the *Lion* was hit by three shells from the *Derfflinger*, one of which damaged her considerably and caused her to slow down. Fifteen minutes later Hipper decided to leave the *Blücher* to her fate. With the *Indomitable* ordered to finish her off and his other ships still closing the rest of the enemy, an annihilating victory was within Beatty's grasp. Unfortunately, at 1100 he saw what he took to be a submarine's periscope on the *Lion's* starboard bow and, suspecting a U-boat trap, signalled his squadron to turn 90

degrees to port, then hoisted, 'Course NE'. With the *Lion* lagging well astern of the rest of the squadron, Beatty gave the further order: 'Attack the enemy's rear'; and because the flags for 'Course NE' were still flying, both were read together as: 'Attack enemy bearing NE'. This being the *Blücher's* bearing, Beatty's second-in-command, Rear-Admiral Moore, allowed the *Tiger*, *Princess Royal*, and *New Zealand* to swing round and join the *Indomitable* in completing the destruction of the German lame duck. By the time Beatty could board a destroyer and rehoist his flag in the *Princess Royal*, Hipper had vanished over the horizon.

'The sinking of the *Blücher* and the flight of the other German ships was a solid and indisputable result', wrote Churchill. But it would have been more decisive if Moore had not concentrated on destroying one crippled vessel instead of pursuing the main enemy force. As important, while the British Navy remained in ignorance of a serious defect in the turret design of all its dreadnoughts, the Germans profited from the near loss of the *Seydlitz*, and corrected theirs before the High Seas Fleet's next encounter.

The Kaiser vented his anger at the loss of the *Blücher* on von Ingenohl; he was superseded by the cautious Admiral von Pohl who never allowed his ships to venture beyond Horns Reef. But his U-boats were authorised to begin a new campaign. The Royal Navy's submarine offensive was never more than ancillary to the operations of the British battle fleet, in spite of conspicuous successes in waters denied to the latter, notably the Baltic and the Sea of Marmara. But German U-boats achieved some startling results. On 22nd September 1914, *U9* sent the armoured cruisers *Aboukir*, *Cressy*, and *Hogue* to the bottom of the North Sea, all within an hour. The *Hawke* followed them on 15th October, and the pre-dreadnought *Formidable* in the Channel early on 1st January 1915.

Germany was not, however, content with operations which only hampered the Grand Fleet's blockade and threatened de Robeck's Dardanelles bombardment force. When the Kaiser's dream of a swift victory on land dissolved into the nightmare of trench warfare, the German Admiralty realised the potency of the U-boat as a weapon for attacking the merchant shipping on which Britain depended for the sinews of war. Against unleashing unrestricted

U-boat warfare there was, however, one obstacle; international law recognised no distinction between submarines and surface ships and both were required to board a merchant vessel to check whether she was carrying contraband and to ensure the safety of her passengers and crew before sinking her. But the time needed to comply with this rule was enough to expose a U-boat to destruction by British light craft. The solution was to defy international law; to sink without warning. To do this, Germany declared a 'war zone' round the British Isles on 16th February, 1915, in which 'every merchant vessel will be destroyed without it being possible to avoid damage to the crews and passengers, it being impossible to avoid attacks being made on neutral ships in mistake for those of the enemy'.

In spite of the multiplicity of steps improvised by the British Admiralty to counter this campaign, including an Auxiliary Patrol of more than 1,000 small ships, and the innovation of Q-ships, it achieved considerable success. It was, indeed, fortunate that it did not last longer than six months. Initial neutral protests were as nothing to the outcry that followed *U20's* attack on the *Lusitania* on 7th May 1915, which cost the lives of 1,198 of her passengers and crew. When the world raised its voice in scandalised horror, the Kaiser banned further attacks on passenger liners. But this restriction did not prevent another serious incident, and on 19th August *U24* sent the liner *Arabic* to the bottom of the Irish Sea. This time the U.S.A. protested so strongly that other counsels prevailed. On 5th October, by which time Britain had lost 900,000 tons of shipping, the Kaiser issued orders to cease all forms of submarine warfare on the west coast of Great Britain and in the Channel.

In the first month of 1916 von Pohl was found to be mortally ill and was succeeded in command of the High Seas Fleet by Admiral Scheer. He was an aggressive admiral who was not slow to demonstrate a more forward strategy. A British minesweeping flotilla was overwhelmed by German light forces on the Dogger Bank in February before Beatty or Tyrwhitt could reach the scene. Further operations were planned in an endeavour to trap weaker elements of the Grand Fleet. The first attempt, in March, failed because the Admiralty learned of it too late to order the Grand Fleet out. Ten days later, when the Harwich Force attacked the Zeppelin sheds at Tondern, Scheer left the Jade intent on

Admiral von Scheer, Commander-in-Chief of the High Seas Fleet at Jutland, was out-manoeuvered by Jellicoe and found himself cut off from his home bases in Germany by the Grand Fleet. Two attempts to break through ended in failure, but during the night he managed to force his way through the destroyer flotillas behind the British fleet

Tyrwhitt's destruction. Beatty sped south to his rescue, and early on the 26th it looked as though the British battlecruisers would come face to face with the High Seas Fleet without Jellicoe's support. Fortunately for the British a rising gale decided Scheer against risking action in a storm.

The High Seas Fleet put to sea again on 21st April, when fog prevented the two fleets meeting. Jellicoe's ships were refuelling as Scheer's battlecruisers left harbour to bombard Lowestoft. The Admiralty only learned of this because the *Seydlitz* was damaged by a mine. The Grand Fleet and the Harwich Force were immediately ordered out, Tyrwhitt in time to sight four German battlecruisers at first light on the 25th. Although not deflected from their first objective, the German ships were obliged to answer a call for help from their light cruisers before they could bombard Yarmouth.

Even so, the Germans made no attempt to destroy Tyrwhitt's small force, instead they chose to retire eastwards at high speed towards Scheer's battle fleet, which by then had already reversed course for home. Tyrwhitt took the Harwich Force after them but the Admiralty, fearing the outcome, called off the chase. On receiving the signal to Tyrwhitt, Beatty's battlecruisers, coming south at full speed, also turned for home, not knowing that the enemy ships were less than 50 miles away.

From the bombardment of Lowestoft Scheer learned that the High Seas Fleet had crossed the North Sea too far to the south to trap part of Jellicoe's fleet. So he designated Sunderland as the next target for Hipper's battlecruisers, with U-boats stationed off the British bases to cause losses as the Grand Fleet emerged. Extensive Zeppelin reconnaissance was also necessary to make certain that Jellicoe was not already at sea. However, defects in several dreadnoughts compelled the postponement of this operation from mid-May to the end of the month. But the weather at that time was unsuitable for airship patrols, so Scheer chose, therefore, the less risky alternative of showing his fleet off Norway as a means of drawing the British. Hipper, in the *Lützow*, led the 1st and 2nd Scouting Groups of battlecruisers to sea at 0200 on 31st May, accompanied by four light cruisers and three destroyer flotillas. Fifty miles astern, up the swept Channel to the Horns Reef, followed Scheer's battle fleet; seven dreadnoughts of the 3rd Battle Squadron under Admiral Behncke; the *Friedrich der Grosse* (fleet flagship) leading eight of the 1st B.S. under Admiral Schmidt, and six pre-dreadnoughts of the 2nd B.S. (Admiral Mauve), with five light cruisers and four destroyer flotillas.

The Admiralty received sufficient warning of this sortie from intercepted radio messages to order the Grand Fleet out on the evening of the 30th. The *Lion* led Beatty's 1st Battlecruiser Squadron (Admiral Brock) of four ships and 2nd B.C.S. (Admiral Pakenham) of two ships to sea from the Forth, supported by the 5th B.S. of four *Queen Elizabeth*-class dreadnoughts (Admiral Evan-Thomas), 12 light cruisers, and three destroyer flotillas. Jellicoe's battle fleet sailed from Scapa and Cromarty; 24 dreadnoughts, divided into the 1st B.S. (Admiral Burney), 2nd B.S. (Admiral Jerram) and 4th B.S. (Admiral Sturdee), with the 3rd Battlecruiser Squadron of three *Invincible*-class ships (Admiral Hood), eight armoured cruisers, and 12 light cruisers and three flotillas of destroyers. For comparison the two forces are best tabulated:

	Grand Fleet	High Seas Fleet
Battleships:		
dreadnoughts	28	16
pre-dreadnoughts	—	6
Battlecruisers	9	5
Armoured cruisers	8	—
Light cruisers	26	11
Destroyers/Torpedo-boats	77	61

Around noon on the 31st the Admiralty misinterpreted its intelligence to the extent of telling Jellicoe and Beatty that Scheer was still in the Jade. So at 1415, having reached a position 100 miles to the north of the Horns Reef without sighting the enemy, Beatty swung his force round to meet Jellicoe's, 65 miles to the north. Since some 50 miles then separated the *Lion* from Hipper's force on its course for Norway, Beatty would have missed making contact but for the chance that the *Galatea*, the

Admiral Sir John Jellicoe, Commander-in-Chief of the Grand Fleet at Jutland, ascending the ladder to the bridge of the *Iron Duke*. Poor visibility, signalling errors, and the lack of available information did much to rob him of a possible victory

eastern ship of his cruiser screen, moved out to investigate a neutral steamer and sighted the *Elbing*, the western ship of Hipper's screen, doing likewise. Beatty reacted to her enemy report with an order swinging his force back to S.S.E. at 22 knots. But the 5th Battle Squadron was too far to the north to read the *Lion's* flag signal: by the time Evan-Thomas received it by searchlight his powerful dreadnoughts were ten miles astern of the battle-cruisers – a 'failure' (Jellicoe's word) to concentrate that was to have considerable consequences. Beatty was, however, chiefly concerned to ensure that Hipper did not again find safety in flight.

However, the German Admiral held his course in the hope of destroying the British light cruiser squadron; not until he sighted Beatty's battlecruisers at 1530 did Hipper swing round to S.S.E. to lead his opponent towards Scheer's battle fleet. This allowed Beatty to close the range to 15,000 yards by 1545, when both sides opened fire. The Germans did the greater damage. The *Lion* was only saved from destruction by the rapid flooding of her midship turret magazines. The *Indefatigable* was struck by a salvo from the *Von der Tann* soon after 1600, and rent by an explosion that left only two survivors. Not until Evan-Thomas managed to bring his 5th B.S. into action with its steady gunnery was the *Von der Tann* hit and damaged and two of the *Seydlitz's* turrets put out of action. The British did not, however, keep their margin of nine ships over the enemy's five: at 1626 the *Queen Mary* met the same fate as the *Indefatigable*. But Beatty remained unperturbed: 'There seems to be something wrong with our bloody ships today', was his now legendary comment as he ordered his force to close the range, and whilst the 5th B.S. smote the *Moltke* and the *Von der Tann* again and again, a destroyer's torpedo flooded the *Seydlitz*.

At 1638 Rear-Admiral Goodenough, in the light cruiser *Southampton*, dispelled Jellicoe's and Beatty's illusion that Scheer's dreadnoughts were still in the Jade with an electrifying report: 'Have sighted enemy battle fleet bearing S.E. course N'. In spite of the loss of two battlecruisers, Beatty had been justly confident that his eight remaining heavy ships could destroy Hipper's five; but now he had to escape from overwhelming strength and lead Scheer north into the maw of Jellicoe's battle fleet. With the enemy's dreadnoughts only 11 miles away, he ordered his

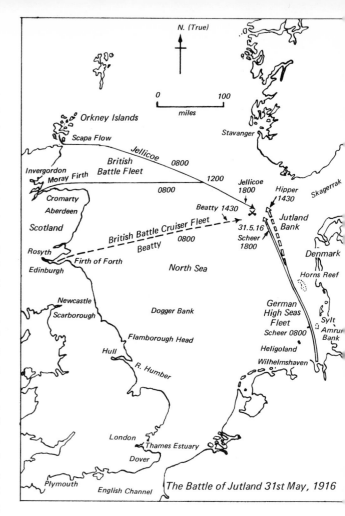

The Battle of Jutland 31st May, 1916

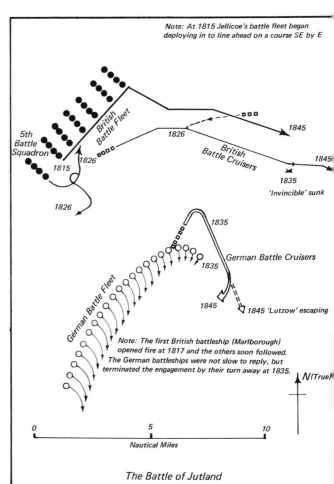

Note: At 1815 Jellicoe's battle fleet began deploying in to line ahead on a course SE by E

Note: The first British battleship (Marlborough) opened fire at 1817 and the others soon followed. The German battleships were not slow to reply, but terminated the engagement by their turn away at 1835.

The Battle of Jutland
The first clash between the battle fleets

ships to reverse their course. But again there was a delay in passing this signal to Evan-Thomas; by the time the 5th B.S. turned, it was within range of Scheer's battle fleet. Fortunately the *Queen Elizabeth* class were stoutly armoured; they not only withstood this onslaught but inflicted further damage on Hipper's battlecruisers, and on the head of Scheer's line. Goodenough held on until he could report the details of Scheer's battle fleet from a range inside seven miles.

Jellicoe had reacted to the *Galatea's* sighting report by increasing his battle fleet's speed to 20 knots, and sending the 3rd B.C.S. on ahead. By the time the *Iron Duke* received Goodenough's report, Scheer's battle fleet was only 50 miles away. Nonetheless, Beatty realised that if his C-in-C was to make contact he must prevent Hipper giving warning of the British battle fleet's approach. To this end he maintained a speed of 25 knots after turning to N.N.W., whereby his battlecruisers drew out of range by 1710, leaving the 5th B.S. to continue their effective engagement for another quarter of an hour. Beatty then swung round to the north-east to prevent the pursuing Hipper from sighting Jellicoe, and the eight British heavy ships inflicted so much further damage on their opponents that by 1800 Hipper was in full flight to the east.

Much of consequence happened around 1800.

Jellicoe's battle fleet was approaching Scheer's in six columns, each of four ships in line ahead disposed abeam. To deploy this compact body into single line of battle the C-in-C depended on his advanced forces for news of an enemy that was still beyond the horizon. But his admirals and captains failed him: though the two fleets were closing at a combined speed of 40 knots, none gave him the bearing and distance of Scheer's flagship. Moreover, when the *Marlborough*, leading his western column, sighted Beatty's flagship, Jellicoe learned the disturbing fact that the *Lion* was 11 miles nearer the *Iron Duke*, and on a more westerly bearing, than he had supposed her to be. He would sight Scheer's battle fleet 20 minutes earlier than expected; he had that much less time in which to deploy before the two battle fleets came within range.

The 3rd B.C.S., pressing ahead since 1510, could not help him because Hood had steered S.S.E. to prevent the enemy escaping by the Skaggerak. This took him to the eastward of Hipper, contact being made when one of his light cruisers, H.M.S. *Chester*, encountered the 2nd Scouting Group. Speeding to the *Chester's* rescue, Hood's battlecruisers reduced the *Wiesbaden* to a smoking wreck, and left the *Frankfurt* and *Pillau* in little better condition. The German light cruisers were only saved from annihilation by the appearance of Hipper's battlecruisers.

But none of this was reported to Jellicoe. He was left in doubt over the position of Scheer's battle fleet until 1801, when the *Lion* appeared out of the mist on the *Iron Duke's* starboard bow and replied to Jellicoe's repeated query: 'Where is enemy battle fleet?' with 'Enemy battle fleet bearing S.S.W.'. This was just in time for his quick brain to make the vital decision on which the future course of the action would depend. At 1815 the Grand Fleet began deployment on the port wing column, steering S.E. by E., whereby he not only crossed the enemy's 'T' but put the Grand Fleet between the High Seas Fleet and its base.

Shortly before 1800 the 1st Cruiser Squadron of armoured cruisers sighted the 2nd S.G., turned in pursuit, and met disaster. Hipper's 1st Scouting Group and Scheer's 3rd Battle Squadron loomed out of the haze only 7,000 yards away. Admiral Arbuthnot's flagship, H.M.S. *Defence*, was destroyed with all her crew; H.M.S. *Warrior* was so crippled that she had to be taken in tow, only to sink early

HMS *Indefatigable*, photographed just before Jutland. She was the first of the three British battlecruisers to be sunk in the action, hit during Beatty's chase of Hipper's Scouting Force to the southward

Admiral Beatty's flagship, HMS *Lion*, very nearly suffered the same fate as the other three battlecruisers which blew up. She was hit on the midship turret, and only saved from destruction by the prompt flooding of the magazine. This photograph taken from the German battlecruiser *Derfflinger* shows the explosion of the shell on 'Q' turret. On the left, destroyers of the British 13th Flotilla can be seen taking up position to attack with torpedoes

The German battlecruiser *Seydlitz* photographed in Wilhelmshaven after her return from Jutland. She was hit about 24 times by heavy shells and also by a torpedo, and had more than 2,500 tons of water in her. She had to be beached at the entrance to the Jade River and pumped out before she could enter Wilhelmshaven

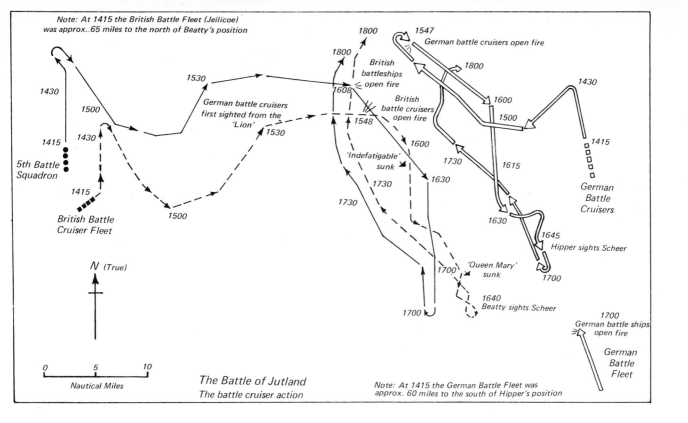

The Battle of Jutland
The battle cruiser action

Note: At 1415 the British Battle Fleet (Jellicoe) was approx. 65 miles to the north of Beatty's position

5th Battle Squadron

British Battle Cruiser Fleet

N (True)

0   5   10
Nautical Miles

German battle cruisers first sighted from the 'Lion'

German battle cruisers open fire

British battleships open fire

British battle cruisers open fire

'Indefatigable' sunk

'Queen Mary' sunk

Hipper sights Scheer

Beatty sights Scheer

German Battle Cruisers

German battle ships open fire

German Battle Fleet

Note: At 1415 the German Battle Fleet was approx. 60 miles to the south of Hipper's position

next morning; H.M.S. *Black Prince*, likewise seriously damaged, blundered into Scheer's battle fleet during the night and was sunk. The visibility round this aptly-named 'Windy Corner' was so bad that Evan-Thomas did not sight Jellicoe's battle fleet until it was too late to take the 5th B.S. into its proper station ahead of the fleet; and when turning towards the rear, the *Warspite's* helm jammed. By the time Captain Philpotts had extricated his ship from turning two involuntary circles under fire, she had suffered so much damage that she had to return to Rosyth.

The German C-in-C., with his battleships already in single line ahead, remained unaware of the approach of the British battle fleet until 1817. With Jellicoe's deployment cloaked by the pall of smoke over the battleground, Scheer's illusion was not shattered until the *Marlborough, Agincourt,* and *Revenge* opened fire, followed by many more. At last, after nearly two years of waiting, Jellicoe had brought the High Seas Fleet to action. The *König, Grosser Kurfürst,* and *Markgraf* suffered hits, whilst Scheer's gunners were unable to score. But Hipper's force gained one more dramatic success. Beatty's four surviving battlecruisers, reinforced now by Hood's 3rd B.C.S., were speeding to the van of their battle fleet when they were heavily engaged with Hipper's ships; at 1829 a shell from the *Derfflinger*

struck the midship turret of Hood's flagship, H.M.S. *Invincible*, which blew up leaving only six survivors. But Hipper's ships were in a worse state than the surviving British ones. The *Derfflinger* had 180 killed and wounded, all the *Von der Tann's* turrets were out of action, and the *Lützow's* speed was so much reduced that Hipper had to transfer his flag to the *Moltke.* Scheer's van would have suffered as badly had he not ordered his battle fleet to reverse course, so that by 1845 the whole of the High Seas Fleet was heading westward into the mist.

Nothing exemplifies Jellicoe's difficulties more than the brevity of this first clash between the battle fleets. In spite of the skill with which he had enmeshed the High Seas Fleet, poor visibility had allowed Scheer to extricate his ships after the *Iron Duke* had fired only nine salvoes. The effective counter to Scheer's turn was a resolute chase, but the British C-in-C would not risk his battleships by following closely after an enemy whom he believed would cover his retreat with torpedo attacks and by sowing mines in his wake, a possibility that gained support when a torpedo from the crippled *Wiesbaden* struck the *Marlborough,* flooding a boiler-room. Because this might be a mine, Jellicoe waited half an hour after Scheer's 'battle turn' before altering as far as S.W. by S. However, at 1855 Scheer again reversed course to steer straight for Jellicoe's line.

As soon as Goodenough reported that the enemy was again steering east, Jellicoe swung his ships back to south. And by 1910, when Hipper's battlecruisers and leading German battleships appeared out of the mist to starboard, the British C-in-C knew that he was again crossing his opponent's 'T'.

The *Marlborough* sighted three ships of the *König* class and opened fire at 10,750 yards. The *Lützow* and *Wiesbaden* suffered so much that they sank during the night. Beatty's ships joined in at 1920, 'making splendid practice'. The Germans replied to little effect: only the *Colossus* was hit, her damage slight. To save his fleet from destruction, Scheer signalled his battlecruisers to 'close the enemy and ram'. The 1st Scouting Group 'hurled themselves against the enemy', but they were not required to complete their death-ride; at 1917 Scheer changed his order to operate against the enemy's van while he extricated his stricken fleet by a second 'battle turn' of 16 points. By 1935, after an engagement of just 15 minutes, compared with 25 on the first occasion, the German heavy ships were again heading west into the mist.

Scheer's destroyers covered this retirement, closing to under 8,000 yards and firing 31 torpedoes, of which ten reached the British line. But Jellicoe believed his battle fleet to be threatened by many more, of which he expected 30 per cent to score hits unless he turned away so that his ships outran the torpedoes' range. Not until years later did he acknowledge that when a turn away would result in losing contact, the more risky alternative of a turn towards might be justified. As it was, he supposed the enemy's temporary disappearance to be due to no more than a thickening of the mist; when the torpedo threat was over, he turned only to the parallel course of south-west. Not until 2000, when Scheer was some 15 miles away, did the British C-in-C turn his battle fleet to west.

Concerned at being headed so far from his base, Scheer had, however, altered to south at 1945. The *Iron Duke* was then only 12 miles to the east, and the two fleets were soon again in contact. Around 2025, the German battlecruisers came under heavy fire from Beatty's force, before the latter turned their guns on Mauve's pre-dreadnought squadron which was now leading Scheer's battle fleet. The two light cruisers *Caroline* and *Royalist*, stationed in the van of Jellicoe's line, sighted Scheer's battle fleet, but Admiral Jerram believed them to be British battle-

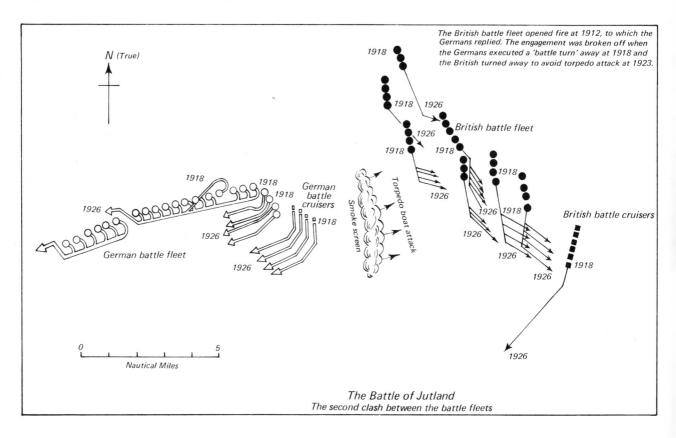

The British battle fleet opened fire at 1912, to which the Germans replied. The engagement was broken off when the Germans executed a 'battle turn' away at 1918 and the British turned away to avoid torpedo attack at 1923.

The Battle of Jutland
The second clash between the battle fleets

Three British battlecruisers were sunk during the Battle of Jutland, all from the same cause.
Hit in their turrets, flames from the exploding shells travelled down the ammunition trunks and
ignited the magazines. This photograph shows HMS *Invincible* broken in two by such an
explosion, with only her bow and stern visible above water

The British flagship at Jutland, HMS *Iron Duke*, photographed at Scapa Flow in 1918. By this period of the war, British battleships had been equipped with scouting and spotting aircraft, and the launching rails can be seen fitted on the guns of 'B' turret

cruisers and continued to lead the battle fleet in silence on a parallel course.

These were the last encounters between the two fleets before nightfall. But since Scheer had twice fled from the guns of a force which now stretched for ten miles between the High Seas Fleet and its harbours, Jellicoe could have high hopes of another 'Glorious First of June' when the sun rose in five hours' time.

Scheer was so determined to gain the sanctuary of the Horns Reef that he accepted the hazards of an engagement during the night. Jellicoe rejected the idea of a night action as leading to possible disaster, owing to the presence of torpedo craft in large numbers and to the difficulty of distinguishing friend from foe. Knowing that there were two other swept channels to the Jade as well as Horns Reef, Jellicoe decided to steer to the southward where he should be in a position to renew the engagement at daylight. At 2117 he closed up his battle fleet into its night cruising order of four columns in line ahead disposed abeam.

He did not ignore the Horns Reef route; his destroyers were disposed five miles astern where they would be in an excellent position for attacking the enemy should he turn to regain his base during the night.

Such news as Jellicoe had gleaned from his ships

around this time led him to believe the High Seas Fleet to be well to the north-west. In reality it was only eight miles away because, at 2114, Scheer had altered to S.S.E. Two hours earlier Scheer had decided to assist his fleet's escape by sending all available destroyers to attack the Grand Fleet. But the 2nd Flotilla approached when there was still enough light for it to be driven off, and was too far astern to achieve anything when it tried again half an hour later. Joined by the 3rd Flotilla it set course for the Skaw and returned to Kiel. The 5th and 7th Flotillas fired four torpedoes at one of the British flotillas at 2150 without result, and then passed astern of the Grand Fleet on a course for the Horns Reef.

Throughout the night there was a series of clashes with the British destroyers as Scheer forced his way through behind the British battle fleet. Both sides lost ships, the Germans three light cruisers, two destroyers, and one pre-dreadnought; the British one armoured cruiser and five destroyers. Nevertheless, in spite of their losses, the Germans had gained their major objective. By dawn, the whole battle fleet was through and safely within reach of its base.

Although the fighting through the night had been severe and had been easily visible from the bridges of the British battleships, no ships actually engaged against the German heavy ships reported to Jellicoe that the enemy fleet was breaking through. Even more extraordinary, some of the battleships in the rear of Jellicoe's night formation, and notably the 5th Battle Squadron, actually sighted German battleships, but failed to report them to the C-in-C and took no action towards engaging them.

The Admiralty itself was also far from blameless. During the night three vital signals from Scheer were decyphered, each of them indicating beyond doubt that the High Seas Fleet was making for Horns Reef. None of them was passed to Jellicoe, and so he held on to the southward. Had he received even one of them he could have altered the course of the fleet and brought Scheer to action in the early morning of 1st June.

It was a most unsatisfactory ending. For two years the Grand Fleet had been hoping and praying for just one chance of a full-scale meeting with the High Seas Fleet. Now they had had it, and a possible victory had been denied them, partly by the North Sea mist of the evening of the 31st, partly by a series of signal failures at critical moments, partly by an administrative breakdown in the Admiralty which failed to provide the Commander-in-Chief with the vital information it had gained during the night, and partly, it must be admitted, by a lack of decisive action by the captains of those battleships which, in the night, had sighted Scheer's ships as they made their way through the wake of the Grand Fleet.

By four o'clock on the morning of 1st June, Jellicoe received a signal from the Admiralty which made it plain beyond all doubt that Scheer was safe within the swept channel beyond Horns Reef. Sadly, Jellicoe swept northward with the fleet in the faint hope of finding one or two damaged ships or stragglers. He found none. During the morning of 2nd June the battlecruisers reached their base at Rosyth; in the afternoon the battle fleet was anchored in Scapa Flow. At 9.45 p.m. that evening Jellicoe signalled to the Admiralty that the fleet was again ready for sea at four hours' notice.

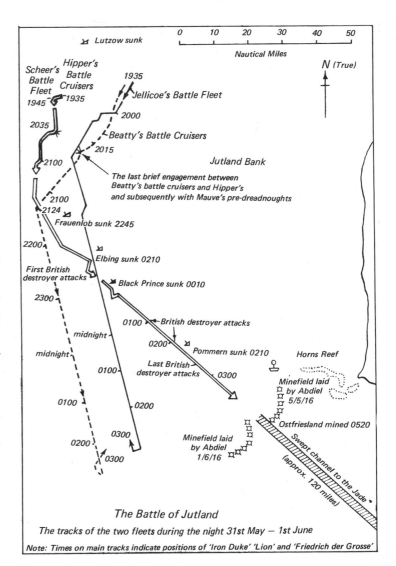

The Battle of Jutland

The tracks of the two fleets during the night 31st May – 1st June

Note: Times on main tracks indicate positions of 'Iron Duke' 'Lion' and 'Friedrich der Grosse'

CHAPTER 19

U-boat Warfare – The unrestricted campaign – Introduction of convoy – German operations against the Scandinavian convoys – The attack on Zeebrugge – Surrender of the High Seas Fleet

GEOFFREY BENNETT

Both Britain and Germany claimed a victory at Jutland, but Scheer was quick to realise that, whatever the German people might be led to believe, his officers and men were not so gullible. To restore morale he took the fleet to sea again in the middle of August for a dawn bombardment of Sunderland by von Hipper's 1st Scouting Group, supported by the battle fleet. The Grand Fleet sailed to intercept, and at 1400 on the 19th the ships were cleared for action. But chance denied Jellicoe the battle he so earnestly desired. Zeppelin *L13* sighted Tyrwhitt's light cruisers and destroyers north-east of Cromer and reported them to Scheer as battleships. Believing he had a detachment of the British battle fleet within reach, Scheer turned towards them. By the time he realised that he was chasing phantoms, *U53* had sighted Jellicoe's fleet and revealed how nearly the High Seas Fleet had been trapped by overwhelming force. Nor did it return to Germany without damage; the submarine *E23* put a torpedo into the *Westfalen* as she was hurrying back to the Jade.

The 24 U-boats which Scheer deployed for this abortive operation scored two successes; they sank the light cruisers *Nottingham* and *Falmouth*. The Admiralty reacted to this danger by endorsing Jellicoe's cautious strategy, for the Grand Fleet, in which it would take a year to remedy the deficiencies revealed at Jutland, was still the keystone of the allied cause. When next warned on 18th October that Scheer intended a sortie the Grand Fleet was not immediately ordered out; it was brought only to short notice for steam. Nor was it required to sail. A few hours after the High Seas Fleet left the Jade the submarine *E38* torpedoed the light cruiser *München*

and Scheer, fearing a submarine trap, hurried back to harbour.

The German C-in-C had a further set-back in November. Sailing the *Moltke* and a division of dreadnoughts to cover the rescue of *U20* and *U30* which had stranded on the Danish coast, he nearly lost the *Grosser Kurfürst* and *Kronprinz* to torpedoes from the British submarine *J1*. Two raids on the Straits of Dover were, however, more successful. On 28th October torpedo-boats sank a British destroyer and six drifters; a month later they bombarded Margate. The latter sortie revived the public criticism that had followed earlier bombardments of the British east coast and the Government decided to appoint a more vigorous First Sea Lord. At the end of November Jellicoe was moved to the Admiralty in London and Admiral Beatty took over command of the Grand Fleet.

Jellicoe was also needed at the Admiralty for a more important reason. In 1916 the German Navy began to reap the harvest of a building programme which would augment its underwater fleet by more than 300 submarines. With the German Army's growing demand for a naval offensive that would help achieve a breakthrough on the Western Front came a note from the U.S.A. to all belligerents which seemed to provide the Kaiser with a solution to the contradictory advice of his civilian and Service advisers. This was a proposal that merchant ships should no longer be armed. And when the British Government rejected the proposal, it was supposed in Berlin that Washington would adopt retaliatory measures to compel London's compliance. This was construed into believing that it would be safe to

The *Orion, Monarch, Conqueror,* and *Thunderer* taking up formation at sea. All four of these ships fought at Jutland, where they formed the 2nd Division of the 2nd Battle Squadron. The *Thunderer* later became the cadets' training ship after the war

renew U-boat warfare against merchant shipping provided that passenger ships were exempt from attack. But when on 24th March 1916, *UB29* torpedoed the S.S. *Sussex,* which was carrying a number of American passengers, a note was received from Washington threatening the severance of diplomatic relations unless Germany at once abandoned submarine warfare against merchant ships. This was enough to force the restriction of U-boats to legitimate targets for the next nine months.

But Jutland, and the failure of Scheer's subsequent sorties, persuaded the Kaiser to change his mind once more. Accepting Scheer's contention that victory could only be attained by destroying the economic existence of Great Britain, he ordered unrestricted U-boat warfare to begin for the third time on 1st February 1917. The Admiralty reacted by intensifying its previous anti-submarine measures, only to find that it was fighting a losing battle against this new form of blockade. In the first three months of unrestricted warfare 1,250,000 tons of British merchant shipping had been sunk, a figure which rose to another 1,500,000 tons in the next four months. This was a rate which Britain's shipbuilding resources could not hope to match. In spite of the belated introduction of stringent rationing, the country's reserves of essential foods dropped to six weeks' supply. So, too, with the sinews of war; for shortage of oil the Grand Fleet's exercises had to be curtailed.

Admiral Sir David Beatty, who commanded the British battlecruisers in the Battle of Jutland, succeeded Admiral Jellicoe as Commander-in-Chief of the Grand Fleet at the end of 1916. It was on him that fell much of the burden of the campaign against the U-boats when they opened their unrestricted warfare against shipping in 1917

Rear-Admiral Duff, whom Jellicoe had appointed to head a new anti-submarine division of the Naval Staff, suggested adopting the traditional proven method of protecting seaborne trade by sailing merchant ships in escorted convoys. Jellicoe contended that Britain lacked the destroyers to provide the necessary escorts. Not until May, a month after the entry of the U.S.A. into the war removed this objection, did Jellicoe allow a trial convoy to be run. And it needed another three months before he agreed to all shipping being escorted through the war zone. Thus it was not until the last four months of 1917 that the convoy system became effective and the rising graph of merchant shipping losses was reversed.

Because of the grievous loss of merchant shipping in 1917, combined with his reluctance to introduce the principle of convoy protection, Jellicoe was dismissed as First Sea Lord and replaced by Admiral Sir Rosslyn Wemyss at the end of the year. By May 1918 the convoy system had become so effective that the tonnage of newly built British ships exceeded the tonnage lost by enemy action. As important, because U-boats were forced to seek their prey around the convoys where the allied anti-submarine forces were concentrated, the number of submarines sunk in 1917–18 was as high as 132, a rate of loss in both craft and crews that Germany could ill afford.

Up in Scapa Flow Beatty made no change in the Grand Fleet's strategy. However, as an anti-U-boat measure he began running the Scandinavian trade in convoy. He realised that this would provide attractive targets for tip-and-run surface raids but believed the risk to be acceptable; and when six months elapsed without incident, it seemed that he was justified. In truth, Scheer was otherwise occupied. In the summer of 1917 the High Seas Fleet was convulsed by mutinies caused by inactivity, short rations, callous officers, and subversive propaganda. The allies might still be powerless to break the German Army's stranglehold in Flanders, but the British Navy's blockade was sapping the German people's will for war. It was October before Scheer suppressed this revolt and was free to operate against the Scandinavian convoys. On 16th October he sailed the two new light cruisers *Brummer* and *Bremse* for a foray against the Lerwick-Bergen route. Evading detection by Beatty's patrols the two ships reached a position 60 miles to the east of the

Shetlands at dawn on the 17th where they sighted an east-bound convoy escorted by two destroyers, the *Strongbow* and *Mary Rose*. Both were quickly sunk, and nine out of twelve merchant ships followed them to the bottom before the cruisers returned unscathed to Germany. Six weeks later eight German destroyers made a similar raid. Four boats went west, to sink two stragglers from a south-bound convoy off Berwick on 11th December. The other four reached the latitude of Bergen on the 12th where they sighted six merchant ships, escorted by the destroyers *Partridge* and *Pellew*. The *Partridge* was sunk and the *Pellew* so disabled that she could do nothing to prevent the enemy sinking the whole convoy.

German minesweeping activities in the Heligoland Bight provided the next opportunity for action. After the Harwich Force, under Admiral Tyrwhitt, had had a successful encounter with German destroyers protecting the minesweepers, intelligence from the Admiralty revealed that Scheer intended in future to provide them with battleship cover. Since the Grand Fleet had now been strengthened by five U.S. dreadnoughts of Admiral Rodman's 6th Battle Squadron, and the battlecruiser force had been augmented by the *Repulse, Renown, Courageous*, and *Glorious*, he could afford to risk a surprise attack to gain a rich prize. On 16th November Scheer's minesweepers were escorted out by two destroyer flotillas supported by Admiral von Reuter's 2nd Scouting Group and the dreadnoughts *Kaiserin* and *Kaiser*. Forewarned, Beatty sailed his battlecruisers, now commanded by Admiral Pakenham, accompanied by Admiral Madden's 1st Battle Squadron.

Shortly after 0800 next day the minesweepers were surprised by British light cruisers. They retired homewards at full speed as von Reuter hurried to their rescue, only to come under fire from the *Courageous* and *Repulse*. Von Reuter reversed course and headed for the protection of the battleships. A running fight ensued until 0930 in which neither side scored more than an occasional hit. By then Admiral Napier in the *Courageous* judged that the minefield risk was too great for the larger British ships to advance and hoisted the recall. The *Repulse* ignored it and, with the 1st Light Cruiser Squadron, pressed on and was rewarded by sighting the *Kaiser* and *Kaiserin*. The British ships swung away to the northwest to lead their opponents to where Pakenham and Madden's squadrons were waiting. But it was to no

Opposite: The sinking of HMS *Audacious*, a battleship of the 'Iron Duke' class, after striking a mine laid by a German U-boat. Her loss early in the war came at a time when Jellicoe had six other battleships refitting and under repair, the only period in the war, if the Germans had known it, when their fleet was equal in strength to that of the British

avail; the German battleships would not leave the safety of the German minefields even though the *Hindenburg* and *Moltke* were hurrying to their support. So the action came to an inconclusive end with no significant losses or damage on either side.

In January 1918 the British Government concluded that the failure of the previous autumn's offensive in Flanders was of such consequence that the Grand Fleet should do nothing to provoke a fleet action, even though it now had 43 dreadnoughts to Scheer's 24. Subject to maintaining the blockade, the Navy's overriding task was to defeat the U-boats. The rest of the nation's effort must be devoted to enabling its Army to hold back the Germans, who were now being reinforced from their eastern front following Russia's collapse, until the full weight of the American Army could be put into the line in 1919. A fleet action was, nonetheless, possible. The Scandinavian convoy débâcles obliged Beatty to cover the Lerwick-Bergen trade with a division of dreadnoughts which might yet draw the High Seas Fleet. And although the British C-in-C welcomed such a chance to avenge Jutland, he feared that the Admiralty might fail to give him enough warning for the Grand Fleet to reach the scene before the covering force was overwhelmed.

April 1918 showed that this fear was not groundless. The Admiralty gleaned no news of the High Seas Fleet's sortie from the Jade on the 22nd, its quarry a homeward-bound convoy covered by battlecruisers and light cruisers. Beatty remained ignorant of the crucial fact that the German battle fleet was moving as far north as Stavanger. Fortunately, Scheer's intelligence was 24 hours in error: the convoy of which he was in search had already crossed the North Sea. And when he ordered von Hipper's battlecruisers to search for it, the *Moltke* lost a propeller, an accident which obliged Scheer and von Hipper to break radio silence. This was enough for the Admiralty to order Beatty to sea. But the High Seas Fleet was already retiring to the south, with the *Moltke* in tow of the *Oldenburg*. By nightfall it had crossed ahead of the Grand Fleet's line of advance, to reach the Jade without incident except for the near-loss of the *Moltke* to a torpedo fired by *E42*.

The British Navy throughout the war laid numerous minefields in the Heligoland Bight at a depth where they were a danger to U-boats leaving and returning to German ports submerged; but channels could be swept through these fields too easily for them to be an effective deterrent. Mine barriers at a greater distance from Germany were needed if U-boats were to be prevented from reaching the shipping lanes off the west coasts of the British Isles. The northern barrage, from the Orkneys to Norway, was a project of such magnitude that it had to await the U.S.A.'s entry into the war, and was not completed before hostilities ended. Indicator nets were laid across the Dover Straits as early as January 1915; when fouled by a U-boat they ignited warning flares as a signal to patrol craft. *U32's* near-destruction in the nets on 6th April 1915 alarmed Berlin into denying their U-boats this route through the Channel, which lengthened their journey to and from the Irish Sea by 1,400 miles and cut their time on patrol by seven days.

The Admiralty was, however, unaware of this ban; they noted only that the nets accounted for very few U-boats. Admiral Bacon, commanding the Dover Patrol, tried to lay nets sufficiently heavy to be a physical obstruction but the difficulties of doing this across 20 miles of tide-swept water proved insurmountable. This failure was not, however, of importance until December 1916 when, coincident with beginning the third unrestricted U-boat campaign, Berlin not only withdrew their ban on the Channel passage but also sent large torpedo-boats to wreak havoc among British patrol craft. Bacon reinforced these with destroyers, which led to several spirited actions, notably one in which the *Broke* rammed and sank *G42*. Such fights were, however, only a prelude to an exploit aptly described by Churchill as 'the finest feat of arms in the Great War and unsurpassed in the history of the Royal Navy'.

Germany had put Bruges, in occupied Belgium, to good use as a U-boat and torpedo-boat base. Six miles inland, and connected to the North Sea by canals, nothing could attack such craft there except aircraft, against whose bombs the U-boats were given concrete shelters. The British Government recognised the vital importance of the ports at which the two Bruges canals entered the sea, Ostend and Zeebrugge, as early as November 1916; and Jellicoe's pessimistic declaration in June 1917 that, unless these were denied to the enemy the allies would lose the war, was enough for the Prime

Minister, Lloyd George, to accept the heavy casualties expected of an advance by the British Army through Flanders designed to capture them. This was a near-disastrous failure. Bacon proposed a blocking attack on Zeebrugge and Ostend from the sea, but showed too little enthusiasm for such a venture to satisfy the new First Sea Lord, Wemyss, who sent Keyes to relieve him early in 1918.

The new Admiral quickly produced his own plans. A landing force of 1,300 volunteers was given special training and a small armada of vessels assembled in the Thames estuary. Many of these were specially adapted for their role. The old cruiser *Vindictive* was equipped with flame-throwers, mortars, and a dozen long-hinged brows along her port side; the cruisers, *Brilliant, Iphigenia, Intrepid, Sirius,* and *Thetis* were filled with 1,500 tons of concrete, and provided with scuttling charges; submarine *C3* carried explosives in her forward compartments; and the upper works of the Liverpool ferries *Iris II* and *Daffodil* were protected with bullet-proof plating.

After two starts had been aborted by winds that prevented coastal motorboats laying the heavy smokescreens required to cloak its final approach, this force left the Swin on the eve of St. George's Day, 1918. Shortly after 2300 Commodore Lynes turned one part of it away to the south towards Ostend, whilst Keyes, in the destroyer *Warwick*, led the remainder towards Zeebrugge. Here the smoke-screen and heavy bombardment by monitors and aircraft proved their worth. The German defences were not alerted until shortly before 2350, when the *Vindictive* suddenly appeared out of the darkness only 1500 yards from the end of the mile-long mole. One minute after midnight Captain Carpenter placed his ship alongside amidst a hail of shot and shell that decimated the waiting storming party. While the *Daffodil* held her there, the naval storming party crossed the *Vindictive's* brows. Their objective was the 5·9-inch battery at the mole's seaward end, where they encountered strong opposition. The Royal Marine storming party and a naval demolition party followed, to destroy as much material on the mole as time would allow. Their task was

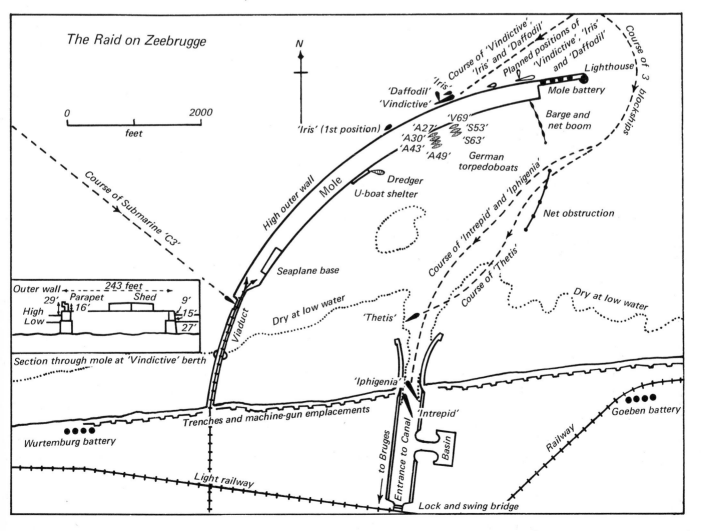

The Raid on Zeebrugge

The blocking of Zeebrugge, St George's Day, 1918. The wrecks of the two blockships *Iphegenia* and *Intrepid* are shown in the mouth of the Bruges Ship Canal. In spite of the gallant attempt to make the canal impassable to U-boats, a new passage was dredged around the blockships within 48 hours

The surrender of the German High Seas Fleet. A photograph of Scapa Flow showing heavy ships of the enemy's fleet at anchor in the British naval base after having been delivered under the terms of the armistice signed in 1918

facilitated by the submarine *C3* which Lieutenant Sandford rammed into the girders supporting the viaduct which joined the mole to the shore. Her detonation by a time-fuse, after her crew had been taken off by a picket-boat, breached the viaduct and prevented the arrival of German reinforcements. Coincident with Sandford's exploit, H.M.S. *Thetis* emerged from the smokescreen and steamed past the head of the mole, only to be stopped by a net obstruction. She then grounded at the entrance of the dredged channel. While the Germans concentrated their attentions on her, the *Intrepid* and *Ighigenia* were taken right inside the canal entrance. As soon as both these cruisers had been sunk, Carpenter recalled his storming parties. By 0115 the *Vindictive* had re-embarked the survivors and was on course for home.

Keyes believed the Zeebrugge raid, which cost the British 214 killed and 383 wounded, with the destroyer *North Star* sunk, was completely successful in blocking the Bruges ship canal. Lynes's attempt to do the same at Ostend was a failure because the Germans had moved the buoy marking the entrance. Both the *Brilliant* and *Sirius*, the blocking ships, stranded a mile to the east, where they had to be sunk after their crews had been rescued.

Keyes quickly prepared another raid on this port. On 9th May the *Vindictive*, now converted into a blockship, reached the entrance to this canal. But there, at the crucial moment, her captain was killed, and before another officer could take his place the ship had run hard aground and had to be abandoned. To add to Keyes's chagrin at this second failure, his own flagship, H.M.S. *Warwick*, was mined and had to be towed home to Dover.

With characteristic determination he planned a third attempt on Ostend. But the Admiralty withheld approval when they learned that another attempt to block Zeebrugge would also be needed. The Germans had been able to dredge a channel round the blockships in time for four small torpedo-boats to clear this canal as soon as 24th April, and by 14th May it was being freely used by torpedo-boats and U-boats. But if in this respect unsuccessful, Zeebrugge was not attacked in vain. The news that the Royal Navy had carried out this direct assault on an enemy-held port came shortly after German troops had broken through the British line at St. Quentin and proved an inspiration that upheld the allies' flagging spirits until their armies were able to launch a successful counter-attack at Chateau-Thierry on 18th June. In Germany, where the Grand Fleet's blockade had brought morale to a low ebb, the news came as a stunning blow heralding final defeat.

By June 1918 the convoy system had won the long-drawn battle against the U-boats. Germany now had no other weapon with which to disrupt the flow of supplies across the Channel and Atlantic, nor to prevent the allied armies being reinforced by a million fresh U.S. troops. The German spring offensive was halted short of Paris, and was followed with a crushing allied riposte on the Marne. On 8th August the British armies advanced nine miles; four weeks later the Germans were in full retreat all along the Western front.

By the end of September, when Bulgaria and Turkey sought an armistice to save Sofia and Constantinople, Germany was menaced by a danger greater than defeat on land. Brought near to starvation by the Grand Fleet's blockade, the people were raising the red flag of revolution. To avert a tragedy such as that to which Russia had succumbed, the German Chancellor appealed to President Wilson, who replied that no negotiations were possible so long as U-boats continued sinking passenger ships. Scheer, who had now assumed an office equivalent to that of the British First Sea Lord, responded by abandoning unrestricted submarine warfare on 21st October.

This freed his U-boats to support a planned sortie by the High Seas Fleet. Led by von Hipper, his successor in command of the High Seas Fleet, two groups of light cruisers and torpedo-boats were to raid the Flanders coast and the Thames Estuary, which was expected to draw the Grand Fleet south against a main body of 18 battleships, five battle-cruisers, and six destroyer flotillas.

The Admiralty had already warned Beatty that an attempt to draw the Grand Fleet was being planned. But he was not required to sail. When von Hipper ordered his ships to raise steam late on 29th October, their crews refused to obey their officers. They had no wish to be sacrificed in battle when they knew the end of the war was near.

On 11th November, before von Hipper could restore discipline, Britain, France, Italy, and the U.S.A. granted Germany's request for an armistice, and at 1100, hostilities ceased on all fronts. The

A closer view of some of the surrendered German ships. In the foreground is the battlecruiser *Hindenburg*, behind her, to the left, is the battleship *Kaiser*. Astern of the *Hindenburg*, right, is the battlecruiser *Derfflinger*

armistice terms required Germany to surrender all her U-boats, and to send her High Seas Fleet to an allied port for internment. On 20th November Tyrwhitt's Harwich Force began receiving 150 U-boats to await scrapping. Next day the Grand Fleet sailed for the last time, to meet and escort five battlecruisers, 11 dreadnought battleships, 10 light cruisers, and 50 torpedo-boats into captivity. They were brought into Rosyth and eventually taken to Scapa Flow where they rusted at their anchors in those gale-swept waters whilst the allies wrangled over a peace treaty.

This might not be the annihilating victory to which the Royal Navy had looked forward since August 1914, and for which the Grand Fleet never

ceased to hope in spite of the disappointing results of Jutland. But, as Captain Richmond wrote in his diary for 1916: 'It is absolutely necessary to look at the war as a whole; to avoid keeping our eyes only on the German Fleet. What we have to do is to starve and cripple Germany, to destroy Germany'. And this the Royal Navy undoubtedly achieved. Many a good vessel has struck its flag in battle; many another has faced destruction rather than surrender; but the annals of naval warfare hold no parallel to 21st November 1918. As the Admiralty rightly signalled: 'The surrender of the German Fleet, accomplished without shock of battle, will remain for all time the example of the wonderful silence and sureness with which sea power attains its ends.'

Oiling at sea, a drawing by Sir Muirhead Bone made in 1916 showing the view from the bridge of a battleship with a tanker alongside

CHAPTER 20

The Royal Navy between the two World Wars – The Washington Naval Treaty of 1921 – International naval limitations – The Fleet Air Arm – The Gun and the Torpedo – Rearmament in Britain

PETER KEMP

The victory over Germany in 1918, gained at such heavy cost in human life, raised as many naval problems as it settled. The challenge to British sea power had been met and vanquished, but there were other factors now to bear on the British concept of the standard of naval strength required to maintain her imperial role. Until 1914 this standard had been set at a strength equal to that of any two other navies which might combine against Britain. But the war had brought to full fruition the naval aspirations of the United States and Japan, and there could be no possible return to the old days of a two-power standard.

Nor was it economically possible. The financial stringency of the post-war years made the replacement of major warships quite unacceptable in terms of budgetary expenditure; moreover the United States had declared her intention of maintaining a navy 'second to none', and was prepared to meet any British attempt to reintroduce a two-power standard by outbuilding Britain. In the face of such a situation there was no other course but to strive for some sort of international agreement on naval limitation.

Before all this became apparent, however, there was another problem to be solved between those allies who had combined in the war to crush the German naval threat. Under the terms of the armistice the major units of the German High Seas Fleet had, as mentioned earlier, steamed across the North Sea and on 21st November had surrendered to the British Grand Fleet. They now lay at anchor in Scapa Flow, where their status could be said to be prizes of war. There were claims from the different allies for a share of the surrendered ships, and any

such distribution could easily upset the existing balance of naval power. The situation had the makings of inter-allied discord, and a British proposal to solve this particular problem by taking all the ships out into the Atlantic and sinking them in deep water did not find much favour among those other nations who saw in the German ships potential and valuable additions to their existing fleets. The deadlock was eventually solved by the Germans themselves who scuttled the ships on a pre-arranged signal from the German admiral.

The major problem, however, still remained. In 1918 Britain was still the heart of a great empire, and her interests were essentially the same as those which had operated over the past four centuries. More than any other nation she depended on the sea, and her whole economy rested on the ability to operate her merchant fleet, at that time by far the greatest in the world, over the sea routes of the world. This ability required naval power to safeguard it against any naval threat, from whatever quarter, that might arise. The huge merchant ship losses in the war that was just over pointed the moral.

From the British point of view the current problem was a double-ended one. On the one hand was the need to maintain adequate sea power to protect the essential sea communications of a world-wide empire; on the other, the extent of this sea power in relation to that of the other maritime nations. The prospect of a new race in naval armaments was economically too daunting to contemplate, and the only alternative was the abandonment of the two-power standard which Britain had hitherto thought necessary for her security upon the seas.

One of the early carriers, HMS *Argus*, converted from a passenger/cargo ship being built
for Italy. In her original conversion she had two flight decks, one forward for launching aero-
planes and one aft for seaplanes. A later conversion gave her the single flight deck shown in this
photograph. After the war she was used for landing trials, and a Blackburn spotter can be seen
just after landing. The year was 1928

The 20 years between the two world wars of this century was mainly notable for the development of naval aviation. Aircraft had been used at sea during the First World War, but it was not until 1917 that one was successfully landed on a carrier at sea. This photograph shows HMS *Eagle* in 1920, one of the very early carriers.

The international agreement for the limitation of navies was finally hammered out in Washington in 1921–2, in spite of considerable difficulties. These arose in the main through the attempt to try to evaluate the relative strengths of ships of different size within the same general classification. One striking example arose in the case of cruisers. For her imperial policing role Britain needed a large number of cruisers of around 5-6,000 tons with a maximum armament of 6-inch guns. The United States however had no uses for cruisers of this size; her needs were best served by cruisers of 10,000 tons carrying 8-inch guns. This, of course, was but one facet of the international wrangling which had begun with the talks at Versailles on the terms of a treaty of peace and were continued by argument and counter-argument until the talks at Washington resulted in an uneasy agreement.

The Washington Treaty laid down the maximum overall size of the navies of Great Britain, the United States, and Japan in the ratio of 5:5:3, with those of France and Italy held at 1·75 on the same scale. There was also limitation within the individual classes of ship, such as battleships, carriers, cruisers, etc., both by tonnage and size of gun, and an agreed limitation of new building of major warships. There was also a requirement that Great Britain and the United States should scrap some of their older battleships to reduce their overall tonnage within the maximum allowed. This was in fact the one-power standard which, until now, the British government had always considered as below the margin of safety necessary for a maritime empire such as Britain's. It took some time to digest the fact and accept that it was to be a permanent feature of the future pattern of naval strength, but in 1925 it was officially recognised as government policy following a recommendation of the Committee of Imperial Defence.

International talks on possible measures of disarmament, in an endeavour to reduce still further the level of naval forces, were held in Geneva in 1927, but nothing was achieved. Britain went into the talks with a suggestion that submarine warfare should be outlawed by international agreement, but the suggestion foundered on the rock of bitter French opposition. Three years later a further naval conference was held in London, and there was an agreement, reached with much difficulty, to prolong the prohibition of new battleship construction among the major naval powers until 1937. But it was made obvious during the discussions that Japan had no intention of allowing herself to be bound irrevocably by the decision, and that when it suited her purposes she would withdraw unilaterally. Ever since the Washington Treaty Japan had felt aggrieved by what she considered a derogatory limitation of her navy in comparison with those of the United States and Britain, and the 5:5:3 ratio had rankled. Already she had her own aspirations to the foundation of an empire in Asia and the Pacific, and her plans, not as yet fully appreciated in the West, called for a large measure of naval expansion. It was her actions in the East in the middle 1930s, together with those of Germany after Hitler came to full power in 1933, that brought to an end all attempts to reach international limitations of armaments.

Finally, still in the international field, an agreement on relative naval strengths was signed between Britain and Germany in 1937. Under the terms of the armistice signed in 1918 the German navy had been cut down to minuscule proportions and a total prohibition had been enforced on the building of submarines. Under cover of technical missions in adjacent countries, the ban on submarines had been sidestepped and a lot of research and training in submarine warfare had been achieved. In addition, one or two submarines had been built clandestinely. German naval rearmament had become a reality when Adolf Hitler became Chancellor of Germany in 1933, and the naval agreement between Britain and Germany signed in 1937 was an acknowledgement of this reality. German rearmament was accepted up to a level of 35 per cent of the British strength, with a clause, in the case of submarines, accepting 100 per cent of British strength if Germany should consider her safety should require it. So far as it went, the agreement was satisfactory to Britain in the overall balance of European naval power which it created, but it contained no mutual inspection clause. Each country agreed to declare to the other the size and armament of all new naval building. In the event, both in battleships and cruisers, Germany built much larger and more heavily armed ships than she actually declared.

Within Britain herself, the normal rundown from wartime to peacetime strength was progressing during the years immediately following the ending of the war. As a guide to the armed services in their future planning the Government announced that, for the purpose of framing the annual Service Estimates of money required, it could be assumed that there would be no major war for ten years. The announcement was made in August 1919, but in 1923 it was given the force of a Cabinet rule, which made it self-repeating as year succeeded year. In 1931, when the strength of Hitler's National Socialist party first began to give an inkling of probable developments in Germany, the three Services called the government's attention to the serious deficiencies in their forces, the Admiralty declaring that they were such as to render the fleet incapable of affording adequate protection to essential trade in wartime. The warning went unheeded, but in the following year the Committee of Imperial Defence once again drew attention to the danger, and this time the government agreed to the withdrawal of the ten-year rule. Although the withdrawal allowed realistic planning towards more balanced forces to proceed,

Britain like the rest of the world was still suffering the effects of the great economic depression of 1929–31, and all new expenditure on rearmament had to be deferred.

It was a series of world events, following each other with a growing rapidity, which forced the government's hand and set the Royal Navy on the road of rearmament and a greater readiness for war. In September 1931 Japan launched her invasion of Manchuria and as a result the British government decided to go ahead with the development of Singapore as a naval base, a project which had been long delayed in the interests of economy. In January 1933 Hitler became Chancellor of Germany, and within nine months had virtually put the country under a war economy with a huge impetus in the rate of rearmament. The naval implication, as expressed in Britain by the three Chiefs of Staff, was the requirement for all existing British battleships to be modernised (no new ones could be built, under the terms of the London Conference, until 1937); all naval bases and fuel depots to be brought up to date; a big expansion of anti-submarine equipment to be put in hand; and a considerable enlargement of the Fleet Air Arm undertaken. The British government accepted the requirement but being unwilling to put the question of rearmament to the electorate, cut the recommended expenditure by one-third. Nevertheless, within the balance remaining, the British Admiralty was able to order one new aircraft carrier. There was still sufficient unappropriated tonnage remaining within the carrier category to cover this new major addition to the fleet.

But world events refused to stand still and quickly overtook Britain's modest rearmament programme of 1934. In 1935 the United States passed her Neutrality Law which barred any reliance by Britain on the manufacturing capacity of that great nation for war material. In the same year Italy launched her invasion of Abyssinia, and six months later, in March 1936, Germany marched into the Rhineland in contravention both of the Treaty of Versailles and the later Locarno Treaty. The occupation of the Rhineland was a herald of the coming war.

The reaction in Britain was swift. The three Chiefs of Staff lost no time in working out a new schedule of rearmament, which was issued as part of a memorandum with the title *Planning for a War with Germany*, in which they estimated the probable date

An early experiment made in HMS *Furious* to prevent aircraft when landing falling over the side. Parallel rows of wires acted as guides to the undercarriage, while collapsible barricades were used to slow up the aircraft. The machine in the photograph is a Parnell Panther, a two-seat reconnaissance aircraft, which was perhaps notable for having a folding fuselage instead of the more usual folding wings

of outbreak as the latter part of 1939. On the material side they costed the essential expenditure over the next five years at between £1,760,000,000 and £1,811,000,000. It was a phenomenal sum in the circumstances of the time and one which the government sought to reduce. In the end they managed to cut it down to an overall figure of £1,570,000,000, but only at the expense of much desirable military hardware.

Nevertheless, even at this reduced figure the British Navy was at last enabled to make a start in equipping itself for the inevitable war which all now recognised as coming. A supplementary Naval Estimate in 1936 made provision for the construction of two new battleships, one aircraft carrier, five cruisers, nine destroyers, four submarines, and six escort vessels. The Estimates for 1937 added three more battleships, two more fleet carriers, seven cruisers, sixteen destroyers, seven submarines, and three escort vessels. Except in escort vessels, which

were in fact going to be needed more than any other class of ship in the new war, the new orders were designed to give the British Navy a healthy superiority over the German and Italian navies combined. But there was still one fly in the ointment. The government laid down an order that the whole rearmament programme was to be implemented without interfering with normal civilian manufacture. Trade was to take preference over defence.

This order was rescinded in March 1938 when Hitler marched the German armies into Austria, convincing the British government that the irrevocable step towards war had been taken and that the timing of its outbreak was merely a matter of political juggling. But by then it was too late. Some of the new cruisers and most of the destroyers, submarines, and escort vessels ordered in 1937 and 1938 could still be completed by the date foreseen by the Chiefs of Staff as the most likely to see Europe again plunged into war, but none of the battleships or carriers could be ready before 1940 at the earliest. It is true enough that the agreement signed at Munich on 30th September 1938 gained a few months for the British rearmament programme to speed up, but even if it did, it gained the same months for Germany who undoubtedly made better use of them in the matter of war production.

None of these events were, of course, within the control of the British Admiralty. They were all political events to which the Royal Navy had to gear its demands for its annual Estimates. But within the Navy itself there were two reactions to the lessons of the First World War which were to have a considerable influence on the eventual shape of the Royal Navy as it faced up to its second major test in the 20th century in the war of 1939–45.

The first of these was the failure within the British Admiralty and throughout the Royal Navy to recognise the dominant naval weapon of the First World War. For four centuries it had been the big naval gun, and traditional beliefs and enthusiasms were hard to dislodge. Part of this continuing belief in the gun stemmed from the traumatic experience of the battle of Jutland in 1916, from which so much had been expected and so little achieved. The actual battle itself was studied and discussed, fought and re-fought, time and time again in Staff College and other presentations in an attempt to discover why the German High Seas Fleet had not been blown out of the sea by the greater gun power of the Grand Fleet. But while this battle was studied in great depth and from every conceivable angle in an attempt to vindicate the dominance of the big gun, there were no attempts similarly to analyse the wellnigh disastrous attack on merchant shipping by the German U-boats during the First World War or to discover the lessons to be learned from a study of that campaign. Throughout the twenty years of peace which separated the two world wars, fleet exercises and manoeuvres were all

The forward deck of HMS *Furious*, with early naval fighter aircraft parked. The *Furious* started life as a fast battlecruiser, armed with 18-inch guns, but was taken in hand for conversion in 1917 to a carrier. It was in the *Furious* that the first ever deck landing at sea was performed on 3rd August 1917

designed to culminate in the meeting of battle fleets in a final gun battle, and there was not a single fleet exercise whose object was to study the problem of trade defence.

In part this was due to the successful solution in 1921 of the problem of underwater detection of submarines, when the asdic (now named sonar) installation was evolved from a mainly French invention. Although in its early stages it suffered from many inhibiting factors, including an inability to determine the depth at which a submarine was submerged, it gave a great confidence that the problems of underwater attack on merchant ships had been successfully solved. Had there been any real study of the U-boat campaign of 1917 and 1918, it would have been quickly discovered that the main successes of the U-boats had been achieved through attack on the surface at night, conditions in which a submarine, because of her low silhouette, is not only virtually invisible to the eye but also immune from asdic detection. But no such study was ever made, and British confidence that the asdic had solved the trade defence problems for good and all was rudely shattered in 1940 when the U-boats again reverted to their tactic of the surfaced night attack.

The other half of this failure to appreciate the problems which would face the Royal Navy in a future war was a corollary of the dominance of the gun theory, that the true dominant weapon was the torpedo. If this had been recognised – and almost the whole of First World War experience pointed towards it – it is hardly conceivable that naval thought and inventiveness would not have been directed towards discovering an effective means of defence against it. Indeed, in the matter of trade defence, the answer was already there. During 1918 many British convoys with destroyer escorts had been attacked by U-boats, and merchant ships had been sunk out of them. But in cases where an air escort was provided in addition to a surface escort, the convoys were immune from attack even though no aircraft at that time carried any weapon suitable for use against a submarine. A reasonably simple analysis would have revealed this fact, and events in the great U-boat campaign of 1939–45 were to prove its truth.

The second of the influences which affected British naval development between the world wars was the

The German 'First Sea Lord', Grand Admiral Raeder, photographed after a meeting with the Italian Admiral Ricardi (left) in Italy in 1941. Grand Admiral Raeder was relieved of his command by Hitler in January 1943, and was succeeded in the high command by Admiral Doenitz

long struggle for control of the Fleet Air Arm. During the First World War, naval flying was in its infancy, but until April 1918 it was under the direct control of the Admiralty. As a result of the recommendations of a committee under the chairmanship of General Smuts, the Royal Naval Air Service and the Royal Flying Corps, which was its military counterpart, were amalgamated to form a third independent Service, the Royal Air Force. Thereafter, the Navy lost all control of its aircraft.

The First World War had seen the birth of naval flying and a doctrine of operational procedure was in the process of development. But with the ending of the war it appeared to the Admiralty that the Royal Air Force was showing much more interest in, and spending much more of its available money on, the shore-based element of its overall responsibility than the seaborne element. Within two or three years of the merger the Admiralty began to mount a campaign for the return to naval control of seaborne flying, mainly on the grounds that naval training and expertise on the part of pilots and observers was a necessity if there were to be any meaningful co-operation with the fleet. The Admiralty's campaign for the return of the Fleet Air Arm was equally strongly resisted by the Royal Air Force.

As the controversy developed, both sides to the argument put all their energies into the campaign for control and none towards the problem of working out a correct strategic and tactical doctrine of naval flying. On the technical side the problems of landing on the deck of an aircraft carrier at sea were successfully solved with the development of an efficient arrester system whereby the aircraft was caught by transverse wires across the flight deck, but in the design of aircraft there was considerable dissatisfaction in the Royal Navy. With its faith pinned so firmly to the land-based aircraft and its bomb as the expression of air power, it was probably unrealistic of the Admiralty to press for specialised research into aircraft designed purely for the sea role, but nonetheless the growing importance of air power in its relation to sea power did call for aircraft of specialised design and not sea adaptations of machines developed for operations from shore bases.

The struggle for control raged with increasing bitterness until 1937, when the government finally decided that the Fleet Air Arm should return to the Royal Navy both administratively and operationally. It was an easier transition than it might have been, for since 1923 all observers in Fleet Air Arm

In 1939, when war was inevitable, Admiral Sir Dudley Pound was brought back to London from the Mediterranean to become First Sea Lord. As such, he guided the destiny of the Royal Navy until he died in office in 1943, by which time the war at sea had been virtually won. This was one of the last photographs taken of him, on the bridge of the ship which took Mr Winston Churchill for his last meeting with President Roosevelt

aircraft had been naval officers, and naval personnel had been trained as pilots up to 70 per cent of the total, although they held rank in the Royal Air Force in addition to their naval rank.

The main casualty, however, of the years of inter-Service quarrel had been the lack of any attempt on the part of either Service to work out a strategic and tactical doctrine. The blame for this must rest as much on the Royal Navy as on the Royal Air Force, for there was still an innate conservatism among many senior naval officers which was unable to visualise the influence of air power on naval operations. It was bound up to some extent in the belief that, at sea, the big naval gun was still the arbiter of naval battle.

Only one of the new carriers, H.M.S. *Ark Royal*, ordered in 1934, was operational when war came in September 1939. Of the aircraft she operated – Gladiators, Flycatchers, Swordfish, Skuas – none was a match for the machines which had been developed in Germany. Even by 1939, when the single wing aircraft had almost completely replaced the biplane ashore, there were few in the Fleet Air Arm who even considered feasible the landing of one of these high-performance, single wing aircraft upon the limited space of an aircraft carrier's flight deck. This was the legacy of years of neglect and of inter-Service disagreement and squabble.

The Munich Agreement, signed in September 1938 and disregarded by Germany within six months, was followed by further aggressions which marked only too clearly the road along which Germany was determined to advance. Early in 1939 naval staff talks with France were held to determine the essential naval strategy as between the two navies in partnership. These quickly reached agreement on the basis of British naval control in home waters and the Atlantic and French naval control in the Western Mediterranean, with the duties of convoy protection and the hunting of raiders shared in proportion to the relative naval strengths.

Hitler's occupation of Czechoslovakia in March 1939 made obvious his next step, as it effectively opened Poland to German occupation. A British guarantee to come to Poland's aid if she were attacked gave notice to Germany that she would have to fight a war on two fronts if she persisted in aggressive adventures, and to make the threat more real, talks were opened with Russia in an attempt to enlist her active support should Germany plunge Europe into war. The talks were doomed to failure, and when on 21st August it was announced that Germany and Russia had agreed to sign a pact of non-aggression, the whole world recognised that it was war.

Thirty-six hours later the British Admiralty took over the control of all merchant shipping movements. On the following day all ships in commission were ordered to their war stations and ships of the Reserve fleet were manned up to full complement. Six submarines were sailed to maintain that part of a line of search across the North Sea which was beyond the range of shore-based aircraft. Four cruisers left Scapa Flow on 26th August to operate a northern patrol between the Faeroe Islands and Iceland and across the Denmark Strait. On the last day of the month the Home Fleet left Scapa Flow to intercept and shadow any German ships that might be encountered at sea. The ships were still at sea when the signal to commence hostilities against Germany was sent out at 11 o'clock in the morning of 3rd September.

The German Navy, too, had been making its preparations. On 21st August the pocket battleship *Graf Spee* left Germany under cover of darkness and made her way unobserved into the South Atlantic. Three days later a second pocket battleship, the *Deutschland*, was equally successful in reaching her North Atlantic war station unobserved. Two supply tankers, one for each ship, were sailed three days later. At intervals between 19th and 29th August seventeen ocean-going U-boats were sent to their Atlantic war stations, and on the 21st seven smaller coastal U-boats took up their positions in the southern North Sea. Six more left Germany on the 25th to occupy patrol areas in the central North Sea.

So, once again, the two navies faced each other in a second war, both of them largely unprepared for the coming conflict and with the Royal Navy to some extent having pinned its faith on a weapon which could no longer command its historic superiority in naval battle. There was still much to learn, and to learn the hard way, before even a gleam of light was to be visible at the end of the tunnel.

Opposite below: The Battle of the Nile. *Opposite above:* The Battle of Copenhagen, showing the two fleets in action, with British frigates anchored in the foreground. Both from paintings by Nicholas Pocock. *Overleaf left:* Three of a series of six Spanish watercolours of the Battle of Trafalgar. *Overleaf top right:* Admiral Sir John Duckworth's squadron forcing the Dardanelles in 1807, from the painting by Thomas Whitcombe. *Overleaf bottom right:* The scene in the fore cabin of HMS *Queen Elizabeth* on 16th November 1918 when Admiral Beatty, C.-in-C. Grand Fleet, read the terms of surrender to the German delegates. From a painting by Sir John Lavery

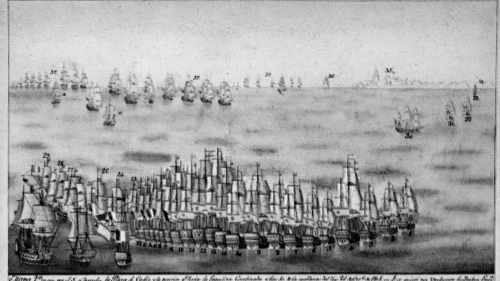

Mapa 2.º en que por S.E. se descubre la Plaza de Cadiz y la prision q.e hizo la Esquadra Combinada á las 10 de la mañana del dia 21 de Oct.e de 1805. en q.e se avistó p.r Barlovento la Esquadra Ingl.a ...

Mapa 4.º que manifiesta el Combate que emprehendido y que sostubieron ambas Esquadras Enemigas desde las 11 y ½ minutos de la mañana del 21 de Oct.e de 1805 ...

Mapa 6.º en que por la parte del N.e se descubre toda la Plaza de Cadiz, é igualmente los 11 Navios de la Esquadra Combinada que entraron en Bahia el dia 22 de Oct.e de 1805 con ...

CHAPTER 21

The Second World War – Operations in Home Waters –
The Norwegian Campaign – Loss of the Glorious –
The Evacuation from Dunkirk

DONALD MACINTYRE

When the Second World War broke out on 3rd September 1939 the Royal Navy alone, and leaving out of consideration the naval forces of Britain's allies, was in a position of unchallengeable superiority over the Navy of Nazi Germany – at least so far as major surface units were concerned. The Royal Navy's capability of combating the assault on her vital merchant shipping by the German U-boat fleet was another matter and is dealt with elsewhere in this volume.

So far as the surface fleets were concerned, when Hitler plunged into war, the ambitious Plan Z, which was to give Germany parity with Britain, was still five years from fruition. Furthermore, although two fast battleships, three so-called 'pocket battleships', two 8-inch cruisers and six light cruisers had been completed, of these only the pocket battleships *Admiral Graf Spee* and *Deutschland* and five of the light cruisers were operational, the remainder being either engaged in training or in dockyard hands. The two pocket battleships had sailed prior to the declaration of war for the South and North Atlantic respectively where, unknown to the Admiralty, they awaited instructions to begin raider operations against Allied merchant shipping.

The British fleet deployed in home waters or in the Atlantic – seven battleships, three battlecruisers, four aircraft carriers, and 35 cruisers – was thus more than adequate to perform the traditional function of sea power by sweeping the oceans clear of German merchant shipping and establishing blockading patrols in Icelandic and Faeroese waters. Surface opposition to this during the first year of war was confined to a half-hearted sortie by the battleships *Scharnhorst* and *Gneisenau* in November 1939, during which they encountered and overwhelmed the armed merchant cruiser *Rawalpindi* in the Iceland-Faeroes Channel before returning to Germany.

The British Home Fleet suffered a number of casualties from submarine attack and mine. The former accounted for the destruction of the battleship *Royal Oak* in the fleet anchorage at Scapa Flow and the carrier *Courageous* in the Western Approaches, and damage to the battleship *Barham* which put her out of action for three months. Mines seriously damaged the battleship *Nelson* and the cruiser *Belfast*. These casualties had little effect on the allied naval superiority, particularly as both the *Scharnhorst* and *Gneisenau* developed defects during their sortie and were under repair until after the New Year.

Thus, when the *Deutschland* and *Admiral Graf Spee* began operations at the end of September 1939, a very large allied force was available to hunt them down; their span of life was inevitably a short one and details will be kept for the next chapter when the German campaign of commerce-raiding by surface units will be recounted as a consecutive whole.

Following the destruction of the *Graf Spee*, no German warships other than submarines remained outside their own territorial waters nor, except for a brief, abortive sortie by the *Gneisenau, Scharnhorst,* and *Admiral Hipper* in February 1940 with the object of attacking the convoys to and from Norway, did the few major operational units venture out into the North Sea until April. German naval effort was confined to minelaying, at first by U-boats but later also by destroyers and aircraft, and to air attacks, the

Opposite above: HMS *Cossack* forcing her way alongside the German tanker *Altmark* in Jossing Fjord in February 1940 to effect the rescue of 300 British merchant seamen. From the painting by Norman Wilkinson. *Opposite below:* This painting by Norman Wilkinson shows one of the two main aspects of the withdrawal of the British Expeditionary Force from Dunkirk in May-June 1940, the men being taken off from the beaches in all types of small ships hastily mobilised for the purpose

majority on merchant shipping along the British east coast.

The mines claimed a number of victims among the merchantmen and, in a confused night action between British destroyers and German minelaying destroyers on 7th December, H.M.S. *Jersey* was torpedoed and badly damaged. A few days later, however, the light cruisers *Nürnberg* and *Leipsig*, covering another minelaying sortie, were torpedoed by the British submarine *Salmon*, both being put out of action for many months.

Though these activities involved British naval forces in continuous defensive operations, and sweeps by the Home Fleet into the Skagerrak in the hope of bringing on an encounter were largely abortive, much consideration to offensive operations was given under the restless spur of the First Lord of the Admiralty, Winston Churchill. The first plan to be examined was an ambitious one to carry the war into the Baltic, using old 'R'-class battleships fitted with super bulges, accompanied by a number of cruisers, destroyers, submarines and auxiliaries. It is fortunate that, in the absence of any possibility of air cover, this outdated scheme, belonging to the era of World War I, was abandoned. Plans were also prepared for motor torpedoboat attacks on German harbours, for passing submarines into the Baltic, as had been done in World War I, and even for attacking enemy ships in harbour by means of oil fuel fires on the surface of the water.

None of these ever matured, however; and, of all the proposals made, only one, by Churchill, to mine the inshore route along the Norwegian coast and so force the important German iron-ore traffic from Narvik into the open sea where it could be attacked, was ever to be converted into action.

The war was, indeed, less than a month old when the naval leaders on either side began to fix their attention on neutral Norway. Churchill was pressing the British Cabinet for permission to carry out the minelaying operation. Grand Admiral Raeder, C-in-C of the German Navy, was at the same time pointing out to Hitler the desirability of gaining bases on the Norwegian coast; by October 1939 he had made definite proposals for the occupation of that country.

Hitler, believing that the allies were planning to occupy Norway themselves, gave orders on 16th March 1940 to set the invasion on foot. D-day was

Admiral Sir Phillip Vian. As a captain he commanded the 4th Destroyer Flotilla during the first two years of the war, and it was in HMS *Cossack* that, in Febuary 1940, he steamed into Jossing Fjord, on the Norwegian coast, to set free 299 British merchant seamen who were confined in the holds of the German supply tanker *Altmark*

fixed for 9th April 1940 and the operation was given the code-name *Weserübung*.

The blatant aggression of this decision is not mitigated by the fact that the allies, acceding at last to Churchill's urging, were indeed planning to mine the Norwegian territorial waters on the 8th and had assembled an invasion force to occupy the principal ports, though only if and when 'the Germans had violated Norwegian neutrality, or there was clear evidence that they intended to do so.' This plan was known as 'R.4'.

Thus each of the antagonists, in ignorance of the other's intentions, was by a remarkable coincidence simultaneously preparing to operate in Norwegian waters; the British with much hesitation and reluctance, the Germans with ruthless determination, *blitzkrieg* tactics, and treachery.

The whole available German fleet was to be used,

divided into six groups; Group 1, composed of the battleships *Scharnhorst* and *Gneisenau* and ten destroyers carrying 2,000 troops for the occupation of Narvik was to sail in company with Group 2, the cruiser *Hipper* and four destroyers with 1,700 troops embarked; after creating a diversion in the North Sea, Group 1 was to continue northwards, the battleships to patrol in the Arctic until it was time to cover the return passage of the other naval units, the ten destroyers to occupy Narvik, while Group 2 would occupy Trondheim.

Group 3, comprising the light cruisers *Köln* and *Königsberg*, the old training cruiser *Bremse*, and some minor units, was to put 1,900 men ashore to occupy Bergen. Group 4, the light cruiser *Karlsruhe* with a few torpedo-boats and smaller units, was to occupy Kristiansand (South) and Arendal with 1,100 men. Group 5, the cruiser *Blücher*, the pocket battleship *Lützow* (ex-*Deutschland*), and the light cruiser *Emden* with torpedo-boats and auxiliaries, was to land 2,000 men to occupy Oslo. Four minesweepers formed Group 6 entrusted with the capture of the cable station at Ekersund. In addition, the old battleship *Schleswig-Holstein* and a number of small craft were to occupy key points on the coast of Denmark, the main assault on which was to be by land. All these groups were to sail in time to reach their destinations and make their assaults simultaneously at dawn on 9th April. They would be preceded by transports disguised as merchant ships carrying troops and military stores, sailing singly. Instructions to commanders of the assault groups called for ruthless action if any Norwegian resistance was encountered.

The British, meanwhile, were planning to lay mines in the Vestfiord and off Bud; by 6th April the forces concerned were on their way, the minelayer *Teviot Bank* and four destroyers for Bud, four minelaying destroyers covered by the battlecruiser *Renown* and eight destroyers for Vestfiord. In case this should provoke a German attack on Norway, troops were embarked, but were to be held in port until evidence of enemy violation of Norwegian neutrality was received, a plan which reveals a lack of appreciation of the bold, swift efficiency of which the enemy was capable.

During 7th April the German Groups 1 and 2 on their way north were located and, on the evening of that day the main body of the Home Fleet from Scapa and the 2nd Cruiser Squadron from Rosyth put to sea. The C-in-C's main concern was to prevent any German break-out into the Atlantic and his forces were directed well out from the Norwegian coast where interception of any invasion group was improbable.

During the 8th several fresh items of intelligence reached the Admiralty. At dawn the destroyer *Glow-worm*, one of the *Renown's* destroyers which had lost touch while searching for a man lost overboard in the wild weather, encountered the destroyers of Group 1 and the *Hipper* off Trondheim. Before being overwhelmed by the latter and inflicting minor damage by ramming the cruiser, the *Glow-worm* had duly reported the enemy. At noon the Polish submarine *Orzel*, patrolling in the Skagerrak, had sunk the German transport *Rio de Janeiro*. Some of those rescued by the Norwegian Navy were in German army uniform and freely admitted they had been on their way to occupy Bergen. At 1400 the *Hipper's* force was sighted by a reconnaissance plane off Trondheim where it was waiting for the calculated moment to turn to arrive off the port at dawn. At 1800 another German force, the powerful Group 5 for Oslo, was reported by submarines off the Skaw.

To the surprise of the C-in-C Home Fleet who, by noon on the 8th, was convinced that an invasion of Norway was under way, the Admiralty's reaction was to cancel 'R.4', order the troops ashore, and the 1st Cruiser Squadron in which they had been embarked, to sea.

By this time it was too late for any movements of the Home Fleet to affect the course of events. The various German groups were beginning their approaches to the ports allocated to them by Operation *Weserübung*. Far to the north, off the entrance to the Vestfiord, the ten German destroyers under Commodore Bonte had parted company with the *Scharnhorst* and *Gneisenau* to head up the long fiord to Narvik while the two battleships plunged on through the tempestuous weather towards their waiting position in the Arctic. Using treachery to overwhelm the two Norwegian coast defence ships that protected their country's neutrality, Bonte would arrive off Narvik at dawn to receive its surrender by its traitorous garrison commander.

Groups 2 and 3 were similarly steering for the entrances to the fiords up which they would successfully bluff their way past the defences to arrive unopposed off Trondheim and Bergen at dawn. Group 5, after brushing aside challenging patrol craft, was steering for the narrows of Oslo Fiord where the forts were to offer the only effective resistance and the cruiser *Blücher* was to be sunk before the remainder pressed on to occupy the capital. Group 4 was to be twice repulsed by the defences of Kristiansand before a misinterpreted signal silenced the forts long enough for the ships to slip by.

Raeder's bold plan had succeeded brilliantly enough though it was not the secrecy on which he had relied which had brought this about; secrecy had been lost at an early stage. Rather was it the misreading of the situation by the British command and the indecision shown. Only in the north did a brief encounter take place early on the 9th when, in the dim and stormy dawn, the *Renown* exchanged salvoes with the *Scharnhorst* and *Gneisenau* between the snow flurries. The *Gneisenau* was thrice hit, suffering additional damage from the heavy seas into which the two German ships fled at high speed to disappear into the Arctic gloom.

During 9th April all the major ports of Norway fell into German hands. Though the cost to Hitler's Navy had so far been small, the problem remained of getting back to their home ports past the opposition of the allied naval forces, now at last partly aware of the true situation. British inability to give the fleet adequate air cover helped to provide a partial solution.

The only carrier in home waters (*Furious*) had been caught not fully operational. With only her Swordfish torpedo-reconnaissance planes embarked, she was still on her way to join the fleet. The R.A.F. was unable to provide fighter cover from its Scottish bases. When, on the afternoon of the 9th, therefore, the Luftwaffe, by this time in possession of Stavanger airfield, attacked the Home Fleet, the C-in-C was forced to abandon plans to attack the German Groups 3 and 4 at Bergen and Trondheim and withdraw to the north and west.

Response to the bold German swoop was thus left, in the south, to the British submarines on patrol in the Skagerrak and Kattegat. The first blow was struck on the evening of the 9th, when the *Truant* waylaid and sank the *Karlsruhe*, returning from the occupation of Kristiansand. The following night the pocket-battleship *Lützow*, returning from Oslo, was torpedoed, crippled, and put out of action for 12

months by the *Spearfish*. The German gunnery training ship *Brumme* and a number of transports also fell victim to submarine torpedoes, though at the cost to the British of the *Sterlet* and *Thistle*.

In addition to these German losses, what they might have suffered had a carrier striking force been present with the Home Fleet was indicated when, on the 10th, two squadrons of naval Skua dive-bombers taking off from the Orkney Islands flew to Bergen and, in a sudden, surprise attack sent the cruiser *Königsberg* to the bottom without loss to themselves.

Only in the far north, beyond the operational range of the Luftwaffe, was an old-fashioned, exclusively ship-to-ship confrontation possible. There, during the 9th, in the absence of any news from Narvik, the C-in-C Home Fleet had ordered the senior destroyer officer in the area, Captain Warburton-Lee, to investigate and 'make certain

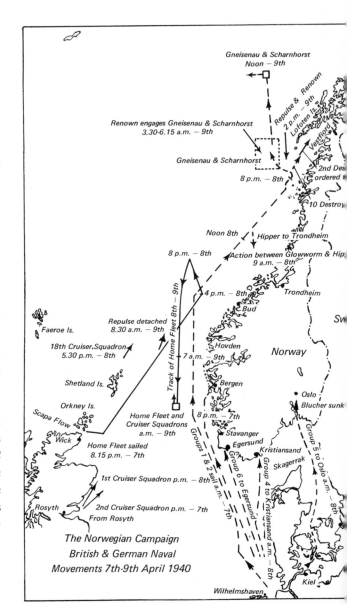

The Norwegian Campaign
British & German Naval
Movements 7th-9th April 1940

Many Norwegian ships, trapped when their country was occupied by Germany, ran the gauntlet to join the Allies. Before sailing, the crews were, where possible, given rubber life-saving suits with an electric lamp fitted. The photograph shows Captain Jensen, of the SS *Taurus*, wearing his suit on arrival in Britain

the tanker which had been sent for the purpose. When the *Hardy* finally led the flotilla seawards, the British flotilla found itself engaged at close quarters by the five fresh opponents.

Two of the Germans were heavily damaged; but in reply, the *Hardy* was crippled and beached in a sinking condition, Warburton-Lee being amongst those killed, the *Hunter* was sunk, the *Hotspur* was damaged but the *Havock* and *Hostile* escaped, the Germans being in no condition to chase.

With the German flotilla thus trapped, the *Scharnhorst* and *Gneisenau* were left to make their way back to Wilhelmshaven which they succeeded in doing, undetected by the British air reconnaissance, the *Hipper* joining them from Trondheim on the 12th.

Warburton-Lee's bold initiative and the success attending it shook the Allied War Council out of its apathy. Action to follow up with an amphibious assault on Narvik was set on foot and during 12th April the cruiser *Southampton* with a small advance force of soldiers left for Narvik, followed on the next day by five troopships with two infantry brigades. The operation, code-name 'Rupert', was to be commanded by Admiral of the Fleet Lord Cork and Orrery, flying his flag in the *Aurora*.

As a first step it was necessary to complete the destruction of the German destroyers at Narvik and, on the 13th, a force composed of the battleship *Warspite* and nine destroyers carried this out in a wild, confused action in the narrow fiords at the cost of three British destroyers heavily damaged.

Allied ambitions were now expanded to include an assault on Trondheim by means of a pincer movement, the two arms of which were to be landed at Namsos to the north and Aandalsnes to the south, each of which lay at the head of a long, narrow fiord.

For the former, half of the troops for 'Rupert' were to be diverted as it was sanguinely considered, after the naval battle on the 13th, that a single brigade would be sufficient to complete the liberation of Narvik. For the latter, the brigade which had been hastily evacuated from the 1st Cruiser Squadron at Rosyth was now re-embarked in the *Galatea* and *Arethusa* of the 2nd Cruiser Squadron.

The first of these expeditions to arrive off its objective was that for Narvik; but though the naval C-in-C, encouraged by the report of Vice-Admiral Whitworth, who had commanded in the battle of

that no enemy troops land'. Arriving at 1600 off the entrance to Narvik fiord with five ships of the 2nd Flotilla, *Hardy, Hotspur, Havock, Hunter,* and *Hostile,* he learned from the Norwegian pilot station that six larger destroyers had preceded him and had occupied Narvik. He at once decided to attack at dawn.

Though, in fact, not six but ten more powerful destroyers would be his opponents, Warburton-Lee's faith in surprise to even the odds was well founded. He arrived off Narvik undetected: his presence was announced by the explosion of torpedoes against Bonte's flagship *Heidkamp,* another destroyer *Schmitt* and merchant ships berthed nearby, and a hail of shells on a third, the *Roeder.* Two other German destroyers received minor damage. Having thus immobilised five of the six enemy ships reported to be at Narvik, Warburton-Lee was in no hurry to withdraw. Unknown to him, however, five more were berthed in side fiords, waiting their turn to fuel from

the 13th, was afire to launch an immediate assault, he was shackled by the fact that his military commander was under strict orders not to attempt a landing against opposition, for which his troops were neither equipped nor correctly loaded in the transports. While attempts were made to resolve such totally opposed views by the two commanders, headquarters were set up at Harstad, some 75 miles from Narvik by sea and the troop convoy was anchored in the vicinity to await the emergence of a plan of action. Whatever chance had existed of a successful frontal assault while the morale of the 2,000 German mountain troops brought in the destroyers remained temporarily shattered by the result of the naval encounters, quickly evaporated; a long siege and a slow reduction of the German defences, for which the melting of the deep snow had to be awaited, was thus embarked upon.

Landings at Namsos and Aandalsnes were made on 17th and 18th April after preparations had been made by landing parties from ships of the Home Fleet. The troop convoys were escorted safely up the narrow fiords by ships of the British and French navies whose far from adequate anti-aircraft armament provided their only defence against attacks by German dive-bombers during the approach and disembarkation. This was achieved with negligible casualties. The fighting now resolved itself, however, into an attempt by ill-organised allied military forces, very poorly equipped for defence against air attack and lacking any tactical air support, to advance on Trondheim against well-trained and equipped German troops whose tactical air support enjoyed complete aerial domination. Meanwhile British anti-aircraft light cruisers, sloops, destroyers, and anti-submarine trawlers, defending the anchorages and the sea supply routes, were the easy targets for a ceaseless succession of attacks by dive-bombers.

Virtually immobilised in the narrow fiords, they fired their guns until the blistering barrels were worn smooth and ammunition exhausted. By all the rules they should have been massacred; but though a number were hit and forced to limp painfully home, only one, the sloop *Bittern*, became a total loss.

Although the two allied expeditionary forces held their own in spite of their lack of air support, their position was clearly, in the long run, untenable and on 27th April it was decided to evacuate them. At both Namsos and Aandalsnes, good organisation,

gallant improvisation, and seamanship of a high order by the destroyers and cruisers enabled all the troops to be embarked under cover of the few hours of darkness and the troopships escorted clear of the fiords before daylight. There, the Stukas made a last effort to overwhelm the prey that had escaped them. They succeeded only in sinking the French destroyer *Bison* and the British *Afridi*.

All central and southern Norway was thus abandoned to the invading German forces and the main allied effort concentrated on the recapture of Narvik. Attempts to hold back the German advance northward to reinforce the garrison failed so long as operations were within range of the German dive-bombers. In the Narvik area itself, only the German high-level bombers could intervene. No allied fighter defences were available until the last week of May when R.A.F. Gladiators brought over in the *Furious*, and a squadron of Hurricanes transported in the carrier *Glorious*, began operations from Bardufoss airfield north of Narvik. But high-level bombing against ships proved to be far less effective than had been prophesied and allied warships were able to operate in support of the investing troops without suffering unacceptable casualties.

Nevertheless it was the arrival of fighter cover and the onset of the spring thaw that at last persuaded the British military commander to open the assault on Narvik on 27th May, two days after news had been received that the allied governments had decided to evacuate the whole of Norway. For events elsewhere now made it crystal clear that the idea of trying to hold Norway with the limited resources at that time available to the allies had never been a valid one. While the six-weeks-long, cautious preparations for the assault had been maturing, in France and the Netherlands the 'phoney war' had erupted on 10th May in the fierce German offensive which, by the 21st, had brought its armoured spearhead within sight of the English Channel and by the 27th forced the British Army back on to the beaches of Dunkirk to await the seemingly hopeless chance of evacuation by sea.

At Narvik, British, French, Polish, and Norwegian troops, backed by the gunfire of allied warships, completed the capture of the town on the 28th. Preparations for evacuation had already begun and on 7th June the first convoy of storeships left for the U.K., followed by the first of two troop convoys which had

Opposite: After the German occupation of Norway in 1940, Norwegian coastal waters were the scene of many naval raids and sweeps. In command of many of them was Rear-Admiral Rhoderick McGrigor, here seen on the bridge of HMS *Campania* during an enemy air attack on a convoy to North Russia

loaded under cover of R.A.F. Hurricanes and Gladiators from Bardufoss and Skuas from the *Ark Royal* which, with the *Glorious*, had joined the naval covering force on 2nd June. The second troop convoy sailed on the 9th.

Only light escort was available for these convoys, though the C-in-C Home Fleet planned to meet them on the second day of their passage. A complete absence of any German naval activity in the last five weeks had bred a certain complacency and there was a serious shortage of escorts owing to the heavy requirements of the Dunkirk operations. Fortunately the continuous fighter cover over the Narvik area had prevented any inkling of the evacuation reaching the Germans.

Equally unknown to the allies, however, was the fact that the *Scharnhorst*, *Gneisenau*, and *Hipper*, now repaired, had sailed from Kiel early on 4th June with orders to mount a raid on the gathering of allied shipping at Harstad. By the 7th, the German squadron, under the command of Admiral Marschall, had reached the latitude of Harstad and made rendezvous with their replenishment tanker. They were thus lying athwart the route of the allied convoys, the most advanced of which, composed of six large passenger liners laden with troops, was reported to the German Admiral by air reconnaissance as some 150 miles south-east of him and steering south. The other troop convoy was also reported forming up off the Norwegian coast, as

also were the *Ark Royal* and *Glorious*, still operating their aircraft from a position further north.

All this activity led Marschall to suspect an allied evacuation; he decided to ignore his orders and set off in chase of the troop convoy. This was in fact already out of his grasp but his southern cast led him during the 8th to an oil tanker escorted by a trawler, both of which were quickly sent to the bottom and with the empty troopship *Orama* which was similarly dealt with, while the hospital ship *Atlantis* in company with her was allowed to proceed unmolested.

Marschall now sent the *Hipper* and his escorting destroyers, which were short of fuel, back to Trondheim, while he himself with the two battleships turned north again. This course could have brought him into contact that evening with the cruiser *Devonshire*, proceeding alone to Scapa Flow with the King of Norway and his entire Government embarked. Or, on the following day, if nothing intervened, he must have encountered the seven liner transports of the second troop convoy. But it was not to be.

The final episode of the allied evacuation had been the embarkation in the *Glorious* of the ten surviving R.A.F. Gladiators and eight Hurricanes, the pilots of which, though none had previously landed on a carrier's deck, had begged to be allowed to fly them on board rather than destroy them on shore. This gallant and successful effort was now to suffer a tragic sequel. Influenced by the difficulty of operating her Swordfish with so many extra aircraft

cluttering the deck, the *Glorious* had no scouting planes aloft on 8th June as she steamed home with an escort of two destroyers, the *Ardent* and *Acasta*. The first she knew of the presence of the *Scharnhorst* and *Gneisenau*, was the sight of their masts rising rapidly over the horizon at 1545 that afternoon.

The *Glorious* turned to flee under cover of a smoke screen laid by the destroyers, but in vain. The German ships, equipped with radar-directed gun-control, overwhelmed and sank her with their 11-inch guns. All but three officers and 35 ratings went down with her, the losses including nearly all the R.A.F. pilots of the Gladiators and Hurricanes.

Nevertheless the encounter may well have prevented a disaster of even greater magnitude by saving the troop convoy and the *Devonshire* with her important passengers. For the *Ardent* and *Acasta*, in a vain effort to save the carrier, made a gallant torpedo attack on the battleships and, before being sunk, the *Acasta* succeeded in torpedoing the *Scharnhorst* and so crippling her that Marschall abandoned the operation and set course for Trondheim, leaving the way home clear for both the troop convoy and the slow stores convoy.

* * *

The ordeal suffered by the British fighting services and their allies which is generally referred to as 'Dunkirk' had, in fact, begun for ships of the Royal Navy as early as 10th May when the German offensive in the west opened with the invasion of Holland and met with little effective resistance. Destroyers had at once been despatched with naval demolition parties to put the Dutch ports and facilities out of action and bring out all merchant ships found there, while cruisers and destroyers brought away the government's gold reserves and the Netherlands Royal Family and Government. The eight days which followed before the Dutch ports were finally abandoned to the advancing German armies provided a foretaste of what to come with operations in mine-infested waters and under continuous air attack. The full fury of the German dive-bombers was not yet experienced, however, and serious casualties were confined to the loss of the destroyer *Valentine* and damage to two others.

Operations moved down the coast with the German advance through Belgium, and on the 19th the destroyer *Whitley* was sunk by bombers. By this

Admiral Sir Bertram Ramsay, who was Flag Officer, Dover, in 1940, organised the withdrawal of the British Expeditionary Force from Dunkirk after the German advance to the Channel coast. Later in the war he was appointed Allied Naval Commander Expeditionary Force, and was responsible for the naval side of the Normandy landings in 1944

time the implications of the headlong German armoured drive towards the Channel and the possibility of the British Army being cut off and having to be evacuated by sea were becoming evident. On the 20th Vice-Admiral Bertram Ramsay (Flag Officer, Dover) began to organise shipping in preparation for the latter eventuality.

Evacuation was by no means decided upon yet, however. When the German advance threatened Calais, reinforcements of a Rifle Brigade and a regiment of tanks were transported there from Southampton escorted by destroyers between the 22nd and 23rd. To Boulogne also the 20th Guards Brigade was transported on the 22nd under destroyer escort.

The following day, however, evacuation of Boulogne was decided upon and additional destroyers were sent which, while alongside in the harbour found themselves taking an intimate part in the land battle, engaging enemy batteries, tanks and machine-gun posts at close range. Two of them, the *Keith* and *Vimy*, came under concentrated artillery, mortar and small-arms fire, their captains being killed on the bridge. And all the while the enemy bombers swooped unopposed until, late in the afternoon, R.A.F. fighters arrived overhead to bring some relief.

In spite of this, only one destroyer, the *Venetia*, was seriously damaged and by the early hours of the morning of the 24th all but some 300 Welsh Guards had been evacuated.

The garrison of Calais, however, was ordered to fight to the last with the object of holding up the German advance on Dunkirk, on which port the main body of the British Expeditionary Force was retiring. Air raids over Calais were incessant throughout the hours of daylight; many of them were concentrated on the destroyers supporting the garrison with bombardments. The *Wessex* was sunk, the *Vimiera* and the Polish *Burza* were damaged. Nevertheless destroyers continued to arrive bringing supplies and ammunition for the troops and taking away wounded or non-fighting elements.

Meanwhile the main body of the British Expeditionary Force had been fighting a number of delaying actions as it fell back on Dunkirk. Already the C-in-C, Lord Gort, had ordered the evacuation of non-essential men and some 28,000 had been lifted by 21st May. That the Navy would soon be called on to mount a large scale evacuation was clear, and planning for Operation 'Dynamo', as it was called, began on the 22nd when 50 Dutch schuyts, coastal craft of some 200 tons which had escaped to England when Holland was overrun, were commandeered. On 26th May the Dunkirk bridge-head was established and the three British Army Corps gradually withdrawn inside it. On the same day 'Dynamo' was ordered to be carried out under the direction of Admiral Ramsay at Dover. Captain W. G. Tennant, R.N. was appointed Senior Naval Officer, Dunkirk.

The modest aim of 'Dynamo', initially, was to evacuate some 45,000 men in two days, which seemed the possible limit. How more than seven times that number were saved in the nine days following 26th May when the operation was ordered to begin, constitutes the miracle that the name 'Dunkirk' has signified ever since.

The conditions under which the evacuation was carried out have to be borne in mind. Dunkirk itself and its inner harbour, where ships normally berthed, had been reduced to rubble. It seemed at first that only from the beaches to the east of the town could the troops be embarked. Fortunately, however, the two breakwaters running seawards to the east and west of the entrance were found to have deep enough water alongside them to berth small ships; after the first day these were used continuously by personnel ships and destroyers and it was from them that by far the largest numbers were embarked.

Nevertheless, as from every little port of England there was gathered a growing swarm of craft – drifters, schuyts, coasting steamers, tugs, lifeboats, yachts, and ships' boats – they, as well as the numerous destroyers and minesweepers brought in from the various naval commands, operated off the beaches of Malo, Bray, and La Panne whence many thousands were embarked by improvised methods that became ever more efficient with experience and under the guidance of naval parties sent across to control the beaches.

Throughout the hours of daylight heavy bombing attacks were almost continuous, and it was soon necessary for the personnel ships – so very valuable on account of their carrying capacity and high speed – to be restricted to night runs. By night German motor torpedoes haunted the route across from Dover. Mines were a constant hazard.

Space does not permit any detailed account of individual ships' experiences during the nine days of ceaseless fighting and manoeuvring by the great host of craft of all sizes that brought about the miracle of Dunkirk. It must be sufficient to give some figures. When 'Dynamo' ended on 4th June, 308,888 men had been evacuated in British ships and craft, 29,338 in allied vessels, these numbers including 26,175 French troops. The greatest number landed in England in a single day was 68,014 (22,942 from the beaches, 45,072 from the harbour) on 31st May. Six British and three French destroyers and eight personnel ships had been sunk, 19 British destroyers and nine personnel ships had been so damaged that they had had to be withdrawn.

Dunkirk will ever remain a heroic epic of sea warfare and of patient, disciplined courage by an army in adversity. Nevertheless it cannot be forgotten that it was an episode, even if a glorious one, in a catastrophic defeat. The 28 destroyers lost or put out of action were to be painfully missed in the months to come as the Battle of the Atlantic grew in extent and fury, and invasion of the British Isles threatened.

CHAPTER 22

*The Second World War – Battle of the River Plate –
German raider operations – The Sinking of the* Bismarck *–
Escape of the* Scharnhorst, Gneisenau, *and* Prinz Eugen

DONALD MACINTYRE

In the previous chapter the course of events in home waters and the Atlantic during the first few months of the Second World War was briefly sketched. It is intended now to recount the operations of German surface ships in the role of commerce raiders as a consecutive whole.

It will be remembered that the pocket battleships *Deutschland* and *Admiral Graf Spee*, attended by supply ships, were despatched, prior to the outbreak of war, to the North and South Atlantic respectively, where they were to remain undetected until ordered to begin operations. These orders were given on 26th September, and four days later the *Graf Spee* sank her first victim off Pernambuco, the S.S. *Clement*, a fact which became known to the Admiralty on 1st October. Within a few days eight allied hunting groups had been formed, composed largely of cruisers but including also the battlecruiser *Renown*, the British carriers *Eagle*, *Ark Royal*, and *Hermes*, the French battleship *Dunkerque* and carrier *Béarn*.

The *Graf Spee*, commanded by Captain Langsdorff, by constantly shifting her hunting ground, refuelling as necessary from her attendant supply ship *Altmark*, to which she transferred the crews of her victims, successfully evaded the hunting groups for two and a half months during which time she sank nine ships, totalling 50,000 tons. The *Deutschland* was much less effective and, after sinking only two ships, was recalled to Germany on 1st November.

The last phase of the *Graf Spee's* career began when, after a diversion into the Indian Ocean, she returned to sink the S.S. *Doric Star* off the South-West African coast on 2nd December and the S.S.

Tairoa on the next day. Three thousand miles away, off the River Plate estuary, Commodore H. Harwood, his broad pendant in the light cruiser *Ajax*, had a presentiment that Langsdorff would no longer be able to resist the temptation of the rich pickings to be found in that area. Harwood's squadron, with the whole length of South America's Atlantic coast to cover, was widely dispersed, the New Zealand light cruiser *Achilles* off Rio de Janeiro, the heavy cruisers *Exeter* and *Cumberland* at the Falkland Islands. Calculating that the *Graf Spee* could reach the River Plate by 13th December, he ordered the *Exeter* and *Achilles* to join him on the 12th.

His intuition had served him well. At 0616 on the 13th the *Exeter*, investigating smoke on the horizon, reported a pocket battleship in sight. In the situation which thus arose there is no doubt that, though opposed by three ships, the *Graf Spee*, with her armament of six 11-inch and twelve 5·9-inch guns could have decisively defeated the *Exeter* (six 8-inch), *Ajax* and *Achilles* (eight 6-inch each), if they had fought as a single unit. Commodore Harwood therefore divided his force into two divisions, the two light cruisers engaging from the east while the *Exeter* steered so as to engage from the south.

Langsdorff, believing at first that he was opposed by a cruiser and two destroyers, began by engaging the *Exeter* with the whole of his main armament while he turned his 5·9-inch battery on the *Ajax* and *Achilles*. Aided by radar, which the British ships did not possess, the *Graf Spee* made accurate shooting at the *Exeter* and soon heavily damaged her. Within 40 minutes the British cruiser had been crippled and left with only one turret in action; by 0730, her speed falling off and unable to keep up with the enemy, she was forced to break off the action to make repairs.

The *Graf Spee's* secondary armament was much less effective and the *Ajax* and *Achilles* had escaped damage. They themselves were scoring hits and though their 6-inch shells could not inflict vital damage to their opponent's stoutly armoured hull, Langsdorff, during his engagement with the *Exeter*, had to shift the fire of one of his 11-inch turrets onto them. And when, at 0716, the *Graf Spee* had turned to concentrate on and finish off the *Exeter*, the accumulated damage from the combined fire of the two cruisers forced Langsdorff to re-engage them and then to steer for the neutral shelter and repair facilities of Montevideo.

Nevertheless the *Graf Spee* was still showing little sign of damage and was shooting as accurately as ever. The *Ajax* was twice hit by 11-inch shells, both her turrets being put out of action and her topmast brought down. Harwood was forced to break off under cover of smoke and to content himself with shadowing as far as Uruguayan territorial waters. Entering Montevideo, Langsdorff obtained a 72-hour extension to the 24 hours normally allowed to a belligerent warship in order to repair his damage.

While a concentration of British warships, including the *Ark Royal* and *Renown*, was hastening to the area, diplomatic representations and successive departures of British merchant ships, each of which was entitled by international law to 24 hours' start before an enemy might sail, thereafter combined to delay Langsdorff's departure. False intelligence put out of the arrival of British reinforcements in the offing then convinced him that to break out could be only suicidal and to no good purpose. On the evening of 17th December he took his ship down river and scuttled her in the estuary. Three days later he committed suicide.

A tail-piece to the *Graf Spee* episode remains to be told. Her supply ship *Altmark*, with some 300 British Merchant Navy prisoners in her hold, evaded intensive searches for her until, on 15th February, she was reported to be off the Norwegian coast. Intercepted by a British force she took refuge in territorial waters in Jossing Fiord. When the Norwegians refused to take action to release the prisoners, which by international law should have been done, the

destroyer *Cossack* entered the fiord, went alongside the *Altmark* and, after a brief hand-to-hand fight, rescued them.

The elimination of the *Graf Spee* removed, for the time being, all threat by German surface ships in the Atlantic. The Norwegian campaign in April, May, and June 1940 left the German Navy with the *Admiral Hipper* as their only operational heavy ship. On 31st March 1940, however, a fresh surface threat was born when the first of a series of disguised merchant ship raiders left Germany. This was the *Atlantis* which, after sinking one British ship in the South Atlantic and laying a minefield off Cape Agulhas, arrived undetected in the Indian Ocean in May to begin a long and successful career of depredations until she was at last intercepted and sunk by the cruiser *Devonshire* in November 1941.

During the spring and early summer of 1940, five other similar raiders succeeded in breaking out to roam the oceans, where they operated against merchant ships sailing independently. With the support of supply ships sent out to attend on them, and by

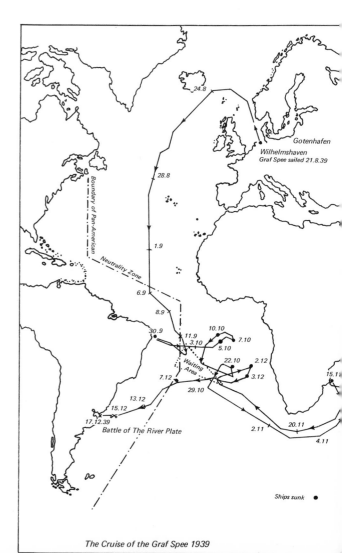

The Cruise of the Graf Spee 1939

Admiral Sir Henry Harwood commanded the South American Division at the time of the action against the German pocket battleship *Admiral Graf Spee*, which had been operating as a raider. The *Graf Spee* was engaged off the estuary of the River Plate by the cruisers *Ajax*, *Achilles*, and *Exeter* and was forced to put into Montevideo for repairs to the damage she received

cruiser *Cornwall* in the Indian Ocean. The other three, *Widder*, *Orion*, and *Komet*, got back to Germany, in October, 1940, August, and October 1941, respectively.

The first of a second wave of four raiders, the *Kormoran*, left Germany in December 1940 and after a career lasting 11 months during which she accounted for 11 ships of 68,274 tons, went down in a mutually destructive encounter with the cruiser H.M.A.S. *Sydney*. In January 1942 the *Thor* set out on a second cruise which ended in October of that year when she took refuge in Yokohama and was soon afterwards destroyed by fire. The *Stier*, which began her cruise in May 1942, came to a surprising end when she encountered the American Liberty-ship *Stephen Hopkins* in hazy weather in the South Atlantic. The merchantship, on being ordered to stop, at once opened fire with her solitary 4-inch gun and, at the short range made such good practice that she fatally damaged the raider before being herself overwhelmed. It is sad to relate that of the gallant crew of the Liberty-ship only fifteen survived to reach Brazil 31 days later in a lifeboat. The *Stier's* crew were rescued by her supply ship *Tannenfels*.

The last German armed merchant raider to be at large on the ocean shipping routes was the *Michel*. Leaving Germany in March 1942, she had accounted for 14 ships of 94,362 tons in the South Atlantic and Indian Oceans before arriving in Japan on 1st January 1943. Sailing again in May 1943 she had sunk only three further ships when she was sunk by the U.S. Submarine *Tarpon* off Japan in October of the same year.

Thorns in the flesh as these numerous, skilfully operated raiders were, their achievements were small compared to those of the German U-boats and the threat posed by them was never a mortal one. A more serious menace were the sorties into the Atlantic made by the heavy units of the German fleet.

The first of these to break out was the pocket battleship *Admiral Scheer*, which entered the Denmark Strait at the end of October 1940 and by 1st November had reached the North Atlantic convoy route. Four days later, after sinking a solitary merchant ship, she sighted the homeward-bound convoy HX84 of 37 ships escorted by the A.M.C. *Jervis Bay*. Ordering the convoy to scatter, Captain Fegen of the *Jervis Bay* steamed out in gallant

constantly shifting their operational area, they engaged the attentions of a very considerable force of British cruisers and armed merchant cruisers during sorties which lasted many months.

One of them, the *Thor*, which left Germany on 6th June, was thrice intercepted by British A.M.C's and on each occasion defeated them without suffering major damage herself. Of these, the ex-liners *Alcantara* and *Carnarvon Castle* were crippled and forced to break off the action; the *Voltaire*, a much weaker and slower ship, was sunk after putting up a gallant fight. The *Thor* then returned to Germany having sunk eleven allied merchantmen totalling 83,301 tons.

Another raider, the *Pinguin*, was at large for ten months during which she sank 136,551 tons of shipping before being caught and sunk by the

defiance to engage his vastly more powerful opponent. Though the outcome could never be in doubt, he succeeded in holding the *Scheer's* attention long enough for the convoy to become widely scattered with the result that 32 of the merchant ships escaped.

Nevertheless the attack disrupted the vital flow of shipping across the Atlantic, causing a serious loss of essential imports to Great Britain. When convoys were resumed the Admiralty was forced to deploy battleships to escort them. Meanwhile the *Scheer*, leaving all this turmoil behind her, had moved far away from the scene to hunt in the South Atlantic before making a remote Christmas Day rendezvous with the *Thor*, *Pinguin*, and two supply ships. Two weeks of refit and replenishment and then the cruise was resumed in the South Atlantic, the Indian Ocean – where the *Scheer* narrowly escaped being caught by a British hunting group – and back to the South Atlantic. At intervals she returned to the refuelling rendezvous in mid-South Atlantic where the *Thor* and *Pinguin* were again met as well as the *Atlantis* and *Kormoran*. A slow, but steady toll of allied merchant ships sunk had reached a total of 16 (99,059 tons) by 11th March 1941 when, having been recalled, the *Scheer* steered for the Denmark Strait and home.

While the *Scheer* had been thus exciting alarm in distant waters, Admiral Raeder had been planning to throw all the available major units of the fleet into the Battle of the Atlantic, including the splendid new battleship *Bismarck*. She and the latest of the 8-inch cruisers, the *Prinz Eugen*, would not be ready until May; but in the meantime the cruiser *Admiral Hipper* reached the North Atlantic on 7th December 1940 and on 27th January 1941 was followed by the *Scharnhorst* and *Gneisenau* under the command of Admiral Lütjens.

The cruiser's low fuel capacity and endurance made her less than ideal for the *guerre de course*. Her mobility thus restricted, she encountered nothing until 24th December when she intercepted a strongly escorted troop convoy. Damaged in a brief skirmish with the escort in thick weather, she returned to Brest where she remained idle until February 1941. She then sortied again and had the good fortune to locate an unescorted convoy in the North Atlantic from which she sank seven ships. Shortage of fuel then forced her to return to Brest, and at the end of March she returned to Germany.

The two battleships were more successful. After a narrow escape from being brought to action by the Home Fleet south of Iceland, they succeeded in passing undetected through the Denmark Strait on 4th February 1941. Arriving on the convoy route they were rewarded on the 8th with the sight of the serried mastheads of the U.K.-bound convoy HX-

RAIDER WARFARE

106. As they approached to begin the work of destruction, however, they sighted the top hamper of a battleship escort. Though this was only the veteran *Ramillies*, engagement with enemy heavy units was no part of a commerce raider's function and Lütjens at once broke off the attack.

The *Ramillies* having reported the ship she had briefly sighted as possibly a *Hipper*-class cruiser, the C-in-C Home Fleet assumed that it might be the *Hipper* herself, or the *Scheer*, about to break back through the northern passage to Germany. He therefore deployed all his available forces accordingly.

Thus Lütjens, waiting south of Greenland for another opportunity, was left unmolested and on 17th February moved out again, heading for a more westerly point on the convoy route. There, as he hoped, he discovered, on the 22nd, a concentration of shipping, 500 miles east of Newfoundland, proceeding unescorted, their westbound convoy having been recently dispersed on leaving the U-boat danger area. Five ships totalling 25,784 tons were quickly snapped up.

They managed to make distress signals before being sunk, however, and Lütjens deemed it wise to quit the area, making across the ocean to investigate the Sierra Leone convoy route. There, once again, on 8th March he found a battleship in charge of the first convoy sighted, this time the *Malaya*, and decided to leave well alone. A luckless independently-routed ship fell into his grasp the next day but, after refuelling in mid-ocean, he steered once more for the Halifax route and again fell in with ships from recently dispersed convoys, sinking or capturing 16 of them to a total of 82,000 tons during the 15th and 16th.

By now all the heavy ships of the Home Fleet, including the modern battleship *King George V*, were seeking the raiders. But Lütjens had been ordered to return to Brest in preparation for the more ambitious operations in conjunction with the *Bismarck* and *Prinz Eugen* planned for May. In spite of intensive air reconnaissance by R.A.F. maritime aircraft and by aircraft from the *Ark Royal*, and although the latter actually sighted the *Scharnhorst* and *Gneisenau* on the 20th, the two ships slipped through the net and reached Brest on the 22nd.

They were to find little rest or freedom to carry out undisturbed the refit of which the *Scharnhorst* was in urgent need. The port of Brest became a regular

Admiral Sir John Tovey, Commander-in-Chief of the British Home Fleet in the operations which ended with the sinking of the *Bismarck*, had a special seat constructed on the bridge of the flagship to give him an all-round view

target for the heavy night bombers of the R.A.F. Though these had failed to damage the *Hipper* before she sailed on 15th March to return to Germany, the damage to the dockyard caused by the nightly raids was to disrupt the work of refit. Then, on 6th April, Flying Officer K. Campbell, in a torpedo-bomber, succeeded at the cost of his own life in torpedoing the *Gneisenau*. Placed in drydock for repairs, she received further damage from four bomb hits five days later.

Raeder's hopes of the two battleships co-operating with the *Bismarck* and *Prinz Eugen* when the latter sortied were thus dashed. Nevertheless, against the opinion of Admiral Lütjens who was to hoist his flag in the *Bismarck*, he persisted with the plan for her and her cruiser consort. The two ships sailed from Gdynia on 18th May and three days later were reported in Korsfiord near Bergen. The C-in-C Home Fleet, Admiral Sir John Tovey, took steps at once to block every exit from the North Sea and

Opposite: The *Admiral Graf Spee*, torn by internal explosions and burning furiously, settles in the waters of the River Plate after being scuttled to avoid further action with British warships which were waiting for her outside territorial waters

239

Arctic. Two cruisers, the *Norfolk* and *Suffolk*, the latter fitted with the earliest effective surface-warning radar set, were patrolling the Denmark Strait. Three more guarded the Iceland-Faeroes passage. From Scapa the battlecruiser *Hood* and the new battleship *Prince of Wales* sailed for Iceland. When Korsfiord was reported empty on the 22nd, the fleet flagship, *King George V*, four cruisers, and the carrier *Victorious* sailed from Scapa and, joined by the battlecruiser *Repulse*, steered for a position south of Iceland.

For the first time the cloak of invisibility provided by the almost constant mists and foul weather in Icelandic waters was to be stripped from the German warships by the eye of radar. Air reconnaissance was grounded on the 23rd; but the *Suffolk*, patrolling between the ice-edge and the north-west corner of Iceland, sighted the *Bismarck* and *Prinz Eugen* that evening and was thereafter, in company with the *Norfolk*, able to shadow and report from the cover of the mist.

The *Hood*, flying the flag of Vice-Admiral L. E. Holland, and the *Prince of Wales* were to the south-west of Iceland when they received the great news. They steered to intercept. An engagement was

imminent in which, at first sight, it might seem that the advantage of strength lay with the British, their eight 15-inch and ten 14-inch guns being opposed to the eight 15-inch and eight 8-inch guns of the German ships. But, in fact, neither the veteran *Hood*, which had only recently emerged from a long refit, nor the new *Prince of Wales*, still suffering from armament defects, had had the opportunity to work up to fighting efficiency whereas the two German ships had undergone extensive and thorough training before sailing. Furthermore, the *Hood*, 25 years old, was armoured in a style and to a degree outmoded by modern concepts of warfare.

The balance of power was tipped even more decisively in the German favour by the tactical situation and by Admiral Holland's reaction to it when the *Bismarck* was sighted on the horizon at 0535 on the morning of 24th May. Steering to close to a decisive range, the British ships were able to bring to bear on the enemy only their forward turrets. The Germans, on the other hand, manoeuvred to keep their full broadsides bearing and, opening fire with great accuracy at a range of 25,000 yards, quickly obtained a hit on the *Hood* which started a fire amidships. At 0600 another salvo

One hit was made on the *Bismarck* by aircraft from HMS *Victorious*, seen above, but the torpedo exploded amidships against her side armour and did no damage. It was about three hours after this attack that the *Bismarck* succeeded in shaking off the pursuit by the Home Fleet

straddled her, one of the shells evidently striking home and penetrating to a magazine. The great ship blew up and within a few minutes had disappeared with all but three of her ship's company. The full weight of the enemy's fire was now turned on the *Prince of Wales* which suffered four 15-inch and three 8-inch hits. With damage mounting and half her main armament incapacitated, she broke off the action under cover of smoke. In company with the *Suffolk* and *Norfolk*, she now settled down to shadow the *Bismarck* until the main body of the Home Fleet could arrive in support early the following day.

In spite of this brilliant initial success Lütjens's commerce-raiding mission had already been frustrated, for two hits by the *Prince of Wales'* 14-inch shells had caused the *Bismarck* to spring an oil fuel leak and had contaminated 1,000 tons of fuel in other tanks. While from all over the Atlantic British forces were being diverted to join the hunt, Lütjens decided he must steer for St Nazaire for docking and repairs. Unperceived by his shadowers, the *Prinz Eugen* was detached to operate on the trade routes.

Admiral Tovey now ordered forward his carrier, the *Victorious*, to launch her squadron of Swordfish aircraft to attack with torpedoes. It was dusk by the time she got within range and in rain, low cloud, and gathering darkness the nine Swordfish, led by Lieut-Commander E. Esmonde, took off. Locating their target by means of their airborne radar, they attacked in difficult conditions, scoring one hit and returning safely to the carrier in the dark.

The battleship's stoutly armoured hull was little damaged. But Lütjens's only hope of avoiding being brought to action now lay in shaking off his shadowers. Early on the 25th he succeeded in doing so, leaving Admiral Tovey faced with the problem of re-locating him in the trackless wastes of the Atlantic Ocean. Lütjens unwisely went on the air with a long radio signal reporting his difficulties, and a stream of wireless direction bearings were signalled to the flagship. A plotting error in the flagship led the C-in-C off on a false scent, but an appreciation a few hours later by the Admiralty that the *Bismarck* was making for one of the Biscay ports brought the

Opposite: In her day the *Hood* was the largest warship in the world, but as she was launched in 1918 she no longer measured up in 1941 to the new conditions of naval warfare. She was hit by plunging fire from the *Bismarck* and disappeared in a huge explosion

Home Fleet back on to a correct course, though a hundred or so miles astern. Throughout the 25th the *Bismarck* was lost to view and it was not until 1030 on the 26th that a R.A.F. reconnaissance flight at last rediscovered her.

Even so it was too late for the Home Fleet to bring her to action unless she could be slowed down. Hope of achieving this now depended solely on the torpedo planes of the *Ark Royal*, floundering northwards through heavy seas from Gibraltar. At 1115 her scouting planes sighted the enemy; at 1550 a striking force of 14 Swordfish took off. Detecting a target by radar, they attacked through low cloud and rain only to discover they had expended their torpedoes on the cruiser *Sheffield*, fortunately ineffectively. The downcast pilots returned to the carrier where their planes were hastily rearmed.

The situation was tense indeed when they took off again. But this time there was no mistake. Diving through the clouds they loosed their torpedoes to score two hits, one of which struck the *Bismarck* on her starboard quarter, wrecking her steering gear and jamming her rudders. A circling cripple, the great battleship's fate was sealed. With the dawn the *King George V* and *Rodney* arrived to hammer her to a wreck with 14-inch and 15-inch shells. But guns alone seemed incapable of sinking her and it was torpedoes from the *Dorsetshire* that finally sent her to the bottom at 1101 on 27th May 1941.

The *Prinz Eugen*, which had meanwhile refuelled in mid-Atlantic, had also by this time abandoned her attempt to follow a commerce-raiding career. Engine defects had arisen and she was on her way to Brest for repairs, where she arrived on 1st June to join the *Scharnhorst* and *Gneisenau*.

There the three ships remained through the summer and autumn, the target for repeated R.A.F. bombing raids which damaged each of them from time to time. Not until the end of January 1942 were all three sufficiently battleworthy to sortie as a squadron to harry the allied merchant convoys as had been intended. But by this time Hitler was convinced that Britain was planning to attack his northern flank in Norway and that the ships were needed at home.

A passage through the northern straits was no longer a feasible operation in the face of increased and improved air reconnaissance and radar equipment, yet to remain at Brest was passively to await inevitable destruction. Hitler, against strong opposition from his Naval Staff, insisted therefore that they should steam boldly home through the Channel. During January 1942 preparations were made which soon became known in England. By 3rd February it seemed certain that the German ships were about to move and that they must take the Channel route.

The motor torpedoboats and motor gunboats of the forces of the Vice-Admiral Dover (Sir Bertram Ramsay) were reinforced by six old destroyers stationed at Harwich, six more motor torpedoboats, and six naval Swordfish torpedo-bombers of No. 825 Squadron commanded by the Lieut-Commander Esmonde who had led the attack on the *Bismarck* launched from the *Victorious* nine months earlier. Such a force was, of course too meagre to oppose the passage of the German squadron but, in the narrow waters of the Channel this task was not primarily one for the Royal Navy but for the Royal Air Force, which was now to have the opportunity to prove the truth of the aerial gospel that capital ships were at the mercy of bomber planes. Of the latter, 33 torpedo-carrying Beauforts of R.A.F. Coastal Command were available, while Bomber Command had some 240 planes suitable for day attack.

That the impending operation was primarily one of aerial attack and defence was equally clear to the

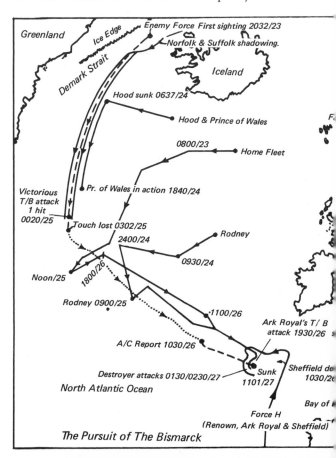

The Pursuit of The Bismarck

HMS *Sheffield*, which came up with Force H from Gibraltar to join in the chase of the *Bismarck*, played a significant part in her destruction. Detached to shadow the enemy while aircraft from the *Ark Royal* attacked, she became herself the target for the first attack by mistake. Dodging the torpedoes, she remained to direct the second aircraft attack onto the true target

German Command, and elaborate arrangements were made for continuous air cover during daylight hours by never fewer than 16 fighters. In addition, large fighter reserves were available at coastal airfields along the route. With such powerful air defence, as well as an escort of six destroyers, 15 torpedo-boats and a large number of MTB's, Vice-Admiral Ciliax, the German commander, was happy enough to accept a daylight passage through the narrows of the Dover Straits which would give him the cover of darkness for leaving Brest and for the greater part of the route up-Channel.

This route, carefully worked out to keep the ships in deep water, where maximum speed could be used and the known British minefields avoided, was itself meticulously swept and marked. Noting this activity, the Admiralty responded by getting the R.A.F. to lay 98 further magnetic mines between 3rd and 9th February. At 2245 on 11th February the German squadron cleared the boom defences of Brest and by midnight was off Ushant steaming at 25 knots.

Warning of any such move had been provided for by R.A.F. Coastal Command in the shape of three night air patrols by radar-fitted Hudson aircraft, one off Brest itself, one along the north Brittany coast, and one between Le Havre and Boulogne. But on the crucial night the first two suffered radar failures and the third had returned to base at dawn before the enemy ships had come within its radar range. Not until 1109 on the 12th was the startling news that the *Scharnhorst* and *Gneisenau* were already approaching the Dover Strait fortuitiously received from the mouths of two Spitfire pilots when they landed back at base after being in combat with fighters of the escort.

There was not a moment to be lost in getting the various British forces in motion. By noon five MTB's had left Dover and steered to intercept; the six destroyers at Harwich, exercising at sea, had set off to attack; three more MTB's set out from Ramsgate at 1225.

The first unit to get into action, however, was the Swordfish torpedo-bomber squadron. It had been intended that the Swordfish should attack simultaneously with the R.A.F. Beauforts; but the slow, short-endurance naval planes could not afford to wait for the others to gather from their dispersed air-fields, some having to come from as far afield as Scotland and Cornwall. Nor, indeed, did the squadron commander consider he could wait for the greater part of the promised five squadrons of fighter escort, which had been delayed. With only 10 Spitfires covering his vulnerable, heavy-laden biplanes, Esmonde led away for the enemy. Two more fighter squadrons, arriving soon afterwards, made straight for the enemy and engaged the German fighters. But they could not prevent some from swooping on their almost defenceless prey. One after the other the Swordfish were shot down; some succeeded in launching their torpedoes but without result; five survivors were picked up from two of the planes. Gallantry had not been enough to bring success to so forlorn a hope.

The little force of MTB's was similarly helpless in the face of the numerous German surface escorts and they, too, achieved nothing. To intercept the racing German squadron, the Harwich destroyers, their veteran hulls vibrating frantically as at high speed they steered for the mouth of the Scheldt, risked the transit of a German minefield in order to achieve interception. One could not stand the pace and turned back with engine defects. The other five pressed on. Making radar contact in mid-afternoon, they finally sighted their targets through the North Sea mists at a range of four miles. For another $2\frac{1}{2}$ miles, under a storm of fire, they drove on, turning to fire their torpedoes at 3,000 yards. Thrusting even closer, the *Worcester* paid for her temerity with heavy damage and casualties. All was in vain, the enemy succeeding in avoiding all the torpedoes.

While this attack was in progress, the first British bombers reached the scene. That this was some four and a half hours after the German squadron had been located is a measure of the lack of preparedness revealed. The nearest R.A.F. Squadron to the operational area was one of seven Beaufort torpedo-planes at Thorney Island, near Portsmouth. Of these, only four were immediately available. On the way to collect a fighter escort over the Straits they became split up and when they finally found the target, attacked singly or in pairs without success, as did the other three of their squadron later.

Another squadron which had to come from Leuchars in Scotland had torpedoes for only nine of its 14 Beauforts. In company with five Hudson bombers they, too, attacked without result. Twelve other Beauforts from a base in Cornwall had to go first to Thorney Island where they arrived at 1430. Not until 1701 did they arrive to pick up their fighter escort above a Norfolk airfield. No fighters appearing, they set off unescorted; in the gathering dusk they failed to find the target.

The aircraft of Bomber Command, trained exclusively for high-level bombing at stationary targets on land, found themselves hamstrung throughout by the high mobility of their targets, the low cloud base which prevented the use of their usual technique, and any possibility of penetrating the enemy's armoured decks. In the event, out of 242 bombers which were organised in three waves, only 39 found targets to attack and scored no hits. Fifteen bombers were lost.

Nevertheless it was Bomber Command which succeeded in preventing the German ships from reaching home undamaged. That mines had been laid by them at the Admiralty's request along the enemy's expected route was mentioned earlier. The *Scharnhorst* was the first to suffer from one of these, being brought temporarily to a standstill at 1431. She was soon under way again, however, little the worse, though trailing behind the remainder of the squadron. The *Gneisenau* had a similar experience off Terschelling at 1955; but when the *Scharnhorst* detonated yet another mine at 2134 from the same minefield, she was holed and severely damaged and limped with difficulty to Wilhelmshaven.

There she was to be out of action for many months. The *Gneisenau* was never to go to sea again. Docked for repairs at Kiel, she was twice hit by heavy bombs on the night 26th/27th February and so heavily damaged that repairs were abandoned.

So ended Raeder's hopes of causing a holocaust of shipping on the vital Atlantic supply routes by means of his surface fleet. The battleship and cruiser sorties had caused great anxiety at times; but in fact their achievements had been negligible in comparison with those of the U-boat fleet. Even more palpably than in the case of the U-boat campaign, their efforts had basically been frustrated by the time-honoured, age-old convoy system.

The *Bismarck* was hit by two torpedoes from the *Ark Royal's* aircraft, one of which damaged her steering gear. She was caught by the British battleships *King George V* and *Rodney*, reduced to a shambles, and finally sunk by torpedoes from the cruiser *Dorsetshire*. She is seen here ploughing into a heavy sea

CHAPTER 23

The Second World War – Operations in the Mediterranean –
The Attack on Taranto – Battle of Cape Matapan –
Convoys to Malta – Surrender of the Italian Fleet

BRIAN SCHOFIELD

Although, in the original British war plans, operations in home waters had been given primary consideration, those in the Mediterranean came next in importance. At the outbreak of the war the appreciation was that with the French fleet operating from its bases in the Western basin and with a British fleet based at Alexandria in the Eastern one, Italy, in spite of her dominant position in the central Mediterranean and the powerful naval and air forces she possessed, could be contained and ultimately neutralised. The use of Malta as a naval base was however precluded by its proximity to the Sicilian airfields and the absence of adequate defences. It was also appreciated that, with Italy hostile, it would be necessary to close the Mediterranean to shipping which in consequence would have to be routed round the Cape of Good Hope.

Italy however did not enter the war on the side of Germany until 11th June 1940, just before the collapse of France, and during the period of the former's neutrality many ships of the British Mediterranean fleet were transferred to other commands. But as soon as an Italian declaration of war seemed imminent, the fleet was reconstituted. Under its Commander-in-Chief, Admiral Sir Andrew Cunningham, it comprised four battleships, one small carrier, one 8-inch and four 6-inch gun cruisers, 16 destroyers, and 10 submarines. The Italian fleet comprised four battleships, seven 8-inch and 11 6-inch gun cruisers, 61 destroyers, and 105 submarines.

With the fall of France on 26th June 1940, Britain was immediately confronted with a strategic situation of the utmost gravity. Should the French fleet fall into enemy hands, not only would Cunningham's fleet be greatly outnumbered, but Britain's ability to control operations in the Atlantic might be jeopardised. To offset the loss of French support, the Admiralty hurriedly assembled at Gibraltar a force, known as Force 'H', under Admiral Sir James Somerville, comprising initially a battlecruiser, two battleships, a carrier, and four destroyers. It was to this force that the distasteful task of immobilising the French forces lying in the North African port of Mers-el-Kebir was entrusted.

When Italy entered the war, she had a further two battleships under construction and nearing completion. Although the Italian fleet lacked carriers, the Italian Air Force was numerically powerful, and had these two services worked in close co-operation they could have made operations by the allies in the central Mediterranean extremely hazardous. But in spite of the insufficiency of the air support available to him, and the enemy's great preponderance in submarines, Cunningham's main consideration was to bring the enemy fleet to action at the first opportunity. He therefore put to sea with his fleet on the outbreak of hostilities in order to test the strength and capability of the Italian air force and in the hope of encountering the enemy's fleet. Although the former made a number of unsuccessful attacks on the British fleet, it was not until after the fall of France that the latter showed any signs of activity.

In response to demands from the Italian army in Libya for supplies of arms and equipment, the Italian fleet began a series of convoy operations across the Mediterranean which were covered by their heavy ships. Lack of adequate air reconnaissance pre-

Opposite: A painting by Norman Wilkinson showing an enemy air attack on a convoy to Malta in 1942

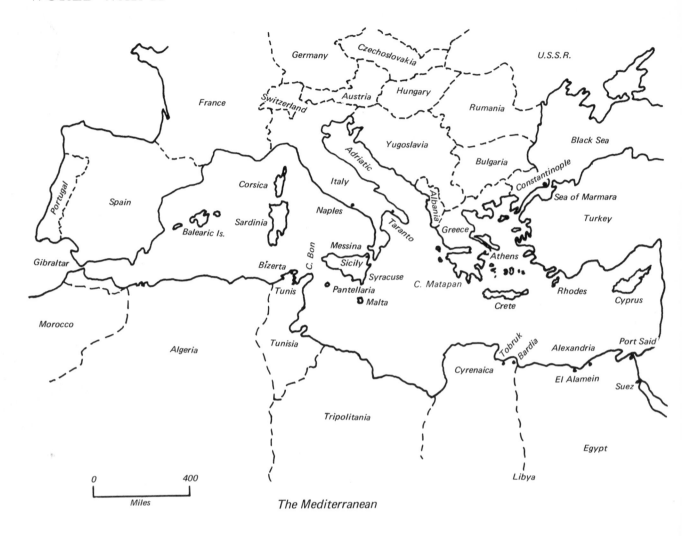

The Mediterranean

vented Cunningham from taking advantage of these brief sorties, but on 8th July a short encounter between the two fleets took place off the Calabrian coast when the British fleet was engaged in convoying supplies to Malta. The action opened at long range, during which the *Warspite* scored a hit on the Italian flagship *Cesare*. Admiral Campioni, the Italian Commander-in-Chief, thereupon retired under cover of smoke, the convoy he had been escorting having reached its destination. While returning to its base the British fleet was subjected to intensive bombing but escaped unharmed.

On 19th July the Royal Australian Navy's cruiser *Sydney* and five destroyers patrolling north of Crete sank one of two Italian 6-inch gun cruisers encountered without loss or damage to themselves.

The brush with the Italian fleet off Calabria made it clear to Cunningham that the two slow and unmodernised battleships in his fleet would be a great handicap in bringing the fast and long range Italian battleships to action, so he asked the Admiralty for another ship like the *Warspite* and also for a carrier to replace the *Eagle* in his fleet, which required docking as a result of the number of near misses which had fallen around her. As a result the battle-ship *Valiant* and the new carrier *Illustrious* were sent to join his flag, which they did on 1st September.

Although the Battle of Britain was in full swing, the British Chiefs of Staff were determined to do all they could to strengthen the defences of Malta, and early in August, using the veteran carrier *Argus* as transport to a point within range of the island, 12 Hurricane fighters had safely reached it. So began a series of progressively more hazardous operations designed to augment and maintain the defences of the island and keep its population from being starved into surrender.

In North Africa, too, the disparity in strength between the British and Italian armies gave cause for concern. An army of 30,000 under General Wavell faced one of 200,000 under Marshal Graziani. While the latter could command the support of nearly the whole Italian air force if necessary, the British had at their disposal only 96 bombers, 75 fighters, 24 Army co-operation aircraft, and 10 flying boats with which to support both land and sea operations in the area.

Towards the end of October a new commitment arose from Mussolini's decision to invade Greece, which resulted in a British occupation of the island of Crete and the establishment of an advanced naval base at Suda Bay, on the north shore of the island.

The transfer to Malta early in October of three Glenn-Martin Maryland reconnaissance aircraft, which because of their superior performance could keep a regular watch on the movements of the Italian fleet, facilitated the execution of a plan which had long been considered. This was a torpedo attack on the Italian battleships as they lay in harbour at Taranto. It took place on 11th November when aircraft from the *Illustrious*, reinforced by some transferred from the refitting *Eagle*, carried out a highly successful surprise attack, as a result of which the new battleship *Littorio* and two older ones of the 'Giulio Cesare' class were sunk where they lay. Of the 21 aircraft which took part in the attack, only two were lost. At the same time light forces under Vice-Admiral Pridham-Wippell swept through the Straits of Otranto where, early on 12th November, they sank three ships out of four in convoy and damaged an escorting destroyer.

The victory at Taranto had a marked influence on subsequent operations by the British fleet. When, a

Admiral Sir Andrew Cunningham, Commander-in-Chief of the British Mediterranean Fleet from 1939 to 1943, with the exception of a short spell in Washington in charge of the British Admiralty Delegation. His brilliant conduct of operations led to the defeat and surrender of the Italian fleet, and in 1943 he succeeded Admiral of the Fleet Sir Dudley Pound as First Sea Lord

fortnight later, an operational convoy was being passed through the Mediterranean under cover of both Force 'H' and Cunningham's fleet, an Italian fleet of two battleships, supported by cruisers and destroyers, sailed to intercept it but returned to base when Admiral Campioni found he was confronted with a superior force and when his calls for support from the air force went unanswered. The ill-timed operations in Greece had in fact made such heavy demands on the *Regia Aeronautica* that it was stretched to the limit of its resources, and Cunningham's fleet returned to Alexandria without firing a gun.

On 9th December Wavell began the offensive operations which drove the Italian army not only out of Egypt but also out of Cyrenaica with the loss of 38,000 prisoners. During these operations ships of the

British Mediterranean fleet bombarded Italian positions at Bardia, Tobruk, and elsewhere, thereby making a useful contribution to the victory. The opportunity was now taken of this favourable change in the situation to supply and revictual Malta.

The Italian defeat in North Africa and lack of success in Greece obliged the Germans to intervene in both these areas. Added emphasis was thus given to the need to interdict the transport of troops and material from Italy to North Africa, and the British government decided to withdraw troops from Wavell's command in North Africa and send them to support the Greeks.

Early in 1941 the Germans transferred a corps of the Luftwaffe to Sicily and it made its presence felt on 10th January during convoy operations to supply Malta, when the carrier *Illustrious* and the cruisers *Gloucester* and *Southampton* were severely damaged by dive-bombers, the latter having subsequently to be sunk. In the Western basin Force 'H' on 9th February made a foray into the Gulf of Genoa during which military targets at Genoa, Leghorn, and Spezia were heavily damaged by air and sea bombardment without loss or damage to the attackers.

The transport of British troops to Greece began on 5th March and as a result of German pressure on the Italian Navy to interfere with this movement, the Battle of Matapan took place. On 27th March, following receipt of intelligence of an intended sortie by an Italian force, which was later found to consist of a battleship, eight cruisers and 14 destroyers, Admiral Cunningham sailed to intercept it. Aircraft from the carrier *Formidable*, which had been sent out to replace the damaged *Illustrious*, succeeded in torpedoing the battleship, which however made good her escape, and they also torpedoed the 8-inch gun cruiser *Pola*, forcing her to stop. During the night this ship, together with the 8-inch gun cruisers *Zara* and *Fiume*, which had been ordered to stand by the stricken *Pola*, and two destroyers, were sunk by the guns of the British battlefleet without damage or casualty to Cunningham's forces.

Meanwhile, at the end of March, Wavell's forces, now too weak to resist the enemy's counter-attack, reinforced as it was by the German Afrika Corps, were driven back to the Egyptian frontier, leaving behind a holding force in Tobruk, which had to be supplied by sea, and which proved a costly undertaking.

HMS *Ark Royal* emerging unscathed from an Italian bombing attack during the action off Sardinia in November 1940. This was a long range action, British ships being unable to catch the faster Italian units, and torpedo attacks by the *Ark Royal's* Swordfish failing to hit and stop them

German dive bombers hit the carrier *Illustrious* in January 1941, setting her on fire. Her after lift was blown out by the bomb hits, and can be seen as a dark shape behind the bomb hole in the flight deck, while steam is rising from the nearly red hot deck as fire hoses spray water on it. In spite of her damage the carrier reached Malta under her own steam, and lived to fight on until the end of the war

In spite of valiant efforts by submarines and aircraft based on Malta to interfere with supplies and reinforcements being sent to the enemy troops in North Africa, the results were inadequate and on 8th April Cunningham sent four destroyers to Malta to assist in this task. They soon scored a substantial success by destroying an entire convoy of five ships. Then, on 21st April, he carried out a successful battleship bombardment of the port of Tripoli to which the bulk of the supplies were being shipped. Almost immediately after this operation the situation of the British troops in Greece deteriorated and their evacuation was ordered. This was carried out by light forces and transports under Vice-Admiral Pridham-Wippell. It began on 24th April and lasted five days. A total of 50,732 men were rescued, of which 16,000 were landed in Crete to strengthen the garrison there, the remainder returning to Egypt.

The arrival of a German armoured division in North Africa led Wavell to call for more tanks as a matter of urgency. In spite of considerable misgivings on the part of both Admirals Cunningham and Somerville, these were passed through the Mediterranean between 6th and 12th May in a convoy of five ships supported by all available ships of both Force 'H' and the Mediterranean fleet. The operation was favoured by cloudy weather which hampered the enemy's aircraft, and only one ship was lost as a result of striking two mines. The opportunity was also taken of restocking Malta with both food and fuel, and light forces bombarded Benghazi. A few days later Force 'H' escorted the carrier *Argus* on another mission to re-supply Malta with fighter aircraft, and this too was successfully accomplished.

On 20th May the Germans launched an airborne

The Battle of Matapan, by Norman Wilkinson. This painting is of the night action when three Italian heavy cruisers, illuminated by searchlight from a British destroyer, were blown out of the water by the 15-inch shells of the British battleships *Warspite*, *Valiant*, and *Barham*

assault on Crete, and the patrols established north of the island to prevent seaborne reinforcement of the enemy's troops came under sustained air attack and heavy losses were incurred. The enemy's complete superiority in the air made sea operations virtually impossible and on 27th May it was decided to evacuate the island. Although Cunningham's forces had had practically no rest since the attack on Crete began, his stirring call to them, 'We must not let the Army down', was answered with a will. During the next five days all available cruisers and destroyers were employed in rescuing the 32,000 men which had formed the island's garrison, and of these 18,600 were brought safely back to Alexandria. But the toll taken of the fleet was heavy and amounted to three cruisers and six destroyers sunk, and two battleships, one carrier, and seven destroyers damaged. Transports, supply ships, and fleet auxiliaries sunk or abandoned numbered 32, with a further 12 lost at sea on passage to Egypt.

The enemy's occupation of Crete and his recapture of Cyrenaica profoundly changed the strategic situation in the Eastern Mediterranean. It was no longer practicable to supply Malta by convoy from Alexandria, but the needs of the island were great and so the attempt had to be made to bring a convoy through from the West. During the month of June no fewer than 142 aircraft reached the island from carriers used to transport them to within safe flying distance of the island. Some of these went on to reinforce the squadrons in North Africa. Submarines also were used to carry essential stores, but these were insufficient to meet the demand. Between 21st and 25th July six storeships with a strong escort of cruisers and destroyers, covered by the heavy ships and carrier of Force 'H', reached the island, and although enemy opposition was strong, it was less severe than it might have been due to the temporary transfer of the German bomber squadrons from Sicily to the Balkans.

The problem of supplying the beseiged garrison of Tobruk was complicated by the need to withdraw a brigade and replace it with fresh troops, a move of about 20,000 men in each direction over a period of

submarine the following day.

Soon after this event a series of disasters befell British forces operating in the Mediterranean, beginning with the loss of the carrier *Ark Royal*, torpedoed on 14th November off Gibraltar after launching fighter aircraft for Malta, and continuing with the loss of the battleship *Barham* on 25th November when she blew up after being torpedoed by *U.331*, and the sinking of the cruiser *Galatea* after being torpedoed by *U.557* off Alexandria on the night of 14th December.

However, the Malta-based sea and air forces so successfully interfered with supplies destined for the Afrika Corps in Libya, sinking among others two Italian cruisers carrying petrol, that Hitler was obliged to order the return of German bomber squadrons to the Sicilian airfields. Then disaster overtook the Malta surface striking force when, on 19th December, the cruisers *Neptune, Aurora,* and *Penelope*, and the destroyer *Kandahar* were mined, the *Neptune* subsequently sinking with heavy loss of life. But even this was not the end of the misfortunes to be

almost three months. In all 72 tanks, 92 guns, and 34,000 tons of stores were transported to and from the town for the loss of 25 naval ships sunk and nine seriously damaged, as well as five merchant ships sunk and four damaged, and two hospital ships.

In September the need arose to send further supplies to Malta, and nine fast supply ships with a powerful escort which included three battleships, a carrier, five cruisers, and 18 destroyers were entrusted with the task. They left Gibraltar on 24th September and in spite of strong air opposition, as a result of which Somerville's flagship the *Nelson* was damaged by a torpedo and one transport, similarly crippled, had to be sunk, the remainder reached Malta safely.

With the transfer of the Luftwaffe from the Sicilian airfields to the Eastern front, Malta enjoyed a respite from bombing which enabled surface forces to be based there once more. On 8th November, two cruisers operating from Valletta intercepted an Italian convoy of seven merchant ships escorted by six destroyers and sank all the former and one of the latter. Another of the destroyers was sunk by a

HMS *Barham*, a 'Queen Elizabeth' class battleship, was torpedoed in November 1941 by *U.331* while the Mediterranean fleet was on an operation in search of a convoy of tankers carrying fuel to the enemy forces in North Africa. Her magazine blew up four minutes after the torpedo hit, and she sank with a heavy loss of life.

suffered by the British fleet, for on 24th December Italian frogmen penetrated the defences of Alexandria and attached charges with delay action fuzes to the hulls of the battleships *Queen Elizabeth* and *Valiant*, both of which were severely damaged as a result. These events unfortunately restricted the ability of the Navy to assist the Army in Libya to exploit their success when, for a brief while, the German and Italian forces there had to withdraw because of shortage of supplies, leaving Cyrenaica once again in British hands.

The return of the German aircraft to Sicily ended the lull in the heavy and sustained bombing attacks on Malta. Paradoxically, because of the improved position on land, it was now possible to restart convoys from Alexandria to restock the island, and to give them fighter cover throughout the voyage. But by the end of January 1942 the enemy had regained possession of the Cyrenaican airfields and had advanced to within 60 miles of Alexandria. Nevertheless on 20th March a further attempt was made to get a convoy of three ships through to Malta. The covering force of four small cruisers and ten destroyers encountered a superior enemy force, which included a battleship, in the Gulf of Sirte. By

the use of smokescreens, through which continuous attacks were made on the enemy, his ships were successfully driven off; a brilliant little action under the direction of Rear-Admiral Vian. Nevertheless, heavy air attacks damaged all three ships of the convoy, of which two were sunk and the third was obliged to turn back.

The acute shortage of British carriers to fly much-needed replacements of fighter aircraft into Malta was overcome by the loan of the U.S. carrier *Wasp*. Since 20th March the island had been under exceptionally heavy attack as part of a German plan to neutralise it and halt the attacks being made by submarines and aircraft operating against supply ships sailing to Libya. In this the enemy was eventually successful, for by 10th May the submarines had been forced to leave. But on the previous day 60 more fighters were flown in from the *Wasp* on her second operation, and this reinforcement effected a dramatic change in the air situation; from then on the enemy was made to pay more and more heavily for his bombing raids on the island. In June attempts were made to resupply Malta both from the East and the West, but only two ships out of the seven loaded with supplies for the island arrived, and the cost in

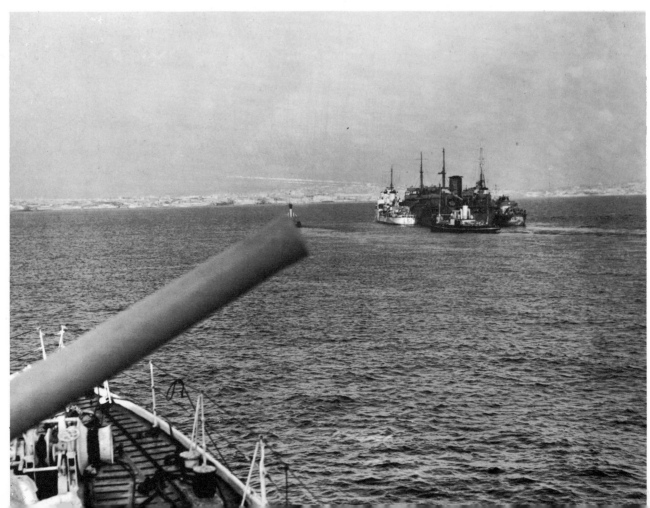

Top: The Battle of Sirte, fought in March 1942, was a brilliant action in defence of a convoy from Alexandria to Malta. Opposed by main units of the Italian fleet, an escorting force of cruisers and destroyers fought off the opposition successfully. In this photograph HMS *Kipling*, one of the escorting destroyers, is closing the enemy to attack with torpedoes

Left: The *Ark Royal* was torpedoed on 13 November 1941 by *U.81* as she was returning to Gibraltar from the second of two sorties towards Malta to fly off RAF Spitfires for the defence of that island. She sank 14 hours after being torpedoed, and within 25 miles of safety at Gibraltar

Opposite: A triumph of endurance; the tanker *Ohio*, twice hit and damaged by German aircraft, reaches the Grand Harbour at Malta. Supported by two destroyers secured alongside, she makes for the harbour entrance. The fuel she carried was vital for the defence of Malta, and had she not got through, the island could not have been held

warships and aircraft lost and damaged was heavy.

Thanks to the improvement in Malta's defensive capability British submarines were able to return, the first one entering harbour on 20th July. As a result, the offensive on the enemy's Libyan convoys was resumed, seven ships being sunk in August. But shortages of food and fuel in the island were growing desperate, and it was obvious that if Malta was not to be starved into surrender, one more desperate effort must be made to fight supplies through. On 10th August a convoy of 14 ships left Gibraltar with a very powerful fleet escort. In spite of the strength of the defence, only five of the 14 ships reached Malta, while the carrier *Eagle*, together with the cruisers *Manchester* and *Cairo* were torpedoed and sunk while fighting them through. But the five ships which reached Malta carried in them just sufficient supplies to stave off disaster. For the time being the island could carry on.

With the British offensive in Libya which began on 23rd October, and the allied landings in Morocco and Algeria on 8th November, the final phase in the struggle to eliminate enemy opposition in North Africa was begun. However, it was not until 13th May 1943 that the remnants of the German and Italian armies were penned in the Cape Bon peninsula and surrendered. In November the improved position on land enabled four merchant ships to be

Another photograph taken during the Battle of Sirte. The convoy was screened from enemy view by extensive smoke screens, through which the British escort emerged at intervals to drive off the Italian battleship, cruisers, and destroyers barring the convoy's path. Here British destroyers are seen coming through the smoke screen on one of their attacks

One of the convoys to Malta in 1942 under heavy air attack. The passage of these vital supply convoys, always hotly disputed by enemy surface and air forces, developed into major fleet actions, and were fought through to their destination with all the bitterness and destruction of modern warfare

escorted successfully to Malta from Alexandria, and on 17th May the first through allied convoy since the Mediterranean was closed in 1941 sailed eastwards from Gibraltar.

In retaliation for the allied landings in North Africa, the Germans invaded unoccupied France and seized the port of Toulon. Admiral Laborde in command of French naval forces there ordered them to be scuttled, but the enemy secured a number of airfields of which he made much use in attacks on allied shipping.

After a pause of two months to enable the necessary preparations to be made, British and American forces landed in Sicily on 10th July, from which island the enemy forces were evicted by 17th August. On 3rd September the British Eighth Army crossed over to the mainland of Italy and the Italian government capitulated. But the Germans, anticipating this event, had made extensive preparations to resist any advance on Naples and Rome, forcing upon the allied armies a long-drawn-out campaign up the whole length of Italy. The naval base of Taranto, in the 'heel' of Italy, was captured almost intact and was soon in full working order. Naples finally fell on 1st October and in spite of extensive demolition of the port facilities by the retreating German forces, an Anglo-American salvage team tackled the job of clearance with such success that by 18th October over 5,000 tons of cargo could be discharged there daily.

The terms of the Italian armistice provided for the transfer of the Italian fleet to allied control, and this was effected between 9th and 10th September when four battleships, eight cruisers, and a number of destroyers anchored under the guns of Malta. A fifth battleship joined them four days later, and one was sunk by German aircraft on passage to the rendezvous. As a result of Italy's capitulation, 101 merchant ships aggregating 183,591 tons came under allied control.

Early in 1944 the Germans began a series of heavy air attacks on allied convoys moving through the Mediterranean, using aircraft which they had assembled in the south of France armed with torpedoes and radio-controlled glider bombs. These were supported by U-boats, of which an increasingly heavy toll was taken, but until ships equipped for fighter direction became available, the air attacks were not successfully countered. After the allied

landing in the south of France, which took place on 15th August, and the capture of the airfields from which the enemy was operating, these attacks came to an end. The last U-boat was sunk on 18th September, and soon afterwards convoy in the Mediterranean ceased.

Allied disruption of roads and railways in Italy obliged the enemy to turn more and more to sea transport to keep his armies supplied and this, together with support of the German armies in the Balkans, laid the scene for allied naval and air operations in the Adriatic, which began in October 1943 and continued to the end of the war. In addition to attacks on enemy shipping, considerable support was given to Yugoslav partisans led by General Tito in their struggle to oust the invader from their country.

The war ended in the Mediterranean at 2.00 p.m. on 2nd May 1945 when German forces in Italy surrendered unconditionally.

Two surrendered Italian battleships, the *Italia* and *Vittoria Veneto*, at anchor in Malta. The arrival of these, and other units of the Italian fleet, was the occasion of Admiral Cunningham's famous signal to the Admiralty: 'Be pleased to inform Their Lordships that the Italian Battle Fleet now lies at anchor under the guns of the fortress of Malta'

Operation 'Torch' was the code-name for the landings in North Africa in November 1942. This photograph shows one of the troopships protected by a smoke screen during the landing at Oran

The use of Antwerp as a port to supply the allied armies advancing into Germany called for the preliminary capture of the Island of Walcheren, guarding the entrance to the River Schelde. The assault on Walcheren was one of the hardest fought actions of the war, carried out by seamen and marines of the Royal Navy. This landing craft was hit within 50 yards of the shore and sank almost at once. Her crew and the Royal Marines on board are abandoning ship

CHAPTER 24

The Second World War – Amphibious Operations –
Invasion of North Africa – Sicily, Salerno, and Anzio – The
Assault on the Normandy Coast

BRIAN SCHOFIELD

In spite of the collapse of France in June 1940 and the consequent withdrawal of British forces from the continent of Europe, by virtue of their dominant position at sea Britain (and later the United States) were able to transport their armies to areas where they could land and engage the enemy at points most favourable to the development of their strategy.

Practical study of how best to exploit this ability revealed the need for special types of landing craft in which men and equipment could be ferried ashore, but an assessment of the number required was so great that had it not been for the entry of the United States into the war, they could not have been provided from British sources alone. Even so, the crippling of the United States fleet at Pearl Harbour and the need to rebuild her naval strength as quickly as possible at first prevented high priority being given to their construction, and it was only after intervention by President Roosevelt that construction of landing craft was made second only to that of aircraft carriers.

Landing vessels are of two main types, (a) ocean-going landing ships and, (b) landing craft which have to be transported to the scene of operations by larger ships. From these a number of specialised types were developed, such as landing ships – Dock, Gantry, Infantry, Personnel, and Tank; landing craft – Assault (known in the U.S. forces as Vehicle and Personnel), Flak A/A, Gun, Infantry, Mechanised, Obstacle Clearance, Personnel, Recovery, Support, Tank, and Rocket.

Almost as soon as the last British soldier was back in England after the evacuation from Dunkirk in June 1940, a Combined Operations Headquarters was set up in London to study the problems of amphibious operations and assault from the sea. A number of raids of increasing audacity and weight were mounted against enemy-held territory in Europe. These culminated in the attack on St Nazaire, the assault on Dieppe, and the capture of the island of Madagascar, all of which took place in 1942. From the two last-named valuable lessons were learned which were used in the planning of subsequent amphibious operations. Chief amongst these was the need for heavy sea and air bombardment of the area to be assaulted to soften up the defences immediately prior to landing, the breaching of anti-tank obstacles before tanks are landed, and that the naval, military and air staffs conducting the operation should be accommodated in one ship, known as a Headquarters ship.

The pattern of an amphibious assault, as evolved from experience in World War II, was basically as follows:

The assault troops and their equipment were embarked in landing ships (Infantry) (L.S.I.) or combat loaders, while the support and follow up troops, heavy equipment and stores were carried in troop transports and specially selected merchant ships. The Headquarters ship and the warships needed to give close support were included in the assault convoy. Two or three simultaneous assaults at divisional strength would be made on either side of the main objective and each beach would be marked by a submarine shining a shaded light to seaward during the approach. When in position about seven miles offshore the L.S.I's would stop or anchor, and lower their assault landing craft

(L.C.A.) manned by assault troops. These would form up into flotillas and proceed inshore so as to touch down exactly at the zero (H) hour selected. As soon as the troops were ashore the L.C.A's would return for more men and equipment while other landing craft were bringing in guns, tanks, vehicles and stores. Of paramount importance was the provision of fire support for the first wave of assault troops. At first this was provided by cruisers and destroyers, but later, when the landing craft (Rocket) and (Gun) had been devised, the enemy defences were subjected to intensive rocket bombardment a few minutes before touchdown.

The above, designated a 'ship-to-shore' landing, was the system used when the assault was preceded by an ocean passage, but there were occasions when troops could be embarked in the craft from which they would land, and this was known as a 'shore-to-shore' landing.

An important feature of all amphibious operations is detailed knowledge of the beaches on which the landing is to be made. It is rare for existing charts and maps of the area to be sufficiently up-to-date, and aerial photographs cannot be relied upon to reveal details such as the gradient and composition of the beach or the existence of false beaches a short distance off the shore which might prevent the landing craft from reaching the beach itself. This requirement was met by the formation of Combined Operation Pilotage Parties (COPPs) which were landed from submarines at night and gathered the required information. It was highly dangerous work, but it paid handsome dividends.

Operation 'TORCH'

In order to reopen the Mediterranean and thereby release an additional million tons of much needed shipping, and to relieve the island of Malta, the support of which was proving increasingly costly, it

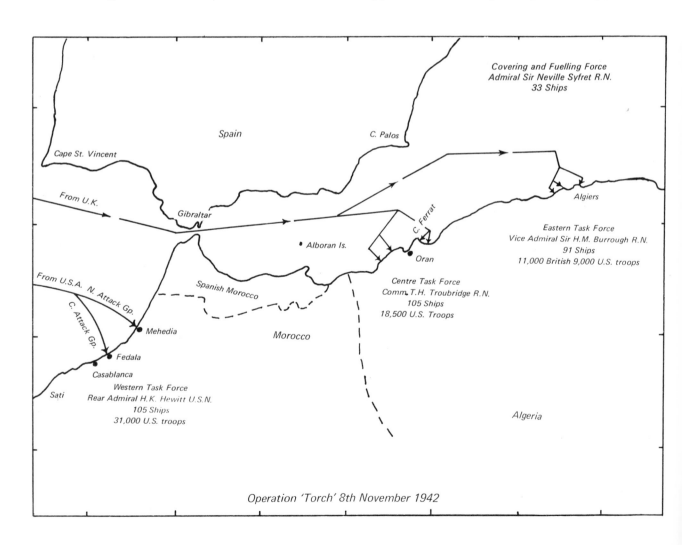

Operation 'Torch' 8th November 1942

was necessary to eliminate the enemy forces in North Africa. In conjunction with an offensive by the British Eighth Army in Libya, a plan was drawn up which provided for landings at Casablanca on the Moroccan coast by 31,000 U.S. troops, and at Oran and Algiers on the Algerian coast east of Gibraltar by 18,500 U.S. troops and a combined force of 11,000 British and 9,000 U.S. troops respectively. In all, 334 ships (including six battleships, five carriers, 15 cruisers, and 81 destroyers) were allocated to the operation. In addition a covering force of three battleships, three carriers, three cruisers, and 17 destroyers was ordered to cruise north of the Algerian landings to prevent possible interference by the Italian fleet.

The assault took place on 8th November 1942, the naval, military, and air commanders being Admiral Sir Andrew Cunningham, General Dwight D. Eisenhower, U.S. Army, Air Marshal Sir William Welsh (Eastern Air Command), and Major-General J. H. Doolittle U.S. Air Force (Western Air Command).

The three widely spaced landings north and south of Casablanca met with considerable resistance from the French and the two to the north also were impeded by the Atlantic surf. Except at the southern landing, where resistance was quickly overcome, bitter fighting continued for three days and ended only on the receipt of a cease-fire order from the French Admiral Darlan, the head of the civil government in North Africa.

In spite of unforeseen difficulties at each of the three landings near Oran, the absence of serious resistance favoured success and all fighting ceased there on 9th November. The landings near Algiers were unopposed, which also was fortunate as many other things went wrong. By the evening of the assault day, Algiers harbour was in allied hands, but German and Italian aircraft soon appeared and inflicted heavy damage on allied shipping.

On the whole the operation was both completely successful and boldly conceived. Losses were much less than expected, amounting to three destroyers, two coastguard cutters, and 16 merchant ships. Fourteen enemy submarines whch tried to interfere with the landings were sunk.

Operation 'HUSKY'

The last remnants of the Axis force in North Africa surrendered to the allies on 13th May 1943,

and preparations began immediately for the next great amphibious operation, the invasion of Sicily, to which the code name of 'Husky' was given.

It was preceded on 11th June by the seizure of the island of Pantellaria, 120 miles W.N.W. from Malta, the airfield on which was needed for the operation. In view of the numerous airfields and the formidable garrison known to be in Sicily, the operation became, as Churchill described it, 'an undertaking of the first magnitude.'

No fewer than 2,590 British, United States, and allied warships, landing ships, and craft took part in it. Under the Supreme Allied Commander, General D. D. Eisenhower, the naval, military, and air Commanders were Admiral Sir Andrew Cunningham, General Sir Harold Alexander, and Air Chief Marshal Sir Arthur Tedder. The area selected for the assault lay in the south-east corner of the island and stretched from just south of Syracuse, round Cape Passero, to Licata. The landing was timed for 0245 on 10th July.

The possibility of reaction by the Italian fleet to an invasion of its homeland was met by the deployment of a powerful British covering force comprising four battleships, two carriers, four cruisers, and 17 destroyers which cruised in an area to the east of Sicily while the landings were in progress.

The weather worsened considerably during the afternoon preceding the landing and caused some interference with the timetable, particulary on the beaches to the north of Cape Passero. The assault force numbered some 181,000 British, Canadian, and U.S. troops, and included an airborne element whose task it was to speed up the capture of enemy airfields. Resistance to the landings was surprisingly light and all the immediate objectives were captured as planned. Rocket-equipped landing craft were used for the first time with excellent effect. Another very successful innovation was the American designed DUKW, an amphibious vehicle of great versatility, into which men and stores could be loaded afloat and driven ashore to where they were needed without disembarking.

Although there were many lessons to be learned from 'Husky', it was a most successful operation. At the time there were some 300,000 enemy troops and 1,000 aircraft in Sicily, and the enemy fought a skilfully conducted retreat lasting 38 days. Three German divisions with their equipment managed to

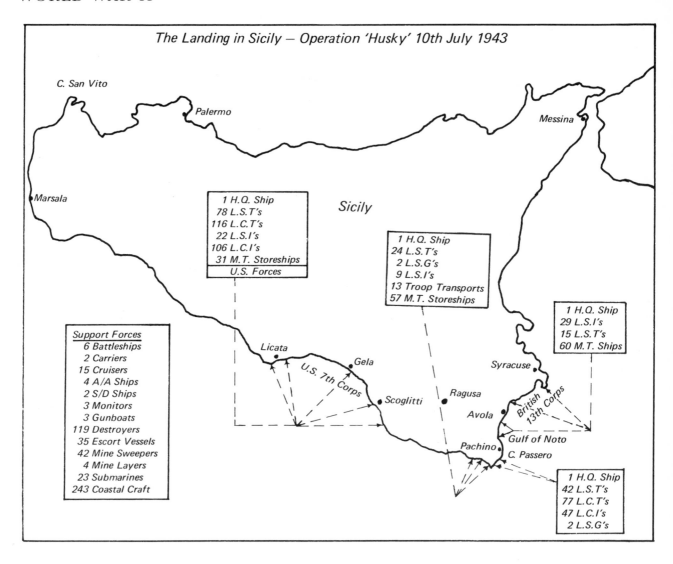

The Landing in Sicily – Operation 'Husky' 10th July 1943

Sicily

C. San Vito

Palermo

Messina

Marsala

1 H.Q. Ship
78 L.S.T's
116 L.C.T's
22 L.S.I's
106 L.C.I's
31 M.T. Storeships
U.S. Forces

1 H.Q. Ship
24 L.S.T's
2 L.S.G's
9 L.S.I's
13 Troop Transports
57 M.T. Storeships

1 H.Q. Ship
29 L.S.I's
15 L.S.T's
60 M.T. Ships

Support Forces
6 Battleships
2 Carriers
15 Cruisers
4 A/A Ships
2 S/D Ships
3 Monitors
3 Gunboats
119 Destroyers
35 Escort Vessels
42 Mine Sweepers
4 Mine Layers
23 Submarines
243 Coastal Craft

Licata

Gela

Syracuse

U.S. 7th Corps

Scoglitti

Ragusa

Avola

British 13th Corps

Pachino

Gulf of Noto

C. Passero

1 H.Q. Ship
42 L.S.T's
77 L.C.T's
47 L.C.I's
2 L.S.G's

get away across the Straits of Messina to the mainland, together with some 7,000 Italian troops, and in view of the great allied superiority on the sea and in the air, there is support for those who argue that with a better plan of attack the escape of these troops could have been prevented.

Hard on the heels of the retreating enemy, and preceded by a massive naval and air bombardment, the allied armies crossed to the mainland of Italy during the early hours of 3rd September. They encountered only token resistance. But faced with the long fight up the whole length of Italy, a country well endowed with formidable river and mountain defence lines, it was obvious that only further amphibious operations could speed the northward advance. The first was to be a landing on the west coast south of Naples, in the Bay of Salerno.

Operation 'AVALANCHE'

The operation, known as 'Avalanche', took place on the night of the 8th/9th September, the amphibious force commander being Vice-Admiral H. K. Hewitt, U.S.N. It involved some 700 warships, merchantmen, and landing craft sailing from five separate ports on six different dates. German aircraft attacked the convoys on passage but caused minimal damage. In the vain hope of achieving surprise, it was decided to dispense with parachute troops and also with a preliminary bombardment of the landing area, in which unfortunately German troops had already replaced the Italians who had thrown down their arms. The plan was to land on two sets of beaches eight miles apart, the British

Xth Corps assaulting the northern group of beaches and the U.S. XIth Corps the southern. The combined forces, designated the Fifth Army, were under the command of General Mark Clark, U.S. Army. A British naval force of four battleships and two carriers escorted by destroyers covered the landings, while close support was provided by three British and four U.S. cruisers. A force of five British escort carriers provided fighter cover over the assault area, while the ships themselves received protection from aircraft of the carriers with the covering force. Aircraft from the U.S. Strategic and British Tactical Air Forces, operating from Sicily, also participated in the defence of the assault area.

The landings began at 0400 on 9th September and encountered varied opposition, which however soon built up as the enemy quickly reacted to the threat. His control of roads and railways, and the air support he was still able to command, enabled him to bring up reinforcements of men and armour and

exploit the gap which existed between the northern and southern groups, so that by the 13th a crisis had developed which lasted for two days. It was only resolved by the continuous gun support provided by the British and American warships and the arrival of reinforcements. The enemy's ultimate withdrawal was hastened by 15-inch gun support from two British battleships which had been hurried to the scene.

When at last General Clark's Fifth Army succeeded in breaking out of the Salerno beachhead and joining forces with General Montgomery's Eighth Army fighting its way north from the toe of Italy, the capture of Naples followed on 1st October. The next major objective was Rome, and to outflank the strong German defences south of that city, known as the 'Gustav' line, it was decided to carry out a landing on the coast at the small port of Anzio, 37 miles south of Rome and 70 miles behind the enemy's line.

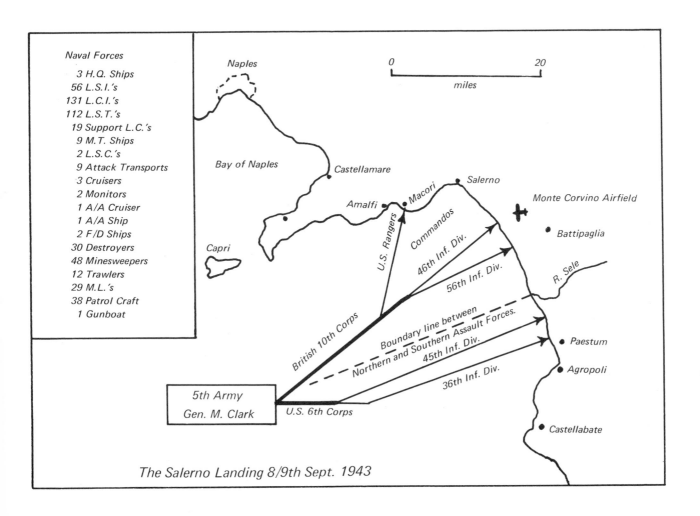

Naval Forces

3 H.Q. Ships
56 L.S.I.'s
131 L.C.I.'s
112 L.S.T.'s
19 Support L.C.'s
9 M.T. Ships
2 L.S.C.'s
9 Attack Transports
3 Cruisers
2 Monitors
1 A/A Cruiser
1 A/A Ship
2 F/D Ships
30 Destroyers
48 Minesweepers
12 Trawlers
29 M.L.'s
38 Patrol Craft
1 Gunboat

The Salerno Landing 8/9th Sept. 1943

Operation 'SHINGLE'

The code name given to the operation was 'Shingle', and the plan envisaged a landing by the 1st British Infantry Division supported by Commandos and the 46th Royal Tank Regiment, to the north of the port and one by the 3rd U.S. Infantry Division supported by the 504th U.S. Parachute Battalion to the south of it. The assault force for the northern landing comprised 119 ships including two cruisers and 11 destroyers, that for the southern one 230 ships, including two cruisers and 13 destroyers. The landing craft required were only made available by delaying their departure for the United Kingdom where they were needed in preparation for the invasion of France, and also by recalling others which had been sent out to India for operations against Japanese held territory.

The assault took place at 0200 on 22nd January in good weather and again without preliminary bombardment other than salvoes of rockets fired from specially equipped landing craft immediately prior to touchdown. Complete surprise was achieved, although some trouble was occasioned by the existence of false beaches in front of the landing areas. The port of Anzio was captured intact by U.S. Rangers, and this proved an invaluable asset. Within 24 hours of the arrival of the first wave of troops, 36,034 men and 3,069 vehicles had been landed, together with a large quantity of stores, and all the preliminary objectives had been secured.

German beach obstacles along the Normandy coast erected to hinder the expected allied assault. Exposed at low water, they were demolished by Commando troops with explosive charges

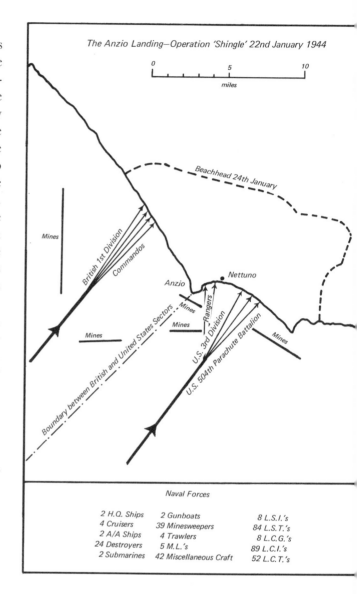

The Anzio Landing—Operation 'Shingle' 22nd January 1944

0   5   10
miles

Beachhead 24th January

Mines

British 1st Division

Commandos

Anzio

Nettuno

Mines

Rangers

Mines

Mines

Mines

U.S. 3rd Division

U.S. 504th Parachute Battalion

Boundary between British and United States Sectors

Naval Forces

2 H.Q. Ships	2 Gunboats	8 L.S.I.'s
4 Cruisers	39 Minesweepers	84 L.S.T.'s
2 A/A Ships	4 Trawlers	8 L.C.G.'s
24 Destroyers	5 M.L.'s	89 L.C.I.'s
2 Submarines	42 Miscellaneous Craft	52 L.C.T.'s

Failure to exploit this favourable situation combined with a rapid German reaction was to lead to a long drawn out and at times critical battle. Reinforcements were poured in and, in spite of gales which at time put a stop to unloading across the beaches, by 29th January 68,886 men, 508 guns, 237 tanks, and 27,250 tons of stores had been landed. The enemy counter-attack began on 3rd Febuary and for two weeks some of the bloodiest fighting of the war ensued. Once again naval gun support proved of inestimable value and the Tactical Air Force was continuously in action supporting the troops. The

enemy made much use of controlled glider bombs and scored several successes with this new and deadly weapon, sinking two cruisers, an ammunition ship, and two landing craft.

The Germans made three all-out attempts to drive the allied forces back into the sea, but by 3rd March stalemate was reached. To the allied navies then fell the task of providing gun support when required and keeping the army supplied for a period of two and a half months, since it was not until 23rd May that the 5th Army succeeded in breaking out of the net which the Germans had closed around it.

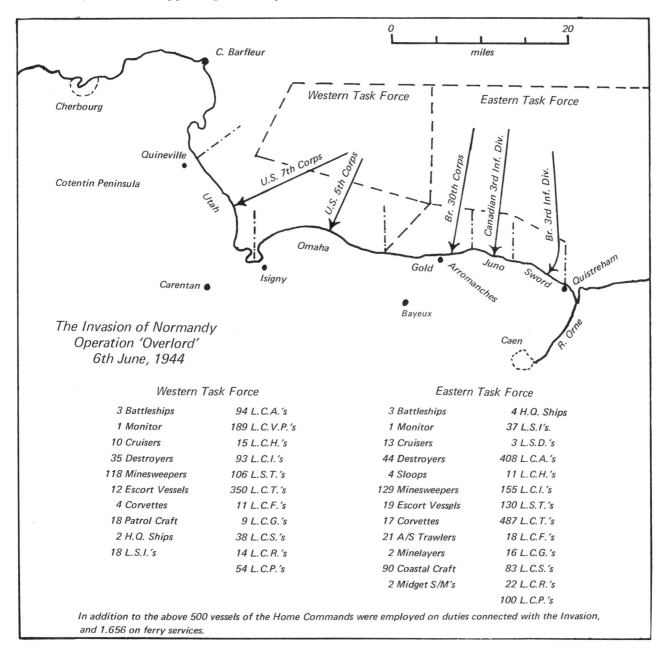

**The Invasion of Normandy
Operation 'Overlord'
6th June, 1944**

Western Task Force		Eastern Task Force	
3 Battleships	94 L.C.A.'s	3 Battleships	4 H.Q. Ships
1 Monitor	189 L.C.V.P.'s	1 Monitor	37 L.S.I.'s.
10 Cruisers	15 L.C.H.'s	13 Cruisers	3 L.S.D.'s
35 Destroyers	93 L.C.I.'s	44 Destroyers	408 L.C.A.'s
118 Minesweepers	106 L.S.T.'s	4 Sloops	11 L.C.H.'s
12 Escort Vessels	350 L.C.T.'s	129 Minesweepers	155 L.C.I.'s
4 Corvettes	11 L.C.F.'s	19 Escort Vessels	130 L.S.T.'s
18 Patrol Craft	9 L.C.G.'s	17 Corvettes	487 L.C.T.'s
2 H.Q. Ships	38 L.C.S.'s	21 A/S Trawlers	18 L.C.F.'s
18 L.S.I.'s	14 L.C.R.'s	2 Minelayers	16 L.C.G.'s
	54 L.C.P.'s	90 Coastal Craft	83 L.C.S.'s
		2 Midget S/M's	22 L.C.R.'s
			100 L.C.P.'s

In addition to the above 500 vessels of the Home Commands were employed on duties connected with the Invasion, and 1.656 on ferry services.

Operation 'OVERLORD'

On 6th June 1944, two days after the allied armies entered Rome, the greatest amphibious operation of the war was launched on the north coast of France. The code name given to it was 'Overlord', but the naval part was known as 'Neptune'. After careful consideration of all the factors involved it was decided that the landing should take place on the Normandy coast, east of Cherbourg. Although this necessitated a longer sea crossing and extra dead flying time for the supporting aircraft, the weaker coast defences and the proximity of a major port were advantages which influenced the selection. The Germans fully expected an invasion to take place but they were uncertain where the blow would fall, and although they had allocated 58 divisions to the defence of France, they also kept 12 in Norway and six in Denmark as a precaution.

The final form of the allied assault decided upon was for two airborne and two seaborne divisions of the U.S. First Army to land at the base of the Cotentin peninsula and strike west and north to seal it off and capture the port of Cherbourg. At the same time one airborne and three seaborne divisions of the British Second Army would land on the beaches between Port-en-Bessin and the mouth of the River Orne, and move east and south-east to protect the flanks of the U.S. First Army.

The sea transport of this force of between 40,000 and 50,000 men with their vehicles and equipment required some 4,000 landing ships and craft, but when a muster was made it was found that this figure could only be met if the date of the assault were postponed from May, as originally intended, to June, to permit the May quota of these vessels under construction to be included.

Until the port of Cherbourg had been captured and restored to use, the success of the operation clearly depended on the ability to land reinforcements and supplies across the beaches. Thus it was decided to construct two artificial harbours which could be towed over in prefabricated sections and sunk off the beaches, one at Arromanches and the other at St. Laurent. These were supplemented by 70 old war and merchant ships, filled with concrete, and also sunk to seaward of the Mulberries, as the harbours were called. Floating piers were devised to enable coasters to discharge direct into trucks at all states of the tide.

Landing craft on D-day going in to the Normandy beaches. Norman Wilkinson was present as
an official war artist at the assault on north-west Europe on 6 June 1944 and painted this picture
from sketches made on the spot

An important factor was the minesweeping organisation, since the enemy was known to have laid extensive defensive minefields off the assault area, and these had to be swept ahead of the assault convoys and the bombarding ships accompanying them. No fewer than 189 sweepers were so employed. The task of dealing with the enemy destroyers, torpedo-boats, U-boats, and patrol craft in the Channel ports and along the French Atlantic coast called for special dispositions of A/S vessels and constant air patrols.

The Supreme Allied Commander for the operation was General Dwight D. Eisenhower U.S. Army and the naval commander of the Expeditionary Force was Admiral Sir Bertram Ramsay. General Sir Bernard Montgomery was in command of the land forces. The assault forces were divided into two groups, the Eastern Force comprising 348 warships (including three battleships, 13 cruisers, and 44 destroyers) and 2,426 landing ships and craft, the Western Force 324 warships (including three battleships, 10 cruisers, and 35 destroyers) and 1,700 landing ships and craft, making a grand total of 5,298 vessels. The assembly and sailing of this vast armada called for a most meticulous and detailed organisation to ensure that every ship reached her appointed rendezvous exactly on time.

Every known form of deception was practised to keep the enemy guessing as to the time and place of the landings.

The Allied Air Forces were entrusted with the task of paving the way for the invasion by disrupting the enemy's land communications, disorganising his radar stations, and shooting his aircraft out of the sky.

An intensive air bombardment of the beach defences was ordered 45 minutes before the assault was timed to take place, and these were to be subjected to rocket bombardment up to the moment before landing. Although the Army would have preferred to land under cover of darkness, the need to ensure accuracy of navigation and for the bombarding ships to be able to identify their targets made a dawn assault necessary. Further to allow for the clearance of the formidable beach obstacles which the enemy had placed below high water mark, the assault had to be timed to take place between three and four hours before high water. Finally, with so

many ships converging on the area and to assist the parachute troops, a moonlight night was desirable. The satisfaction of all these conditions restricted the choice of date to three or four days in any month, and this led to the selection of 5th June as 'D' day. In the event bad weather caused a postponement of 24 hours, and this in turn affected the times of landing, which were different at each beach to suit the tidal conditions, and varied between 0630 at the western and 0745 at the eastern ones.

As daylight faded on 5th June, the minesweepers clearing a path through the minefields were visible from the French coast, but fortunately the enemy ignored their presence, and when at dawn the next day the assault took place, almost complete surprise was obtained. In spite of the rough sea and a wind which caused the tide to rise faster than scheduled, and thus upset the plans for dealing with the beach defences, the five assaults took place as planned, with negligible losses in ships. Sporadic attacks by enemy surface forces were repulsed, and of the 25 U-boats which attempted to interfere with the build-up, seven were sunk and three damaged. Mines of course took their toll, and there was considerable damage to landing craft from uncleared beach obstacles. At all beaches the guns of the supporting battleships, cruisers, and destroyers proved invaluable in neutralising batteries and the enemy seemed stunned by the sheer weight of the assault. Only at one of the western beaches was real trouble experienced, where the enemy was on the alert, the defences particularly strong, and the means for dealing with them inadequate. After heavy losses had been incurred by the assault troops the situation was saved by seven U.S. destroyers which rained a hail of 5-inch shells on the defenders at close range and kept them at bay until sufficient army guns had been landed.

The build-up went well, and by 11th June a beach-head 50 miles wide and 10 to 15 miles deep had been established. Meanwhile the construction of the artificial harbours, which began on 'D' day, proceeded smoothly, but as the size of the expeditionary force grew, so did the demand for food, stores, and ammunition. Then on 18th June a gale blew up and raged for four days, causing great loss and damage and seriously interrupting the landing of supplies. When it subsided, the harbour off St Laurent had been wrecked beyond repair.

The storm emphasised the need to capture Cherbourg as a matter of urgency. This was accomplished on 26th June, but so thorough were the German demolitions that it was three weeks before the first deep draught vessel was able to enter, and it took three months of hard and dangerous work by British and United States salvage teams to restore the port to its full capacity. In spite of these difficulties, supplies to the troops were maintained.

Operation 'DRAGOON'

At the insistence of the U.S. Chiefs of Staff, a landing in the south of France to capture the ports of Marseilles and Toulon was planned to take place as soon as possible after the Normandy landings, but it was not until after the fall of Cherbourg that the necessary landing craft could be spared. The plan involved an assault by three U.S. Divisions and a French Armoured Brigade. In all 880 vessels were involved of which 65 per cent were American, 33 per cent British, and the balance Canadian, French, and Greek. The landings took place at 0800 on 15th August and met with little opposition, being preceded by the dropping of parachute troops. Fighter aircraft from four U.S. and five British escort carriers provided tactical air support and everything went so well that by nightfall on 'D' day 66,390 troops and 8,240 vehicles had been landed. Both Toulon and Marseilles fell on 28th August.

Part of the vast organisation to supply allied forces after they had landed in north-western France was the construction of two artificial harbours on the Normandy coast. Prefabricated concrete caissons, known as Phoenix, were towed across the Channel and sunk in position to form a protective breakwater

269

CHAPTER 25

*The Second World War – The U-boat campaign in the
Atlantic and the Arctic – The Tragedy of PQ 17 –
Convoy ONS 5 – Defeat of the U-boats*

BRYAN RANFT

Even in the days of sail Britain had always been particularly vulnerable to attacks on her seaborne trade, but it was only in the war of 1914–18 that such operations brought her to the brink of surrender. The use by Germany of the submarine against merchant shipping was, by 1917, producing losses beyond the shipbuilding capacity of Britain and her allies to replace, and supplies of essential commodities came down to a few weeks' supply. Only a belated and reluctant recourse to convoy protection by the Admiralty, coupled with the extra resources made available by the entry of the United States into the war in April 1917, brought the defeat of the U-boats in the nick of time.

In the war of 1939–45 the submarine, now aided and supplemented by long-range maritime aircraft, again emerged as the most potent danger to shipping and the greatest threat to allied victory. Only once in the whole war did Mr Winston Churchill, Prime Minister of Britain, admit the possibility of defeat. This was in 1942 when the losses of merchant shipping were at their height and all the protective measures seemed to be failing. He was particularly concerned with the losses in the Atlantic between the United Kingdom and America. This was not only Britain's economic lifeline but also the one essential strategic line of communication by which America's military might be deployed against Hitler. Until the Battle of the Atlantic was won, Germany's armies in Western Europe could not be defeated. Such a defeat was going to be even more difficult, if not impossible, if Russia were beaten or came to terms with Hitler. To keep her in the war it was essential for Britain and the United

States to supply her with large quantities of military equipment, and these must go by sea to Russia's northern ports. It was thus not only the economic survival of Britain but the whole issue of allied victory or defeat which was at stake in the long drawn-out convoy battles of the Atlantic and the Northern Seas.

Hitler's naval commanders were well aware of the strategic importance of mounting a major attack on allied shipping, especially Karl Doenitz, who had been appointed in 1935 to revive and develop Germany's submarine arm. As a submarine captain in 1918, Doenitz had fallen a victim to convoy escorts and knew that since that period technological development had moved against the submarine. The development of sonar and the availability of long-range air reconnaissance and attack had deprived the U-boat of many of its advantages. But Doenitz believed that there was still one method of deployment which could overcome this. He thought that by collecting his submarines into packs and attacking on the surface by night he could exploit their high surface speed and low silhouette. Undetected, they would slip through the escort, sink the helpless merchantmen, and escape in the ensuing confusion. In the few years before the war Doenitz practised these tactics with his growing force, undetected by British Intelligence, and when they were put into use they very nearly achieved decisive success. That he did not succeed was due not only to the belated allied counter-measures but to fundamental weaknesses in his own position. He never had the number of submarines which he thought essential to achieve a decisive rate of

A frequent scene in the Atlantic battle. Norman Wilkinson's picture of a destroyer picking up
survivors from a sunken ship

sinking of merchant ships and, because of inter-Service rivalry, could never rely on the availability of adequate air reconnaissance to locate the convoys and direct his wolf packs to them.

That the German U-boats were ultimately defeated was not in any way due to any peacetime foresight by British and American naval planners but to the ability of the allies to react effectively after the danger had become clear and menacing. In the years before 1939 the Admiralty had thought that Germany would be deterred from waging unrestricted submarine warfare, by remembering that it was this sinking of merchant ships without warning which had brought America into the war in 1917. Moreover the Naval Staff believed that the capacity to locate and attack the submarine had so increased that, in the words of an official document in 1937, 'it should never again be able to present us with the problem it did in 1917.' In consequence, more attention was paid to the threat from surface raiders, which in the event were to account for only 237 allied merchantmen, as compared to the 2,828 which were to be sunk by submarines.

Thus in 1939 the Royal Navy was woefully unequipped to counter the main threat. What escorts there were lacked sea endurance and speed. The Fleet Air Arm had never been given an anti-submarine role. Coastal Command, the part of the Royal Air Force created to work with the Navy, had likewise no appropriate training or weapons systems. There were no standard screening instructions for convoy protection, and training for convoy operations had been neglected. Between the wars there had even been doubts whether the convoy system, which had proved the only way to defeat the U-boats in 1917, should be employed at all, but by 1939 these had been resolved and the protective measures were ready when war began. The sinking of the liner *Athenia* by a U-boat during the night of September 3rd was wrongly taken as showing that Hitler had decided on unrestricted submarine war from the outset, and convoys were immediately introduced.

A complete convoy system could not be organised until November, and in the interval many independently sailing merchantmen were sunk. Even more ominous was the dislike of Winston Churchill, now in control of the Admiralty, for what he considered the 'defensive' method of convoy, and his pressure on

Admiral Karl Doenitz organised the U-boat campaign throughout the war. He had served in U-boats during the First World War and the experience gained then stood him in good stead later, particularly in the introduction of the wolf pack tactics which were so successful up to 1943. This photograph shows him in the uniform of Grand Admiral

A depth-charge attack by an escorting destroyer. As the war against the U-boats developed, this method of dropping charges over the ship's stern was replaced by ahead-throwing mortars; first the Hedgehog, which launched 24 small explosive charges, and then the Squid, which threw three full sized depth-charges

An Atlantic convoy nearing a British port, the ships altering course together. The ability of merchant captains to keep their ships in station within the convoy formation was a prime factor in the ultimate defeat of the U-boats, for it was from stragglers that the U-boats claimed most of their victims

the Naval Staff for more 'offensive' methods of hunting out U-boats. However, in December, with the convoy system completed, not only did sinkings decrease but no fewer than nine of Doenitz's still small submarine force were sent to the bottom. The convoy escorts not only defended the merchantmen but, by being in the zone into which the U-boats had to enter to be within torpedo range, had a much greater chance of locating and destroying them than if they had been employed in searching the wide ocean. In the whole period from September 1939 to April 1940, no effective attacks were made on convoys in spite of the weakness of their escorts. Even more encouraging was the fact that 18 submarines were sunk while only 11 new boats were brought into commission.

This success was short-lived. Just as the U-boat war influenced what could happen on land, so it could be affected by the outcome of campaigns ashore. In April 1940 Germany began her *Blitzkrieg* in Europe. The fall of Norway and then of France gave Germany bases which greatly increased her U-boats' offensive potential in the Atlantic and northern seas, and exposed the mass of shipping in the English Channel to attack from the air and light surface forces. As more submarines with greater endurance emerged from German yards, they could operate further out into the Atlantic. In these distant waters Britain's shortage of escorts with adequate cruising range, and her complete lack of long-range aircraft trained and equipped to deal with submarines, would leave the convoys virtually unprotected. Destroyers, which could have filled the gap, were not now available in adequate numbers. Many had been lost or damaged in the Norwegian operations and in the evacuation of the British Army from France. Others were employed in the Mediterranean where Italy had joined Britain's enemies.

Losses of merchantmen began to rise alarmingly. In June 1940, 58 ships of 284,000 tons were sunk by U-boats in the Atlantic alone, other losses almost doubled this total. It was perhaps fortunate that Germany did not realise the British weakness, and would not give the priority which Admiral Doenitz demanded to the production of submarines and maritime aircraft. Even now there were only some 60 U-boats operational, with not more than eight actually attacking the Atlantic convoys at any one time. Doenitz had envisaged 100 as being decisive. Even

so, the successes in mid-Atlantic were alarming, especially when, in September, there were enough boats to begin regular pack attacks by night. As yet Britain had no counter to these, nor to the attacks by *Condor* aircraft operating from France. Between July and October 1940, which Doenitz called his 'First Happy Time', 217 ships of 1,100,000 tons were sunk by U-boats alone, for the loss of only six submarines. In the same period, six merchant surface raiders operating simultaneously in the South Atlantic, Pacific, and Indian Oceans, sank only 225,000 tons, all of them isolated ships, as they had been ordered not to risk attacking convoys.

Throughout 1941 the submarine, now operating in greater numbers, remained the greatest threat to the convoys in the Atlantic. More escort corvettes were available but it was soon apparent that they were too slow and lacking in endurance for the work. Not until frigates joined the convoy escorts in 1942 was the Navy to have really adequate anti-submarine forces. The lack of long-range aircraft to give cover far out at sea was an even greater weakness. An improvement came in April when Coastal Command was placed under the Admiralty's operational control and more effort was put into anti-submarine work. Even so, the U-boats by operating further west could still be outside the range of the aircraft available.

Before the end of the year the situation was eased by the entry of the U.S. Navy into the Battle of the

The crew of a sinking U-boat climbing up into the conning-tower and others diving from the forward casing, following an attack from an escorting aircraft

A German anti-aircraft gunner manning his weapon during an attack by a Fleet Air Arm Avenger aircraft. The photograph was taken from the attacking aircraft during the run-in

Atlantic, even though the country was not yet at war with Germany. A pattern was created whereby American and Canadian escorts convoyed the merchantmen to mid-Atlantic, where the British took over. But this advantage was counter-balanced by a revival of British political and naval doubts about convoys. There were those who argued that aircraft would be more effective if used offensively in searching for submarines rather than in providing close cover for convoys. Those responsible for the country's supplies protested against the delays inherent in putting shipping into convoy. Yielding to this latter pressure, the Admiralty lowered the speed limit, which exempted a ship from convoy, from 15 to 13 knots. The consequent increase in sinkings was so alarming that the old limit was restored in a few months. Even so, the monthly losses in the year touched the figure of 100 ships of some 500,000 tons.

The full entry of the United States into the war in December 1941 might well have been expected to reduce the allied shipping losses. In fact it produced an immediate increase. With his great understanding of the strategic flexibility of the submarine, Doenitz sent about a dozen to operate off America's eastern coast. There they produced his 'Second Happy Time'. They found shipping sailing in peacetime fashion, with no convoy organisation at all. The greater part of the U.S. Navy was in the Pacific trying to stem Japan's initial onslaught, and what escort vessels and aircraft there were in the Atlantic were employed in the hunter-killer role, which all Britain's experiences since 1939 had shown to be useless. The results were soon apparent. In the first six months of 1942 the United States lost a greater merchant tonnage than she had in the whole of the 1914–18 war. Many of the ships lost were the vitally important tankers which had already survived the perilous transatlantic voyage in convoy. In May, in the face of these figures and urgent British pressure, convoys were introduced and by November were completely established. The results were startling. Losses fell to less than one half of one per cent of sailings and soon the U-boats were withdrawn to less dangerous waters.

It is worth while examining the reason for these unnecessary losses as they emerge in the Official History of United States Naval Operations in the war. Many American naval authorities, like their

Sunderland aircraft of the Royal Australian Air Force attacking a surfaced U-boat in the Atlantic. The first of two Sunderlands damaged the U-boat with a near miss, so that she was unable to dive. The second then attacked, and the depth-charge seen exploding alongside the U-boat succeeded in sinking her

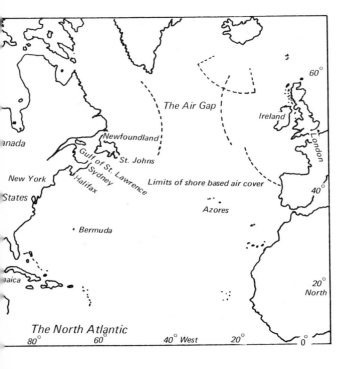

The North Atlantic

An incident during the passage to North Russia of Convoy PQ18 showing a tanker on fire after an attack by German aircraft. Convoys to North Russia normally included one or more small carriers in the escort since the route taken by these convoys was well within range of German Air Force stations in northern Norway

British counterparts, were opposed to what they regarded as the defensive nature of convoy operations and the undoubted delay in shipping voyages and turn-round which they caused. It took the bitter demonstration of these losses to convince them that these disadvantages were more than compensated for by the greater security which only convoy could provide. Never were the principles of the only effective way to counter submarine attacks on merchant shipping more clearly put, than in a letter from Admiral King, the United States Chief of Naval Operations, to General Marshall written in June 1942 when this harsh lesson was being learned.

But if all shipping can be brought under escort and air cover, our losses will be reduced to an acceptable figure. I might say in this connection, that escort is not only one way of handling the submarine menace, it is the only way that gives any promise of success. The so-called patrol and hunting operations have time and again proved futile.

So by mid-1942 both major allies had realised that only by complete adherence to a convoy system based on massive sea and air resources could the U-boat be defeated and the economic and strategic lifelines of the alliance be kept open. But the required resources were not yet available, and Germany was rapidly increasing her submarine building-rate. In the first six months of 1942 the average monthly losses were over 500,000 tons, far above the replacement rate then possible. The number of operational U-boats increased by 151 over the year and by the beginning of 1943 the monthly production rate rose to 45. Germany was winning the war of attrition at sea. Unless something could be done to decrease losses and obtain a killing rate of U-boats which would negate the increased rate of production, the whole war could be lost. When the dreadful year 1942 came to an end, U-boats had sunk a total of 1,160 ships of over 6,000,000 tons. Another 504 vessels had fallen to surface raiders, aircraft, and mines. It was clear that 1943 would be the decisive year. Would the allies be able to bring into the Battle of the Atlantic the ships, aircraft, and equipment necessary to redress the balance, or would the submarine, now appearing in improved types, retain the upper hand?

A simultaneous challenge was being presented in the other major area of the war against shipping, the convoy routes to northern Russia. The sailing of these convoys, which began in September 1941, presented problems even more difficult than those of the Atlantic routes. Their passage lay through some of the world's stormiest seas. Gales, sleet, hail and snow, freezing fog and icy water, were added to the threat of a strategically well-placed enemy. The thermal make-up of the sea made accurate sonar operation difficult. In the winter there were more than 100 days of complete darkness, which made station keeping and close manoeuvring a hideous nightmare. In the summer, when there was no darkness at all, attackers from the air and sea could keep up their attacks without remission. It is not therefore surprising that the loss rate of ships sailing in the Russian convoys was 7·2 per cent as compared with 0.7 per cent on other ocean convoys. Even so, ultimate victory came to the allies through the dogged determination of their merchant seamen and the courage and skill of their naval and air force protectors. No fewer than 40 convoys were sailed. Of the 811 ships in them 720 arrived safely with cargoes of over 4,000,000 tons, including 5,000 tanks and 7,000 aircraft. Ninety-two merchantmen and 18 warships were sunk, but against this the Germans lost one of their major units, the battle-cruiser *Scharnhorst*, three destroyers, 38 submarines, and many aircraft in operations against the convoys. The Russians have never admitted that these supplies were of major importance, but the clamour which they set up when the convoys were interrupted and their acknowledged desperate shortage of equipment in 1941 and 1942 infer that without them victory on the Eastern front would have been delayed.

The fate of one of these Russian convoys in July 1942 was particularly grim and its story brings out all the elements of this hazardous campaign. Convoy PQ17 sailed from the United Kingdom on 27th June with 36 merchant ships, British and American. Those responsible for its safety knew that it would have to face not only sustained attacks from U-boats and aircraft, operating from their Norwegian bases, but also from the heavy surface units which Hitler had moved to northern waters. To meet this complex of dangers a pattern of protection had been evolved which had got previous convoys through without disaster. In addition to its close escort of anti-submarine and anti-aircraft vessels, the convoy could rely on the support of a cruiser force of two British and two American ships. To counter any attack by heavy surface units, including the battle-ship *Tirpitz,* known to be in northern Norway, distant support was given by the Home Fleet with its force of battleships, including the U.S.S. *Washington,* and the carrier H.M.S. *Victorious,* under the command of Admiral Sir John Tovey. So this was going to be a major operation.

Up till 4th July the convoy made good progress. It had lost only three ships to air attack and its escort seemed on top of the developing submarine threat. But in the Admiralty in London it seemed clear to the First Sea Lord, Admiral of the Fleet Sir Dudley Pound, that a far greater threat was developing. His Intelligence showed that not only the mighty *Tirpitz* but also the pocket battleship *Scheer* and the heavy cruiser *Hipper,* were in Altenfiord, well placed to attack PQ17. In a concentrated attack, these three ships could overwhelm the allied cruisers as well as the close escort long before the Home Fleet could arrive on the scene. Admiral Pound decided that the

loss of so many valuable warships could not be accepted, and on the night of 4th July ordered the cruisers to withdraw to the west, and the convoy to scatter and make for Russia independently. These orders, which were based on inference and not on solid fact, were sent in such terms of urgency that the warships round the convoy expected to see the enemy loom over the horizon at any moment. In fact the *Tirpitz* and her consorts did not leave Altenfiord until more than 12 hours after the order to disperse was given, and soon abandoned their plan to attack under the mistaken impression that the *Victorious's* aircraft might fall on them at any moment. The scattered merchantmen of PQ17 were now at the mercy of the swarm of aircraft and submarines which the German naval command sent to pursue them. The small ships of the escort tried to regain control of the situation but could do no more than shepherd small groups of merchantmen out of danger. Between 5th and 10th July 11 ships were sunk by air attacks and 10 by submarine. Of the 36 which had sailed, only 13 ultimately arrived in Russia. During this terrible experience, and feeling that they had been deserted by their naval protectors, it is not surprising that some of the merchant crews panicked

Heavy weather in the Arctic. The escort carrier *Nairana* pitching in a steep sea during the passage of an Arctic convoy. The photograph was taken from HMS *Campania,* a second escort carrier with the convoy

WORLD WAR II

Part of the general campaign of the defence of trade lay in the neutralization of attacks by surface ships as much as by U-boats and aircraft. All these hazards existed in the case of the convoys run to North Russia. This photograph records an air attack on the battleship *Tirpitz* as she lay in a Norwegian fjord by aircraft from carriers of the Royal Navy. A heavy bomb can be seen exploding just forward of the bridge

HMS *Onslow* after the action in December 1942 in which a pocket battleship, an 8-inch gun cruiser, and six destroyers were driven off by the escort of one of the convoys to North Russia. The *Onslow*, commanded by Captain R. St V. Sherbrooke, who was awarded the Victoria Cross for this action, was severely damaged by the cruiser *Hipper*

and abandoned ships which, with more resolution, could have been got into safety.

The destruction of PQ17 was certainly a great disaster. At this distance of time it is possible to see where the responsibility lay. Admiral Pound made the fundamental mistake of not giving enough discretion to the men on the spot. If, instead of issuing the orders himself he had sent out all the information he had to the commanders of the close escort and the cruiser force, and given them discretion to act, there is little doubt that they would have stayed with their charges and prevented the major losses. But this is wisdom after the event and is a matter of assessing responsibility rather than awarding blame.

In the Atlantic the battle came to its final crescendo between January and March of 1943. The U-boats achieved their operational peak of 235 and Admiral Doenitz concentrated them on the convoys. In March, two-thirds of the submarines' victims were in convoy and once again naval opinion began to doubt if the system could stand up to this scale of attack. But, by the end of the month, as yet imperceptibly to those engaged in the battle, the tide was turning. For the first time all the resources and techniques needed for victory became available. Adequate air cover came now both from long-range shore-based aircraft and from aircraft operating from small escort carriers which accompanied major convoys. Airborne and shipborne radar ended the invisibility of the U-boat working on the surface by night. Escort ships had now adequate speed and endurance, and were moreover equipped with more effective anti-submarine weapon systems. In addition, they now existed in such numbers that escort groups could be given adequate training before they went into battle with a consequent rise in efficiency. Additional vessels were organised into support groups to give further protection to hard pressed convoys, and the whole convoy system was supported by a most highly developed intelligence system which enabled the U-boats' movements to be predicted with remarkable accuracy. The bare statistics show what happened as a result of the long battles round the convoys in the Atlantic and British home waters in the spring of 1943.

In April, 245,000 tons of merchant shipping were sunk for the loss of 15 U-boats. In May, 165,000

The enemy continued his attacks on the Arctic convoy route even when within sight of the Russian shore. The snow-covered coastline is visible in the background of this photograph which shows a British escort driving off an enemy aircraft with heavy A/A fire

tons of merchant shipping were sunk for the loss of 41 U-boats. Not only was the balance of attrition changing in favour of the allies but, again unknown to them, the determination of the U-boat commanders to press home attacks was beginning to falter. This was a result of their experiences in such actions as those surrounding the successful passage of Atlantic convoy ONS5 in April and May 1943.

The convoy of 40 ships, mainly old and slow, never achieved its designed speed of $7\frac{1}{2}$ knots. Shortage of shipping due to the heavy losses of the previous years made it essential to utilise every available vessel in order to bring from America the vast amount of stores and equipment needed for the invasion of Europe. When the convoy left British waters on 22nd April it was escorted by a destroyer, a frigate, and four sloops while another destroyer with three additional merchantmen was to join off Iceland.

The escort was under Commander Peter Gretton, one of the most experienced escort group commanders. His attention to the training and general standard of his ships had formed them into one of the most efficient groups in the Atlantic. They sailed by a northern route which was bound to lead the ageing merchantmen into bad weather, let alone into what the enemy might do. The ships were going out to America practically unladen and found station keeping difficult. Two collided on the fourth night out, one of which had to be sent into Iceland for repair. Another had to be detached as being too slow even for the sluggish ONS5.

On the 27th the wind and sea subsided and the human enemy took his first chance. The Germans had a line of U-boats stretched across the possible convoy routes, and the most northerly boat sighted the convoy on the 28th. A radio report from it to U-boat headquarters resulted in an order for all German submarines within reach to concentrate on the convoy. Wireless direction finding indicated that the convoy was now in danger and, duly warned by the Admiralty, at least they were prepared when the attack was made. Visual confirmation soon came; a U-boat was seen briefly travelling at high speed on the surface and was forced to submerge by an attack by one of the frigates. Flying boats of Coastal Command were sent from Iceland and found three U-boats pursuing the convoy on the surface. One was damaged and all were forced to submerge by the aircraft. Below the surface their slow speed put them out of the chase.

Even so, by nightfall a large pack had gathered around ONS5. At least five U-boats were detected on the surface trying to break through the screen. All were forced to submerge by determined attacks from the escorts without achieving their object. Two were damaged and forced to withdraw from the battle. The rest were kept at bay and on the morning of the 29th left the convoy in order to take up positions ahead of its route for attacks the following night. One did remain only slightly ahead and torpedoed one merchantman without damage to itself. But a loss of only one ship from such a strong attack was nothing for the escort to be ashamed of.

For the following five days the weather was again the enemy, with a strong south-westerly gale heaping up mountainous seas. Two more ships had to make for Iceland and the rest were widely scattered. The only comfort was that although the submarines were sitting relatively comfortably below the surface, they could not attack in such appalling conditions. Another result of the gale was that Commander Gretton's own ship was unable to refuel at sea and had to make for Newfoundland on 3rd May, just as the convoy approached the heavy U-boat concentration now lying in wait for it. As a compensation, four destroyers from a support group joined the convoy but three of them had to leave the next day for lack of fuel, leaving only three destroyers and four corvettes with the main body of the convoy.

By now 30 U-boats were gathered round their prey, though one was soon sunk by a Canadian aircraft from Newfoundland. The main attack came on the night of 4th May and continued intermittently for two days. First a straggler was hit and then, overcoming the defence by weight of numbers, the submarines succeeded in breaking through the screen and got among the labouring merchantmen, sinking several of them. In exchange, two U-boats were destroyed and the rest had to break off the attack when fog came down to shield the battered convoy and its escort.

Equipped with excellent radar, the escorts now had the advantage over the blinded submarines. During the night of the 5th at least four attempts to break through the screen were repulsed and four more submarines sunk. At daylight on the next day the U-boats withdrew, refusing to attack any more. True, they had sunk 12 merchantmen, but their own losses were heavy. Six had been sunk by escorts and aircraft, two more had collided and sunk, and several were seriously damaged.

This was defeat, as Admiral Doenitz himself admitted. He had made a major effort to destroy this convoy. No fewer than 60 U-boats had been directed to attack it and the results achieved were highly disproportionate to their own losses. As May continued, further convoy battles went increasingly in favour of the escorts. No fewer than 41 submarines were sunk during the month, and on the 24th Doenitz admitted defeat in the Atlantic by withdrawing his U-boats from attacks on the convoys.

This was not to say that the German submarine arm was completely defeated. It remained defiant to the end of the war, operating in distant oceans as well as the inshore waters of the British Isles. New and faster vessels were produced. The use of the *schnorkel* device enabled submarines to recharge their batteries without coming to the surface and thus much reduced their vulnerability to location and attack from the air. But such were the strength and skill of the allied anti-submarine effort that never after May 1943 was it possible for the U-boat to be a decisive element in the war. The battles of the Atlantic and the Northern Seas had been won, once and for all.

Survivors from a damaged U-boat swimming over to be picked up. The U-boat was attacked and mortally damaged by the corvette *Starwort*, but came to the surface to abandon ship before sinking

Captain F. J. Walker, of HMS *Starling*, became the greatest individual killer of U-boats in the Royal Navy. He is shown here on the bridge of the *Starling* taking a bearing on a U-boat blown to the surface after an attack by depth-charges

The defeat of the U-boats. *U.541*, flying the White Ensign above the Nazi naval ensign, coming in to surrender

The scene on the flight deck of the carrier *Formidable* after she had been hit by a Japanese Kamikaze suicide plane. It was in this form of attack that the British practice of giving carriers armoured flight decks proved its value, for in every case in which a carrier was thus hit, she was again operational within a matter of a few hours

CHAPTER 26

*The Second World War – Operations in the Indian Ocean –
Formation of the British Pacific Fleet – Attacks on the
Japanese Islands – Surrender of Japan*

DONALD MACINTYRE

The prospect of war with Japan while fully stretched in European waters had posed a daunting problem for the British Government and Admiralty ever since the fall of France had added the whole of the Mediterranean to the Royal Navy's sphere of responsibility.

As Japanese ambitions revealed themselves in the summer of 1941 with the occupation of Indo-China, whence the British possessions – Malaya, Singapore, and Borneo – in the South China Sea were directly threatened, plans were made for reinforcing the token force of three old light cruisers and five old destroyers in the Far East.

In the Admiralty's view all that could be done was to build up a defensive fleet, based on Ceylon, which would ultimately comprise seven capital ships – all of World War I vintage – one carrier, ten cruisers, and three flotillas of destroyers. The Prime Minister, Mr Churchill, thrustful as ever, urged the despatch of the modern fast battleship *Prince of Wales* to Singapore which, it was considered, might deter the Japanese from a southward aggression.

Churchill's view prevailed and on 25th October 1941 the *Prince of Wales*, wearing the flag of Acting-Admiral Sir Tom Phillips, left home waters and, after picking up the battlecruiser *Repulse* at Colombo, reached Singapore at the beginning of December.

By that time evidence of Japanese preparations for war, beginning with a southward thrust at Singapore, was coming in. The two capital ships, devoid of any air cover beyond what could be spared from the meagre force of obsolete R.A.F. planes based in Malaya, were likely to be confronted by a vastly superior Japanese fleet. Having failed to deter, they were now being exposed to grave risk to no good purpose.

The Admiralty, with Churchill's concurrence, suggested that Phillips should leave Singapore and go eastwards out of danger; Phillips himself contemplated a retreat to Darwin. But when, on 6th December, a large Japanese troop convoy was reported steering westwards across the Gulf of Siam, such an abandonment of the threatened territory and its garrison became unthinkable.

At dawn on 7th December the surprise attack on Pearl Harbour by the massed planes from the Japanese carrier force eliminated the battle squadrons of the U.S. Pacific Fleet. The Japanese were thereafter free to deploy the whole of their fleet in support of the southward drive. The American, Dutch, and British forces opposing them were left with the choice of retirement in the face of overwhelming odds or of accepting hopeless battle and inevitable destruction to uphold their Services' treasured traditions. They chose the latter.

The first to suffer were the *Prince of Wales* and *Repulse*, not at the hands of the imposing Japanese surface fleet but those of the shore-based, twin-engined naval torpedo-bombers whose potentiality had been greatly under-estimated by the Western world. Based on airfields near Saigon they had flown the 500 miles to Singapore to bomb the town and airfields at dawn on 8th December at the same time as Japanese troops were pouring ashore from their transports at Singora on the Malaya-Siam border.

That same afternoon the two British ships, with a screen of four destroyers, sailed from Singapore with the hope of surprising the Japanese troop convoy, relying upon the R.A.F's exiguous force of out-moded aircraft to give fighter cover. By the afternoon of the 9th Admiral Phillips knew that the latter could not be provided, and when Japanese recon-naissance aircraft were sighted that evening, destroy-ing any element of surprise, he turned back for Singapore. He had in fact been reported even earlier by a Japanese submarine and, on the airfields of Saigon, 52 planes of the 22nd Air Flotilla had been armed with torpedoes and 34 with armour-piercing bombs, taking off at dusk to seek out the British squadron.

The darkness of a moonless tropical night foiled them and they returned to base to wait for fresh information of the enemy's whereabouts. During the night this came in from another submarine, and at dawn the swarm of aircraft took off again. Around midnight, however, on receipt of a signal reporting a Japanese landing at Kuantan, 150 miles north of Singapore, Phillips had altered course for the coast. Once again, therefore, the questing air strike failed to find their objective on their outward journey. Almost at the limit of their range they turned back. At 0945 a reconnaissance plane sighted the British squadron; the message was passed to the leader of the striking force and at 1100 their attack began. The high-level bombers had little success, bearing out previous experience in the European theatre; but the massed torpedo attack could not be avoided by any amount of manoeuvring by the two big ships, manoeuvres that became more sluggish as damage from successive hits mounted.

The *Repulse*, a thin-skinned, lightly protected battlecruiser, was the first to go to the bottom, torn apart by five torpedoes. The *Prince of Wales* survived for another 47 minutes before succumbing to six torpedo hits. Both Admiral Phillips and Captain Leach, his flag captain, were amongst the 840 officers and men lost from the two ships. The destroyers of the screen rescued 2,081 survivors of the attack.

The loss of the only two allied capital ships in the South-West Pacific, and the demonstration of the degree of air superiority held by the Japanese, made it abundantly clear that little or nothing stood be-tween them and their ambition to overrun Malaya, Borneo, and the Dutch East Indies, vital source of oil and other essential raw materials. By the end of January the main ports of Borneo had been occu-pied and bases established in the Celebes. An amphibious expedition had reached out to the south-east to capture Rabaul in the Bismarck Archipelago. On 15th February Singapore surren-dered.

The surviving allied naval units had combined under the command of the Dutch Admiral Karel Doorman to form a striking force prepared to do un-equal battle with the Japanese forces covering the invasion convoys which now made for the main Dutch island of Java. Doorman's squadron, com-posed of the Dutch light cruisers *De Ruyter* (flag) and *Java* and H.M.A.S. *Perth*, the heavy cruisers H.M.S. *Exeter* and U.S.S. *Houston*, three British, two Dutch, and four American destroyers, was concentrated at Sourabaya on 26th February; a force quite imposing on paper but suffering under the handicap of total enemy air superiority besides a heterogeneous armament and an absence of any common signal system or tactical doctrine.

On the 27th Doorman led it to sea to engage the Japanese force covering a transport convoy – two heavy cruisers, two light cruisers, and 13 destroyers. In the Battle of the Java Sea which followed, both Dutch cruisers, one Dutch, and two British destroyers were sunk, and the *Exeter* was crippled by a shell in a boiler room. The remainder escaped to survive a few days only, being intercepted and sunk as they tried to break through the Sunda Strait to retreat to Australia.

The desperate, forlorn attempt by the allies to prevent the Japanese conquest of the East Indies – or even to exact a price for it – had failed. Hard pressed in European waters, the Royal Navy abandoned the Pacific where the U.S. Navy and Australian and New Zealand forces were first to halt further Japanese southward expansion at the Battle of the Coral Sea and in the land campaign to defend Port Moresby. Remnants of the British Eastern Fleet which it had been planned to form – four unmodernised *Royal Sovereign*-class battleships, the modernised *Warspite*, and the carriers *Indomit-able* and *Formidable* comprising its main strength – was assembled in Ceylon under the command of Admiral Sir James Somerville.

A hastily scraped together force of inadequately trained, obsolete ships, with even the value of the two modern carriers limited by the outmoded air-craft that the Navy had still to make do with, it was in no shape to confront the fast Japanese striking force centred on five fleet carriers and four battleships under Admiral Nagumo which arrived off Colombo on Easter Sunday, 4th April 1942. It must be held fortunate that Somerville had been forced to retreat to refuel at his base at Addu Atoll in the Maldive Islands, so leaving a clear field for Nagumo to strike at Colombo harbour. His aircraft found few ships there to attack, the majority having been dispersed; but the cruisers *Dorsetshire* and *Cornwall*, steering to join Somerville, were discovered; a massed attack by dive-bombers sent them both to the bottom in a few minutes.

Fortunately, also, when Somerville arrived in Nagumo's vicinity and, with the intention of launching his low-performance Albacore biplane torpedo aircraft to deliver a moonlight attack, sought to make contact, the Japanese had turned away to the eastward to repeat their attack on Trincomalee. The two fleets thus failed to meet and a battle which could only have been calamitous for the British was avoided.

After refuelling from attendant tankers far out in the Indian Ocean, Nagumo returned and on the 8th launched his strike aircraft on Trincomalee. The little carrier *Hermes,* an old destroyer, a sloop, and two tankers, which had been dispersed down the east coast of Ceylon, were located and suffered the same fate as Somerville's two cruisers.

The Japanese expedition, and a smaller one directed against shipping in the Bay of Bengal, had been planned only as a lightning raid. The two Japanese squadrons now left the Indian Ocean and returned home to prepare for the operation against Midway which was to mark the disastrous turning point in their fortunes.

Until then, however, fears of further westward thrusts by the Japanese persisted. The Vichy-French island of Madagascar and its fine harbour of Diego Suarez whence the convoy route through the Mozambique Channel, serving our North African armies, could be dominated, had for some time been considered likely Japanese objectives and a British expedition planned to occupy them.

A force commanded by Rear-Admiral E. N. Syfret, composed of the battleships *Malaya* and *Ramillies*, the carriers *Illustrious* and *Indomitable*, the cruisers *Devonshire* and *Hermione*, ten destroyers, and a dozen corvettes and minesweepers, assembled during April 1942 at Durban with five assault ships and nine large transports. The assault launched at dawn on 5th May achieved surprise and success. By the afternoon of the 7th a spirited defence had been overcome and Diego Suarez occupied. French resistance elsewhere in the island continued, however, and it was not until 5th November, after further amphibious operations, that the French Governor-General finally surrendered the whole island.

It was not until the beginning of 1944 that the march of events in European waters permitted a beginning of the re-establishment of the British Eastern Fleet, the first major units to arrive being the *Renown*, wearing the flag of Vice-Admiral A. J. Power who was to be Second-in-Command, the *Queen Elizabeth* and *Valiant*, and the aircraft carrier *Illustrious*. In March the Free French battleship *Richelieu*, and the U.S. carrier *Saratoga* also joined.

With this force Admiral Somerville sailed on 16th April 1944 to register the rebirth of a British Eastern Fleet, albeit with the aid of American and French ships, by delivering an air strike on the Japanese-held port of Sabang at the northern end of Sumatra. Complete surprise was achieved, a number of enemy aircraft being destroyed on the ground and in the air, and oil storage tanks destroyed without loss to the allied fleet. During May Somerville took the fleet to Exmouth Gulf on the Australian north coast whence he sortied to deliver, on the 17th, a success-

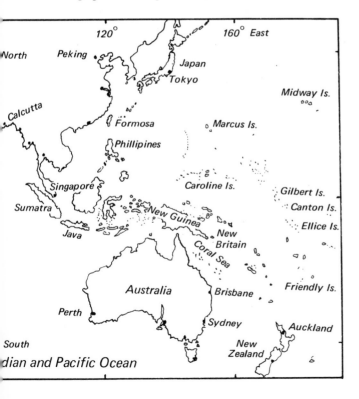

dian and Pacific Ocean

ful attack by 93 aircraft from his two carriers on the dockyard at Sourabaya and a nearby oil refinery.

The *Saratoga* now left Somerville's command to return to the Pacific; but from the U.K. there arrived the *Victorious* in her place, and in July a second air strike, followed by a bombardment by the capital ships and destroyers, was made on Sabang.

The addition of the *Victorious* was the first move in the planned build-up of a carrier force with which it was hoped the Royal Navy could enter the Pacific to fight the Japanese alongside its American allies. A very great deal had to be done before this was feasible, however. For the sort of war being fought in the Pacific, British carriers needed to be largely re-equipped with American naval aircraft in place of the unsatisfactory British types available. Above all, a logistic organisation had to be provided on the lavish scale necessary for support of a carrier fleet operating many thousands of miles from base and therefore required to replenish at short intervals at sea.

Admiral Ernest King, the American Chief of Naval Operations, together with the C-in-C Pacific, Admiral Chester Nimitz, doubted whether British resources could meet these requirements within a useful time. When Winston Churchill, as early as September 1943, offered to send a detachment to the Pacific, King was far from enthusiastic. Such British forces as could be spared from the European theatre, he felt, would be best employed against Japanese oil supplies in the East Indies or, if they came to the Pacific, in General MacArthur's South-West Pacific area where distances from bases were not so great.

Nevertheless the British Government, determined to play a full part in the Pacific War, had begun preparations to send a fleet during 1944. A naval mission was sent to the U.S.A. to study the logistic requirements. The development of Sydney, Australia, as a main naval base was begun, as was the assembly of the huge number of auxiliaries – repair ships, store carriers, ammunition ships, tankers, ferry aircraft carriers – which would make up the logistic tail or Fleet Train.

By the time the second Quebec Conference (Octagon) assembled in September 1944, Churchill felt able to offer the British main fleet grouped round the carriers *Indefatigable, Victorious, Illustrious,* and *Indomitable,* to be joined later by the *Formidable*

and *Implacable.* To command this fleet, to be known as the British Pacific Fleet, Admiral Sir Bruce Fraser was appointed in August 1944. As he would be too senior *vis-à-vis* his American equivalents to command at sea, his headquarters were to be set up at Sydney, leaving the sea-going command to Vice-Admiral H. B. Rawlings. Under him, in command of the carrier squadron, was Rear-Admiral Sir Philip Vian who joined the fleet at Colombo in December 1944.

Meanwhile Fraser had gone to Pearl Harbour to meet Admiral Nimitz, to make himself fully acquainted with what operations with the U.S. fleet would entail, and to overcome American resistance to such an arrangement. His signals to the Admiralty soon made it clear that, with the American advance towards the Japanese homeland since their great victory at the Gulf of Leyte, the fleet would be operating even farther ahead of its most advanced base and its periods at sea would be even longer than before. The logistic problem had increased proportionately.

Meanwhile the first task for the British Pacific Fleet was to work itself up, particularly the carriers, to operational standard. The carriers, mostly newly equipped with American aircraft and with many of their aviators lacking experience and training, were to be employed first in the Indian Ocean in attacks on the oil refineries of Sumatra, a valuable source of supply for the Japanese. The two largest refineries in the Far East, at Palembang in southern Sumatra, were the main targets; but to gain experience, a third – Pangkalan Brandan at the northern end of the island – was to be used in two rehearsals for the main attack.

In the first of these, launched from the *Indomitable* and *Illustrious* on 20th December, bad weather forced a diversion of the attack on to port installations at Belawan Deli and Kota Raja. The *Indefatigable* was added for the second attack two weeks later. Both were completely successful. Nevertheless the latter operation highlighted the shortcomings of the British type aircraft, particularly Seafires – an adaptation of the land-based Spitfire – with which the *Indefatigable* was still equipped. Their low endurance and lack of reliability and robustness compared to their American equivalents raised a number of problems and were to be a source of acute embarrassment when the time came to join the American fleet.

Admiral Sir Bruce Fraser was appointed Commander-in-Chief of the British Pacific fleet on its formation at the end of 1944. Although much of the naval strength of Britain was sent to the Pacific after its work in European waters had been successfully completed, the main burden of the campaign against Japan at sea was borne by the United States Navy

The final operation against Palembang was mounted on 24th January 1945 while the B.P.F. was on passage to its new base at Sydney. Escorted by the battleship *King George V*, three cruisers, and ten destroyers, the four carriers *Indomitable, Victorious, Indefatigable,* and *Illustrious* launched a force of 43 Avengers with a strong fighter escort to attack the refinery at Pladjoe while other fighters were directed to neutralise the airfields round Palembang.

Surprise was again achieved although the approach to the target included more than 150 miles of flight over enemy territory. The refinery was heavily damaged. But in spite of the efforts of the fighters, who destroyed 34 aircraft on the ground and damaged many more, fierce opposition was met during the retirement during which six Corsairs, two Avengers, and one Hellcat were lost. The remainder arrived safely aboard their carriers.

Five days later the assault was repeated against the Soengei Gerong refinery. The enemy were fully prepared on this occasion and losses were correspondingly heavy, 16 aircraft being shot down and another 25 lost from other causes. But the refinery was put out of action for several months, while the enemy also paid a heavy price in aircraft shot down, including some which tried to attack the fleet.

The B.P.F. now resumed its passage to Sydney where it arrived on 10th February. Its first task and a measure of the British desire to integrate fully with their allies, was to scrap the whole of its time-honoured and efficient system of signals and adopt that of the U.S. Navy. On the 28th the fleet sailed for its advanced base at Manus in the Admiralty Islands, which it was to share with the Americans.

Arguments as to how the B.P.F. was to be employed were still going on however, with Admiral King still insisting it should be allocated to the U.S. 7th Fleet in General Douglas MacArthur's command. This was a comparative backwater in the naval war; so it was with much rejoicing that the news was at last received on 18th March that King's objections had been overborne and that the B.P.F. was to form part of the United States 5th Fleet. After a stop to refuel at Ulithi in the Carolines, the fleet, now designated Task Force 57 (though it was in fact of a comparable size only to a Task Group of the American Task Force 58) sailed on 23rd March to take part in the operations already in progress for the capture of Okinawa. Ruffled British feathers were smoothed by a graceful signal of welcome from Admiral Nimitz.

Understandably, however, the 5th Fleet, a huge complex organisation practised in the massed carrier operations of which, with their limited resources, the British had no experience, was chary of opening its ranks immediately to the newcomers. When Task Force 57 began operations on 26th March, Admiral Spruance, the 5th Fleet commander, directed it to operate independently against airfields in the Sakishima Gunto, a group of islands between Formosa and Okinawa, while Task Force 58 operated against Okinawa itself.

Adopting a routine of two or three days of strike operations followed by a withdrawal of from one to three days for refuelling before returning again to the attack, the British Task Force on this first stint remained for 26 days in the combat area. Bomber planes from the carriers made repeated attacks, in an effort to keep the runways cratered – a dangerous and not very rewarding task as the coral strips had powerful gun defences and were easily repaired each night. Meanwhile fighters patrolling overhead fought day-long series of combats with their enemy equivalents.

Japanese offensive capability against ships had by this time been so reduced that nearly all their efforts were being concentrated on the suicide attacks, the 'Kamikaze'. The British Task Force had its first experience of one of these on 1st April when a suicide plane crashed on the *Indefatigable*, hitting her at the base of the superstructure. It was now that the armoured flight deck incorporated in British carriers justified the handicap of the much reduced hangar space which it entailed compared to American carriers. The *Indefatigable* was operational again within a few hours, whereas American carriers similarly hit were forced to return to a fully equipped dockyard for repairs.

A few days later the Japanese began launching massed Kamikaze attacks (Kikusui) against the American Task Force 58. At the cost of many hundreds of planes, they nevertheless managed to inflict such casualties on the fleet that Spruance for a time contemplated a retirement. As many of the attacks were known to be coming from airfields in northern Formosa, he now directed Task Force 57 against them. The raids in full strength launched from the British carriers on 12th and 13th April and again for three more days after a refuelling break, were highly successful and undoubtedly did much to ease the weight of attack on Task Force 58.

Task Force 57 sailed again on 1st May after a brief rest at Leyte to resume operations, the *Formidable* taking the place of the *Illustrious*. In addition to carrier strikes, the battleships and cruisers delivered a bombardment of airfields on Miyaka. While they were away, depriving the force of much of its anti-aircraft gunfire protection, a Kamikaze crashed on the flight deck of the *Formidable* causing many casualties and starting a fire amongst parked aircraft which destroyed 11 of them. Though the flight deck was holed and dented, the ship was once again operating aircraft within six hours. On the same day Vian's flagship, the *Indomitable*, was also hit but escaped serious damage, the Kamikaze's bomb not exploding until his aircraft had bounced over the side.

On 9th May the *Formidable* was again hit and

though once again her armoured flight deck saved her from serious structural damage, 18 of her aircraft went up in flames. In the same attack the *Victorious* was hit near her forward lift; while the fire which resulted was still being fought, yet another suicide plane attacked, but fortunately succeeded only in giving a glancing blow before plunging over the side.

This was the last Kamikaze attempt on the British carriers, though Kikusui continued to attack the American Task Force until 22nd June, some 1,900 Kamikaze in all which sank 27 ships and damaged another 164. By 25th May, however, with Okinawa captured, the B.P.F. was released to return to Sydney for rest and replenishment after 62 days at sea, broken by eight days at Leyte.

At the same time, under the American system of alternating command, Admiral Spruance was relieved by Admiral Halsey; the 5th Fleet then became the 3rd. On hauling down his flag, Spruance signalled his appreciation of the fine work done by T.F. 57 and in his report stated that the B.P.F. had gained sufficient experience to form part of the United States Fast Carrier Force.

Thus when the B.P.F., now T.F. 37, again reported for duty with the 3rd Fleet on 16th July, it was as an integral part of that fleet, one Task Group of it, that it was operated by Halsey. It was to pose some almost insuperable difficulties. During operations the B.P.F.'s full speed, restricted by that of the two battleships, was four knots less than that of the Americans. The low-endurance Seafire and Firefly aircraft had to be adapted to American sortie lengths by the use of long-range petrol tanks, with their many disadvantages.

By dint of strenuous efforts and much ingenuity these difficulties were overcome; but in the vital sphere of replenishment at sea the B.P.F.'s facilities lagged far behind those of the Americans, the Fleet Train having never been quite built up to the quantity or quality required.

And so, as the horrifying atomic climax to the war with Japan drew nearer, the British carrier planes joined those of the American Task Groups in the attacks delivered far and wide over the Japanese homeland and on the remnants of the Japanese fleet. The atomic bombs on Hiroshima and Nagasaki were exploded on 7th and 9th August. The end was now in sight and the majority of the B.P.F. parted

United States and British battleships and cruisers lying at anchor in Tokyo Bay after the surrender of Japan in August 1945. The document of national surrender was, appropriately, signed in the admiral's cabin of the United States fleet flagship

company on the 12th to return to Australia, leaving a token force consisting of the *King George V,* (flag) *Indefatigable, Gambia, Newfoundland,* and ten destroyers to continue operations to the end. This came at 0700 on the 14th with the news of the Japanese surrender.

Admiral Fraser, with his flag in the *Duke of York,* joined T. F. 37 at this time and, after a delay caused by the passage of a typhoon, the whole of the 3rd Fleet anchored on 27th August in Sagami Wan. During the next three days all except the Carrier Task Forces entered Tokyo Bay. The latter remained standing by at sea ready for any emergency during the large-scale airborne landings and landing parties from the U.S. 3rd Fleet and the B.P.F. to take over Yokosuka Naval Base; when it was clear that no Japanese treachery was to be feared, a general reduction in carrier strength allowed the withdrawal of the *Indefatigable* and her destroyers.

Prior to the decision to explode atomic bombs, plans had been prepared for a great amphibious assault on Kyushu. In readiness for this the B.P.F. had been rapidly growing. Besides the *Duke of York* the battleship *Anson* and the new light fleet carriers *Venerable, Colossus,* and *Vengeance* had arrived at Sydney to form a second British Task Group under Rear-Admiral Harcourt to operate with Task Force 37.

Now it was necessary to organise the available ships in Task Groups to proceed to Hong Kong to reoccupy the colony, and to Shanghai to represent British interests. For the former Harcourt took the *Indomitable* (flag), *Venerable, Anson,* the cruisers *Swiftsure, Euryalus,* and *Prince Robert* (R.C.N.) and seven destroyers, the submarine depot ship *Maidstone* and eight submarines, and six Australian minesweepers. This force entered Hong Kong harbour on 30th August after some suicide boats in Picnic Bay, Lamma Island, some of which were seen to get under way, had been dealt with by aircraft from the carriers. The formal surrender was made to Admiral Harcourt on 16th September.

The Task Force for Shanghai, under Rear-Admiral Servaes, went first to Kiirun in Formosa to supervise the repatriation of a number of Commonwealth prisoners-of-war, many of them critically ill from malnutrition. Having seen the survivors taken aboard a hospital ship, Servaes took the cruisers *Belfast* (flag) and *Argonaut* and four destroyers to Shanghai, while the *Bermuda* and a destroyer went to Tsingtao.

Meanwhile Admiral Sir Arthur Power had arrived at Singapore from Ceylon on 3rd September in H.M.S. *Cleopatra* and was followed by H.M.S. *Sussex* carrying senior army officers to negotiate the occupation of the colony, which took place on the 6th when a troop convoy of 26 LCI (L) arrived.

A naval amphibious group consisting of an assault ship with her eight assault craft and a commando carrier with her helicopter-borne commando. The ships in this group are the *Fearless* and the *Bulwark*

CHAPTER 27

*The Royal Navy after the War – The rundown to peacetime
strength – Development of new carrier techniques – Nuclear
propulsion and Polaris – National economy and naval strength*

BRIAN SCHOFIELD

It took two years from the end of World War II to reduce the Royal Navy from its wartime strength of 863,500 officers and men and 3,470 combatant ships to a size compatible with peacetime requirements. These were defined in the Navy Estimates for 1947 as 'to provide a navy sufficiently strong to ensure that the vital lines of supply can be kept open, and to provide such support for the United Nations as may be required, whilst at the same time making a minimum demand on the nation's manpower and material resources.'

By 1948 the ships in commission numbered 615, with 359 in reserve, and personnel strength had been reduced to 167,000. The active fleet at that time included two battleships, four light fleet carriers, 12 cruisers, 34 destroyers, 25 frigates, 26 submarines, and 14 minesweepers.

The war had clearly established the aircraft carrier as the dominant type of war vessel in succession to the battleship, and when it ended the Royal Navy included no fewer than 57 carriers. Another 18, of four different types, were under construction or on order. Not all of these, however, were completed, and of those that were finished, several were either sold or transferred to other navies. The war had also given a great impetus to aircraft development, and at its end it was clear that if carrier-borne aircraft were to hold their own with those coming into service ashore, the carriers themselves would have to be adapted to operate aircraft using jet propulsion.

The first trial landing of a specially modified Vampire jet aircraft took place successfully on board the light fleet carrier *Ocean* on 4th December 1945,

but it was not until August 1951 that an operational Fleet Air Arm squadron equipped with jet aircraft was formed. Four years later the transition from piston-engined aircraft to jets in first line fighter squadrons in the fleet was complete.

The higher landing speed of these aircraft had presented several new problems, the first of which was the need to improve the arrester gear. This was achieved by replacing the friction brakes hitherto used by hydraulic rams, better able to absorb the impact of the heavier aircraft. To prevent an aircraft which had failed to engage an arrester wire from crashing into aircraft parked on the forward part of the flight deck, a flexible crash barrier had been used, but as in jet aircraft the weight of the engine is abaft the pilot, this system involved him in too great a risk of injury. The solution was the 'angled' flight deck by which that portion used for landing on is slewed at an angle of $8\frac{3}{4}°$ to port of the centreline. Thus a pilot failing to hook an arrester wire has a clear run to take off again and repeat the attempt.

It was also found that jet aircraft with their high wing loading could not take off from a carrier's deck using the existing catapult unless it was provided with rocket boosters under the wings. If however one of the rockets failed to ignite, the aircraft would tend to slew round at a critical moment, with possible fatal consequences. This led to the introduction of steam catapults in place of the hydraulic ones then in use, the greater power of which enabled the rockets to be discarded.

Another device introduced at this time was the mirror landing sight. This is a gyro-stabilised instrument containing a mirror in which a light

A Buccaneer strike aircraft being catapulted from the flight deck of HMS *Eagle*. The introduction of the steam catapult provided sufficient power to put these heavy aircraft successfully in the air

Opposite: HMS *Hermes* and HMS *Victorious* anchored off Aden during the British withdrawal from the former colony. Carriers are expected to be phased out of the Royal Navy by 1972, by which time no British forces will remain east of Suez, with the exception of a small garrison in Hong Kong

reflected from the aircraft enables the pilot to tell whether or not he is on the correct approach path. All these inventions were adopted by the United States Navy, which fully acknowledged the contribution made by the Royal Navy to the development of naval aviation.

While all these developments were taking place, work on the two new fleet carriers, H.M.S. *Eagle* and *Ark Royal*, laid down in 1942 and 1943 respectively, continued but at a much reduced pace. The construction of three new cruisers of the *Tiger* class was, however, halted, but an order was placed for the building of eight new destroyers of the *Daring* class, and this represented the sum total of the new construction programme at that time. But Russia's absorption of Czechoslovakia in 1948 alerted the free world to the new danger arising in the East, and there was much criticism of the inadequacy of this programme by those who foresaw the need for Britain to maintain her defences.

In April 1949, the North Atlantic Treaty Organisation came into being, to which Britain undertook to subscribe an unspecified number of ships in the event of war. It was as a result of criticism in Parliament of the decision to appoint an admiral of the U.S. Navy to the NATO post of Supreme Allied Commander, Atlantic, that the British public became fully aware of what had been evident ever since the end of World War II – that the sceptre of the seas which Britain had wielded for so long had passed to the United States.

The outbreak of the Korean War in June 1950 led to a reconsideration of Britain's defence policy. The Navy Estimates for 1951, at £278½ million, were the largest since the war and reflected growing concern over Soviet submarine construction. In March of the following year, 1952, the fleet carrier *Eagle* was commissioned, but three more years were to elapse before her sister ship, the *Ark Royal*, entered service.

When the war in Korea ended on 27th July 1953, the strength of the Royal Navy was 153,000, an increase of 10,000 over the 1950 figure. Some reduction was therefore in order, but few could have foreseen the progressive decline which was about to set in and which has continued up to the present day. Although in the main due to cuts imposed by successive Governments, it has been aggravated by the problem of how to persuade men to re-engage after completing their first period of service, in face of the rapid rise in wages which has taken place in industry.

In 1955 it became evident to the British Government that, confronted with Russia's enormous strength and resources, the nations of the West would have to share the burden of providing the ever more expensive armaments needed to counter this threat and for protecting their important lines of communication. In order to play its part it was stated that:

The Royal Navy requires therefore, carriers operating the latest aircraft; powerful ships armed with guided weapons; escorts capable in co-operation with carrier and shore-based air forces of providing protection for our shipping; submarines and amphibious forces; minesweepers to keep the sea lanes clear for vital supplies. All these ships must be well equipped and maintained in a high state of readiness.'

An outcome of this reappraisal of Britain's maritime policy was a decision to grasp the nettle of the anti-aircraft missile problem which had already been solved in the United States with the production of the Talos – Terrier – Tartar family of missiles. The greatly improved performance of aircraft had placed them beyond the range of even the most modern A/A guns, and missiles alone could now deter them. The construction of the three *Tiger* class cruisers, which had been restarted in October 1954, had advanced too far to make it an economic proposition to equip them with the British A/A missile Seaslug, the development of which was then proceeding, and it was considered preferable to design a ship specially to take it, even though this meant a considerable delay in getting the missile to sea. During trials the Seaslug proved itself to be an exceptionally reliable and efficient weapon, its only disadvantage being that it required a ship of not less than 5,000 tons displacement to carry it and the necessary ancillary equipment. A smaller missile

known as Sea Dart is under development; it can be fitted in ships of about 3,000 tons displacement, and is expected to come into service in about 1972.

In April 1958 a contract was awarded for the development of a close-range ship-to-air guided weapon to replace the 40-mm Bofors A/A guns in H.M. ships, which the rapid progress in the offensive capacity of aircraft had made obsolescent. The aim was to produce the simplest possible weapon capable of destroying an aircraft which had escaped the vigilance of the protective fighter cover. This was achieved by the production of the Seacat missile, employing a common link guidance system by which the controller directs it towards the target using visual guidance until impact occurs. The missile, five feet long and seven and a half inches in diameter, is powered by a solid propellant rocket motor and has a range within the limit of visual control. The warhead in the nose carries a proximity fuse, and the mounting, carrying four missiles, can be reloaded in three minutes. In addition to providing highly reliable close-range defence against aircraft, Seacat can also be used to counter attacks by missiles such as carried by Soviet patrol craft of the *Komar* and *Osa* types. Mountings for Seacat missiles are being extensively fitted in all classes of British ships from carriers to frigates.

In 1957 the steady rise in the cost of defence equipment, coupled with the unsatisfactory state of Britain's economy, led the Government to revise not merely the size but the whole character of the defence plan. The Admiralty dissociated itself from the resulting Navy Estimates, although this fact was never made public, and it had to fight hard to retain the carriers. There were at the time four of these ships operational, two employed on non-flying training and special trials, one under construction, and six in reserve. After much discussion it was agreed that the number in commission should not exceed four and that the principle of the Task Group built around the carrier should be retained, two of which would be maintained in Home and Mediterranean waters, and one in the Far East.

Other proposals included:

(a) a rundown of naval personnel over the next five years to a total strength of 80,000 officers and men.

(b) the scrapping of the four battleships of the *King George V* class. (The battleship *Vanguard* completed after the war was to be temporarily retained in reserve. She was scrapped two years later).

(c) The replacement of eight war-built cruisers by the three ships of the *Tiger* class.

(d) In place of the four cruisers which it had been intended to build to carry the Seaslug weapon, four new fleet destroyers would be laid down. (These ships when completed were in fact of cruiser tonnage but in deference to the 'little navy' party in Parliament, they were classed as destroyers.)

During the period of the Korean war the opportunity had been taken to initiate the construction of two classes of frigates, 11 of which had been delivered, 12 more were under construction, and a further 21 were on order. This programme, designed to provide the fleet with an up-to-date anti-submarine capability, was allowed to stand.

The proposed cut in personnel strength was strongly opposed by the Admiralty. In the opinion of the Board, commitments could not be met with fewer than 110,000 officers and men. After strong representations had been made, a transfer of 7,000 men from the Army strength to that of the Navy was authorised, but as events were to prove, had the Admiralty figure been accepted the grave 'overstretch' which occurred six years later during the Indonesian confrontation would have been avoided.

HMS *Valiant*, a fleet submarine propelled by nuclear power, at speed on the surface. Armed with conventional torpedo tubes, a powerful sonar, and modern anti-submarine weapons, one of her tasks will be defence of the fleet against enemy submarine attack

Other economy measures included the merging of the two Reserve organisations into one body to be known as the Royal Naval Reserve.

In 1958 the Government reaffirmed the decisions outlined above and also announced that the construction of a nuclear-powered submarine was proceeding with the valuable co-operation of the United States. In Britain the development of nuclear reactors had been confined to those needed for electrical power stations ashore, but in 1957 the Admiralty, in association with the United Kingdom Atomic Energy Authority and the Yarrow Admiralty Research department, began the study of their use for marine propulsion. There was much leeway to be made up since besides the American achievement in completing the U.S.S. *Nautilus,* the world's first nuclear-powered submarine, Russia was within two years of completing the world's first nuclear-powered surface ship, the ice-breaker *Lenin,* which had been launched on 5th December of that year.

After the war experiments carried out in the United States showed that at a depth below that affected by surface wave action, a submarine with a hull shaped like a teardrop could attain a speed far in excess of that of a similar powered surface ship. With the greater power now possible using nuclear propulsion, it was clear that submerged submarines would be able to operate at very high speeds almost indefinitely, and out-distance any surface ship seeking to attack them. There was clearly a great future in vessels of this type.

The engineering skills required for the design and operation of a nuclear propulsion system are much higher than those needed for any comparable conventional one. The United States had learned all these by experience, and with great generosity this knowledge was placed at the disposal of the Admiralty when the decision was taken to build a nuclear-powered submarine. Further, under an agreement concluded in 1955 between Britain and the United States, a complete nuclear reactor and all the ancillary machinery was purchased in the latter country, thereby enabling H.M.S. *Dreadnought,* the first British nuclear-powered submarine, to enter service much earlier than would otherwise have been possible. She commissioned on 17th April 1963.

Following on the construction of the prototype H.M.S. *Dreadnought,* five vessels of the *Valiant* class were ordered of which two have since been completed. They have a submerged displacement of 4,500 tons and speed of over 30 knots. Their reactor cores and the associated machinery are of British design, and their armament includes six 21-inch torpedo tubes and the latest type of sonar. It is understood that consideration is being given to equipping them with a rocket-assisted weapon which would greatly increase their offensive capability. Orders for two more of these submarines of an improved type have been placed.

One of the most outstanding engineering achievements of this nuclear age has been the development by the United States of the Fleet Ballistic Missile system. Following the successful trials of U.S.S. *Nautilus,* it was decided to design a solid-propellant ballistic missile capable of being launched from a submerged submarine. This bold and imaginative project, to which the name Polaris was given, was brought to fruition on 20th July 1960 when the U.S. nuclear submarine *George Washington* successfully fired two Polaris missiles from a submerged position off Cape Canaveral (now Cape Kennedy).

Britain, meanwhile, was planning to contribute to the deterrent forces of the West throughout the 1960's by using her 'V' bombers fitted with stand-off weapons, firstly Blue Steel and later the U.S. developed Skybolt. However the cancellation of both these weapons led the British Government in

Britain's first Polaris submarine, HMS *Resolution,* photographed at sea on her return from trials. She was commissioned into the Royal Navy in October 1967. She carries 16 A-3 Polaris missiles with British nuclear warheads, each with a range of 2,500 nautical miles

January 1963 to enter into an agreement with the United States Government for the purchase of sufficient Polaris missiles to equip four (later changed to five and subsequently reduced by the present Government to four) nuclear-powered submarines. Each submarine carries 16 missiles.

Since its first inception the Polaris missile has passed through three stages of development, beginning with the A1 having a range of 1,200 sea-miles, followed by the A2, 1,500 sea-miles, and the A3, 2,500 sea-miles. It is the last named type which has been purchased for the Royal Navy. A special nuclear warhead has been designed in Britain for these A3 missiles which it is understood is more sophisticated than that carried in the U.S. submarines armed with these weapons.

After nearly eight years of operation the deterrent credibility of the Polaris submarines remains unimpaired and there are no indications that the problem of locating them in the deeps of the ocean will be overcome in the foreseeable future. Whether, in view of their cost and the United States predominance in this field, the small contribution which Britain (and later France) are able to make has any real strategic significance is open to argument.

The Anglo-French operations off Port Said and Suez in 1956 revealed a weakness in Britain's organisation for conducting amphibious warfare in spite of the experience gained in World War II. As a result it was announced in the Navy Estimates for 1958/59 that the light fleet carrier *Bulwark* would shortly be taken in hand for conversion to a 'commando' carrier. Her fixed wing capability was removed and alterations were made to enable her to operate 16 Westland Whirlwind helicopters and to carry a Royal Marine Commando of 750 men. The work was completed in 1960 and the following year the ship proved her value when on 1st July the Ruler of Kuwait called for help to resist the threat of attack by Iraqi forces. In 1962 H.M.S. *Albion*, a sister ship of the *Bulwark*, joined the fleet after a similar conversion. During the confrontation with Indonesia following on the formation of the state of Malaysia on 16th September 1963, these two ships played an important role. The Royal Navy's amphibious forces have been further strengthened by the construction of the two Assault Ships (Amphibious Transports Dock) *Fearless* and *Intrepid*, which carry troops and helicopters as well as landing craft which can be floated out of the well where they are carried. They joined the fleet in 1965 and 1967 respectively.

During the debate on the Navy Estimates for 1963/64 in the House of Commons, particular attention was drawn to Russia's development of a maritime strategy as part of her overall policy to extend Communist influence throughout the world, and to the need for Britain to maintain her naval strength. However, the modest increase in the Estimates, amounting to some £21 million, was largely absorbed by rising costs and the provision of funds for the construction of the four nuclear-powered Polaris submarines referred to above.

Just before adjourning for the summer recess, after many months of hesitation, the Government announced that the Royal Navy was to get a new carrier by 1971. She was to be a ship of about 53,000 tons and would embody many new features. But a year later it was announced that her design was to receive further study, indicating that no action had yet been taken to implement the decision announced the previous year.

Meanwhile the modernisation of the existing carriers continued, H.M.S. *Eagle* undergoing a four and a half years reconstruction costing £31 million which was completed in May 1964. She was fitted with a new armoured deck, new steam catapults, a new island structure, and much new and highly sophisticated electronic equipment. This last included Type 984 radar and the comprehensive display system associated with it. From its ability to provide a continuous supply of information on the tactical air situation in three dimensions simultaneously, it is known as 3D radar. Also fitted was Type 184 Sonar, the first British all-round scanning, medium-range instrument of this type to enter service.

On 1st April 1964 an historic event took place with the absorption of the functions of the Board of Admiralty (together with those of the War Office and Air Ministry) by the Ministry of Defence. Although the three Services retained their separate identities, the key note of the reorganisation was interdependence. As a result of the change the historic office of First Lord of the Admiralty disappeared. The Board of Admiralty was replaced by an Admiralty Board subservient to a Secretary of State for Defence who was vested with complete authority to control both

HMS *Fearless*, one of two new assault ships recently commissioned into the Royal Navy. This photograph shows the dock at the after end of the ship which, when flooded, allows her assault craft to be floated out

defence policy and the machinery for the administration of the three Services.

In October 1964 a new Government was voted into office in Britain and it immediately set in train a series of studies on defence policy designed to halt the rising trend in defence expenditure. One such, on the rationalisation of air power, produced a sound and balanced report advocating a pooling of resources for the deployment of tactical air power by the Royal Navy and the Royal Air Force and an end to the unprofitable controversies between the two Services which had soured their relations for nearly fifty years. The report envisaged the retention of the carriers as floating air bases complementary to and not in competition with static air bases ashore.

It was in every way a sensible and workmanlike recommendation, but the Government chose to ignore it and in the *Statement on the Defence Estimates* for 1966 announced that aircraft operating from land bases would take over the strike-reconnaissance and air defence functions of the carrier after the mid-1970's. This decision brought about the resignation of the Minister for the Royal Navy and the First Sea Lord, but in spite of this gesture the Government refused to alter its decision.

One of the arguments which the Government used in support of its decision to phase out the carriers was the intended purchase in the United States of 50 F.111K variable geometry strike aircraft for the Royal Air Force. These it was claimed, by virtue of their high performance, would be able to take over the overseas strike and reconnaissance duties hitherto performed by the Fleet Air Arm. Two years later the order was cancelled on a demand by the Treasury for further economy in defence expenditure, and ironically enough the cancellation charges which have to be paid amount to almost as much as the cost of a new carrier.

It will be remembered that the 1957 cuts left the Royal Navy with four operational carriers, the *Ark Royal*, *Eagle*, *Albion*, and *Bulwark*. The last two, as has been mentioned, were subsequently converted into Commando ships and their places were taken in 1958 by H.M.S. *Victorious*, after extensive reconstruc-

The Commando carrier *Albion* with her Wessex v helicopters on deck. Commando carriers
have demonstrated their value and versatility in scores of situations around the world

tion, and in 1959 by H.M.S. *Hermes*, the last of the *Albion* class to be completed. A fifth ship, H.M.S. *Centaur*, took the place of any ship paid off for refit or reconstruction. This situation persisted until 1966 when the *Centaur* was placed in reserve and, the following year, as a result of a serious fire while in dockyard hands, H.M.S. *Victorious* was scrapped.

Of the three carriers remaining the *Ark Royal* is being modernised at a cost of £30 million, and both she and the *Eagle*, also modernised, are capable of at least another seven years of service. When her refit is complete, the *Ark Royal* will be capable of operating the McDonnell F-4K Phantom II fighter aircraft, 50 of which have been purchased in the United States, but the *Eagle* will not. Surprisingly none of the special reconnaissance type of Phantom RF-4 aircraft have been ordered, so that when the carriers are paid off there will be no aircraft available with a high speed reconnaissance capability.

Both carriers can operate the Buccaneer S.Mark 2, two-seater, all-weather strike aircraft, which is unquestionably the best all-round strike aircraft in existence today. The construction of an improved version of this aircraft, designated Mark 3, with

better radar and some of the equipment from the cancelled TSR2 aircraft, was proposed by the Naval Staff of the Ministry but turned down. If approved it would have given the Fleet Air Arm and the Royal Air Force an aircraft superior to the cancelled F.111K. Now that the Anglo-French variable geometry aircraft project has fallen through, no successor to the Buccaneer is in sight.

A serious situation affecting both the Royal Navy and the Royal Air Force will shortly arise due to failure to provide a replacement for the Fleet Air Arm's airborne early warning Gannet aircraft, which are nearing the end of their effective life. These aircraft provide an indispensable element in the protection of surface ships from both missile and air attack, and are also invaluable ashore to provide troops with warning of attack by low flying enemy strike aircraft.

In the long-range maritime reconnaissance field, the Royal Air Force's obsolescent Shackleton aircraft will be replaced by jet-propelled Nimrods, which it is claimed will provide an improved platform for the conduct of maritime operations. Unfortunately only 38 Nimrods have been ordered, a

Opposite: A model of the new Type 42 destroyer which is expected to join the fleet in the 1970's in substantial numbers. They will be armed with the new Sea Dart missile, though some may be completed with an anti-submarine capability based on the new Ikara weapon

number which would appear to be quite inadequate to meet the commitment.

After the withdrawl of the carriers, almost half the Royal Navy's offensive potential will be devoted to anti-submarine warfare, the balance being divided between submarines, including the Polaris element, and amphibious warfare. The Royal Navy can boast of ships and equipment as good as, if not in some cases better than, can be found in any other navy in the world, but the size of the British Navy is tailored to fit the Government's economic policy. It is the Government's hope that British forces will not be required to operate outside the North Atlantic and Mediterranean areas, and it argues from this that carrier-borne aircraft can be dispensed with. But the primary function of maritime forces is the protection of shipping, and since this is a world-wide commitment, these forces must be highly mobile and of course include an air component. Ironically, the Royal Navy is well equipped with support ships enabling it to operate for long periods independent of shore bases.

Since the Royal Air Force cannot now provide the Royal Navy with effective air cover outside the North Atlantic and Mediterranean areas, it would appear desirable to devise some means for the retention of fixed wing aircraft in H.M. ships without recourse to carriers. The solution to this problem may lie in the employment of V.T.O.L. aircraft operating from smaller and less sophisticated ships, such as perhaps the new cruisers which, it has been announced, are to be built. Rotary wing aircraft such as the Sea King helicopters cannot fulfil this role. And there is still the question of the provision of airborne early warning aircraft, the importance of which cannot be overstressed.

Looking further ahead, everything points to the primacy of the nuclear-powered submarine once the problem of the lack of environmental intelligence has been overcome. The Soviet Navy appears to be well ahead in this field, and has equipped some of its nuclear submarines with missiles which could be used effectively in an anti-ship role, and especially against a group of ships such as a convoy. It is with attacks such as these that the Royal Navy must be prepared to deal.

Finally, notwithstanding the progress which has been made within the NATO organisation for co-operation between the naval forces of member nations, there is an urgent need to carry this much further. It does not make sense for each country to contribute whatever maritime forces it fancies without having first discussed the requirement with its allies and considered their composition from the point of view of collective security as well as that of national defence.

INDEX

302

ACKNOWLEDGEMENTS

All colour illustrations are reproduced by courtesy of the National Maritime Museum, with the exception of the painting at bottom of page 223 which is reproduced by courtesy of the Imperial War Museum, the painting on page 153 which is reproduced by courtesy of The National Trust, Berrington Hall, Herefordshire and the three Water Colours on page 222 which are reproduced by courtesy of Peter Kemp.

The Editor and Publishers are grateful to the following for permission to reproduce all black and white photographs in this book: The National Maritime Museum for photographs on pages 8, 10, 14, 15, 17, 19, 20, 22, 24, 25, 27, 28, 31, 37, 38, 39, 41, 42, 44, 46, 47, 48, 49, 50, 52, 54, 57, 59, 60, 61, 64, 65, 69, 71, 72, 73, 76, 79, 80, 82, 90, 91, 93, 95, 98, 100, 102, 105 (bottom), 107, 108, 110, 111, 112, 113, 114, 115, 116, 117, 120, 121, 122, 124, 128, 133, 134, 137, 138 (top), 141, 142, 145, 146, 148, 150, 151, 159, 161, 162, 165, 166, 246, 252, 267, 271; The Imperial War Musuem for photographs on pages 168, 171, 173, 174, 177, 180, 183, 184, 186, 190, 192, 193, 195, 196, 199, 200, 203, 204, 208, 210, 213, 214, 216, 217, 218, 219, 226, 229, 231, 232, 234, 237, 238, 239, 240, 241, 243, 245, 249, 250, 251, 253, 254, 255, 256, 257, 258, 264, 269, 272, 272–3 (bottom), 273, 274, 275, 276, 277, 278, 279, 281, 282, 287, 289; The Navy Department, Ministry of Defence for photographs on pages 63, 68, 75, 103, 105 (top), 106, 118, 127, 138 (bottom), 188, 211; Crown Copyright for photographs on pages 290, 292, 293, 294, 295, 297, 298, 299; The Musée de la Marine, Paris for photographs on pages 94, 123, 158; The Tower Armoury, Ministry of Public Buildings & Works for the photograph on page 84; The National Trust, Berrington Hall, Herefordshire for the photograph on page 96; The Henry E. Huntingdon Library for the photograph on page 105 (centre); and The Tate Gallery, London for the photograph on page 152.

Maps were drawn throughout by E. H. Roberts.